HEADS & HEADLINES
The Phrenological Fowlers

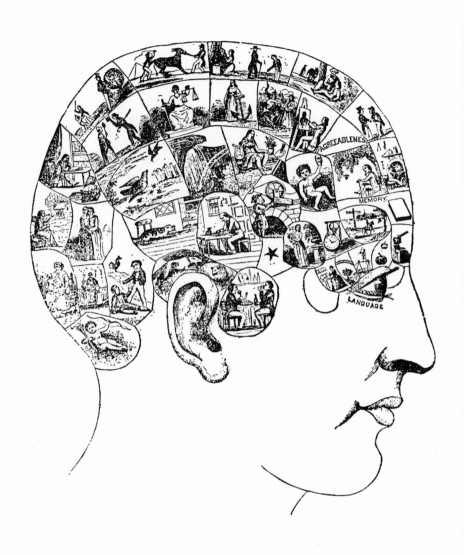

HEADS & HEADLINES

The Phrenological Fowlers

MADELEINE B. STERN

UNIVERSITY OF OKLAHOMA PRESS
NORMAN

By Madeleine B. Stern

The Life of Margaret Fuller (New York, 1942)

Louisa May Alcott (Norman, 1950)

Purple Passage: The Life of Mrs. Frank Leslie (Norman, 1953)

Imprints on History: Book Publishers and American Frontiers
(Bloomington, 1956)

We the Women: Career Firsts of Nineteenth-Century America
(New York, 1963)

The Pantarch: A Biography of Stephen Pearl Andrews (Austin, 1968)

Heads & Headlines: The Phrenological Fowlers (Norman, 1971)

JUVENILES

So Much in a Lifetime: The Story of Dr. Isabel Barrows
(New York, 1965)

Queen of Publishers' Row: Mrs. Frank Leslie (New York, 1966)

International Standard Book Number: 0-8061-0978-5

Library of Congress Catalog Card Number: 77-160506

ACKNOWLEDGMENTS

. . . .

M̲Y HEARTY THANKS goes to the following who, by providing information, source material and encouragement, helped to create this book: Miss Gertrude L. Annan, former librarian of the New York Academy of Medicine; Prof. Harold Aspiz, Department of English, California State College at Long Beach; Dr. Eric T. Carlson, Department of Psychiatry, The New York Hospital-Cornell Medical Center; Mr. Harold Celnick of New York; Mr. Wilson Dupre, New York Historical Society; Mr. Jack T. Ericson, Head, Manuscript Division, Syracuse University Library; Mr. Charles E. Feinberg of Detroit; Mr. Herbert Finch, Curator and Archivist, Collection of Regional History and University Archives, Cornell University; Mr. William H. Helfand, Director of Marketing, Merck Sharp and Dohme International, New York City; Dr. James J. Heslin, New York Historical Society; Mr. Robert W. Hill, former Keeper of Manuscripts, The New York Public Library; Mr. and Mrs. Arthur C. Holden of New York; Mr. C. R. Jones, Associate Curator, New York State Historical Association, Cooperstown, New York; Prof. Brenton H. Smith, Department of History, University of Kentucky.

My gratitude also goes to the editors of the following journals for permission to reprint parts of my articles on phrenological matters: *American Jewish Archives*; *American Literature*; *The Book Club of California Quarterly News-Letter*; *Brigham Young University Studies*; *Coranto*; *The Cornell Library Journal*; *Occasional Notes Norlin Library University of Colorado*.

Other acknowledgments appear at appropriate places in the Notes.

Finally, for the generous, unstinting use of her own extraordinary phrenological faculties, I thank my friend and partner, Leona Rostenberg.

MADELEINE B. STERN

New York, New York
February 17, 1971

INTRODUCTION

. . . .

NINETEENTH-CENTURY America was the spawning ground in which reform was generated and flourished. For its many ills—slavery and the oppression of labor, currency irregularities and improper soil cultivation, rigid marriage laws and injustices to women, alcoholism and national dyspepsia—the country sought a swift and easy panacea. It loved the newness in its varied forms, embracing many crusades in quick succession, from abolition to crop rotation, from temperance to land reform, from the pot-hooks of shorthand to spirit rappings and magnetic experiments, from graham bread to the bloomer dress, from cold baths to communal societies. "Every possible form of intellectual and physical dyspepsia brought forth its gospel. Bran had its prophets. Everybody had a mission."[1]

In that exhilarating century and on that fertile soil, man was kindled by the belief that perfection was attainable. His gods were wise and beneficent, his religion a kind of optimistic deism. The discoveries of the scientists seemed designed to fortify those beliefs, and the layman relished their neat classifications that made every fact a compartment in a "glorious fabric." The nineteenth-century American especially sought to know himself, for he—a sovereign individual—was a microcosm of that fabric. He heeded the injunction written in gold capitals upon the Temple of Delphos: "Know Thyself."[2]

Before an audience of such sovereign individuals, who breathed with gusto all the winds of change, a German physician in 1832 delivered a series of lectures that unfolded to eager America yet another newness, a panacea that would cure all its ills, a reform so pregnant with possibilities that it promised to obviate the need for all other reforms. Dr. Johann Spurzheim, disciple of the Viennese physician Franz Joseph Gall, had come to the United States to tell the country about a comparatively new science called phrenology.

The name was a combination of two Greek words meaning "discourse on the mind." In its simplest form, phrenology postulated that since the brain was the organ of the mind and shaped the skull which neatly cased the brain, there was an observable concomitance between man's mind—his talents, disposition, and character—and the shape of his head. To ascertain the former, one need only examine the latter.

Phrenology had had its origin in Vienna, where, not unlike a Viennese physician of a later century who would found another science of the mind called psychoanalysis, Dr. Franz Joseph Gall had made some startling observations. Early in life, as a student of nature, he had noted that those of his classmates who "had good memories had large foreheads." Later in life, as a physician fascinated by the anatomy and physiology of the brain, he had continued his observations of the correlation between character and the head:

> I collected in my house . . . quite a number of individuals of the lower classes of society, following different occupations; such as coachmen, servants, &c. I obtained their confidence, and disposed them to sincerity by giving them beer, wine, and money; and when favorably inclined, I got them to tell me of each other's good and bad qualities, and most striking characteristics. . . . I ranged the quarrelsome on one side, and the peaceable on the other, and examined carefully the heads of both. I found that in all the former the head, immediately behind and on a level with the top of the ears, was much broader than in the latter. On another occasion, I assembled separately those who were most distinguished for their bravery, and those most distinguished for their cowardice. I repeated my researches, and found my first observations confirmed. . . . I there-

fore began to conjecture that the disposition to quarrel might really be the result of a particular organ.[3]

From such conjectures, corroborated by empiric research, proceeding from the known to the unknown, Dr. Gall had by the last decade of the eighteenth century developed his new science of the mind. Its tenets were simple. The brain is the organ of the mind, just as the eye is the organ or instrument of sight. The brain is, however, not a unitary organ but a congeries of organs, the mind consisting of a corresponding number of faculties. Each mental capacity therefore manifests itself through its own cerebral organ, the size of which indicates its power of function. Moreover, the size of the organ can be increased by exercise, just as a muscle can be strengthened, and so man is literally the master of his own mind.

At a time when, despite the early insights of Aristotle and Michael Servetus, Thomas Willis and Emanuel Swedenborg, some thinkers still placed the soul in the heart or the stomach, Dr. Gall's radical, "materialistic" views resulted in his enforced departure from Vienna in 1805. He did not leave alone, for he had enlisted the support of an ardent disciple, Johann Gaspar Spurzheim, who continued to proselytize for the system all over Europe. By 1828, when Gall died, Spurzheim had convinced many of Europe's scientists that, in spite of the sneers at calves' heads and tincture of gall, the proper study of mankind was indeed man and that the proper method of that study was phrenology.[4]

America had not yet been convinced. Thanks to the pioneer efforts of the imposing, stately Dr. Charles Caldwell of Transylvania University, who had met Gall and Spurzheim in Paris and had written the first book on phrenology to be published in the United States, a few phrenological societies had been formed, the earliest in Philadelphia in 1822.[5] As Mrs. Trollope was to observe, "Americans love talking"; when it came to demands for subscription fees, however, many of the phrenological societies of the 1820's simply expired.[6]

In 1832 Americans discovered that they loved listening as well as talking and that although phrenology had had no past in their country, it surely had a glorious future. Indeed, America, learning of phrenology in the 1830's, was akin to twentieth-century America learning of Freudian analysis. On June 20, 1832, Johann Gaspar Spurzheim set sail from Le Havre to plant the banner of phrenology firmly in the soil of the New World. Arriving in the heat of summer, he found cholera raging in New York and swiftly moved on to the hub of America. On September 17 he began a course of eighteen lectures at Boston's Athenaeum. The tall, distinguished Dr. Spurzheim, his "countenance beaming with superior intelligence," promptly captivated his listeners—the fashionable and the learned, the gay and the grave, the skeptic and the Christian—expanding their horizons as he elucidated the new doctrine.[7] And indeed the new science seemed to have a special relevance for the new country.

> The Phrenologists of Boston, and the Other Citizens of America, who, trained to liberty, untrammelled by prejudice, and disdaining every species of mental bondage, sought, from the opposite side of the globe, an Instructor, well knowing how to emancipate Minds from the despotism of Error, and establish the commonwealth of Truth and Nature, Freedom and Morality, Reason and Religion. Every city, every village, every university, every school of art and academy of science, thirsted for the promised stream of knowledge.[8]

How much it promised, this simple philosophy of the mind, to America, that fertile ground for newness! It seemed in truth the philosophy of a free country, this doctrine that man's character could be read from the shape of his skull and improved by the exercise of various mental functions. To a nation in love with facts, Spurzheim brought a whole body of facts about the mind upon which he set "the finger of Scientific Certainty." To a nation sympathetic with the new, he brought a new doctrine shedding light upon the dark recesses of the mind. To a nation avid for the practical, he brought a "practical system of mental philosophy." Since the shape of all things was a sure sign of their nature, the skull became "a more correct index to . . . character, than the pen of a ready writer." Man, who had been studied piece-meal in the past, could now be studied as a unit, for he was in-deed one—a whole creature, whose physical and mental faculties were closely interrelated. To a nation captivated by the neat and simple classifications of science, what system was more beautiful and perfect in its arrangements?[9]

Man's brain was a three-story house with a skylight. In the base the instincts had their being; above them resided the animal propensities; in the top story sat reason and, illuminated in the skylight, towered spirituality. There was a place for everything, and everything was in its ordained place. The domestic organs, clustered in the lower portion of the back of the head, were grouped together in a charming society of their own. Amativeness (or sexuality) was at the side of Philoprogenitiveness (or parental love); nearby was Adhesiveness (or love of friends); Inhabitive-ness (or love of home) completed the family circle. An infinite wisdom had placed related organs side by side "and thus greatly facilitated their reciprocal intercourse." In man—the microcosm of the best of all possible worlds—every organ was placed just where it was best fitted for its special function.[10]

To the Americans attending the lectures at the Athenaeum, here was a system beautiful, neat, scientific, and practical by which man could learn to know himself. "As eight musical notes contain, by their repetitions and combinations, the whole realm of music; as twenty-six letters in the English alphabet by their combinations make its whole literature, so [the] . . . faculties of the human mind . . . make and maintain all the variety of char-acter, talent, propensity, and peculiarity which is seen in the dif-ferent persons whom we meet."[11] Since, by measuring a skull, one could analyze a character, determine its weaknesses and correct them, ascertain its aptitudes and encourage them, the ramifications of phrenology seemed limitless. There need be merely a universal examining of heads to arrive at a universal omniscience.

The response to Spurzheim was electric. As Harriet Martineau observed, "When Spurzheim was in America, the great mass of society became phrenologists in a day, wherever he appeared; . . . all caps and wigs . . . [were] pulled off, and all fair tresses dishevelled, in the search after organization."[12] And having, in less than two months, kindled the phrenological flame into a bonfire, Spurzheim—dubbed by Emerson one of the world's greatest minds—suddenly and dramatically died; his brain—the organ of that mind—was preserved in alcohol in the laboratory of Harvard Medical School. "The Americans at first welcomed him as a stranger—early they acknowledged him as a friend—too early they wept over him as a Brother."[13] When he died on November 10, 1832, he died in the arms of America. His death only heightened the fervor with which his doctrines had been greeted.

On the day of Spurzheim's funeral, the Boston Phrenological Society was founded in the printing house of Nahum Capen, Spurzheim's friend, business manager, and publisher. Other societies sprang up elsewhere, wherever there were enthusiastic advocates of the new system. Although some dismissed Spurzheim as "an imported mountebank," there was no doubt that he had introduced to the free America of 1832 a practical philosophy of the mind.

The times were ripe and the soil receptive for the system. Despite detractors who would deride the new science, phrenology would, for a time, take hold. "Plaster casts of heads, and lithographs marked with the organs" would be "sold by thousands." There would be a "universal feeling of heads." Lecturers would go "from town to town, explaining the new science, and giving public and private examinations."[14] Periodicals would be published to promulgate the new philosophy, and a library of phrenological books would rapidly be issued. Many of the country's greatest men would accept its pronouncements, Henry Ward Beecher preaching them from his pulpit, Horace Greeley affirming them in his *Tribune*, Horace Mann and Samuel Gridley Howe applying them to educational reform. Errand boys and candidates for political office would be appraised by its standards. The greatest poets of the century—Whitman and Poe—would cull from phrenology a new vocabulary. Because the science was ardently embraced by so many thinkers of the nineteenth century, that century cannot be thoroughly understood without a knowledge of phrenology.

Yet Spurzheim alone could not have revealed all its diverse manifestations and possibilities to the people. His thoughts had carried on the winds of reform to a nearby college—Amherst— where two undergraduates found in them a meaty subject for debate. One was Henry Ward Beecher, the future Unitarian minister who would deliver from Brooklyn's Plymouth Church sermons that shook the country. The other was his classmate Orson Squire Fowler, an upstate New Yorker whose life would be shaped by Spurzheim's message and whose family would soar to eminence on the wings of Spurzheim's ideas.

The seed that the German doctor planted took root in this country largely because Orson Fowler devoted his life to nourishing it. And so, to understand the nineteenth century and its devotion to phrenology, one must also understand that upstate New Yorker and his family, who gave to the country a practical answer to the Sphinx's question, What is man?

CONTENTS

· ·

ILLUSTRATIONS

. . . .

The Fowler office from 1892 to 1902
Nelson Sizer
Edgar C. Beall, M.D.
Students and faculty of the American Institute
of Phrenology
Jessie Fowler analyzes the presidents

LINE DRAWINGS

HEADS & HEADLINES
The Phrenological Fowlers

Men are like open books, if looked at properly.

HENRY WARD BEECHER

Phrenology has melted the world's conscience in its crucible, and cast it in a new mold with features less those of Moloch and more like those of humanity.

OLIVER WENDELL HOLMES

Phrenology declares the equal rights of all men.

PHRENOLOGICAL JOURNAL (1875)

Phrenological biography is far superior to any other biography, and is destined eventually to become the only clear, certain, and satisfactory method of estimating character and talents.

PHRENOLOGICAL JOURNAL (1842)

THE FAMILY

I

With his birth on October 11, 1809, Orson Squire Fowler immediately became a pioneer, for he was said to have been the first white child born in Cohocton, Steuben County, New York. In a year that gave to the world such giants as Darwin, Gladstone, Lincoln, Tennyson, and Oliver Wendell Holmes, this distinction was perhaps not great, and the fact that Fowler's designation as the town's first white baby was probably erroneous dims his claim to priority.[1] Yet the role of pioneer was his from birth, and during a lifetime of nearly eighty years he would never step out of character. Orson Squire Fowler, heir to the zeal and the errors of missionaries, was the descendant of men who had always plowed new ground.

His first American ancestor, William Fowler, had migrated from Lincoln, England, in 1676, settling in Bradford, Vermont. His grandfather Eliphalet had served in the Revolutionary Army. And so Orson had inherited the blood of those who ventured to new places and championed new ideas. He had inherited much else besides. One of his ancestors, dubbed "the Giant of America," had captured a five-hundred-pound shark, shouldered it, and carried it alive to shore; this same ancestor's portrait showed him grasping a bear and "carrying it on his hip."[2] Although Orson had inherited a "weak stomach" and a "consumptive tendency," he was also the heir to great intellectual strength. As he boasted, "I am able to perform an amount of mental labor . . . which would kill any but a descendant of 'the giant.'" He would be able to perform such labors for many decades, for he had also inherited longevity from his ancestors, the youngest of whom had died "at eighty while healthy, of poison."[3]

Orson's mother gave him his literary leanings, for she "wrote manuscript by the bushel, and in a style at once graceful, flowing, perspicuous, and elegant, consisting mostly of sermons, or, rather, of essays on religious subjects." At least in the quantity of his writings, Orson would follow in his mother's footsteps. Martha Howe Fowler, besides being a devout churchgoer—she was admitted to the Congregational Church of Cohocton even before its formal organization—was a granddaughter of Jemima Howe, who had been captured by the Indians. A delicate plant in the twenty-four-mile wood where her children were born, she would wither early. Orson would recall: "Of my own sainted mother I remember distinctly but two things—laying my head back in her open lap while she kissed, caressed, and fondled me; and her death. Both are indelible."[4]

Orson's father, Deacon Horace Fowler, left more varied impressions. Born in Guilford, Connecticut, he had journeyed to upstate New York, settling in Cohocton in 1806. Carrying his ax wrapped in a linen cloth on his back, he had moved into the wooded wilderness, made a clearing with the help of a yoke of oxen, and built a log house. He had married three years later and begun his family. Although his own formal education had been limited to six weeks, he would encourage learning for his children; his home in Cohocton would be the scene not only of church meetings and discourses on abstinence but of readings. Mirth was not encouraged, for "after he became a deacon he repressed all his jokes," believing it wicked to laugh. He conquered his children less by physical violence than by convincing their consciences and so making them condemn themselves. Upon one occasion, however, he subdued Orson by ducking him in the rain trough—the boy's introduction to the effectiveness of hydrotherapy.[5]

Cohocton, where Orson grew up, was hilly, upland country,

"separated into ridges by deep and narrow valleys." As a child he saw its first sawmill built, its first schoolhouse, its first tannery. While he played and learned to study his conscience, Indians fished, hunted, and traded. The Cohocton River, which flowed through the center of the town, was filled with speckled trout; the forests, with deer and bears; at night, above the voice of Deacon Horace reading aloud, the howl of the wolves could be heard. Bounties were offered for wolves' skins and panthers. To the boy it was "a wild and mountainous section of country, on the head waters of the Susquehannah, Oswego, and Genesse [*sic*] Rivers."[6]

Orson was not alone when he explored the woods or fished the streams. His brother, elegantly named by a literary mother Lorenzo Niles Fowler, was born less than two years after Orson, on June 23, 1811; a sister, Charlotte, followed three years later, on August 14, 1814. The three were to be closely united in their pioneer work for the better part of their lives. In childhood Orson's resemblance to his father and Lorenzo's to his mother were already apparent. Lorenzo would be less dashing and more equable than his older brother, who managed to combine a grave sobriety with electric magnetism. Charlotte united the best qualities of both parents—the vitality and compact organization of her father, the temperament of her mother.

In a home where laughter was frowned upon, character development was demanded. Appeals were frequently made to conscience; long before the boys had heard of a science of the mind, they were made aware of mental disciplines. In other ways their "boyhood was quite like that of other boys born in log cabins, . . . helping 'father' clear off a new and very stony farm . . . ploughing among roots and stones together."[7] While they divided their days between attendance at the district school and assisting on the farm, they studied the human nature of Cohocton.[8] There was the town miser who buried his gold and watched it on dark and stormy nights; there was the preacher who boarded with the Fowlers and accepted a colt as a parishioner's yearly subscription; especially after their mother's death, there was the Sabbath-school teacher Mrs. Andrews, whom Orson worshiped as his "polestar."

Martha Fowler died of consumption at the age of thirty-six in August, 1819. Orson later said:

> Losing my mother at nine, working now at home and then away, of course craving female sympathy without knowing it, a childless Mrs. Andrews, sometimes my Sabbath-school teacher, by her affectionate aid in reciting, made me love her as if my mother. I learned the more Scripture verses when I knew she was to hear me recite them, . . . hated to go to Sunday-school "barefoot," lest she might think the less of me; and about half worshipped her up to sixteen, when I left home to study.[9]

There was no question in the mind of any member of the Fowler family about the purpose of the boys' studies—both were to become ministers. Orson, the elder, left home first, taking his preparatory studies under the Reverend Moses Miller, the tall and distinguished pastor of the First Congregational Church in Heath, Massachusetts, known to the townspeople as Father Miller. Since Father Miller was a prime mover in the establishment of Amherst College, Orson early set his sights on that institution. His work with Moses Miller was followed by studies under the Reverend Benjamin F. Clarke at Buckland, Massachusetts, and later at Ashfield Academy.[10]

In addition to his studies, he practiced other disciplines. In 1825 he joined the Congregational Church.[11] Suffering upon several occasions an "affection of the lungs," he limited his diet to sweetened buttermilk and "a syrup recommended by a neighborhood doctress."[12] Early in life he started writing. "When but a mere boy, [he] took great pleasure in composing essays, and when on his way to New England to obtain an education, he spent an entire week at the house of an uncle, in writing and re-writing an article on 'Dress,' leaving off *only* to *eat and sleep*." His first published article would concern the subject he knew best at the time —agriculture—and this would be followed by contributions to the *Temperance Recorder* (priced at ten cents a volume or the price of three glasses of grog).[13]

Long before those articles appeared—the year after his mother's death—Orson's father had married Mary Taylor, a "grand-niece of that Mrs. Phillips, of Maryland, whose daughter was the first sweetheart of George Washington." She herself came from Heath, Massachusetts, "whence so much brain power has permeated the life of New York," and she came well recommended into the Fowler family. Horace's second wife was "a well educated New England school teacher [who] had excellent mechanical talents, was proficient in housekeeping, millinery, dressmaking, tailoring and nursing." Besides being "a good theologian," she was well endowed with "the missionary spirit."[14]

Out of the second marriage were to come another trio of children—Samuel, Almira, and Edward—all of whom would combine the missionary spirit of their mother with the determined pioneering of their father. They would introduce the Fowler family to social and medical reforms that harmonized well with those reforms their half brothers and half sister had championed. Indeed, the six Fowlers would, in their diverse ways, eventually embrace most of the reform movements of a reform-ridden century.

By the time the second trio of Fowlers was emerging from Steuben County, Lorenzo Fowler was a student in the classical department of Amherst Academy and his older brother Orson had graduated from Amherst College. There the young man with the high forehead and strong nose, the piercing blue eyes and the somber yet electric personality, had learned still another discipline—the science of the mind—which he was prepared to explain to all mankind and so lead human nature to perfection. The pioneer had found new fields to plow; the would-be minister had been called to his life's mission.[15]

Orson had left home with four dollars in his pocket and all his possessions on his back; his journey to fortune had begun with a four-hundred-mile walk.[16] Amherst College, where he matriculated in 1829, was a young and flourishing institution dedicated to the task of "civilizing and evangelizing the world."[17] Under the presidency of Heman Humphrey, orthodox Congregationalist and strong temperance man, its students began their day with compulsory prayers at 4:45 on summer mornings and at 5:45 in the winter. Discipline was strict, with fines levied for "not keeping study hours, for firing a gun, and for playing musical instruments on the college grounds." Recreation consisted chiefly "in tea-drinking with the family of some professor, who . . . split doctrinal hairs over the cheering cup."

To pay his college expenses, Orson worked as hard as he had on his father's farm. By sawing, splitting, and carrying wood up several high flights of stairs for his fellow students, he supported himself. At the same time he began an experiment in dietetics which, combined with his physical labors, had dire results:

> The college Mess constituted my first dietetic experiment—a dozen students uniting . . . appointing a contractor, who hired a room and cook, bought provisions, and was captain-general of the mess . . . averaged from sixty to eighty cents *per week*, for food alone. . . . I took a great amount of exercise all through college, by sawing dry hickory wood in two twice, and backing it up four and *five stories* for only *seventy-five cents per cord*, thus earning most of my collegiate expenses. But over-working with underfeeding wore in upon an excellent constitution.

Indeed, they "wore in" so much that they brought about a return of Orson's old illness. Set back a year, he was placed in Amherst's class of 1834.[18]

There were compensations for this setback as well as for the austerities of Amherst life. There were compensations in the teaching of the great professor of chemistry and natural history Edward Hitchcock, who sharpened and broadened the minds of his students by pointing out analogies and connections where they had seen only contrasts and antitheses. There were compensations in the college societies, where opinions could be aired and debated; there were compensations for Orson in some of his class-

8

mates, among them a disorderly but eloquent young gentleman named Henry Ward Beecher.

Beecher's room was always, according to Orson, "in the greatest disorder, his clothes, books, &c., strewed about in all directions and in utter confusion—some upon the floor, others in chairs, or the windows, and others under or upon the bed."[19] He seldom bothered with his recitations, instead organizing a course of "reading and study of his own." One day it would be said of the class of 1834, "The average ability of that class should have been high, as Henry Ward Beecher stood at the foot!" Although Beecher may not have shone in the classroom, he glittered upon more social occasions. When Henry Clay visited the college, it was Beecher who made the presentation speech that accompanied the gift of a Bible. His large, full eyes transfixed his audience when he declaimed before the Athenian Society, which alternated in weekly debate with Orson's society, the Alexandrian. There was much to debate at Amherst in the early thirties, from teetotalism to theological orthodoxy, from poisons (against which the Antivenean Society was formed) to anti-Masonry. As president of the Society of Natural History, Beecher had the opportunity to elicit not only new curiosities for its cabinet but new topics for its podium.[20]

The winds of reform were blowing gently over the eastern seaboard, wafting in the air of Amherst new thoughts, new phrases: free inquiry, association, New Harmony. In 1832 yet another word was added to the college vocabulary, a new hypothesis for debate in the Society of Natural History. For Beecher here was a new science for enthusiastic exploration, a new subject for eloquence. For Orson Squire Fowler it was more.

While official Amherst, endorsing more orthodox "metaphysical mysticisms," looked down its nose at Spurzheim's phrenology, the new science caught the imagination of a few members of the faculty. It especially caught the imagination of the tall, sober upstate New Yorker who, destined for the ministry, had a professional interest in philosophies of the mind. Orson Fowler, afire with phrenology, had, although not yet fully aware of it, been

9

called to another ministry. Like all converts, he was a zealous proselytizer, and, like all proselytizers, he inspired some scoffing amusement. The college wits saw in Orson's devotion to phrenology a delicious opportunity for fun, and Henry Ward Beecher was not averse to joining in the sport. Beecher's sister Harriet was later to write:

> In the course of his sophomore year, Mr. Beecher was led, as a mere jovial frolic, to begin a course of investigation which colored his whole after life. A tall, grave, sober fellow had been reading some articles on Phrenology . . . and avowed himself a convert. Quick as thought, the wits of college saw in this an occasion for glorious fun. They proposed to him with great apparent earnestness that he should deliver a course of lectures on the subject in Beecher's room.
>
> With all simplicity and solemnity he complied, while the ingenious young inquirers began busily arming themselves with objections to and puzzles for him. . . . The fun waxed hearty, and many saw nothing in it but a new pasture ground . . . for an endless harvest of college jokes.[21]

The "jokes" culminated in plans for a colloquy on the question "Is phrenology entitled to the name of science?" Either to give the quietus to the subject by the selection of a strong opposing speaker or merely to provide further amusement to the skeptics, the eloquent Henry Ward Beecher was invited to uphold the negative, Alonzo Gray taking the affirmative. In preparation, Beecher sent to Capen's in Boston for Spurzheim's books, and his disorderly room promptly became more disorderly with the addition of phrenological notes, busts, and pamphlets. As he read and thought, however, Beecher found he was catching the contagion, and as for the objections to phrenology, he believed he could "knock them to pieces." When he arose to address the Society of Natural History on the subject, he gave a brilliant speech—but not in support of the negative. Exposing the futility of objections to phrenology, he defended its fundamental principles. Instead of ridiculing the new science into oblivion, he announced himself a convert to its tenets.[22]

With Beecher in the phrenological camp, Orson Fowler renewed his ardor for the system. Skeletons and busts found their way to the cabinet of the Society of Natural History. Readings in Magendie's *Physiology* and the phrenological works of Gall, Spurzheim, and Combe opened new vistas to Orson in his explorations of mental philosophy. The college was filled with heads —all awaiting analysis. For two cents apiece, Orson obliged. Beecher, he announced, had "an impassioned temperament" and "a strong social brain," with "very large Benevolence" and "Amativeness fully developed." A man with "a small brow and big in the lower part of his head, like a bull [was] not likely to be a saint." Nor did the cranial irregularities of professorial skulls escape investigation. Orson would one day recall the first days of his enthusiasm at Amherst:

> As I . . . entered upon the collegiate study of mental philosophy, my more especial object was to compare Phrenology, as an expositor of the mind, with Brown's, Stewart's, and other metaphysical text-book systems, and found it immeasurably their superior. Meanwhile I learned the location of a few of the organs and Faculties, from inspecting the heads of fellow-students, among whom I began to be so noted for making correct "hits," that they flocked around me, all curious to hear what I would say about themselves individually, and each other. . . .
>
> Two College Classmates gave me my first satisfactory *test* of the truth of Phrenology. One was smart, the other dull, but both were excessively conceited, and both their heads projected far out and back to a peak at their crowns, where Ambition is located . . . the smart one having a good sized forehead, the dull one a low, narrow one. Their characters thus corresponded perfectly with their Phrenology.[23]

Orson Fowler especially delighted in analyzing himself, for without self-knowledge he could never know the world. On the positive side, he found his intellectual faculties of Comparison and Language remarkably developed; on the negative side, he considered himself deficient in the faculty of Ideality or aesthetic perception—a result, he claimed, of his having been brought up in "the back woods." He lacked a "shrewd, pecuniary, bargaining, acquisitive talent," and his Amativeness was "only moderate."[24] He would devote much of his life to strengthening—with no small success—all the faculties in which he regarded himself deficient.

Meanwhile, still looking upon phrenology as a stepping-stone to the ministry, Orson continued to pursue his studies. Between preparing his commencement address and distributing temperance publications for the lay preacher and book manufacturer John C. Holbrook of Brattleboro, Orson found time both to examine and to inspire his brother Lorenzo.[25]

Lorenzo had thus far been an amiable follower in his brother's footsteps. He too had worked on the farm, attended district school, and pursued studies that would lead him to the ministry. With Dansville and Hadley behind him, he attended Amherst Academy while his brother was at the college. At sixteen he had "helped to form the first teetotal temperance society . . . in America," and even during a visit to dissipated, intoxicated Natchez, he had refrained from demon rum. Now, in his early twenties, he shared his brother's devotion to the new science of the mind, and where his brother phrenologized he was also prepared to phrenologize.[26]

The heads of members of the family were especially convenient for practice. Orson's young half brother Samuel was a likely subject, for his cranial developments indicated a rich variety of talents, although his Benevolence was too large to drive a bargain and his Veneration too large to meet the tricks of trade.[27] Sister Charlotte, who had attended Franklin Academy in Prattsburg, New York, displayed in her cranium a fine blending of faculties and temperaments, all of them boldly led by the mental. Even as a young girl, Charlotte was a staunch believer in the rights of her sex, and at the very beginning her approach to phrenology was linked with her interest in woman's rights. She later wrote:

> It is to Mrs. [Sarah Josepha] Hale that the writer . . . was indebted for her start in Phrenology. In the *Ladies' Magazine and Literary Gazette*, published in Boston, which that distinguished lady edited, appeared in 1832 a succinct article from her pen on Phrenology. . . . Mrs. Hale was a personal friend of Spurzheim and did all she could to aid him in his work in Boston, where she then resided. It was to her that Spurzheim said, "It should be woman's work to introduce Phrenology, and give it a start in America. . . ." In a conversation with Mrs. Hale on female education, Spurzheim remarked, "Excepting Christianity, Phrenology will do more to elevate woman than any other system has ever done. It gives her a participation in the labors of mind."[28]

With the help of her older brothers, Charlotte eagerly participated in those labors. The examination of heads was for the Fowler family a highly contagious act. No sooner had Charlotte been taught the rudiments of phrenology than she proceeded to teach them to others—in a class at Ludlowville, New York. No sooner had her head been examined by Lorenzo than she proceeded to examine a theological student, Joel Wakeman, in Painted Post, Steuben County.[29] To the three older Fowlers, just completing their education, men were indeed "like open books, if looked at properly."[30]

On August 27, 1834, Orson Fowler delivered his commencement address at Amherst on "Temptation—Its influence on guilt" —a subject that surely involved considerable self-analysis.[31] He had learned much from his years at college, not the least the ability to analyze himself. He had learned less perhaps from the formal curriculum than from his discussions with Beecher and his readings in nonrequired texts by Spurzheim.

Now his trunk was packed with books and notes and clothes, and the stagecoach was at the door. His mind less filled with Butler's *Analogy* and Paley's *Moral Philosophy* than with Combe's

13

Elements of Phrenology, Orson Squire Fowler climbed aboard. Never would he feel more alive than at this moment when, at the age of twenty-four, he was "related to the past by memory, [to the] present by experience, and [to the] future by anticipation."[32]

O. S. AND L. N. FOWLER

. . . .

II

Orson had delivered his first lesson on phrenology in Brattleboro, Vermont, where, as an Amherst undergraduate, he had peddled temperance tracts for John C. Holbrook. Armed with a simple chart and a few handbills, a knack for reading character and a conviction that with his new science he could solve the riddle of the Sphinx, Orson Squire Fowler cleared forty dollars and began his professional career. To the meetinghouses and town halls, the church vestries and schoolhouses of New England, he would now introduce a new limner of human nature, a new peddler of Yankee notions, a new purveyor of unsurpassed panaceas for human ills. With Orson's first venture, the itinerant practical phrenologist was born. He recalled many years later:

> My Professional Life began thus. A classmate, after our graduation in 1834, came to Brattleboro', Vt., to lecture on the "Battles of the Revolution," a re-hash of collegiate lectures by Professor Fiske, but failed. This fired me with an ambition to try *my* hand at lecturing on Phrenology, since I had nothing special to do after graduating, and before the next term began at Lane Seminary, Ohio, which I designed to enter, in preparation for the orthodox pulpit.
>
> One night I lay awake "till broad daylight," first thinking out whether or not I should make the attempt, which I finally resolved to do; next studying up my form of notice for my proposed handbill and advertisements; and finally studying our improvements in my chart, in giving the definitions of the Faculties . . . and spent nearly a week on it; bought paper, hired printer, and got out a

15

thousand copies, along with my handbill; ordered a bust, and thirty-two dollars' worth of works on Phrenology, opened my lectures, threw out my card, charged men twelve and a half cents for a phrenological chart, marked, and ladies and children six and a quarter cents; cleared forty dollars in the place, and started for Saratoga, meanwhile writing to my brother, L. N. Fowler, who had come from Amherst Academy home to Cohocton . . . to come back, and meet me. . . .[1]

Orson Fowler—henceforth Professor Fowler—and his brother Lorenzo had taken to the lecture circuit, joining the ranks of the most popular entertainers on the eastern seaboard. They had much to offer their audience, Lorenzo explaining the basic tenets of phrenology in his succinct, matter-of-fact style, while Orson elaborated eloquently and enthusiastically on its grandiose possibilities. Their chart, at first a mere slip, then a larger sheet, defined the faculties in degrees or sizes. Their handbill promised a demonstration of "the truth of phrenology in any, and in every honourable way which the ingenuity of the incredulous may devise or propose."[2] America became more and more head conscious. If scoffers came to mock and raise objections, others came to be convinced, and in many a town it was noticed that the ladies had begun to dress their hair "with the object of showing the right phrenological organs."[3]

The Fowler brothers were more than lecturers; they were practical phrenologists. At the end of each discourse on theory, the public was invited to an applied demonstration.[4] When a subject offered his head for analysis, the Fowlers would first consider his "temperament." Coarse, large features indicated a bilious temperament—a man whose physical strength predominated over the mental—a hewer of wood and drawer of water; thin hair, small muscles, pale skin, on the other hand, suggested the nervous temperament of one drawn to study, thought, and poetry. The Fowlers gradually became adept at sizing up character from a glance, installing their subject in the niche of his particular temperament —vital, motive, or mental. Each of the brain's organs had its "natural language," betrayed by a gesture, a walk, a laugh, a handshake, a sneeze. Physiognomy was eloquent to any who could read expression in the lines and contours of a face. Kindness bent the head forward; Dignity carried it upward and backward; Firmness produced straight posture. To the Fowlers, all shapes and outlines indicated character, and all resulted from the "pregnant brain."

Even before they had examined a skull, the brothers had gauged the temperament of their subject. Size was their next point of interest; to determine this, they measured the horizontal circumference of the head with a tape. Form too was significant; placing their hands upon the sides of the subject's head, they investigated its shape. With one hand on the forehead and the other on the "basilar portion," they proceeded to study the relative developments of those regions. Applying the balls of their fingers, they moved the scalp slightly, becoming thoroughly familiar with the head they were examining. They rarely looked for bumps—although their work would so often be denigrated as "bumpology." Rather, they looked for distances between the various organs.

Having determined the general size and shape of the skull, they proceeded to more specific areas, investigating the individual organs or faculties. Since the organ of Amativeness, for example, occupied the cerebellum at the base of the back part of the head, the Fowlers, to explore it, felt along the middle line toward the base of the skull. There, below a small bony projection called the occipital process, behind the bottom of the ears, lay the sought-for organ of Amativeness. Having found it, they determined its size, designated by numbers from 1 to 7. If the organ was extremely small—1, 2, or 3—it required cultivation; if it was inordinately large —7—it required control and repression. The earliest charts, marking the various faculties by size, were in great demand by the subject, who, intent upon knowing himself, could contemplate the size or power of his Combativeness, Destructiveness, his Firmness and Ideality, his Acquisitiveness and Cautiousness. As they manipulated, the Fowlers talked; their language, racy and vivid, painted

17

character in broad strokes. Here was a loquacious man like "a full jug, turned upside down, with the stopper out." Here was another "probably to be seen on Bloomingdale Road . . . behind a fast trotter every pleasant day."[5] As they practiced, their fingers became twenty feelers and they themselves "two wizards of manipulation" who could "take a man's character right out from his keeping, and hold it up before . . . a whole meeting-house full of folks."[6]

The meetinghouses were full, for the lectures themselves were free, the only charge being made for the examination. Often the Fowler finds were dramatic.[7] At one public analysis, the moment Orson touched the head of his subject he recoiled "as from a serpent, exclaiming, 'No Conscientiousness! not a bit! No Approbativeness! No feeling of shame!'" It was subsequently discovered that the shameless gentleman had been arrested for the manslaughter of a female slave. The detached skull of a murderer whose history was unknown to Orson evoked his comment, "A snake in the grass." Although they peddled a new science, the Fowlers did not forget that they were also showmen. Double tests were a popular form of entertainment, Orson examining in Lorenzo's absence, Lorenzo repeating the test in Orson's absence. If their analyses did not concur, they became the butt of derision and their science was castigated as humbug. Blindfold tests were also provided on demand, and even double blindfold tests:

> Audiences have been found who demanded not only an examination before them of any stranger from their body, but that such examination should be conducted by the lecturers *blindfolded*! . . . But not only this: the one brother has been taken away and kept in another room, whilst the other conducted his blindfold examination; then he has been led forth and required to go through the same ordeal.[8]

Other ordeals were demanded of the traveling crusaders. Clergymen disguised themselves "with the loud colors and cut of a commercial drummer's clothing," entering the hall with a "slouching rudeness in language," all to mislead the examiners. For the same purpose a physician "dressed as an insane man, with his hair ... disarranged, his eyes staring, and his general expression wild." The Fowlers faced not only this testing of the testers but the scoffing of wits, the bigotry of the intolerant, and the opposition of those who held that phrenology was both materialistic and fatalistic.[9]

They replied to all such charges, Lorenzo declaring with some casuistry, "The fact that Phrenology recognizes the difference between the brain as the medium of mental manifestation and the mind as a spiritual essence, destroys the objection brought against the science that it leads to materialism."[10] Neither did it lead to fatalism, for although born with undeveloped faculties, man could develop them and so was never damned by his birthright. The objection of some scientists and physicians that the "external of the brain does not harmonize with the external of the skull" was waved away. Undaunted by their accusers, the Fowlers simply retorted, "It is an old trick of agitators and bigots to raise the hue and cry of infidelity, atheism, materialism, heresy ... against new doctrines in religion, and new discoveries in philosophy and science." Their polestar was "Truth," Orson announced in his answer to a pseudonymous opponent called "Vindex." The brothers were harassed almost as much by "*barefaced plagiarists*" who "styled themselves eminent professors of the science" and aped their technique and copied their charts. Yet imitation was flattery, and satire presupposed a general familiarity with the new science.

The Fowlers, moving from upstate New York to Baltimore and on to St. Louis, were indeed making the country aware of this modern psychology. They went to Providence (where they examined Margaret Fuller),[11] to Hawthorne's Salem,[12] somewhat later to Mark Twain's Hannibal, feeling a multitude of heads, analyzing the foibles of a nation, and giving its writers a new vocabulary. Mark Twain would remember those itinerant practical phrenologists in recollections that brought them back to life:

In America, forty or fifty years ago, Fowler . . . stood at the head
of the phrenological industry. . . . One of the most frequent arrivals
in our village of Hannibal was the peripatetic phrenologist and he
was popular and always welcome. He gathered the people together
and gave them a gratis lecture on the marvels of phrenology, then
felt their bumps and made an estimate of the result, at twenty-five
cents per head. I think the people were almost always satisfied with
these translations of their characters—if one may properly use that
word in this connection; and indeed the word is right enough, for
the estimates really were translations, since they conveyed seeming
facts out of apparent simplicities into unsimple technical forms of
expression, although as a rule their meanings got left behind on the
journey. Phrenology found many a bump on a man's head and it
labeled each bump with a formidable and outlandish name of its own.
The phrenologist took delight in mouthing these great names; they
gurgled from his lips in an easy and unembarrassed stream, and this
exhibition of cultivated facility compelled the envy and admiration
of everybody. By and by the people became familiar with these
strange names and addicted to the use of them and they batted them
back and forth in conversation with deep satisfaction—a satisfaction
which could hardly have been more contenting if they had known
for certain what the words meant.[13]

By the time the phrenologists had found their way to Hannibal,
Orson's mind had overflowed with newer schemes, his life had
undergone some change, and he himself had examined a host of
remarkable heads.

As he journeyed, alone or with Lorenzo, to Troy or Worcester
or New Haven, human nature was unfolded to him encased in a
variety of skulls.[14] All skulls offered for a reading were meant to
be anonymous; "I don't . . . know you from a side of sole leather"
was a fitting salutation from phrenologist to subject. Although
this anonymity could scarcely extend to the Siamese twins whose
heads passed under the brothers' sensitive fingers, it did apply in
many cases. A beggar at Orson's doorstep, lifting his hat in greeting, exhibited to the professor's penetrating eye enormous Causality in the forehead—an observation corroborated when the beggar

turned out to be a student of the ten lost tribes of Israel and a man who had fallen upon evil days.

The measuring tape was passed around a diversity of heads by the Fowlers. In Nashville, Orson made a reading of John A. Murrell, the preaching bandit-king, concluding that he had "natural Ability, if it had been rightly called out and directed." The sculptors Hiram Powers and James V. Stout sat for their phrenological portraits, as did the actor Edwin Forrest. Writers were especially drawn to the new method of reading character; Bryant and Fitz-Greene Halleck submitted to the test. In the well-developed head of Lydia Maria Child, Lorenzo, unaware of that strong-minded woman's identity, detected the "self-directing" intellect and "radical notions" of one who "enjoys herself with a book and pen more than in household arrangements, or general society." Reformers pursuing their hobbies took time for an analysis—Mrs. Nicholson "of vegetarian boarding-house notoriety" and the "Old Wizzard" Samuel Thomson, who had developed a system of therapy based on the emetic weed lobelia and in whom Orson found the organ of Acquisitiveness markedly developed. The abolitionists Theodore Weld, Isaac Hopper, Arthur Tappan, and John Greenleaf Whittier were also tested.

Of all the early analyses performed by the brothers, none had a more lasting influence than Lorenzo's reading of the hypersensitive fifteen-year-old Clara Barton. Having arranged two courses of lectures in Oxford, Massachusetts, Lorenzo was invited to board with the Bartons. Mrs. Barton, deeply troubled by her daughter's withdrawn shyness, consulted the professor, who advised her—to the world's future benefit—to "throw responsibility" upon the girl. When the founder of the American Red Cross later wrote *The Story of My Childhood*, she spoke with emotional gratitude of that remarkably effective psychological analysis:

> Two courses of lectures by L. N. Fowler were arranged for our town. . . . He very naturally became the guest of my father and mother.
>
> These two courses . . . covered nearly a month of time. How can

the value of the results of that month, extending through a lifetime, be put into words? How measure the worth of the ideas, the knowledge of one's self, and of others, growing out of it? Aside from this was his aid and comfort to my mother in her perplexity concerning her incomprehensible child. I recall the long, earnest talks, in which it was evident that I was the prime subject, although not clearly realizing it at the time. . . . My mother remarked that none of her children had ever been so difficult to manage. "Was I disobedient, exacting or wayward?" asked Mr. Fowler. Oh no! she often wished I were, she would then know what to do, for I would make my wants known, and they could be supplied. But I was so timid and afraid of making trouble that they were in constant fear of neglecting me; I would do without the most needed article rather than ask for it, and my bashfulness increased rather than diminished as I grew older. . . .

Mr. Fowler replied that [certain] characteristics were all indicated; that, however much her friends might suffer from them, she would always suffer more. "They may be apparently outgrown, but the sensitive nature will always remain. She will never assert herself for herself—she will suffer wrong first—but for others she will be perfectly fearless." To my mother's anxious question, "what shall I do?" he replied, "Throw responsibility upon her. She has all the qualities of a teacher. As soon as her age will permit, give her a school to teach."[15]

By the mid-thirties, when Lorenzo made his historic analysis of Clara Barton, the Fowler family had undergone several changes. The boys' stepmother had died and had been replaced by their real mother's sister, Susan Howe, whom Horace Fowler had married in October, 1835.[16] In 1836 the Fowlers—Horace, Susan, and the three younger children—moved to Jackson, Michigan. At about the same time Orson himself embarked upon his first marriage. On June 10, 1835, the forcible, persuasive, eloquent phrenologist, who had by then abandoned all thought of a theological career, married a young widow from Fishkill, New York, Eliza Chevalier, daughter of the merchant Elias Brevoort.[17] No phrenological analysis of Eliza appears to be extant, but since their marriage was the first of three for Orson, it may be inferred that she stimulated his taste for the institution and helped develop the mental organ of Amativeness in which he had once found himself deficient.

Orson's mind, "literally overflowing with its subject," imparted not merely to his wife but to his brother and his subjects an "exhilarating freshness and enthusiasm" for phrenology. His style formed a perfect complement to his brother's matter-of-fact, concise, penetrating manner.[18] Together they now set out to conquer the nation's capital, where they opened a temporary office. There, one of their first patrons was an opponent of phrenology, Dr. Thomas Sewall, who believed that "nature does not reveal her secrets by external forms." He came incognito, Orson recalled, "to test the science; confessed to the striking correctness of my delineation; that he had written a book against Phrenology, and wanted me to examine the skulls from which his objections were drawn, &c. I replied that I cared nothing for his book or skulls; that Phrenology should stand or fall by its *experiments*; that he might select any of his friends . . . blindfold me himself . . . and in that state I would describe them: that *he* should write out their special traits from what he knew of them; that *my* remarks of them should be reduced to writing; and that if his friends, who were to be the umpires, did not say that my description came nearest to their characters, I would give in. . . . The Blinders were put on by Dr. Sewall himself, some lady pressing her gloves up between my eyes and the bandage, and chose and brought forward some subjects . . . and among them slipped *himself* into the chair for reinspection."[19]

Orson was apparently equal to the demands and ordeals—and the heads—of the capital.[20] In the head of Senator John Tyler he found such towering Self-esteem and Firmness that he described the future president as a man who "would veto bills." In addition to the heads of "about twenty Indians of the Cherokee delegation to Congress," many senatorial skulls were manipulated by the Fowlers. Orson came to know the intimate habits of several of the nation's notables.

When I visited Washington to take the busts of our great men, I was forcibly struck with the fact that they all took a great amount of physical exercise. Speaker Polk habitually rose about daylight, and took a walk of two hours before breakfast. . . . John Q. Adams informed me that he uniformly rose before the sun to take his exercise. . . .

Benton told me that he required his servant to spend all his strength in rubbing him at least two hours daily, with the stiffest, hardest brush.

Frequently, as I was going to take my walk, have I met Webster returning from his.[21]

Meanwhile, Lorenzo devoted his attention to a subject of prime interest to a practical phrenologist—art. The phrenological bust was and would continue to be as much a tool of the phrenologist's trade as the tape measure. The quick and cheap manufacture of plaster casts therefore concerned the phrenologist in general and Lorenzo in particular, for he had

been much interested for several years past in statuary and the arts. . . . My business likewise being of that nature, which leads me to notice individual mental peculiarities, I have embraced every opportunity of becoming acquainted with American artists; taking measurements and casts of their heads.

This interest would continue throughout his life. Both brothers agreed that "the importance of combining a knowledge of Phrenology with the arts . . . is very great. . . . In a few years every artist must be a phrenologist."

In Washington the phrenologists were making every effort to become artists, a task in which they were aided by Alburtis D. O. Browere, the son of an obscure New York sculptor, John H. I. Browere. The elder Browere, fired with the ambition of creating a national gallery of busts of notable Americans, had invented a secret method of making life masks. He had used his process to take casts of Adams and Madison, Lafayette and Clay, Gilbert Stuart and Thomas Jefferson. Unfortunately, Jefferson's complaints of the discomfort suffered during the procedure all but ruined the sculptor's career. When Browere lay dying of cholera in 1834, he directed "the heads to be sawed off the most important busts and boxed up for forty years." As for his process, its secrets were imparted only to his son Alburtis, a painter, who honored his father's memory by adding draperies to busts made from the life masks. Alburtis allied himself for a time with the Fowlers, an arrangement immortalized by the "Browere del." which appears at the foot of at least one of their early phrenological charts. Alburtis Browere taught the Fowler brothers the art of making phrenological busts, an art in which they would in time "introduce several improvements." By 1841 they would announce that they were "now able to take with ease and safety, fac-similes of the living head, as correct almost as life." As early as 1836, when Aaron Burr died on Staten Island, they paid an unnamed artist fifty dollars to take a cast of his head; through the years they would spend "many thousands of dollars in taking casts from the heads of distinguished men."[22]

Partly for the purpose of housing those casts, Orson Fowler set up an office in Philadelphia in 1838.[23] While Lorenzo lectured and plied his trade in New York, one of Orson's in-laws joined the Philadelphia office, which became known as Fowler and Brevoort. John Brevoort, who combined his phrenological activities with *bel canto*, proved a disappointment to Orson, who complained: "I took him into my office, not as a partner, but as an apprentice ... till I found he was disgracing me and the science by dissipation and other vices, when I discontinued my connection with him. ... More than once I have taken him out of the Sheriff's hands." Despite these trials, the office flourished for a few years at 210 Chestnut Street. Known as the Phrenological Museum or Athenaeum, it contained the "rarest assemblage, perhaps, on this continent of unique skulls, and casts of persons now living ... nearly, if not wholly, unparalleled in the series of cranioscopal formations." Despite the disorder of the establishment, where heads were often "heaped up in confused piles," the display was so varied as to be "unsurpassed in this country." The Philadelphia office was, however, more than a museum and more than an examination room, for it provided the background for yet another of those fresh ideas with which Orson Fowler's seething brain overflowed.

The *American Phrenological Journal and Miscellany*, patterned after the *Edinburgh Phrenological Journal*, began operation in Philadelphia in October, 1838, and would continue, through crises and near suspensions, until 1911—the longest-lived periodical ever devoted to the cause.[24] The magazine's first real editor was a young medical student, Nathan Allen, who had been Lorenzo Fowler's classmate at Amherst Academy. While he worked for his degree at the Pennsylvania Medical College, preparing his thesis on the "intimate connection of mental philosophy with medicine," Allen edited the *Phrenological Journal* under the aegis of the Fowlers. The magazine was filled with the Fowlers' analyses of skulls, as well as with articles reprinted from the *Edinburgh Phrenological Journal*. During the early years of its existence Orson learned at firsthand the all but insurmountable difficulties of issuing a periodical on a comparatively new subject with insufficient funds and poor health. In 1842 he elaborated his trials and expenses, along with his plans and purposes in undertaking what would become the most important phrenological magazine in the country:

> In the spring of 1837, I formed the resolution of commencing this Journal . . . at $1,00 [$1.00] and of becoming its editor, in order to make it a record of those coincidences between character and developments which I had observed. . . .
>
> Nathan Allen became its editor, with 1500 paying subscribers, to whom the first ten Nos. of Vol. II. were sent, though few of them had renewed their subscription. At length, seeing how loth they were to pay for what they had already got, I gave positive instructions to have it sent to those *only* who had *paid*. So deeply had it involved me at the close of Vol. II, that I wished to stop it; for, its expenses were really enormous, and together with those incurred by collecting specimens for my cabinet, and heavy rents of places to exhibit my collection, kept me groaning under an intolerable load of debt, to pay which, I was obliged to labor far beyond my

strength, and prevented time for taking exercise, till the failure of my health at last compelled me to close my office and travel. My brother insisted on giving up the Journal, and I really felt that I *could* no longer sustain it, yet it was my *idol*, that for which mainly I lived, and the great object of my life and labors. This, together with the persuasions of its Editor, (who was pursuing a medical course, while editing the Journal,) prevailed on me to continue it through vol. III, which closed with about 400 paying subscribers,— *not enough to pay its Editor.* My brother then absolutely refused to continue his support, and tried to dissuade me from keeping up the Journal, partly because it kept me loaded down to the water's edge with debt, but mainly on the ground that I had not the kind of mind requisite properly to conduct it. In this opinion the Editor also concurred.

Above all, my *wife* entered her protest against its continuance. She plead that it was not only swallowing up all my earnings, and depriving my family of the comforts of life ... but that I was ruining my health, and fast shortening my days by excessive labor and being harrassed by debt—and all to support the Journal. Between these conflicting motives, I remained undecided for more than six months. The only encouragement I had came from my *sister*, who held up my hands, and told me I *could* write what the public would be glad to read. This decided me to continue it through its fourth volume, which commenced with not a hundred of its former subscribers....[25]

It was no wonder that Orson's health was affected. In addition to the *Journal*, he was issuing other phrenological publications, the earliest of which had been his *Phrenology Proved, Illustrated and Applied.* In that work, copyrighted in 1836, Orson had had as collaborators his brother Lorenzo and Samuel Kirkham, a grammarian with large Causality who was presumably to correct any syntactical lapses in return for instruction in phrenology. The combination was productive. *Phrenology Proved* was what it was intended to be—a practical manual designed for an American audience and destined to go into numerous editions; and Kirkham was so thoroughly indoctrinated with the science of the mind that he willed his skull to his wife.[26]

Orson's wife, however, was understandably less interested in her husband's skull than in his earning capacity, for their family had begun to increase—Orsena arriving in 1838, followed by Charlotte Howe.[27] Fowler's sister, for whom the new child was named, had meanwhile been invited to partake actively in the phrenological crusade by writing, proofreading, office managing, and, as Orson put it, "holding up his hands."[28] Under the demands of his lectures and analyses, the *Journal*, and his own publications, Orson's hands needed considerable holding up. To alleviate his exhaustion, he depended not only upon his sister but upon a system of "extra breathing," which he called the breathing cure or pathy, and which he clinically described as the

> most efficacious of all the cures. The Author hit upon it thus. When he first established his Philadelphia office, in January, 1838, he opened courses of lectures in several places at once, thus lecturing every evening. They brought such crowds for examinations, as finally to completely exhaust him, compelling him . . . to dismiss callers, crawl up stairs by the banisters, and throw himself upon the lounge; when he involuntarily fell to panting, or breathing deep and fast, as if perishing for more breath. . . .
>
> This Extra breathing soon made him dizzy, by thinning a part . . . of his blood. Reaction presently sent the blood bounding and rushing throughout his system, producing a prickling sensation. . . .
>
> Lecture Time arrived, after about half an hour's breathing. He arose . . . much stronger than he had supposed possible, . . . walked . . . two and a half miles, to Northern Liberty Hall, gave altogether his best lecture of the course, and walking home, set down to his desk and wrote . . . *until after sunrise* the next morning, without food or sleep.[29]

George Combe, following Spurzheim's footsteps, arrived in the United States with his wife, Mrs. Siddons' daughter, and excited public interest in the science to a new peak. His thin silvery hair exposed his own "beautifully developed frontal and coronal regions," and even his Scottish burr did not prevent his listeners from responding to his earnest lectures. He felt that "in addressing

28

an American audience, the speaker enjoys the inestimable advantage of breathing the air of Liberty; and only in such an atmosphere can Phrenology flourish."[30] As a result of both Combe's lectures and Orson's practical demonstrations, phrenology certainly flourished for a time in Fowler's Philadelphia office.[31] There, Charlotte or Orson Fowler received their distinguished visitors: the impressive Dr. Charles Caldwell, who was shown a portrait of George Combe painted by Rembrandt Peale; the eminent actor and elocutionist James E. Murdoch; Napoleon's erstwhile "body servant," who burst into tears when he saw a copy of Antomarchi's death mask of the Little Corporal. Another visitor would one day become an important member of the Fowler firm and be a strong supporter of phrenology for half a century. Nelson Sizer, inspecting the Philadelphia office in 1839, "felt that the American Phrenological Journal was the organ of a great cause, and the office and cabinet of its publishers, the Fowlers, must be regarded as the headquarters of Phrenology in America, and that, whatever I could do to aid and strengthen headquarters, would be in the right direction for promoting the cause." By rounding up paying subscribers, Sizer not only "promoted the cause" but decided the fate of the *Journal* for another year.[32]

Despite the faltering of the *Journal*, into whose depleted coffers Orson continued to pour the earnings from his analyses, the cause was gaining ground and converts of far greater renown than Nelson Sizer were joining the ranks of believers.[33] Richard Cobden in England and Sarah Grimké and Samuel Gridley Howe in America hailed the movement. Indeed, Howe, who was to acknowledge his debt to phrenology in the education of the blind, would not allow a "woman servant to be engaged until . . . she had removed her bonnet, giving him an opportunity to form his estimate of her character." Along with hundreds of heads cast by the Fowler method, that of Samuel Gridley Howe would adorn the Phrenological Cabinet.

With converts came competitors, minor phrenologists armed with charts and busts, aping or emulating the Fowlers in the vestry rooms and lecture halls of the East.[34] Some were humbugs who practiced not phrenology but bumpology and read fortunes instead of skulls; others, including Amos Dean of Albany and John Bell of Philadelphia, were eminent exponents of a new and highly plausible science.

By 1842, when both converts and competitors were flocking to the standard, the Fowlers made two important changes in the conduct of their business. Nathan Allen had resigned from his editorship of the *American Phrenological Journal* as soon as he received his medical degree. His place was taken by Orson Fowler, who described his "Proposed Course" in full if ungrammatical detail:

> In assuming the Editorship of the American Phrenological Journal, the public will doubtless expect a statement of the proposed manner of conducting it. My experience in lecturing upon, and practising, Phrenology . . . in most of the cities and villages, and in many of the country towns in the Union, has made me fully acquainted with one predominant characteristic of our age and nation, namely, a desire for Facts. . . . It was *mainly* to furnish a medium for recording and circulating . . . phrenological facts, that this Journal . . . was established, and that I have sacrificed so much in its support.
>
> Since the publication of 'Phrenology Proved, Illustrated and Applied,' all my time and energies have been consumed in augmenting my cabinet, and in defraying the expenses of this Journal . . . I have finally resolved to give the results of those examinations and observations to the public through its pages. . . .
>
> From my extensive intercourse with the mass of American minds, I believe them to be thoroughly *practical*. . . . To this leading characteristic of our age and nation, I shall endeavor to adapt the Journal.[35]

Shortly before he assumed editorship of the periodical, Orson closed his Philadelphia office, moving the Cabinet to New York. There, in the spring of 1836, Lorenzo had set up his shingle on Park Row, next to the old Park Theatre. The following year he had joined forces with T. Barlow and Rufus Dawes, announcing the "New-York Phrenological Rooms [at 286 Broadway] for Phrenological Instruction, where they will test the Science to individuals or classes with or without manipulation by anatomical specimens, by Busts, Casts, Statuary, Books, Charts."[36] These temporary quarters had merely heralded the first permanent New York office of the firm, an office the brothers would occupy until 1854.

Clinton Hall, on the southwest corner of Beekman and Nassau streets, had been built for the Mercantile Library Association in 1830. In time the lower portion of the building was rented to insurance companies, banks, booksellers, bootmakers, shirtmakers, hotel keepers, and the phrenologists O. S. and L. N. Fowler. "When the brothers Fowler opened their first office in New York, the centre of business interests was the vicinity of Broadway, Nassau and Fulton streets. . . . On the corner of Beekman and Nassau, in . . . a favorite landmark of old New Yorkers, Clinton Hall, American Phrenology had its head-quarters." By 1842, when the Philadelphia office was closed, the New York Cabinet housed nearly one thousand specimens and, like Clinton Hall, this "Repository of Curiosities" was becoming a landmark of the metropolis. Through purchases from George Combe and exchanges with the London phrenologist Anthony De Ville, the Fowlers amassed in time a sizable and fascinating collection that included:

casts of the whole head, masks of distinguished men, of thirty Indian chiefs, all taken from life . . . the whole of G. Combe's collection, with many from the Boston and Edinburgh collections, casts of sculls of murderers, thieves . . . lions, tigers, hyenas. . . . They have now at command the means of ready access to nearly every tribe of Indians on our western frontier, and through one of the missionaries at Green Bay . . . to many of the interior tribes. By means of exchanges with other phrenologists . . . especially with Deville of London, and the Phrenological Society in Paris . . . they have at command the means of collecting into one splendid American cabinet all the valuable phrenological specimens . . . in the civilized world. . . .

31

They have moulds of all their most valuable specimens, and of Combe's collection, so that they can supply societies and individuals with sets of 20, 50, 100 or more specimens . . . at about cost, and nearly 50% less than casts can be purchased of the regular artists in this line, namely at 25 cts. each, for casts of animal heads and human sculls, and from 37½ to 50 cts. each for busts or casts of heads.[37]

O. S. and L. N. Fowler were in business. Their stand at Clinton Hall would attract almost as many visitors as Barnum's Museum and would witness the development of the brothers not only as phrenologists and proprietors of a phrenological journal but also as publishers on a large scale. It would also form the background for some of the most colorful reform movements in the country.

Lorenzo Fowler had been vouchsafed a personal and dramatic vision of the possible relationship between phrenology and those reform movements. Upon his return from a phrenological tour in the West and South, in the course of which he had been "almost constantly employed in examining heads, which, of course, required the equally constant exercise of his organs of size, individuality, form, locality, eventuality, comparison, and language," he had observed "that these organs . . . had very much increased." Orson explained, "The exercise of particular mental faculties, causes the exercise, and consequent enlargement, of corresponding portions of the brain."[38] What further proof was needed that the mental faculties were improvable and that through exercise the size of the cerebral organs could be increased? What ramifications such a concept suggested! James Freeman Clarke has said:

One of the real benefits of this study was that it inspired courage and hope in those who were depressed by the consciousness of some inability. . . . Phrenology also showed us how, as Goethe says, our virtues and vices grow out of the same roots; how every good tendency has its danger, and every dangerous power may be so restrained and guided as to be a source of good.[39]

32

By extending good and curbing evil, phrenology could advance not only the individual but mankind. Teaching, with dramatic certainty, the improvability of human nature, it opened the way to the perfectibility of the entire race. Thus phrenology could be used as the basis for guidance and the fulcrum of reform. With missionary zeal, the brothers described their broadened purpose in the *American Phrenological Journal*: "Society *must* be reformed, and this science, under God, is destined to become the pioneer in this great and good work."[40]

Armed with their fortified conviction, O. S. and L. N. Fowler of Clinton Hall were ready to lay the phrenological "axe of reform" at the root of almost every evil in American society.

PHRENOLOGICAL PANACEAS

. . . .

III

THE FOWLERS' statement that "The organs can be enlarged or diminished . . . even in adults" was simply a technical way of saying that "Man is not compelled to carry all his faults, excesses, and defects to his grave."[1] This belief appealed especially to Orson Fowler, who, never satisfied with things as they were, constantly experimented with new ideas. The doctrine was also particularly pertinent to nineteenth-century America. The concept of reform through self-knowledge was first of all, eminently practical; second, it was audaciously idealistic; third, it was good business. In their *American Phrenological Journal*, the publishers could proclaim as early as 1844:

> Let *practical* Phrenology be encouraged; for, it has done a work in this country which nothing else could have achieved; and by establishing, and popularizing, and generalizing Phrenology, it has laid the foundation on which those glorious superstructures of reform now so rife—now sweeping into oblivion the evils that enthral society, and placing man upon the true basis of his nature—are based.[2]

It was not only phrenologically sound but patriotic to say, "We are free to choose what course we will pursue, and our bodies, our brains, and our features readily adapt themselves and clearly indicate the lives we lead and the characters we form." With the self-knowledge given by phrenology came freedom of choice; with freedom of choice came the possibility of improvability—that "practical watch-word of the age"; with improvability came

34

the hope of reform. By their insistence upon this aspect of practical phrenology the Fowlers truly Americanized the science.[3]

At the end of the forties, the Fowlers announced that the work of the *American Phrenological Journal* had just begun and that its object was "to Phrenologize Our Nation, for thereby it will Reform The World . . . Mould The Now Forming Character of Our Republic . . . Perfect our Republic . . . reform governmental abuses. . . . Let its teachings become national. . . . We love our country, and are determined that it shall be the better for the American Phrenological Journal."[4]

Although their declaration of reform was couched in hyperbole, the Fowlers were convinced of its practical applicability. They went so far as to formulate a "Self-Improvement Directory Table," assuring patrons that, "as every one should be his own doctor, so every one should be his own phrenologist. . . . Our whole population should Grow Up phrenologists."[5]

Perhaps their simplest, most obvious demonstration of practical improvability was related to mnemonics.[6] In 1842 the brothers presented to the public a manual entitled *Fowler on Memory: or, Phrenology Applied to the Cultivation of Memory*, a work frankly "adapted to the come-at-it-at-once disposition of our age and nation." In the manual Orson described his own experience in mental self-discipline:

> I have practised giving *written* descriptions of character along with charts; and, when a company was examined, or when several examinations were made in succession, being compelled to postpone the writing till I had more leisure, I charged my memory with . . . the size of every organ in each person examined; and . . . with *what I said* about each, until I could write them out, which often was not till days afterward, and till hundreds in the mean time had been examined.

For the purpose of "charging memory," he lectured without notes and wrote from recollection only. Charlotte too "pursued this course," charging "her mind with facts" during the day, which

35

she recorded in her diary at night. Along with the art of doubling or improving memory, Orson advocated, in this same year, 1842, speed reading—"Teaching Children to Read in a Month"—and the study of foreign languages through conversation.

Indeed, the Fowlers' interest in what has come to be called child guidance formed the base of their phrenological edifice of reform, for they believed that "a Child is more valuable than any other human being."[7] In book after book written by one or both of the brothers, in their *Journal*, in lectures, and in their private and public examinations, they insisted upon the natural rights of the child not only to education but to phrenological analysis at Clinton Hall. "A child's head should be examined as early as at two or three years of age, then again at twelve, and again at fourteen or seventeen." They bitterly condemned the mother who, during an interview in the Cabinet, threatened her child, "If you don't sit still, Mr. Fowler will take you and throw you out of the window." To all parents who visited the establishment on Nassau Street, they taught the "secret of managing children" by understanding their peculiar natures and organizations and by adapting their training to those organizations. The progressive, individual education advocated at Clinton Hall frowned upon punishment, for "no chastisement can ever be inflicted without the exercise of Combativeness and Destructiveness in the punisher." Persuasion and affection were to take the place of compulsion, and children were to be taught from observation rather than from books. The wizards of manipulation struck blow after blow at the educational system which, as early as the 1840's, they considered antiquated.

The Fowlers' own pedagogical methods and precepts were startling in their modernity:

> Even before children are three months old, crowd Objects upon their notice. . . . As they grow older . . . take special pains to explain all, and even to excite curiosity to know still more. Take them often into your fields, gardens, shops. . . . Accompany them often to the museum.

They noticed that the mother whose skull revealed to them strong parental love often tried to retard her sons, dressing them "in infantile kilts" and refusing to "let them be men." Railing as loudly against overprotectiveness as against repression, they took a far-sighted view of the evils of current pedagogy.

> War has its origin in the wrong government of children. So slavery and licentiousness arise from the wrong direction of the youthful mind, and in its imperfect development. The training of children is at the very foundation of society. As is their training so is society. . . . Reformers . . . commence at the beginning.

The Fowlers did indeed commence their reform with the child, the fountainhead of life. "We hear much," they would one day say, "of 'Human Rights,' 'Man's Rights,' and 'Woman's Rights,' but Children's Rights are almost entirely unrecognized." The Fowlers recognized those rights early, as did the secretary of the Massachusetts Board of Education, Horace Mann, who would confess, "I declare myself a hundred times more indebted to Phrenology than to all the metaphysical works I ever read. . . . I look upon Phrenology as the guide of Philosophy and the hand-maid to Christianity." Throughout the forties, the *American Phrenological Journal* pleaded for the introduction of phrenology into the schools. When the Eatontown Institute was established "on Phrenological principles," Almira Fowler attended it, and the school received several puffs in the *Journal*. Retarded children had their rights too, and when the New-York Institute for the Physical and Mental Training of Imbecile, Idiotic, Backward, Nervous, Insane and Epileptic Children was established, the firm was listed among the founder's "friends."

Clinton Hall was not only the seedbed for the kind of education that would flower in a later century; it was also the center for what would eventually be called vocational guidance and employment counseling.[8] The Fowlers' success in this department of improvement and reform was so great that newspaper advertise-

37

ments for office help frequently read: "An Apprentice Wanted. ... It will be necessary to bring a recommendation as to his abilities from Messrs. Fowler." Certain firms would not engage employees until their heads had been submitted to a phrenological test. Only then could a railroad conductor or a purchasing agent, a domestic servant or a mechanic be selected with any guarantee of success. By this means alone would businessmen be enabled to "choose reliable partners and customers; merchants, confidential clerks; mechanics, apprentices having natural gifts adapted to particular branches; ship-masters, good crews."

For those in search of a calling, the Fowlers provided in most convenient form a list of the "Developments" that would qualify them for success in particular pursuits. The lawyer, they decided, required large Eventuality to recall his cases, while the prime need of the mechanic was large Constructiveness. Where the perceptive faculties should dominate in the physician, the statesman needed above all a well-balanced intellect. Editors should be endowed with "large Individuality" as well as "large Language, to render them copious, free, spicy, and racy"; the phrenologist, whose aptitudes the Fowlers knew so well, required "a first-rate head" marked by good perception and excellent memory, strong Comparison and Human Nature, Constructiveness and Ideality.

With seemingly scientific exactitude, the Fowlers expanded their list of professions and occupations, matching them with the desired faculties. For merchant and dressmaker, organist and carpenter, poet and printer, the wizards of Clinton Hall drew up the individual requirements. To them it was no more difficult to advise about the choice of vocation than for the "mariner with his compass to direct his ship over the boundless ocean," for they had "the compass of the mind, by which they could direct with unerring certainty, the steps from childhood to youth, from youth to manhood."

Their compass was the phrenological examination. Lorenzo tersely explained, "Find out your peculiarities of mind, and decide at once on the profession or business you wish to pursue ...

then cultivate the faculties that are necessary to qualify you for success in the . . . calling you have chosen." Armed with charts of their natures, young men went forth from the Fowlers aware that they would be "self-made or never made," encouraged to become the sculptors or tradesmen, the sailors or clerks, the poets or architects of the nation's future. The early choice of the right profession—a choice to which the compass of Clinton Hall was an ineffable guide—would result not only in the happiness of the individual but in "the prosperity and material good of the next generation and greatly enhance the happiness of the race, besides abolishing poverty and nearly abolishing crime."

The belief that crime could be abolished by means of phrenology was part of the Fowler credo.[9] The brothers frequently visited prisons and almshouses to lecture and examine, to test both phrenology and the criminal. Lorenzo recalled:

> While at Baton Rouge, La., a few years since, I was invited to . . . the State prison, to examine the heads of several convicts. Soon after I entered, they selected eleven prisoners, and I made remarks upon each individual, describing the crime of which they had been respectively guilty, pointing out their phrenological developments to the warden of the prison. In every instance, my delineations were said to be appropriate to the life and crime of the individual.

Obviously, if phrenology could be so accurate after the crime, it could be equally accurate before the crime, detecting the excessive development of the organ of Destructiveness before it erupted into criminal behavior. In the phrenological canon there was no such thing as "total depravity," since the mind consisted not of a "single malign force" but of "a set of faculties to be studied and governed." It followed naturally that punishment and repression were ineffective; only the "reform . . . of the faculties which are concerned in passion" could prevent crime.

In a letter to the inspector of Sing Sing Prison, Lorenzo Fowler explained his ambitions and intentions regarding his work with criminals:

I wish to present to the Board of Inspectors of Mount Pleasant Prison, through you, my desire to secure the following privileges— First, to visit from time to time the male and female departments of the Prison, and converse with those who wish respecting their various natural dispositions, propensities, capacities, & also their habits, education, and parentage,—And believing as I do that there are intimate relations between the shape of the brain and natural tendencies of the mind, & as there is no other class in the community so favorable to observations of this kind, I wish 2ndly to make such observations as will be satisfactory on this point, & 3rdly, to take such drawings of different persons as is necessary to illustrate my observations....

Privileges of this kind have been granted me without reserve in many of the States, so that I do not ask it as a matter of curiosity, but for the sake of science only.[10]

For the "sake of science" and the abolition of crime, Lorenzo formed an informal alliance with the strong-minded Mrs. Eliza W. Farnham.[11] Mrs. Farnham, who had been brought up in a backwoods section of New York State by a nagging aunt and an alcoholic uncle, had attended a young ladies' seminary in Albany, where Lorenzo Fowler had examined her head, finding it "masculine" with "immense" Causality. Thanks to such natural endowments, Mrs. Farnham had in 1844 achieved the position of matron of the female department of Sing Sing Prison. Having caught the phrenological contagion, she introduced phrenological books into the prison library, invited Margaret Fuller to lecture, and, with Lorenzo Fowler's help, edited Marmaduke Blake Sampson's *Rationale of Crime*. With Fowler's blessing, books and lectures, music and kindness were used in the treatment of Sing Sing's women prisoners. Mrs. Farnham's assistant Georgiana Bruce, who had tasted the joys of communal life at Brook Farm, brought her piano to the prison. For a time the Fowlers could rejoice. The power of kindness, coupled with phrenological understanding, was on its way to reclaiming the criminal.

Since phrenology was "directly at war with the gallows," the

Fowlers were at war with capital punishment, pleading, with George Combe, that "our prisons be converted into physiological, educational, and religious Reformatories." Although Eliza Farnham was shortly dismissed from Sing Sing and branded as a Fourierite and Socialist, an infidel and "a woman of ill fame," the brothers continued their crusade, working to introduce phrenological testimony in court trials and later acting as American publishers of a monthly magazine devoted to criminal reform, *The Prisoners' Friend*.

Their views on the treatment of criminals corresponded with their views on the understanding of the insane, and, just as they visited prisons, they visited asylums and retreats for lunatics.[12] Confronted by a woman patient in a strait jacket, her lips foaming as she screamed wildly, Orson placed his fingers "upon the organ of Destructiveness, which was very large, and felt excessive heat there, and *there only* . . . whenever my fingers touched the organ of Destructiveness, she would cry out." Case after case seemed to confirm the Fowlers' conviction that insanity and moral imbecility could be recognized before they led to crime and could even occasionally be cured. It was obvious to them that the man who had been struck upon the temple and who indulged "in immoderate laughter at everybody" had simply received an "injury . . . upon the seat of Mirthfulness." When leeches and crushed ice were applied to that "seat," a cure was eventually effected. Lorenzo wrote, "By showing the reciprocal relations between 'Body and Mind,' Phrenology enables us to retain a proper balance between our physical and mental functions, to restore lost equilibrium, and to treat successfully the various phases of insanity and other disorders." Orson said: "Much of the wickedness of mankind is on a par with insanity. It is . . . caused by the sickness of the Organs of the erring faculties, not by depravity of purpose."

To cure the sickness of crime and wickedness, the Fowlers brought to the asylums and prisons of the East their gift of seeing "manners in the face" and character in the head. Indirectly they also helped reform the treatment of the criminal and the insane.

41

In 1842 Lorenzo examined the head of Pliny Earle, who doubted "if any of my nearest relatives or most intimate friends could have given a more accurate synopsis of my character." Earle was to become one of America's pioneer psychiatrists, first president of the New York Psychological Association, and author of *The Curability of Insanity*; his early introduction to the "practical utility of phrenology" may well have played some part in his treatment of the insane.

Indeed, during the forties it seemed to the Fowlers that almost every aspect of life could be approached phrenologically. The heads of all races, nations, and sexes, differing widely in form, differed also in character. Exploring expeditions should therefore, they held, be accompanied by a phrenologist who would advance the understanding of ethnology.[13]

Meanwhile, in their New York office the Fowlers, equipped with their measuring tapes and casts of heads, were advancing another cause. In their crusade for sex education, Orson and Lorenzo Fowler pioneered in eugenics and marriage counseling.[14]

Against the prudery, false modesty, and ignorance that made sex a forbidden subject, they waged a daring campaign. Lorenzo wrote: "Is it not absurd for any one to advance the opinion that it is too *delicate* a subject, to improve the human race. . . . If it be *really too delicate* to discuss the principles necessary to be known and observed before one is qualified to enter upon the duties incumbent upon this change of condition—then it will most certainly be entirely *too delicate* to get married, and absolutely *shocking* to become parents." To "improve the human race," Orson lectured frankly on marriage despite threats that the gaslights would be turned off in the lecture room and he himself imprisoned. In the examining room the Fowlers encouraged their visitors to face those "domestic evils which lead to . . . vice and misery." Tearing away the veils of "morbid delicacy or prudish affectation" from the subject of sex, the Fowler brothers must be counted among America's pioneer sex educators.

Some of their advice was sheerest nonsense. "Bright red hair should marry jet black." "Red-whiskered men should marry brunettes." "Those very fleshy should not marry those equally so, but those too spare and slim." "Curls should not marry curls— except those easily taken off." Yet much of their marriage counseling was not only wise but beneficent in its effects. Orson, with his contagious enthusiasm and robust, sledge hammer style, accepted as his province more and more of the matrimonial problems that found their way to Nassau Street. And his doctrine was applied successfully in the field too, as Nelson Sizer reported to the *American Phrenological Journal*:

> Husbands and wives, having quarrelled and separated, being "unequally yoked," or, from the unrestrained indulgence of antagonist faculties, have applied to me for examination and advice, which has subsequently been adopted, and they now rejoice under the fragrant foliage of the domestic olive-branch. I have rode for miles among mountains and storms, with some young man or widower, to examine the head of his prospective wife. . . . Husbands and wives are beginning to regulate their connubial habits, and settle their disputes . . . *by the aid* of *phrenology*.

The basis of all the advice given in Nassau Street was the sound belief that since "getting married is the *most responsible* act we can do," "we should be educated for married life." Clients were cautioned to "avoid marrying cousins" and to shun "hereditary diseases." Although early marriages might be a "fruitful source of imperfection," clients also were advised to "marry your first love" and to "gratify each other's faculties." Interrupted love was "the Cause of Licentiousness." Intercourse was more pleasurable when "spiritual love . . . sanctified the sensual. All else is vulgar, debasing . . . and . . . yielding comparatively but little pleasure, because of the small amount of brain called into action." Orson was candid enough to add that the mental organ of sexual passion was relatively smaller in woman than in man—this being his own "inductive observation . . . which his extensive practice entitles to some consideration." Some kind of planned parenthood should be upheld, for the "increase of children beyond all expected ability ... to educate their ... natures, is ... a positive and undeniable moral sin."

Using guidelines dictated by temperament and phrenological development, the Fowlers drew up charts that would enable their clients to choose "congenial companions for life." Lorenzo balked only when one bold young man presented *two* ladies for phrenological analyses at the same time in order to be guided in his selection. In general, the matrimonial advice issued from Nassau Street was direct and clear. "Persons of the same temperament, especially if on *the extreme* of that temperament, should never be united." Indeed, insanity might result if two entirely nervous temperaments combined. Rather, the motive temperament should wed the vital, and "strongly feminized men ... should marry strongly masculinized women." On the other hand, there must be certain "compatibilities of organic development," and those in whom Amativeness was very large—number 7 on the phrenological chart—should obviously not marry those whose Amativeness was very small—number 1. Love was governed by "exact scientific rules." One had merely to consult the phrenologists of Nassau Street in order to study and apply them.

For those who preferred to learn the grammar of love without a teacher, the Fowlers provided several manuals on the subject, all written and published by themselves. Orson's *Matrimony: or Phrenology and Physiology applied to the selection of Suitable Companions for Life; including ... Directions to the Married for Living Affectionately and Happily Together*, written in one week, was published in 1841 while the firm was still in Philadelphia; an edition of five thousand copies was sold in three months, followed by a second edition of ten thousand, which was exhausted in four months. His *Love and Parentage, applied to the Improvement of Offspring* appeared in 1844 with a universal dedication to "All who have ever tasted the sweets of Love; or felt its sting; or consummated its delightful union: or who anticipate its hallowed cup of tenderness." As a supplement to *Love and Parentage*, Orson issued *Amativeness: or Evils and Remedies of Excessive and Perverted Sexuality*, a book that fulminated against matrimonial excess and "self-abuse" or "solitary libertinism."

Lorenzo's pen, though never so prolific or flowery as his brother's, was not idle. In 1842 he published *The Principles of Phrenology and Physiology applied to Man's Social Relations; together with an Analysis of the Domestic Feelings*, a work in which he advocated togetherness in family life and discussed in matter-of-fact detail all those faculties concerned in man's so-called social relations, from Amativeness and Adhesiveness to Philoprogenitiveness and Union for Life. Lorenzo's *Marriage: Its History and Ceremonies; with a Phrenological and Physiological Exposition of the Functions and Qualifications for Happy Marriages* listed the requirements for married life in convenient form and stated:

> We see, through the light of these sciences [phrenology and physiology], that man was created a social being, on scientific principles, for the sake of constituting him a special agent of his race; and that perfect love between the sexes depends on these principles and fixed laws.

The Fowlers, in their books and examinations, exposed those laws, boldly pried open the blind eyes of love, championed a primitive form of eugenics, advanced sex education, and served as marriage counselors to the matrimonially perplexed. At one time they even considered the formation of a society "to apply Phrenology to ... matrimonial alliances"; the columns of the *American Phrenological Journal* were opened to questions and answers on the "Choice of a Wife" ("What kind of a woman [ought a man to marry] who has a predominance of the sanguine temperament ... is about five feet nine inches in height; has blue eyes, dark . . . hair . . . large Amativeness, and rather a narrow forehead"). One satisfied customer, Jesse W. Goodrich, a poet and lawyer of Worcester, Massachusetts, went so far as to publish his own phrenological character as described by Orson Fowler, along with his verses, in a volume intended not only as a "Memento to his Kindred and

45

Friends" but as a means of finding a wife. Goodrich, a bachelor, though not a "confirmed" one, bound in an extra copy of his phrenological reading with the following explicit instructions:

> Will each of those, to whom this friendly memento is sent, please cut out this extra leaf,—mark in the right hand dotted spaces, left blank for that purpose, the sizes of *their* respective organs, *according to their own charts* . . . and return the same together with their daguerreotype . . . to me.

It is not known whether Goodrich's method succeeded, but it assuredly merits classification as an ingenious forerunner of computerized mating.

Upon occasion, as the years passed, the *American Phrenological Journal* even accepted matrimonial advertisements. The periodical was especially receptive to one signed by "A Reformer" of Harrisburg, Pennsylvania, who announced, "I am 25 years old, a vegetarian and reformer in general, and would like to become acquainted with a lady of suitable age—one that believes in the reforms of the present day."

The Fowlers themselves had not only advocated those "reforms of the present day" but had clearly shown how phrenology could advance them. In penal reform, in the understanding of the insane, in vocational and child guidance, and in marriage counseling, they had applied the principle that to phrenologize the nation was to reform the world. The manipulators of Nassau Street were "phrenological reformers" who believed that economic hard times were caused not by the Democrats or the Whigs or the Bank of the United States, but by the excessive exercise of Acquisitiveness on the part of the people. They had found the brokers whom they had examined "as a class, almost destitute of *Conscientiousness*." Lorenzo considered the Seminole War in Florida an outcome of the extreme prominence of Inhabitiveness in the head of the Seminole chief Osceola.[15] Society was engulfed by evil, from inequity in trade and property to folly in fashion and dress, from

46

gluttony and alcoholism to national dyspepsia. The universal panacea could be found in the science that dissected man and exposed him "fully to view," in phrenology and in those reforms that "would rescue mankind from the jaws of a premature grave." The Fowlers regarded sickness and premature death as sinful—health, a duty. They were convinced that the world's bedlam could become a Garden of Eden if man followed not fashion and the abuses of society but the laws of nature.

To those reforms that concerned the mind of man they now added reforms that concerned man's body and physical well-being. The seers of sexual and social harmony joined the ranks of the prophets of bran and the poets of brown bread. The phrenologists who traced psychology in the skull were about to become physicians without benefit of medicine.

A reform in fashion closely connected with their work in sex education was the aspect of dress reform known as antilacing.[16] To the Fowlers' many popular mottoes they added the cautionary maxim, "Natural Waists, or No Wives." Antilacing societies were formed and the evils of tight lacing attacked in the columns of the *American Phrenological Journal* and in book after book written or published by the brothers. "Tight lacing," Orson warned, "is gradual suicide; and, what is quite as bad, kindles impure desires." By "compressing the organs of animal life," the corset hindered circulation, restricted the muscles, deranged the nervous system, and caused a horrifying array of illnesses from stomach cramps to consumption, from premature parturition to cancer of the breast. To Orson's list of grievances against tight lacing, Lorenzo added the mournful complaint, "The fashions of the day are carried to such an extent that we can have no correct idea of the natural form of a fashionable lady." Tight corsets, along with hogshead skirts and shoulder balloons, were "a lasting reproach on the taste of the times." Engravings of women with and without tight corsets graphically depicted the folly of "*self-immolation* upon the altar of fashion"; in private and in public,

in speech and in manual, the brothers exhorted the daughters of
Zion to "break away from the shackles of . . . fashionable liber-
tines" and clothe themselves in "the garb of natural beauty."

To the sons of Zion, the Fowlers directed a message against another fashionable habit, indulgence in the "noxious weed."[17] In
attack after attack, tobacco, with its corollary spitting, was condemned as "an enemy to the constitution." Far more revolting
than the habit was Orson's language in describing it. "The dog
re-eating his vomit is disgusting, but tobacco-spittle is far more
so." As with tight lacing, the Fowlers attributed moral effects to
indulgence in tobacco, which "depraved the nervous system" and
caused a "sinful, sensual tone or cast of the love-feeling, which
constitutes the very essence of licentiousness." Because of its
"vitiating influence on amativeness," Orson concluded that "no
man can be virtuous as a companion who eats tobacco." Like tight
lacing, tobacco was the cause of a long line of diseases, from insanity and loss of memory to neuralgia of the rectum, epilepsy,
and—shades of the twentieth century—cancer. By the end of the
decade, prize essays on the subject would be sponsored by the
firm and the headquarters of the American Anti-Tobacco Society
would be at 131 Nassau Street in the Fowler office.

There too the crusade was waged against a third deadly evil—
alcohol.[18] Like corsets and tobacco, alcohol excited man's animal
nature and weakened his moral and intellectual powers. "Two-
thirds of the idiots and insane in the land," Lorenzo calculated,
"have been the immediate result of one or both parties having
been accustomed to steep their brains, scorch their blood, and
wither their muscles by the free use of this liquid fire." Alcoholism, the Fowlers held, incited gambling and swearing, intensified
Destructiveness which led to murder, and was closely allied with
prostitution. Why, Orson asked, is " 'her house whose steps take
hold on hell,' always in close proximity to the grog-shop? Why
do all harlots take strong drink?" Without citing chapter and
verse for this dubious assumption, and indeed without answering
his rhetorical question, he proceeded to offer a remedy. Orson's

thirty-two-page *Phrenology versus Intemperance* was "Entered according to Act of Benevolence, in the year 1841, By A Tee-Totaller, in the Clerk's Office of the Public Good." The lecture held that "no individual of ordinary intellect could become thoroughly imbued with the spirit of Phrenology, without becoming a thorough-going temperance man."

Temperance men, antitobacco men, and antilacing women basked in the congenial climate of Clinton Hall. There they were joined by the vegetarian men, who promised a return to innocence and peace through a Pythagorean diet.[19] Of all the vegetarians who congregated at Clinton Hall, none was more effective perhaps than the Fowlers' friend Sylvester Graham, who lectured there. Graham, whom Emerson dubbed the "poet of bran bread and pumpkins," advocated the virtues of hard mattresses and stale bread. By these rigorous means he had apparently overcome the severe dyspepsia of his early life, but during the 1840's, when the Fowlers were associated with him, his "mental developments" still had a dyspeptic cast. Endowed with "large combativeness" as well as "extreme cautiousness," he could not have been an easy companion. Indeed, when he died in 1851, it was said of him: "His vanity . . . was excessive. . . . He was obtrusive, and . . . such was the irrepressible energy of his will, that though sometimes he . . . went up like a rocket, he was as sure to come down like a stick. He wore every body out who listened to him. . . . His memory is associated with bran-bread."

Despite the dyspeptic nature of this health reformer, the Fowlers welcomed him and his views at Nassau Street, along with his colleague William Alcott, who advocated a diet of ass's milk to cure cancer and of cow's milk to cure fits. By the time the decade had ended, applications for vegetarian wives and husbands would appear in the matrimonial correspondence of a Fowler periodical, and the American Vegetarian Society would be organized at Clinton Hall to promulgate the view that "if we believe in a millennium, we must, inevitably, give up our belief in animal food." The glories of "fruit and farinacea," along with the evils of alcohol and tobacco, were publicized. Orson Fowler described in detail for his followers his own frugivorous diet, which, though it varied slightly with the changing seasons, maintained a decided monotony:

> With the first appearance of strawberries annually, he [Orson] picks or buys, mashes, sweetens, and adds water or milk, and breaks in brown bread. This dish constitutes his only diet for breakfast and supper, and often for dinner, when he eats three diurnal meals. When strawberries disappear, raspberries—he prefers the black . . . supply their place, till they give way to currants, whortleberries and blackberries. Give me this diet, and you are quite welcome to all the flesh-pots of modern cookery. . . .
>
> This gone, pears and peaches take their place. . . . This diet serves me till November. . . . I sometimes vary the dish by stewing . . . pears in water, and add molasses, eaten with bread. . . .
>
> For dinner—which . . . I frequently omit—I . . . sometimes eat peas, beans, eggs broken into water and boiled but little, or butter-milk . . . or the apple or cherry of pot-pies and dumplings eaten with bread. . . .
>
> My winter and spring diet consists mainly of bread and apples . . . homminy . . . Indian and oat-meal gruels . . . wheat mush . . . honey.[20]

All things considered, it is little wonder that Orson frequently omitted not just the "flesh-pots of modern cookery" but all the farinaceous feasts of the food reformers. Like his eating habits, Orson's bathing regimen was rigorous. To alleviate painful throbbings, he wore wet bandages over his heart and often wrapped himself in wet sheets and blankets. In so doing, he followed the precepts of one of the age's most extraordinary health reforms—hydropathy, or the water cure—and allied himself with its equally extraordinary practitioners.[21]

Russell T. Trall, who had studied under a physician and attended medical lectures, founded a water-cure establishment in New York in 1843, basing his teachings upon those of the Silesian Vincenz Priessnitz. According to Lorenzo, whose diagnoses were always perceptive, Trall had a high head and "all his thoughts were lofty." He was also blunt, unpleasantly candid, and indifferent to the opinions of others. His lofty thoughts were aimed at universal health and eventually an "earthly millennium" through the emancipation of mankind from dependence upon doctors and the "drugopathic system." Water—in wet sheet packs or sweating cradles, in douche baths or wet girdles, in sitz baths or river baths or plunge baths—was the cure-all dispensed at Trall's New York Hygeio-Therapeutic College on Laight Street and advocated in the Phrenological Rooms of Clinton Hall.

Along with Trall, Joel Shew was a frequent visitor to, and lecturer at, the Fowler Cabinet. Having been "badly impregnated with minerals" as a result of his daguerreotypic business, Shew had studied medicine and set up a water-cure establishment in his home on New York's Bond Street. While he ministered wet sheets and sitz baths to his patients, his wife offered kindness. Indeed, she has a claim to fame for having supplied not a hard mattress but a feather bed for Edgar Allan Poe when he settled in his cottage at Fordham.

While the practitioners dispensed packs and douches, the Fowlers advanced the cause of cold water in their own way. In April, 1848, they took over publication of the *Water-Cure Journal, and Herald of Reforms*, edited by Joel Shew, and in little more than a year increased its circulation from one thousand to twenty thousand. Believing that hydropathy would "soon surpass all other systems of the healing art," the Fowlers sponsored a journal that advocated accouchement with the water cure and home treatment for fever and ague, reported Benvenuto Cellini's "Cure by Cold Water," and even sported a "Cooling and Refreshing" design on its cover.

The *Water-Cure Journal* was actually the organ of the American Hydropathic Association, of which Lorenzo was a vice-president. With the *Water-Cure and Health Almanac*, compiled from back numbers of the *Journal*, as well as with other publications, the Fowlers continued their crusade for pure water. They were undaunted by satires and lampoons that depicted icicles in the caves of Nova Zembla and described invalids dosed with water until they "kicked the bucket." Even the ravages of cholera, which broke out the day after Shew's Clinton Hall lecture on water treatment as a cure for that disease, did not dismay them. Both business and the *Water-Cure Journal* were resumed after a few weeks' suspension. Indeed, by 1850 the firm was looking forward to "a great universal Hydropathic Convention" along with "a Hydropathic Reading Circle in every neighborhood."

In order to supply the demands they had helped create, the Fowlers published not merely a journal on the subject of water cure but an entire *Water-Cure Library*. The causes of sex education and child guidance, temperance and hydropathy, antilacing and antitobacco—all the reforms touted in the Phrenological Cabinet—required appropriate reading matter. As the Fowlers supplied books for those in search of health of mind and body, they found that the salubrity of mankind went hand in hand with increased business at Clinton Hall. They were adding to their renown as phrenologists a reputation as large-scale publishers. For the extended range of their activities they needed an expanded staff. Providentially both their family and their firm had been enriched during the forties by two new members: a husband for Charlotte, a wife for Lorenzo. The former would enlarge the scope of the business; the latter would eventually extend the horizon of the reform movements agitated at Clinton Hall.

"SELF-MADE OR NEVER MADE"

. . . .

IV

SAMUEL Roberts Wells was exactly what the Fowler brothers needed.[1] Less fanatical than Orson, he still believed in the
"good time coming." Less gifted in psychological insight than
Lorenzo, he still had a keen understanding of his fellow man.
Though he had some interest in medicine, he was not restricted
by scientific disciplines, and so he accepted phrenology not merely
as a reform of the day but as a way of life. Primarily he was a
vigorous businessman, ready to sell phrenology to the public as
any merchant would sell his wares. Tall, impressive, graceful, he
inspired confidence and, with his genial temperament and winning manners, was bound to influence his public. Moreover, he
had an attribute that, above all others, must have endeared him to
the firm of O. S. and L. N. Fowler. Samuel Roberts Wells was
inclined to overwork.

He had been born in West Hartford, Connecticut, on April 4,
1820, but his father had soon moved to the near-wilderness of
west central New York, settling on a farm near Little Sodus Bay
on the shore of Lake Ontario. There—like the Fowler boys before
him—he had cleared the land and tilled the soil, in addition to
trapping in the forest and sailing on the lake. He too had been
beset by dreams, at first vague reachings for "light and knowledge," which crystallized at length into the ambition to study medicine at Yale College. After brief sessions at the district school,
young Wells was apprenticed to a tanner and currier in the neighborhood, reading medicine at the same time. Thus he familiar-
ized himself with business methods while he studied human ills.

53

When he was only sixteen he happened to see, in Ithaca, New York, a phrenological chart marked by one Charlotte Fowler, who, at twenty-two, had already shown some proficiency as a manipulator. The chart introduced him to the new science. A few years later he would be introduced to its delineator.

Meanwhile Samuel set aside a few hundred dollars for his future education and learned that the Fowler brothers were delivering a course of lectures in Boston. After attending these lectures, he immediately "determined to be a student of the Fowlers, and joined them for that purpose in their professional ramblings, studying the theory, listening to their delineations, and taking daily lessons in that department." Young Wells was a believer, though a genial one, and, besides accepting the precepts of phrenology, he dedicated himself to all the other reforms advocated by the Fowlers, from hydropathy to temperance, from vegetarianism to antilacing. In addition, perhaps more perceptively than Orson and Lorenzo, he saw in those reforms the means not only of enlightening the public but of creating and developing a large publishing business. This would be his forte as the years passed —providing the American reading public with a library of self-improvement books. Like his friend Horace Greeley, he would be, in his own gentle and courteous way, a tribune of the people, preaching the gospel of health and improvability. Like the firm of which he would soon become a partner, he personified the motto "Self-Made or Never Made."

In 1843 Samuel Wells abandoned his medical ambitions to join the Fowler brothers in New York. To them both, as well as to sister Charlotte, he was an attractive addition to Clinton Hall. Above the "common height," "symmetrical in form," he "spoke in gentle tones, and was polite and winning in his address. His hair was dark and plentiful; his beard full; his forehead broad and high—in a sentence, he had the look of a refined and cultivated gentleman." On October 13, 1844, the thirty-year-old Charlotte and the twenty-four-year-old Samuel exercised their organs of

Union for Life, and shortly thereafter Samuel Roberts Wells became a member of the reorganized firm of Fowlers and Wells.

It was a time for marriages. Less than a month before Charlotte became Charlotte Fowler Wells, her brother Lorenzo had taken a wife, enriching the Fowler family with one of its most colorful members.

In March, 1844, Lorenzo had left Nassau Street for a phrenological journey that took him to Nantucket Island, where he examined the head of Walter Folger, the astronomer-mathematician-navigator who called himself a clock- and watchmaker but whose neighbors called him "as odd as huckleberry chowder."[2] While manipulating that gentleman's remarkable head, Lorenzo was introduced to Lydia Folger, daughter of Walter Folger's brother Gideon. Six months later they would be married.

It was small wonder that Lydia Folger took hold of Lorenzo's heart and mind.[3] Born in 1822, she was almost eleven years younger than he, and yet, even in her early twenties, she had that "commanding presence, charm of manner, [and] excellent command of English" that would invariably impress the world in which she moved. Just then, on Nantucket, the combination of her faculties strongly impressed Lorenzo Fowler. Her plump, rather full face gave indication of her strong vital temperament, and in her conversation with the young phrenologist she revealed those scholarly and scientific interests which she may have inherited from no less distinguished an ancestor than Benjamin Franklin.

The daughter of Gideon and Eunice Folger, Lydia was a descendant of Peter Folger, from whom Benjamin Franklin had also been descended through his mother. Lydia's ancestry was also shared by such strong-minded women as Lucretia Mott and Maria Mitchell, and the family propensity for knowledge in general and science in particular persisted in Lydia. Like astronomy itself, her own "elementary principle" seemed to direct her upward, a course she followed by being "a very ardent student" who enjoyed "intellectual training somewhat in advance of that which was customary for young ladies in her day." Lydia spent her girlhood to such good effect that she would one day become not merely a lecturer and a writer but the first woman professor of medicine in the country.

At that moment, in 1844, she had another role—that of "May-queen" about to "usher" Lorenzo Fowler into what would be described as "a long glad summer of happy wedded life." So impressed had he been with Lydia's bearing, learning, and warmth that he returned to Nantucket on April 2 to take phrenological notes on her character. His analysis is interesting, both as a perceptive reading and as a form of courtship:

> This lady has a brain of full size, and a physical organization well adapted to its exercise. The relationship . . . between the body and the brain is more perfect than in many. . . .
>
> Her mind is very susceptible to impressions. . . . She is constantly taking lessons. She learns something from everything she sees, hears, or reads. She observes and obeys the language of nature. . . . She is purely a child of nature. . . .
>
> Her phrenological developments are mostly full, large, or very large. . . . The strongest elements of her mind are of a moral nature. . . . Her next strongest are the social and intellectual faculties. . . . She is seldom carried away by impulse or the excitement of the moment. . . .
>
> Her social and domestic nature is strongly developed. . . . [She] can not enjoy herself without mate or companion. . . . She has strong parental feelings . . . well adapted to the care of children. . . . She has the disposition to defend and maintain her rights . . . resolute and executive . . . does not stop at trifles or multiplied difficulties when she has an object to accomplish. . . . Her desire for nutrition is rather strongly developed. . . . She does everything with both eyes open, and seldom makes a mistake . . . cautious and deliberative . . . firm, decided, and persevering . . . ambitious to a high degree . . . affable and agreeable . . . dignified. . . . She enjoys herself alone, and delights to allow her mind to dwell upon subjects entirely disconnected with matter or sense. She is evidently fond of fiction, as also of the wonderful and uncommon. . . .

She not only learns from books, but from observation and experience. She has a decided preference for experimental philosophy, and for the philosophy of mind. She is also fond of natural history. ... She has a clear and original mind.[4]

The child of nature Lydia Folger found a phrenologically suitable companion for life in the student of nature Lorenzo Fowler. On September 19, 1844, they were married in Nantucket.[5] Although Charlotte Wells would have no children, and Orson's would not share in the firm's activities, the Lorenzo Fowlers would have three strong-minded daughters, one of whom would carry the phrenological standard into the far from congenial climate of the twentieth century.

Meanwhile, in the more sympathetic nineteenth century, the firm of Fowlers and Wells organized itself for the threefold purpose of phrenologizing America, reforming the world, and expanding a self-made business. Now that there were three members of the firm, a division of labor was feasible. Orson explained in the *American Phrenological Journal* of December, 1845:

We have always before been distracted between a multiplicity of engagements which allowed time to perfect none. Lecturing, examining, writing, running after paper, following up printer and binder ... [we were] compelled to write by *snatches* ... interrupted ... *incessantly*, now by a business applicant, now by one who wants to talk on Phrenology, next by a letter. ... Thus it has been ... from the beginning until now. But he [i.e., Orson] has now obviated this great barrier ... by having formed a partnership with his brother L. N. Fowler, and brother-in-law, S. R. Wells, by which he can now retire to his study and write more to his liking. His brother, after the 1st of January, will always be found at the Journal office, until we can take more eligible quarters, to fulfil all professional applications. Having devoted all his energies to making examinations, and distracted by neither authorship nor publishing, L. N. Fowler is probably as well calculated to *examine heads*, and to delineate character, and give advice, as any other man in the world. ... Heretofore *a Fowler* has not always been at our office.

57

Hereafter, one of them will be at the service of professional applicants. . . .

S. R. Wells is the business, publishing man of the firm. . . .

Nor will that excellent sister, to whose devotion to the Journal it owes in part its continuance, be severed from its interests. She is yet to be as devoted and efficient a helper as she has ever been.[6]

By 1845 the pattern was established: Orson, the writer, producing page after page for the *Journal* and text after text on phrenology and matrimony, antilacing and temperance; Lorenzo reading head after head in a succession of private or group examinations; Samuel Wells serving as publishing arm and business manager—the three aided in their varied endeavors by the sympathetic and omnipresent Charlotte. Division of labor was phrenologically sound and all but a guarantee of good business. "Do you wish to have a firm that shall be successful in making money?" Lorenzo asked. "Select one partner who can buy the goods, another who can sell them, and a third to be the financier. *Let each attend to his own department and not attempt to do the work of the others,* and success will surely come."[7] Besides attempting to follow this sage injunction, the firm of Fowlers and Wells had all the advantages of being literally a family affair. Even the paterfamilias Horace, residing in Hanover, Michigan, was numbered among the agents who distributed Fowler publications. In the mid-1840's, when phrenology and related reforms were palatable cure-alls to thousands, Fowlers and Wells were intent upon spreading those *"glorious truths . . .* on a larger scale than the Fowlers alone had been able to do." They would write and publish and phrenologize in a manner that could be described only as wholesale, in order, as they put it, "by selling the more, to *spread our doctrines* the farther."[8] The very air of Nassau Street breathed of expansion and success.

The Philadelphia office had long since been discontinued, and all the Fowler efforts were now concentrated on Clinton Hall. Some years before, they had moved next door to 131 Nassau Street—still in the Mercantile Library Building—but in "rooms

. . . larger, and every way better"; toward the end of the decade they occupied two adjoining stores in the same premises.[9] They needed the rooms for their ever expanding Phrenological Cabinet, which, combining the attractions of Barnum's American Museum, a freak show, and a scientific repository, was fast becoming one of New York's show places.[10]

Visitors to Clinton Hall were surrounded by busts and casts, specimens and mummies, paintings and drawings of animal and human, the savage and civilized, the criminal and virtuous. They were surrounded indeed by human nature, whose varied aspects and astonishing forms a guide was ever eager to expound. Since admission was free, visitors often came in droves, and either Orson, Lorenzo, Samuel, or Charlotte would take time to conduct them round the Cabinet.

The displays had been assembled from literally all over the world. There were casts and specimens from "the cream . . . of the celebrated Edinburgh collection" of George Combe and skulls from as far away as Canton, China, sent by a captain who sailed with "a phrenological crew" and who was "a thorough-going phrenologist." The firm announced:

For years an artist was kept in requisition, to take Casts and Busts of persons of eminence in talent and virtue, and of those who were notorious for crime.

For many years arrangements were kept open with the friends of peculiar people, to let us know when they died, so that a cast of their heads could be obtained, and many a dark, rainy night have the proprietors traveled miles to make a cast of some deceased person.

They have visited prisons and attended executions for the purpose of taking the casts of heads, and large sums of money have thus been expended sometimes, as a premium, for obtaining the head of some singular or vicious character. Travelers, captains of ships, soldiers on the frontier, have brought home specimens of the skulls of the different nations of the world, and contributed them to this collection.[11]

59

The visitor might examine the busts and casts, the life masks and death masks of pirate, robber, murderer, cannibal, and idiot as well as of the most benevolent and brilliant. There was indeed a grand variety on display: in one corner, the head of John Quincy Adams, "old man eloquent"; in another, that of the executed pirate Gibbs. Here was the bust of Horace Greeley, recently added to the collection, as well as that of a black woman whose brain, diseased in the area of Veneration, caused her to "pray incessantly from morning to night." An African stood side by side with a Choctaw chief, Michelangelo near Black Hawk, a wild boar in close proximity to a Bengal tiger. The heads of Julius Caesar, Captain Cook, and Napoleon Bonaparte recalled the past, while those of Bryant and Clay, De Witt Clinton and Peter Cooper illumined the present. Eventually a congenial family circle of heads was formed. Lorenzo, Lydia, Orson, and Charlotte and Samuel Wells were united in plaster casts upon which the heads of Spurzheim and George Combe looked kindly down. To remind all visitors of the joys of reform, the cast of a temperance lecturer was added to the Cabinet, along with that of a "writer on Health."

Cabinets, the Fowlers believed, were "required in every town and district in the land," for "to learn, we must first Observe, and to do this, must have Things to look at." There was much to look at in the Phrenological Cabinet of Clinton Hall, where, the firm advertised, "Strangers, as well as citizens, will find . . . an agreeable place to spend a few moments, when at leisure. No one can look on the vast number of familiar faces therein contained without being deeply affected."

Having been "deeply affected," the visitor might proceed to a lecture on phrenology, temperance, or vegetarianism, free or costing only twelve and a half cents, before savoring other, somewhat more expensive, advantages offered by the firm. In phrenological classes at the Cabinet, costing twenty-five cents each, "those who wish may become acquainted with this interesting circle," learn the different temperaments, and place "each other's hands on organs that are large or small."[12] Private lessons were, necessarily, priced higher—one dollar a session—although, since "to lecture to and instruct woman in Phrenology" was Orson's "great delight," he frequently gave his services free to a lady. In 1848 Charlotte started a phrenological class for women, a project which, it was said, "opens a new field. Popular prejudice forbids a lady perambulating the country and teaching her own sex the science of mind, but by private classes and lectures, she may do much good."

There was much to teach to both ladies and gentlemen, for such was the exuberantly fluid nature of phrenology that the faculties themselves were being increased from time to time as new organs were discovered. That interesting organ of Union for Life, for example, had been found situated conveniently between Amativeness and Adhesiveness, and subsequently the organ of Alimentiveness would be neatly subdivided to set off Bibativeness, giving a fondness for liquids, from that faculty which gave a fondness for solid food. Before his death Spurzheim had raised the number of organs to thirty-seven, a number that was gradually increased to thirty-nine, forty-one, and, by some, forty-three.[13]

After a lecture or a lesson, the visitor may well have been inclined to purchase a memento. Symbolical heads engraved by the New York wood engraver William Howland, and priced at twenty cents, represented Firmness as a mule, Appetite as Mr. Greedy devouring apple dumplings, and Benevolence as the Good Samaritan. According to Lorenzo:

Each representation in the head is designed to show the qualities of mind in that region. . . . Comparison represented by an alchymist [*sic*] before his crucible, analyzing and comparing; Combativeness, by two boys contending; . . . Acquisitiveness, by a man counting his money; Causality, by Newton philosophizing upon the falling apple; . . . Sublimity, by the Niagara Falls.[14]

For those who wished a more lasting token of a day at Clinton Hall, a phrenological bust, "showing the exact location of all the

Organs of the Brain," was available at $1.25. The cast, the size of the human head, was made of plaster of paris and was described as "one of the most ingenious inventions of the age." It could be sent by express or freight; indeed, the firm of Fowlers and Wells served its mail order customers well, even reading characters from daguerreotypes, "the ¾ pose preferred."[15]

There was, however, no doubt that the presence of the actual head was advantageous, if not absolutely essential, for an analysis, and many visitors, having learned to know others from the grand display of casts at Clinton Hall, were enticed into the examining room to "know themselves."[16]

Those who submitted to the manipulations of Lorenzo, Orson, or his assistant B. J. Gray—who was soon to leave for the gold fields of California—came away in the early days with a chart, later with a sixty-page pamphlet upon which the faculties of the subject were marked in seven degrees: very small, small, moderate, average, full, large, and very large. As early as 1843 the *Phrenological Journal* boasted,

"What distinguishes O S F [owler]'s practice most of all from that of other phrenologists is, that whereas *they*, besides the *oral* predication, give only either a mere chart containing the names and functions of the organs, with the relative size of each in the person examined, marked opposite,—or a simple written predication, without the sizes of the organs; *he*, for no greater fee, gives *a book* containing 60 18mo pages and 6 pages of engravings, in which several pages are appropriated for a statement of the relative sizes of the organs.

The Fowler firm, in other words, gave more for the money, their fee ranging from one dollar for a verbal examination with booklet to three dollars for a lengthier handwritten analysis. The great and near great, the known and the unknown flocked to Clinton Hall, for what delights were greater than to hear a discourse on their own temperament and mental manifestations, their talents and dispositions, while a bearded, affable examiner with a comforting manner whipped out his tape to measure the circumference of their heads? They came as the decade rolled on —the dancer Fanny Elssler, the learned blacksmith Elihu Burritt, of whose head Lorenzo made a cast. Horace Greeley, dropping in at Nassau Street, was informed that his brain was large and in the right place and that brown bread and cold water were his salvation. The writer Joseph Neal, the sweet singer of Hartford Lydia Sigourney, and the Poughkeepsie clairvoyant Andrew Jackson Davis bared their heads to the wizards of manipulation. Brigham Young came incognito with "most of his . . . apostles" to hear the encouraging diagnosis, "You, sir, have vital force sufficient to live a hundred and fifty years." Indeed many came incognito, perhaps to test the tester, among them Lucretia Mott, whose very large "Reflectives" could not be hidden despite her anonymity. By and large, the analyses were sugarcoated and hence decidedly palatable to the visitors. Nonetheless Lorenzo especially had a way of saying "a great many sharp things of people who desire it, but in such a good-natured way as not to chafe and harass them."

Perhaps the most provocative of the analyses made at this time was one not by Lorenzo but by Orson, on February 27, 1847. The man who sat for his phrenological portrait was engaged in the wool trade at Springfield, Massachusetts, and was on a visit to New York; he wore a beard and had a strong, rugged, almost granite face. Orson had never seen him before, nor did he have any information about him. His written analysis, still extant, included some perceptive observations:

You are very active both physically and mentally—are positive in your likes and dislikes, "go the whole figure or nothing" and want others to do the same.

You . . . would rather lead than be led. . . . In making up your mind you are careful and judicious, but are firm as the hills when once decided. . . . You like to have your own way, and to think and act for your self—are quite independent and dignified, yet candid, open, and plain; say just what you think. . . .

63

> You are too blunt and free-spoken—you often find that your
> motives are not understood.[17]

The man Orson examined that winter day in 1847 would indeed
"go the whole figure or nothing" and find his motives "not understood." His name would reverberate through the nation in a
dozen years. It was John Brown.

When Orson was not flourishing his measuring tape, he was
flourishing his pen, as, to some extent, were all the scribbling
Fowlers. For the mill of partner Wells, who managed the publishing department of Fowlers and Wells, all the Fowlers provided
grist by the bushel. Their themes were more or less the same, and,
though the titles of their books were varied, their texts had a kind
of steadfast monotony. Orson expounded his publishing credo in
the preface to the American edition of Andrew Combe's *Principles of Physiology*, which he edited, "I shall publish no work
which I do not think eminently *calculated* to *do good*." Moreover, "so that all, especially the *labouring* classes," might learn
from them "the comforts and happiness of a virtuous and healthy
life," his books were practical and low-priced. They were also
fresh and racy, "intensely American" in style, full of graphic
colloquialisms and slipshod grammar. He had no time at all to re-
write and seldom had time even to read his manuscripts before
they went to press. Their composition frequently "caused a sickness probably consequent on *night* writing." They also caused a
considerable amount of paper consumption. In addition to his
purely phrenological writings *The Christian Phrenologist* and the
Synopsis of Phrenology, a host of books on related subjects flowed
from his agile pen: *Physiology, Animal and Mental; Self-Culture,
and Perfection of Character; Memory and Intellectual Improvement; Temperance;* and *Hereditary Descent,* books that studied
man "not by sections, but as a Unit" in order to clarify "the reciprocal bearings and complex inter-relations of the multifarious
laws of his being." This view of man as a whole being proved popular, and Orson's books sold in the thousands: fifteen thousand

copies of *Memory* in one year, and the entire edition of *Education and Self-Improvement* in three months.[18]

Although Lorenzo was less prolific, taking, in this single respect, "more after his father" and finding writing rather difficult, he too produced a few phrenological best sellers—for example, *Principles of Phrenology and Physiology applied to Man's Social Relations* and *Marriage: Its History and Ceremonies*, the latter selling eight thousand copies within two years.[19] His wife also joined the ranks, writing for the "use of Children and Youth in Schools and Families" her trilogy of *Familiar Lessons—on Physiology*, *Phrenology*, and *Astronomy*. Since it was as important for children as for adults to "know themselves," Lydia Folger Fowler supplied them with manuals advertised in her husband's *Journal* and published under the supervision of her new brother-in-law.[20]

The days of the Fowlers were full indeed. Despite the division of labor in the office, Orson especially seems to have worked almost compulsively, as his schedule indicates:

I have lectured to crowded houses, in close rooms, every evening in the week, Sabbath evening (on temperance) included, and I seldom lecture much less than two hours, and usually longer, and in a highly energetic manner, and examine heads all day, from the time I rise in the morning till lecture time, and often after lectures till midnight, and have followed it for ten years, and am now more vigorous than when I began. When I am not talking incessantly, (and I always speak loud,) I am writing characters or composing my works, most of which have been written after the exhausting labors of the day and evening. . . . And even now, while writing this paragraph, the clock has struck three in the morning. For four months, I have rarely retired till after 12, and frequently written till daylight.[21]

During the day—a day that ran from 8 A.M. until 10 P.M.—the Fowlers usually remained in their Clinton Hall office, "prepared to wait professionally upon those who may wish 'to know themselves as others know them.' " Between these demanding analytic sessions, they took time to write their manuals and to edit the

Phrenological Journal. Classes and lectures were crowded into the day or held in the evening. These experts in mnemonics lectured not from notes but from memory, wherever they could create a demand. From Clinton Hall to St. Luke's Buildings, from the church at the corner of Christie and Delancey streets to Boston's Marlboro Chapel, they wandered, armed with their phrenological busts and their measuring tapes, to spread the doctrine abroad. "Let me plant a course of lectures in a little village," Orson wrote, "containing but a single tavern, a blacksmith shop, and a dozen houses, and the people flock in from their mountains and valleys for ten miles in all directions, and fill up any meeting-house that can be found."

Even an attack of smallpox which Orson suffered in the early 1840's did not keep him long from his work. Subsisting on only two daily meals, he fortified himself for his intellectual labors by hard physical work. In October, 1842, he and his wife had purchased about twelve acres of land not far from Fishkill, and there, "crowbar in hand," he would clear away stones to fit him for his winter's labors. He must have had little time to exercise his educational theories on his own children, Orsena and the baby Charlotte. Holidays were merely a different version of work. A visit to his father in Michigan was combined with a lecture tour; lecture tours were in turn combined with specimen collecting for the Cabinet. He labored, he said, for love—for love of the science of phrenology. The money he made—nearly seventy-five thousand dollars by the early 1840's—he spent upon the *Journal*, the Cabinet, and "the cause of Phrenology." During the same crowded period he seemed to have been spending himself upon that cause too.

Lorenzo was not very different. He too worked, if not compulsively, steadily. He made frequent lecture tours, accompanied by his wife, who also lectured. In the South and the North, Lorenzo examined heads and gave characters "even to the splitting of a hair." Having analyzed the Philoprogenitiveness of so many others, he found his own rewarded with the birth of his first daughter, Amelia, on June 23, 1846. By that time the Clinton Hall office was alive with activity. The examining room was the scene of a succession of analyses; the Cabinet was filled with visitors; classes of the curious assembled for lectures. New York was becoming phrenologized.

The presses hummed too. The publishing department of Fowlers and Wells, under the stewardship of Samuel Wells, continued to apply Orson's credo, to "publish no work which I do not think eminently *calculated to do good.*"[22] Wells, whose faculty of Acquisitiveness was certainly not underdeveloped, was able to combine the reforming zeal of the Fowlers with brisk business. There is no doubt that during the second half of the decade the Phrenological Cabinet was the "central distribution point" for almost universal reform. From its presses flowed manuals on temperance and vegetarianism, water cure and physiology, as well as Justus Liebig's treatise on *Chemistry* and Cornaro's *Discourses . . . on a Sober and Temperate Life*. Phrenology was regarded in its broadest sense as a window opened upon "Human Rights" and "bearing on legislation, as well as on moral, political, and self-government." The firm, under Wells' aegis, published prize essays on tobacco by its favorite hygienists Trall, Shew, and Alcott—all to demonstrate its "deleterious effects . . . on the human constitution." A *Water-Cure Library* was issued, as well as a series of *Almanacs*—a *Tobacco and Health Almanac*, a *Water-Cure Almanac*, and of course the *Phrenological Almanac*, which, priced at six cents a copy, supplied an apparently almanac-hungry public with tide tables, times of eclipses, phrenological news, and character readings from a variety of heads, including those of Eliza Farnham and Walter Folger, Edwin Forrest and Sylvester Graham. The *Boston Medical and Surgical Journal* commented, "The sale of the Phrenological Almanac in 1846—a popular mode of disseminating the elements of the subject, a sort of sandwich for creating a reading appetite—exceeded 90,000, and it is presumed that 150,000 will be required to meet the demand in 1847."

On the cover of the *Phrenological Almanac* was inscribed the motto "Nature's Printing Press is Man, her types are Signs, her books are Actions." Thanks to the activities of Samuel Wells, it almost seemed as if "Nature's Printing Press" was the press of Clinton Hall, where "The Works of Gall, Spurzheim, Combe, and Graham, together with all works on Phrenology, Physiology, and . . . the Water-Cure [were] for sale, wholesale and retail." The firm boasted that each year the sales of its books doubled while the subscription list of the *Phrenological Journal* rose steadily.

The *Journal* endured and survived the vicissitudes that confront most specialized periodicals.[23] The "pecuniary embarrassment" under which it had labored during its early years was finally overcome; its debts were liquidated, and it not only could pay its bills but could furnish capital for increased engravings, new type, and superior paper. Agents were consigned copies "at the rate of 100 Nos. for $10," although Orson understandably preferred amateur agents who labored for love. "Those who obtain subscriptions *for pay* do well, but how much better those who labor for the *cause*! . . . The Journal goes for *the cause*—for Man—instead of for the 'almighty dollar.' "

The text of the *Journal* certainly did go "for *the cause*." It offered, along with the phrenological developments of scholars, artists, and statesmen, exposés of "Existing Evils" and proposed "Their Remedy," advocating reforms based upon phrenological principles. The phrenological circle was completed when Fowlers and Wells offered their own publications as premiums for subscribers. Results were substantial, the subscription list rising from less than six hundred in 1842 to more than twenty thousand in 1848, and the firm's promise to send "a *monthly* Phrenological Journal, down the stream of time to convert thousands to Phrenology" seemed on its way to fulfillment.

The *Journal* won converts not only to phrenology but to another so-called reform of the age—animal magnetism. In its columns, as well as in books published under the firm's imprint, this aspect of the newness of the forties was warmly endorsed. For a short time phrenology and magnetism embraced one another in a union as fascinating as it was productive. Out of that union came the exploration of thought and of dreams. Out of it too came the search for the poet incarnate as, for a strange moment in time, the self-made wizards of Clinton Hall harked to the music of a *danse macabre*.

POE AND THE GLORY THAT WAS
CLINTON HALL

V

THROUGH the mysterious workings of some strange historical pattern seemingly interwoven in the sciences and pseudosciences of the mind, animal magnetism bore close resemblances, both in its origins and in its progress, to phrenology.[1] Like phrenology, animal magnetism had been a European import. Its Franz Gall had been another Viennese physician, Franz Anton Mesmer, "the great enchanter," who in the eighteenth century had developed a theory of hypnotism based upon the existence of some "external, visible agent," some magnetic force or fluid which permeated the universe and insinuated itself into the nervous system of man, a force which he termed animal magnetism. Like phrenology's Spurzheim, Charles Poyen had been the apostle of animal magnetism, introducing the provocative theory in Boston. The excitement in New England stirred up by his lectures and experiments followed the pattern set by phrenology. "Unreasonably and stubbornly doubted . . . contumaciously discredited and opposed" by some, animal magnetism or mesmerism was accepted by others as a "discovery . . . interesting and sublime . . . calculated to exhibit the power and dominion of the human will."

In the wake of Poyen's lectures flowed a stream of converts —mesmerists, and clairvoyants, psychographers and etherologists, psychometrists and surgeons who performed operations during the "magnetic sleep."[2] The contagion struck with epidemic force. Sophia Peabody Hawthorne succumbed to it, despite her husband's objections, as did Harriet Martineau, who claimed that "the highest faculties are seen in their utmost perfection during the

70

mesmeric sleep." In England, John Elliotson began a periodical called the *Zoist: A Journal of Cerebral Physiology and Mesmerism*; in America, La Roy Sunderland, a revivalist Methodist preacher from Rhode Island, left the church to exercise his hypnotic powers and edit the *Magnet* and later the *Spiritual Philosopher*.

Many of Sunderland's "cerebral experiments" were conducted before the admiring eyes of the Fowlers. Never content with being spectators, however, they soon joined the animal magnetists themselves, experimenting with mesmerism and actually treating patients by that method. Orson explained the technique:

> Animal Magnetism consists in the magnetizer passing his hands from the top of the patient's head down the patient's face and arms, and shaking them at each pass, to shake off the diseased magnetism. The Author has cured and been cured of headache, teethache, neuralgia, and other aches and pains . . . by this means.[3]

Indeed, the Fowlers went further, even magnetizing patients before surgical operations. During a trance induced by Lorenzo, a New Bedford woman had a tumor removed. Orson found that he also could magnetize water until it turned into salts. Their powers were often extremely convenient. During a lecture interrupted by a coughing young lady, Lorenzo was able to relieve the cough, as well as the class, by making "a few passes over the pole of the lungs in the face" of the cougher, telling her "she would not cough again." Orson was so convinced of the widespread beneficence of Mesmer's theory that he believed a knowledge of magnetism would "greatly aid the farmer to improve his stock and promote vegetation."[4]

The Fowlers soon advanced a step forward and combined phrenology with animal magnetism. Their discovery that the phrenological organs could be excited by means of animal magnetism was called phreno-magnetism or phreno-mesmerism, "the exercise of the faculties of the mind by Mesmerism."[5] As the *Phrenological Journal* put it, phrenology and magnetism were "twin brothers by nature" and "ought never to be separated in practice."

Orson and Lorenzo gave frequent exhibitions, both public and private, of this all but incredible combination. After placing their subject in a magnetic trance, they applied their fingers to one or another phrenological organ, and "in every *single* instance the *Faculty* thus magnetized leaped instantly into ... activity." They touched the organ of Devotion, and the magnetized patient clasped hands and prayed; they touched Adhesiveness, and the subject grasped a hand; they touched Combativeness, and the hand struck out. Lorenzo magnetized a lady's Alimentiveness, and when she awoke from her magnetic sleep her appetite had been restored. Orson magnetized another lady's Acquisitiveness, so that she could bargain successfully while shopping. A third young lady, under Orson's beneficent influence, was left with her "moral sentiments highly charged."

Though some objected strongly to a phreno-magnetism that seemed powerful enough to cast out devils, the Fowlers were able to draw many enthusiasts. An observer from the *Cazenovia Eagle* gave an interesting account of the conversion of the local citizenry:

> We have been disposed to class the believers in Animal or Phreno-Magnetism, as members of the same fanatic fraternity with Miller-ites, Bentonian gold humbuggers, & c.; and until recently, have had no evidence to doubt but that they were deservedly so classed. ...
>
> On Thursday evening last a number of our citizens attended his [O. S. Fowler's] lecture [on phreno-magnetism], at the Presby-terian Church; at the close of which he proceeded to magnetize a lad. ... In about fifteen minutes the boy [was] ... in a magnetic sleep. Mr. F. then proceeded to make experiments in Phreno-mag-netism by touching the different organs, which produced corre-sponding action. ... when *tune* and *mirthfulness* were magnetised, the boy would sing and laugh. ... *philoprogenitiveness*, he would caress and fondle any object given him. ... *destructiveness*, he would dash away the object.[6]

With their interest in this hybrid science of the mind came the

Fowlers' investigation of the mental phenomenon of dreaming.[7] They experimented with the idea that "pressure applied to the organs during sleep will cause dreaming." They insisted—as did other philosophers of sleep—that dreaming itself was a kind of "incomplete sleep" that proved the mind was not one single faculty but a congeries of faculties, for if the mind were one separate power, it "would be either all awake or asleep at the same time." Many years later the *Phrenological Journal* would carry an article entitled, "Will the Man of the Future Be Able to Control His Dreams?"

In that article it would be said that Edgar Allan Poe had been among the first to "institute and make *memoranda* of experiments looking to the actual analysis of transition between waking and dreaming." Whether or not the Fowlers during the 1840's were aware of Poe's "drowse-fancies" and views on "bridging the Lethe between waking consciousness and dream-consciousness," they were aware of Poe. Indeed, the man who would soon become Poe's publisher, Justus Starr Redfield, had his headquarters in the same building with Fowlers and Wells.[8]

The partners of the Phrenological Cabinet were as fascinated by the phenomenon of the poet as they were by the phenomenon of dreaming.[9] The phrenological requirements of authors and poets were invariably included in their manuals on vocational guidance, and they relished giving analyses of Shakespeare's characters as well as of poets living and dead. They had noted that Language, which gave a "fulness under the eyes," was very large in the head of Charles Dickens, and they concluded almost reverently:

> Poets require the highest order of both temperament and developments. Poetry depends more on the physiology than the phrenology. It consists in a spiritual ecstacy which can be better felt than described. Not one in many thousands of those who write verses have [sic] the first inspiration of true poetry.

In addition to large Ideality and Language, the poet required a

73

certain type of temperament—the mental or nervous temperament characterized by a slight frame and an oval face, with features delicately cut. Endowed with such a temperament, a man or woman would exercise more mind than body and so be particularly well adapted for the literary, artistic, or poetic life. The Fowlers delighted in searching out an embodiment of this mental temperament that bespoke the poet. Although Emerson had it in "great predominance," and although Bryant also had a "remarkable head," they did not exactly fit the picture of the poet incarnate with which the firm hoped to enrich their manuals. It was not until they hit upon the poet of dreams and of nightmares, of the grotesque and the arabesque, that they found their quarry. In the pages of the phrenological handbooks written or published by the firm, the face of Edgar Allan Poe would for decades mirror the mental temperament of the poet.[10]

Like the Fowlers, Poe had demonstrated a deep interest in mesmerism and animal magnetism. While books on mesmerism flowed forth from the Phrenological Cabinet—eventually an entire "Library of Mesmerism and Psychology,"[11] including Joseph Haddock's *Psychology*, John B. Newman's *Fascination*, and John Bovee Dods' *Philosophy of Electrical Psychology*—the *Phrenological Journal* had instituted a new department, running article after article on the subject, from "Experiments in Magnetism" to "Electricity the Great Acting Power of Nature."[12] In September, 1845, the *Journal* carried an essay entitled "Mesmeric Revelation —By Edgar A. Poe," which had been reprinted from the *Columbian Magazine*. Prefaced to Poe's narrative, the Fowlers inserted the following remarks under the general heading "Magnetic Developments":

> As chroniclers of magnetic occurrences, we cannot well refuse admission to our pages of an article as important as the *subject matter* of the following "Magnetic Revelation,"...claims to be....
>
> The following was written by Edgar A. Poe, a man favorably known in the literary world; so that it may be *relied* upon as authen-

74

tic. Its mere literary merit, the reader will perceive, is by no means inconsiderable. Read and re-read.[13]

They themselves had apparently read with the deepest absorption the dialogue between Poe the magnetizer and Mr. Vankirk the magnetized. They had agreed wholeheartedly with Poe's sentiments on the general acceptance of mesmeric phenomena, and had been profoundly shaken by the death of the sleepwalker at the end. Their dismay must have outdistanced their delight when they soon learned that the narrative they had accepted as fact was mere fiction. In the October issue of the *Journal* they published a retraction:

> *Retraction*, when convinced of error, is due on its own account, and evinces a highminded love of *truth*. . . . The article in his last number, quoted from Mr Poe, proves not to be that "magnetic revelation" it claims for itself, but simply the production of its author's own brain.
>
> The Editor was first led into the error of supposing it a veritable magnetic disclosure, by a verbal account given of it by a magnetizer; which was such as to induce him to procure and peruse it; and secondly, by knowing that the literary clique to which Poe belongs, Joseph C. Neal included, had given much attention to magnetism. Without the least suspicion, therefore, that it was not genuine . . . he gave it the insertion it really merited, provided it had been genuine. . . . he *takes back* all responsibility concerning it, and regrets its occupancy of his pages.[14]

Poe's reaction to this retraction has apparently not been recorded. Indeed, while he reviewed and studied one or more books on phrenology and described many of his own characters and the "literati" in phrenological terms, and although he doubtless must have known of the Fowlers, there is no positive evidence that they ever met. Yet the opportunity existed for such a meeting, either in the early days in Philadelphia, when the firm plied its trade on Chestnut Street, or later at Clinton Hall. The motive too existed, for

Poe's preoccupation with the dark mysteries of the mind might well have led him to the Golgotha of Nassau Street.[15]

In any event, either from life or from a picture, the Fowlers analyzed Edgar Allan Poe and, after his death, published their perceptive findings along with his portrait in the *Phrenological Almanac*:[16]

> This gifted son of genius and misfortune died at Baltimore, in October, 1849, aged thirty-seven. His phrenological developments, combined with the fiery intensity of his temperament, serve to explain many of the eccentricities of this remarkable man. His mother was an actress of great merit, and he inherited from her strongly developed and highly excited faculties, an unusual degree of intellect, Ideality, Sublimity, Spirituality, and Language. We mean that he inherited in sublimated embodiment all of ORGANIZATION that his mother possessed, together with all that unearthly intensity and ethereality which her profession as an actress awakened. Left an orphan at an early day, and being constitutionally averse to restraint, and surrounded as he was by associates ill adapted to moderate and mold the wild enthusiasm of his nature, he released himself from the control and roof of his foster-father, Mr. Allan, and boldly shot off in a tangent, gleaming like a meteor in the heavens, to delight and amaze, attract or astonish. Such was he in social life and in the world of letters. Ambitious, sensitive, and critical in a high degree, he found himself surrounded by those who could neither understand his nature, appreciate his talents, nor sympathize with his erratic spirit. The wine-cup was the bane of his being, and brought out the worst phases of his character; and although his friends claim that this one fault was the procurer of all his waywardness and gained him all his enemies, yet we believe that, artificial excitement aside, he was from the very nature of his organization a wandering star, which could be confined to no orbit and limited to no constellation in the empire of mind.

In the *Phrenological Journal*, where the presence of Poe's "Mesmeric Revelation" had once been regretted, Poe's portrait was now published as the embodiment of the mental or nervous temperament.[17] For years thereafter that portrait would appear

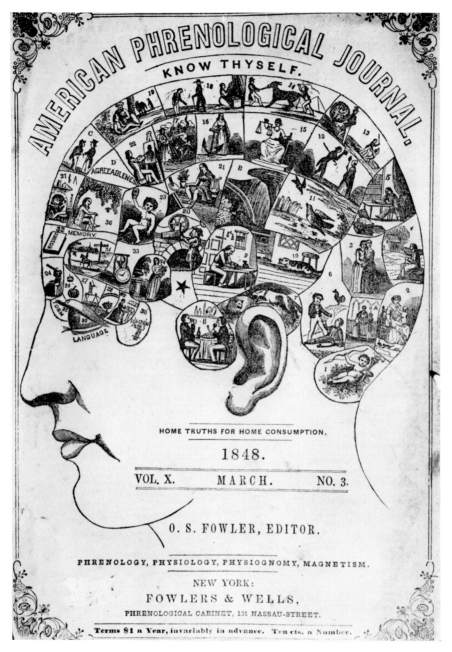

AMERICAN PHRENOLOGICAL JOURNAL.

KNOW THYSELF.

HOME TRUTHS FOR HOME CONSUMPTION.

1848.

VOL. X.   MARCH.   NO. 3.

O. S. FOWLER, EDITOR.

PHRENOLOGY, PHYSIOLOGY, PHYSIOGNOMY, MAGNETISM.

NEW YORK:

FOWLERS & WELLS,

PHRENOLOGICAL CABINET, 131 NASSAU-STREET.

Terms $1 a Year, invariably in advance. Ten cts. a Number.

Symbolical head

From *American Phrenological Journal,*
Vol. XII (1850)

Lorenzo N. Fowler

From William Windsor, *Phrenology*
(Big Rapids, Mich., 1921)

Orson S. Fowler

From William Windsor, *Phrenology*
(Big Rapids, Mich., 1921)

The Fowler office from about 1838 to 1854

From *American Phrenological Journal,*
Vol. 80 (1885)

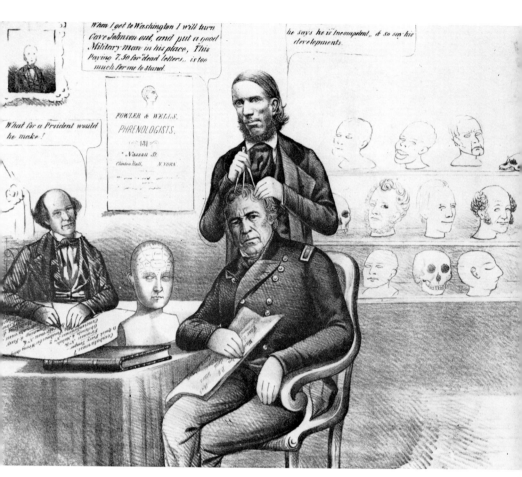

Political caricature (1848)

The New-York Historical Society

The faculty of Philoprogenitiveness. Original caption reads: "DEFI-NITION—*Love of children, animals, pets, and horses.* LOCATION—*Philoprogenitiveness is the second social organ, and is situated directly above Amativeness, in the back part of the head, and is number two in the Symbolical Head.*"

From Lydia F. Fowler, *Familiar Lessons on Phrenology* (New York, 1848)

The faculty of Destructiveness. Original caption reads: "DEFINI-
TION—*Resolution; energy; cruelty; desire to kill.* LOCATION—*Destructiveness is situated on each side of the head, over the ears.*"

From Lydia F. Fowler, *Familiar Lessons
on Phrenology* (New York, 1848)

Object lesson in heads

From George Combe, *Lectures on
Phrenology* (New York, 1839)

in the pages of the firm's manuals—the picture of one whose "dark
. . . eyes . . . carried a vein of sadness and shadow," whose "entire
life was an intense excitement," the poet incarnate who was also
the poet of Golgotha.[18]

Poe's bust graced the Phrenological Cabinet soon after his
death in 1849.[19] In the same year the firm was enriched by the
addition of an important new member. Another self-made man,
destined to remain with the office for more than half a century,
was invited to share the fortunes of the brothers Fowler and
Samuel Wells by becoming a professional examiner.

Nelson Sizer was the right man in the right place.[20] He had all
the attributes—hereditary, temperamental, and phrenological—to
dispense sound vocational and matrimonial advice from the inner
sanctum of Nassau Street. With his strong, compact figure and
well-developed vital system, his sharp, long nose, full beard, and
high ridged brows, he even looked the part of a trustworthy examiner. The descendant of a sailor from the Azores who had settled in Connecticut, Sizer had been born in 1812, the son of
Fletcher and Lydia Bassett Sizer of Chester, Massachusetts. By
his ancestry he was one-eighth French, one-eighth Scottish, with
the balance divided between English and Anglo-American. Thus
he combined "sound English vitality, the Scotch framework and
locomotive force, and the activity and cheerfulness"—along with
"the heavy . . . eyebrow"—of the French. Nelson Sizer was built
to endure.

From his mechanic father he had acquired an easy familiarity
with tools; from the farms of the Berkshire hills he had come to
know something of agricultural processes. At the age of fourteen
he began work in a woolen mill, which he managed three years
later. By the time he was twenty-seven he had labored at carpentry, become partner in a paper mill, and contributed articles to
the local press. He worked, it was said, "eighteen hours a day for
ten months in the year, and twelve hours a day the rest of the
time." As with Samuel Wells, an inclination to overwork was
a decided advantage at the Phrenological Cabinet.

Like the Fowlers, Sizer had first become interested in phrenology when Spurzheim lectured on the subject, but he did not pursue it as a career until 1839, when, after his wife's death, he abandoned the business of paper manufacturing and burned his bridges behind him. At that time Sizer began lecturing on the science of mind, and, thanks to his animated and earnest style, abounding in "comparisons and illustrations," he had some success. That same year he visited the Fowler Philadelphia office, which impressed him as "the headquarters of Phrenology in America." As *"most* efficient" agent for the firm, he rounded up *Journal* subscribers, continuing after he joined forces with Phineas Lyman Buell in 1841.

Buell, who had been born "with a hereditary taint of melancholy," had found in phrenology, which he studied under Orson's assistant Samuel Kirkham, both the cause of and the means of escaping from that "disordered manifestation of mind." His melancholy exorcised, he became for a while a highly suitable partner, with whom Sizer roamed the country as the Fowlers had done, lecturing, manipulating, making character delineations, writing *A Guide to Phrenology*, and frequently sending both subscriptions and letters to the office of the *American Phrenological Journal*.

After the termination of his partnership with Buell and after a second marriage, based upon phrenological selection, Sizer continued on his own, expanding his experience in practical phrenology. By the time he was thirty-seven, he had had ten years in the field and was eminently equipped to join the staff of Fowlers and Wells. An abstainer from coffee and tobacco, he had early cast his lot with the Methodists, who, he believed, "did not bar out, by inflexible decree, nine-tenths of the human race." Though he was touched with the *"reforming* spirit," there was nothing wild or visionary about him. He "engaged in nothing which does not promise to be useful and successful." To the practice of phrenology he lent an aura of earnestness, steadiness, and profound respectability. Nelson Sizer was not only a practical phrenologist but, like Samuel Wells, a practical man.

He began his career as resident examiner with a delineation of Horace Mann, an experience he recalled decades later:

> When I became examiner in the office of Fowler[s] and Wells, photography . . . had not yet made the faces of all public men common. Horace Mann was introduced to me as a subject for examination by Mr. Samuel R. Wells. I had no idea who my subject was, for from that day to this it has been the custom in this office, when an eminent stranger came in and the business department met him and knew his rank, he was introduced to me . . . unknown, unnamed. During the examination, I never felt more inspired or more as if I were walking a tight rope across the gorge of Niagara, but there was enough in him to make me feel strong. When he went from the examination-room into the business department, with his name still unknown to me, he asked Mr. Wells how it was possible for a stranger to know him so well.[21]

Horace Mann would also proclaim, perhaps in part thanks to Nelson Sizer, "Whoever disseminates true Phrenology is a public benefactor."[22]

If only because of the duration of his career, which would in time encompass three hundred thousand professional examinations, Nelson Sizer would come to be known as a giant in the field. With his melodious, wide-ranging voice, his "strong physical forces," and his quiet, steady dedication, he became a pillar in the temple of phrenology founded by the brothers Fowler.

That temple was further enlarged by the end of the forties.[23] Samuel Wells' cousin Lester A. Roberts, of Connecticut, who had read law for a time, joined the firm as cashier. Charles Sheppard, soon to establish the first Turkish bath in this country, served as business assistant, along with Rodney D. Wells. The literary department of Fowlers and Wells was broadened by the presence of the prolific Daniel Harrison Jacques, a native of Massachusetts, who had studied medicine and theology and edited a labor journal. Putting his busy pen to work in the cause of phrenology, Jacques would write one manual after another for the firm, in one of which he would immortalize his employer Samuel Wells as the prime example of the American type or temperament.[24] In the domain on Nassau Street, Approbativeness obviously vied with Self-Esteem.

With a larger staff came increased business, and with increased business, the need for additional personnel. By 1850 Fowlers and Wells were advancing another reform of the age at the same time as they expanded their own office corps. The Phrenological Cabinet was one of the first firms to employ phonographers—those experts in the system of shorthand invented by Isaac Pitman and brought to America by the abolitionist Stephen Pearl Andrews in the hope that it would provide a shortcut to reading for the underprivileged and the enslaved.

Phonography was hailed in the *Phrenological Journal* as "this most promising field of human progression."[25] Lectures on the subject were held at Clinton Hall, and in time the firm became a headquarters for books not only on water cure and vegetarianism but also on this aspect of reform. The periodical *Universal Phonographer* was published by Fowlers and Wells along with books on phonography that eventually filled *A Complete Catalogue of Works for Shorthand Writers*. Phonographic envelopes, mottoes, pencils, and gold pens were sold, and both the Declaration of Independence and the Constitution of the United States were available in phonographic type.

Believing that phonography was to writing what the railroad was to travel, the office "used phonography in its editorial work, in the writing of books and in its professional phrenological consultations . . . [and] was among the very first in New York to adopt it." Especially in the consulting room of Fowlers and Wells, the use of Pitman's system met an urgent need. The *Journal* explained: "Written descriptions of Character are becoming every day more and more in demand. So much, indeed, has this branch of our business increased, that we are obliged to keep a Phonographic Reporter in our office, to report and write character from the lips of the examiner." From the lips of Lorenzo Fowler or Nelson Sizer, "these mental portraits" were recorded in hooks and dashes and later transcribed as guides to self-knowledge and self-culture. While the phrenologists learned the art of dictation, short-hand reporters were trained in their office, and in time two expert reporters were "constantly busy in writing character delineations."

About mid-century it indeed seemed that a phrenological bust might adorn every mantel and that the right to a phrenological examination might be regarded as one of the inalienable rights of every American.[26] The *Journal* welcomed the "thousands of new converts to our glorious science"; while "the voice of the Fowlers was heard far and wide," other voices joined and swelled the phrenological chorus. *Synopses* and *Epitomes of Phrenology* were published as far west as Conneaut, Ohio. Women phrenologists were venturing west, and Orson, returning from his own winter tour, was moved to say:

> Emigration liberalized the public mind, because the bolder minds and freer spirits of older countries, states, and towns, always settle the new, having first left behind many of their erroneous doctrines and contracted customs. This idea he found fully verified throughout the West. Hence Phrenology is there readily embraced and thoroughly diffused, and enters largely into the every-day household usages and ideas of the people.

From Mark Twain's Hannibal to Buenos Aires, where a "phrenological professorship" was established, this science of the mind was disseminated.

In the East, Beecher preached phrenology from his pulpit, stating that "the views of the human mind, as they are revealed by Phrenology, are those views which have underlayed my whole ministry." In a letter to a young lawyer, Horace Mann advised, "The principles of Phrenology lie at the bottom of all sound mental philosophy, and all the sciences depending upon the science of Mind; and all of sound theology, too."

Phrenology, answering the needs of the *Zeitgeist*, permeated the life of the times. It sifted into the language, for, as Harriet Beecher Stowe would observe, its terminology was as convenient in treating human nature "as the algebraic signs in numbers." It even found its way into equitation, for Abraham Lincoln's sponsor and employer Denton Offutt wrote a book entitled *A New and Complete System of Teaching the Horse. On Phrenological Principles.* In Utica, a phrenological room was opened in connection with a public bathhouse. In New York, Clinton Hall was enshrined as a mecca in the verse of one J. H. Cook:

> Ye stranger forms, that often come
> Old Gotham's stirring scenes to greet,
> Call at *one hundred thirty-one*,
> On Nassau's famous, busy street.

On Nassau's "famous, busy street," a Phrenological Tract Society was formed, with Lorenzo as vice-president, Wells as treasurer, and Charlotte as home secretary, to furnish at cost tracts on all the reforms of the age. In May, 1849, a convention was called at Clinton Hall, and the American Phrenological Society was established, with Orson chairing a committee to draft a constitution. The first lecture before the newly formed society was given by Nelson Sizer on the "History, Progress, and Prospects of Phrenology."

The prospects of the science seemed golden. Yet, although many concurred that phrenology was "the mighty engine for propelling human nature onward in its track of illimitable progression," some continued to scorn it as quackery and its practitioners as "*professors* of the celestial humbug."[27] For these, David Reese's view of the phrenologists of the thirties still applied:

> They mark on the skull of some luckless wight, or upon their plaster busts, the mystic numbers of the . . . organs; and then draw black lines around each in imitation of "the illustrious expunger," who is probably a phrenologist, . . . they provide casts in imitation of the brain itself; and they mark these with their magic figures

... until every man may hold the model in his hands, and by the aid of phrenology, read the arcana of his own brains. And, provided with these paraphernalia of office, every wiseacre of the party is at once dubbed a *professor* of the celestial humbug.

Others persisted in objecting to phrenology as fatalistic, materialistic, immoral, and anti-Christian, destroying all sense of individual responsibility. "Multitudes," they warned, "go to the science *for the purpose of easing a loaded conscience*, by learning that their delinquencies and vices are constitutional." The old debate of the thirties was carried on. Early in the new decade, the physicians John Augustine Smith and Frank H. Hamilton attacked, while Andrew Boardman and Orson Fowler defended. By the end of the decade the Cincinnati clergyman Nathan L. Rice joined the fray with his *Phrenology Examined, and shown to be Inconsistent with the Principles of Phisiology* [sic], *Mental and Moral Science, and The Doctrines of Christianity*.

Some controversialists were satisfied with undermining not the theory but the practitioners, especially those notorious charlatans and pretenders who denigrated the science. "Dollars-and-cents *quacks*," fortune-telling phrenologists, and ignorant humbugs still roamed the country, and against such swindlers the Fowlers themselves railed, demanding in the *Phrenological Journal*:

> What shall we say of those who use this noble science as a *coy-duck* ... to bring victims within their power? There is a *gambling* phrenologist ... from Ohio, ... who practices this science simply to secure notoriety and make those acquaintances which will enable him to prey upon the unsuspecting.

For some of their more candid remarks, the Fowlers were threatened with a libel suit by Robert H. Collyer, erstwhile "Professor of Mesmerism and Psychography," whom they castigated as an "immoral Phrenologist, and magnetizer."

Unfortunately, to many observers the omnipresent Fowlers, whose writings were "to be found in almost every town and village," were not distinguished from the quacks and became prime targets for abuse. Because of his belief in man as a "constitutionally moral and religious" being, Orson was accused by some of "rank infidelity" and by others of "truckling to religion and currying its favor." In a review of Spurzheim's *Phrenology*, *The Ladies' Repository* remarked: "With Dr. Combe phrenology reached its zenith. In the hands of the Fowlers, and many other itinerant self-seekers, it has degenerated to the reputation of a humbug." Walter Edgerton published *A Brief Review of Certain Phrenological Works of O. S. Fowler* in the hope that his comments would assist all benighted individuals "in escaping the snare of the 'FOWLER.' "

In singling out the firm for special abuse, assailants simply added further testimony to their popularity and their success. Rival phrenologists, advertising themselves as "superior to Fowler," had the same effect. And so too did the impostor against whom the *Phrenological Journal* fulminated in 1849: "Calling himself L. N. Fowler of Fowlers and Wells," and wearing "dark pants, a linen sack coat and a black oil-skin cap," this impersonator of Lorenzo had collected subscriptions for the *Journal*, hired a horse and carriage, and promptly absconded with the proceeds.[28]

There was no doubt that by this time Fowlers and Wells were manipulators not only of heads but of big business.[29] Their publishing department, under Samuel Wells, claimed to have the largest mail-order list in the city. Their market extended "from Nova Scotia to New Mexico, including the Canadas, and all the Territories on the American continent." Orson's books alone sold by the thousands, and in New Haven "at one time his popularity ... was so great that a bookstore in which his books only were sold was established." Without the help of the general book trade, the firm's phrenological charts were published in "immense numbers," and "almost half a million of his [Orson's] various productions were now in the hands of the American public."

The self-made Fowlers, with Samuel Wells, Nelson Sizer, and their staff, could look about them at 131 Nassau Street and see the results of their handiwork. Their Cabinet had become a veritable museum filled with busts and plaster casts; in their examining room one head after another was bared for examination while reporters recorded the results in shorthand. On tour, Lorenzo and his wife Lydia spread the phrenological doctrine and the laws of good health as Orson produced yet another manual to improve mankind. Over the family domain in Clinton Hall the bustling Charlotte Wells still presided, proofreading, managing, supervising. Soon the business would branch out still further, in Boston and in Philadelphia. Soon too the second group of Horace Fowler's children—Samuel, Edward, and Almira—having come of age, would make their impress directly or indirectly upon the firm and its activities.

Just then, however, with Clinton Hall running smoothly, effectively, and profitably under the aegis of Samuel and Charlotte Wells and Nelson Sizer, there was time at last for the Fowler brothers to engage in pursuits other than strict business. Lorenzo and Lydia could devote themselves to study or more extended lecture tours. Orson could indulge an interest that had of late become more and more compelling. He would of course not forsake the "first and only occupation of his enthusiastic youth, and the idol of his matured . . . years." He would merely turn aside temporarily from phrenology to fulfill a desire that had grown with his "professional peregrinations."[30] Orson's teeming mind had produced yet another plan—the design for a house on the land he had bought near his wife's birthplace in Fishkill. His new project would vigorously exercise his organs of Inhabitiveness and Constructiveness—not to mention his faculty of Hope. It would also excite the wonderment and imitation of the eastern seaboard, for the phrenologist-turned-amateur-builder was about to exert a profound and startling influence upon the development of American domestic architecture.

THE OCTAGON HOUSE

Orson started out with a tract of land and an idea. The land was in Dutchess County, New York, on the Post Road between Fishkill and Poughkeepsie, about two miles south of Wappingers Falls. He had begun buying land in that area—where his wife's family, the Brevoorts, had their home—as early as 1842, when he and Eliza had paid $675 at public auction for twelve acres of Fishkill soil. Later he had added more parcels of land on both sides of the road as his idea matured.[1]

The idea was simple. He wished to build a cheap and comfortable home for himself and his family, and, having offered guidance in so many fields from his sanctum in Clinton Hall, he wished also to instruct others in building, "especially to bring comfortable dwellings within the reach of the poorer classes."[2] He was not at all troubled by the fact that he was not by education or training equipped for architecture. If every man could be his own physician, every man could be his own architect. Besides, architecture came quite naturally within the ken of phrenology. As the *Journal* explained, "Phrenology points out an organ of Inhabitiveness, or love of Home, as well as of Constructiveness, so that building cheap houses, and telling the Poor—for it also points out an organ of Benevolence—how to build themselves cheap and good houses, comes properly within its sphere."[3] In other words, since Orson Fowler was phrenologically suited for architecture, there was nothing to deter him from going forth and building himself a house.

Indeed, the Poughkeepsie clairvoyant, Andrew Jackson Davis,

had had a vision of Orson as architect long before he had commenced building. On January 16, 1847, the seer had written,

> The other day, when I met Mr. O. S. Fowler, I seemed to see an architect, whose plans are large, and various, and desirable, with an unusual number of windows and doors in his proposed superstructure, but either lacking the suitable building material, or else not properly and congenially assisted by efficient carpenters and masons.[4]

The vision was prophetic. In time, after "suitable building material" had been discovered, the structure and superstructure of Fowler's extraordinary edifice would dominate the surrounding country and bemuse the local citizenry.

Before he had hit upon that "building material," indeed, while his house was still in the planning stage, Orson Fowler did what came naturally to him—he wrote a book. Seizing his pen before he gripped his shovel, he produced in 1848 a manual entitled *A Home for All: or a New, Cheap, Convenient, and Superior Mode of Building*, a book that inveighed against current architectural errors in judgment and taste, introduced an astounding number of modern conveniences in building, and suggested a comparatively unusual shape—the octagonal—for domestic dwellings. His publishing credo was now applied to his architectural purposes. The reformer who touted the benefits of bran bread and cold water adapted his reform concepts to building. Long in advance of Louis Sullivan, Orson Fowler upheld the doctrine that "form follows function." Long in advance of the housing administrations of the twentieth century, he attempted to bestow upon the common man the benefits of good housing. On the high tide of nineteenth-century individualism, he launched the concept that every man could be his own builder.

Published by Fowlers and Wells, *A Home for All* was well reviewed in May, 1848, by *Holden's Dollar Magazine*, which said that while the book was "novel" and "excellent," "Mr. Fowler's architectural aphorisms are sensible, but peculiar." "Mr. Fowler's architectural aphorisms" would be quoted and referred to in near-ly every contemporary building and carpentry manual. His book, with important revisions, would go through at least seven editions in nine years, becoming what art historians have called the "main instrument of propagation for octagonal house plans throughout the United States."[5]

In the preface of a revised edition, Orson outlined the purpose of his book, recalled the architectural observations he had made in the course of his travels, and reviewed the steps that had led him to abandon temporarily the plaster casts of Clinton Hall for the fields of Fishkill:

> To cheapen and improve human homes . . . is the object of this volume. . . . It delineates a new mode of inclosing public edifices and private residences, far better, every way, and several hundred per cent. cheaper, than any other; and will enable the poor but in-genious man to erect a comfortable dwelling at a trifling cost, and almost without the aid or cost, as now, of mechanics. Except in a single particular, and this he has greatly improved, this mode is the invention of the author, and occurred thus. Till past forty, his profession engrossed too much of his time and means to allow him to procure a comfortable home; yet for ten years he has been making observations, in all his professional peregrinations, and cogitating by months, upon the best mode of building the home of his future years.[6]

While *A Home for All* went through one printing after another under Samuel Wells' supervision, its author began to practice what he had already preached. Living in a house in Fishkill Village, a small agricultural community some five miles west of the Hudson and some sixty miles from New York, Orson Fowler, between 1850 and 1853, built the "home of his future years." Although his manual suggested do-it-yourself techniques for the amateur build-er, the house that Orson envisioned for himself was hardly of such nature or dimensions that "the poor but ingenious man" could emulate.

It was to be an extraordinary house. Perched upon an oval

knoll, it would in time command "a full prospect of . . . the . . . 'Highlands,' and . . . the Cattskill [*sic*] Mountains . . . together with the opposite banks of the noble Hudson." The view it presented to others would be equally "noble."[7] Octagonal in shape, the completed house contained 60 rooms, including entries, a basement, three stories, and a twenty-foot glass-domed octagonal cupola. On the main floor were four large octagonal rooms—the parlor, sitting room, dining room, and amusement room—all connected by folding doors, as well as four other side rooms, all adjoining. Each of the upper floors contained twenty rooms.

Many visitors were to stroll through "Fowler's Folly," but none gave a more vivid report than the writer for *Godey's Lady's Book*, who observed:

> The appearance is noble, massive, grand, and imposing, especially as seen from a distance. Its position, on an eminence in the basin of the Hudson formed by the Highlands, renders it "the observed of all observers," from all the regions round about. Its scenery, as viewed from the top of the cupola, is surpassingly grand, far-reaching, and picturesque. It has piazzas all around at each story, which make delightful promenades. Its main, or through entry, is in the ground or first story, devoted to work and storage; and its storeway is in the centre, which greatly facilitates ready access from each room to all the others, and saves steps, and which is lighted from the cupola, in the centre of which is a glass dome, which also lights its stairway and the right centre rooms.[8]

Orson believed that "men's habitations correspond with their characteristics," and hence a fancy man would build a fancy cottage, a practical man a convenient home. By such a standard, Orson Fowler, who built "a superb villa," was most assuredly "a superior man."[9] He was also a man who, despite the demands of creditors, despite the money poured from Clinton Hall into the Fishkill octagon, was thoroughly enjoying himself. Going off to lecture when funds were low, he returned with replenished coffers and renewed zest to the work of construction. Nelson Sizer's opinion—that "O. S. is digging along with his mudwall castle, large enough for ten families. The whole thing a magnificent piece of folly"—disturbed Orson not a whit.[10] "No labor of my life," he wrote, "has given me more lively delight than the planning and building of my own house; and to all it can likewise be rendered almost intoxicating."[11]

To that intoxication Orson Fowler gave himself almost completely. For each of his plans he had a purpose, and there was considerable method to his seeming madness. He would have sixty rooms, "but not one too many,"[12] for by the time the house was ready his household would number sixteen, including his wife, two daughters, his father and stepmother, a few Brevoort relatives, and several Irish laborers.[13] In addition, any Fowler family home required: a playroom for children, a dancing room, and a gymnastic room for unlaced ladies; a wash kitchen for rough work and a milk room below stairs; a woodhouse, a lumber room, and sauce cellars; a dressing room for every bedroom and closets innumerable; a library and a room for minerals, shells, and portraits; a prophet's chamber and an author's studio. Verandas surrounded the house, not for ornament but for viewing. Indeed, Orson deplored the finicky ornamentation of Greek Revival houses with their "finified carvings and cornicings,"[14] and his own house was relatively free of such gimcrackery. He deplored too the smoky chimneys, poor cellars, and ratholes of many contemporary structures, and he determined that his house, avoiding all such inconveniences and nuisances, would be a perfect home.

For his selection of the octagon shape, Orson also had his reasons.[15] Although the form had been applied architecturally for centuries—in the Florentine Baptistry of Saint John and the Chapter Houses of York and Westminster—it had seldom been adapted to domestic architecture. Orson Fowler saw the octagon for what it was—the geometric shape closest to the sphere. Hence, he deduced, it would allow for more room than the conventional square or rectangle; providing such economy of space, it would also admit increased sunlight, eliminate square corners, and actually facilitate communication between rooms. Orson would utilize corners that did remain for storage areas or closets. Here in truth was a form that not only followed but expedited function.

Here was a form that could be part of an architectural reform, loosing mankind from bondage to the traditional boxlike house. Orson demanded:

> Why continue to build in the same Square form of all past ages? ... Nature's forms are mostly SPHERICAL.... Then why not apply her forms to houses? ... Since, ... a circle incloses more space for its surface, than any other form ... the nearer spherical our houses, the more room for the outside wall, besides being more comfortable. ...
>
> The octagon, by approximating the circle, incloses more space for its wall than the square, besides being more compact and available.

It was, in short, a shape "more beautiful, more capacious, and more consonant with the predominant or governing form of Nature—the spherical."[16]

It was from nature too that Orson Fowler took the materials with which he built his octagonal house. After he had begun the construction with conventional planks and plaster, he had interrupted his labors for a lecture tour through Wisconsin. There, near Jaynesville, in the town of Milton, he had met Joseph Goodrich, an innkeeper and trader who introduced him to nature's building material.[17] Goodrich had made the long wagon journey from the East to "the then almost unknown Wisconsin" to trade with the Indians of Prairie du Lac, not long after O. S. and L. N. Fowler had opened their Cabinet. On the western prairies where he had settled, lumber and building stones were scarce, but the land was rich in gravel, coarse sand, and lime. From those materials Goodrich had made a mixture which he called grout or gravel wall, and with this bounty of nature he had built in 1844 a combination residence, store, and tavern known to the local citizenry as Goodrich's Folly but destined to make architectural history as one of the first concrete buildings in the United States.

Both Goodrich—an antitobacco man—and his tavern—a temperance hostelry—appealed to Orson Fowler. With his "corpulent frame" and "beaming face," Goodrich looked the part of the jovial and generous innkeeper who would "fill your shirt for a shilling." So convinced was he of the durability of his construction materials that "for 6 cents per blow, he would let a man pound with a sledge upon his parlor walls, and let any one bang away on his blacksmith shop till they were tired." Orson accepted the challenge, hammered without indenting the wall, and, although he had ordered the timber for "the house of his life," immediately upon his return countermanded the order "except for the floor timbers." Since New York State was as rich in gravel lime as Wisconsin, he would proceed with the Goodrich recipe and avail himself of the bounty of Fishkill.

As the octagon form followed nature, so this mixture of coarse gravel, lime, sand, and broken slate came from nature. It was "better than brick or wood and not ¼ as expensive." Hence it was irresistible to Orson Fowler, who wrote: "Nature's building material is abundant everywhere, cheap, durable, and complete throughout. . . . The superiority of this plan must certainly revolutionize building, and especially enable poor men to build their own homes." All the credit he claimed was "that of appreciating its superiority" and applying it to the construction of his octagonal house.[18]

With his own hands he dug, shoveled, and wheeled the material into the mortar beds. He was surrounded not by phonographers and editors but by assistants doing odd jobs and errands. For the plaster casts and phrenological heads that had been the appurtenances of his life he substituted wheelbarrows of lime and hogsheads of water. The phrenologist had abandoned himself to the intoxicating joys of scaffolding and gravel walls, window sills and door arches. He kept careful account of his expenses, concurring with Joseph Goodrich that his walls, which prevented drafts better than frame walls and preserved an even temperature, were "four times cheaper than wood, and six times cheaper than brick."

It cost me 44 days' work, of common $12 per month hands, to put up my wall. . . . It took six days and a half of my carpenter's labor, at $1^{00} per day, which, added to the other, makes $26^{50}, and two and a half days of the mason to lay the window sills, and the arches over windows and doors, and to level off the wall, and put on the boards, ready for the floor timbers.

"I leave you," he gloated, "to either proceed in the old horse-jog mode of building, or adopt this new railroad style."[19]

The new "railroad style" was indeed fast and cheap, designed for the age of the railroad and of the common man. With his use of the octagon form and of Goodrich's gravel wall—facetiously called by his neighbors "Fowler's brick"[20]—Orson was convinced that he had discovered "NATURE'S style of architecture."[21]

Only a man of nature could improve upon nature. It was the age of patents and inventions as well as the age of the common man, and Orson Fowler was as alert to the conveniences of central heating as he was to the practicality of Goodrich's gravel wall. By the time his sixty-room octagonal villa was complete, it boasted not merely a room for every child and a room for every whim and every activity but all the modern conveniences known to the mid-century. In place of the fireplaces and grates of the "horse-jog" age, it used hot air and hot water furnaces. The building was filled with speaking tubes and dumb waiters to lighten the burdens of the housekeeper. Each room had its own ventilator. Glass was employed wherever possible. "I can not resist the growing conviction," Orson proclaimed, "that *glass* is *Nature's* roofing and flooring material. . . . It could be run in all sorts of forms and molds of beauty, interweaving, as in carpets, any varieties and combinations of beautiful figures." With gas illumination, refrigeration, and running water, Fowler's octagon was "perhaps the most modern house in America in its day."

In its use of the indoor water closet, it was especially modern. Orson had decided views on this subject, which he candidly shared with his public. The water closet—"a real necessity in a prime house"—should, he believed, be placed under the stairs. "To

squeamish maidens and fastidious beaux, this point is not submitted, but matrons, the aged and feeble, are asked, is not such
a closet a real household necessity and luxury?"[22]

While Fowler's Folly rose on its knoll over the Hudson valley,
A Home for All underwent revision and enlargement. The 1853
edition of that significant architectural handbook recommended
not only the octagon form but the gravel wall method of building.
Meantime, the builder cultivated his garden when he was not
improving his home, and at the end of a long day's labor he could
climb to the top of his octagonal cupola and look far off, into the
highlands and into the future.

Orson could be gratified that the purpose for which each of his
sixty rooms had been designed found fulfillment.[23] The bedrooms
and dressing rooms were occupied by a household that included
not only his immediate family but several of his in-laws as well
as his workmen. Neighbors who could not resist the attractions of
Fowler's Folly dropped by to see the latest in central heating or
exchange views on the cultivation of fruit trees and berry bushes.
Receptions were held in the parlors for visitors who, taking the
steamboat that plied between New York and Fishkill, arrived in
droves to marvel at the monumental octagon—among them such
notables as Amelia Bloomer and Lucretia Mott, Horace Greeley
and Charles A. Dana. Gardner Howland, the shipping merchant
who owned the California Isthmus route, brought his daughters
to behold the wonder of the eastern seaboard. Beecher, a summer
resident of Fishkill, came to reminisce about Amherst or compare
ideas on mental philosophy as he partook of Mrs. Fowler's vegetarian table.

Fowler's architectural creation was admirably suited to large-
scale lectures. The distinguished-looking host with flowing beard
and piercing eye discoursed on phrenology at his Fishkill residence
every Monday evening in August and September, dropping his
words of wisdom free to all except "tobacco chewers," who were
requested to "leave old 'soldiers' behind." Classes for "Learning

Phrenology" ("tuition $20 in advance") were advertised in the *Phrenological Journal,* where it was announced that board for students was obtainable in the neighborhood or with Orson's family at four dollars a week. To bring additional students into the area, Orson lectured on "Home Truths for Home Consumption or the Laws of Our Being" at Finch's Hall in Peekskill, following up his preachments with professional examinations at John Williams' Hotel. The like-minded flocked for a time to the Hudson valley. Fowler's co-worker Russell Trall was consulting physician in the Highland Home Water-Cure in Fishkill Landing. Having feasted on bran bread and gloried in the architectural possibilities of the octagon, visitors could climax their Fishkill sojourn with an invigorating shower, douche, or plunge bath.

In time, thanks to the astounding influence of Orson's book *A Home for All,* some water cure establishments in New York State would themselves be built in the shape of octagons.[24] Scarcely a "Cottage Builder's Manual" during the 1850's could omit reference to Fowler's book, while any mention of an artisan, nurseryman, or roofer in *A Home for All* guaranteed the workman a flood of inquiries. Fowlers and Wells announced that it was receiving orders for the book from France, England, China, and the Sandwich Islands. The firm initiated an architectural department, selling not only Orson's manual, but "Works on Architecture" by Downing, Ranlett, and Gould; one of its periodicals offered "The Builder" as a feature, and by 1860 it numbered among its "New Publications" a *Manual of House Architecture.* Daniel Harrison Jacques applied his busy pen to the subject in *The House: A Manual of Rural Architecture,* in which he announced: "In this country everybody builds a house. . . . Everybody, then, should know something about domestic architecture."

During the 1850's, especially in the eastern part of the country, it seemed indeed that the house "everybody" was building was of the gravel wall variety and octagonal in shape. According to the *Phrenological Journal,* "A new era in the art of building seems to

95

be dawning upon the world." It was an era marked by the octagon and gravel wall house. Under the heading "Gravel-Wall Builders Wanted," the *Journal* announced:

> Applications by hundreds have been made to us for architects who can superintend the construction of houses on the new gravel-wall plan. ... Should a sufficient number of applicants signify their desire to learn, we will form a class ... to show all about both the mode of fixing the boxboards, and mixing and depositing the mortar and building the walls.[25]

Summering at Little Sodus Bay on Lake Ontario, Lorenzo, arrayed in "a straw hat a shirt and overalls," built himself a small gravel wall octagon house. The firm's engraver William Howland followed suit with an eight-sided cottage, and John Brown's son John did likewise, erecting a two-story octagon in East Williamsburgh, New York.[26] Along the Hudson and the Connecticut valleys, in New England and the Middle West, the eight-sided structures sprang up. Thanks to that amateur enthusiast Orson Fowler, another fad was added to a fad-ridden decade—the octagon. Octagonal schoolhouses and churches, barns and carriage houses, smoke houses and chicken houses, "associative dwellings" and lodging houses, windmills and pigsties dotted the landscape—all visibly proclaiming that there could be eight sides to a building. Even a séance chamber built by a spiritualist summer colony in New York State would follow the Fowler precept.

At least one thousand octagon houses were built in the United States, most of them by 1857, the panic year when the fad subsided. In that year too Orson Fowler—doubtless overwhelmed by the drain upon his financial resources—leased the octagon that had started the frenzy. Its earlier history was happier than its end would be.[27] In September, 1857, Orson rented it, with its 130 acres and its household furniture (except for an "Eolian . . . instrument") to a New York real estate operator, William A. Riker, for $2,500 annually. Converted by its lessee into a boarding house, it was the dread scene of a typhoid outbreak the following summer—the partial result of cesspool seepage through Orson's "impermeable" gravel walls. It was then, when the boarders fled in terror, that Orson, whose own life had undergone some change, sold the octagonal Folly that had been his dream. Transferred in 1859 to his daughter Orsena, now married to Melville Smith of Minneapolis, it remained in her hands only a few months before it left the family forever.

The house would stand some four decades, passing through a series of ill-starred owners. During the Civil War it served Andreas Cassard as the "Cuban Institute and Military Academy." When the academy failed, the octagon was once again metamorphosed into a boarding house under the proprietorship of one Mrs. Cunningham. Mrs. Cunningham was unfortunately and erroneously confused with the Mrs. Cunningham who had been indicted for the murder of the dentist Harvey Burdell, and, despite her protestations, her boarders hastily departed as the rumor of her murderous propensities spread. By 1880, after another unsuccessful attempt at converting it into a boarding house, the sixty-room octagon stood empty on its knoll over the highlands. Ten years later the younger generation of Wappingers Falls and environs illuminated the building with torches and cavorted through it in a carnival that resembled a witch's dance. The local press called the occurrence "A Ball in a Deserted House":

On a recent night, the Fowler House . . . which has been deserted for years, was the scene of festivity and fun. A large party of young people from Wappingers Falls and elsewhere took possession [of] it and had a grand carnival which lasted throughout the night. There was abundant room to dance in, and when tired of dancing the young people wandered about the . . . rooms, played hide-and-seek in the spacious corridors, and promenaded the building generally. The old building, illuminated from cellar to turret, presented a picture as grand as unusual, and to those who did not know the cause, it appeared that the spooks and goblins with which it has been thought the old pile was inhabited, were on the rampage.[28]

By 1894, after the house had been bought and sold on the New

York Stock Exchange "for apparent considerations of from $10,000 to $50,000," it was an "old pile" indeed. The windows were broken, the roof and woodwork decayed, the verandas rotted away. Soon the walls—those walls that Orson had called "NA-TURE'S style of architecture"—began crumbling. The Fishkill paper made its lugubrious observation: "A much larger portion of the walls of the old Fowler house . . . has fallen within the past few days and the house is more of a ruin than ever." The great octagonal structure that had been the delight of its builder, the wonder of the Hudson valley, the impetus to changing architectural whims, was now "a public hazard." In August, 1897, the *Fishkill Weekly Times* commented: "the tottering walls of the Fowler House . . . were razed . . . and now the site is covered with a heap of broken debris. The work of razing was done by a few dynamite blasts, Fred C. Haight being the demolishing engineer."

Orson Fowler did not live to see his octagonal creation dynamited into a heap of debris, for by the time it was razed he had been dead for ten years. He did live to see its decay and gradual ruin, and once, only a few years before he died, it was said that he visited the house and climbed the outer stairway to the roof, "running up the ladder like a cat." Much had changed since he had built that stairway, designed that octagon, written his *Home for All*. Both the home and its architect had reflected time's metamorphoses.

So too had the firm he had founded. When Fowlers and Wells was selling Orson's manual to readers in China and the Sandwich Islands, it was selling another book destined eventually for all the world. While Orson Fowler was finding in his Fishkill octagon a delight "almost intoxicating," the Phrenological Cabinet was greeting a young visitor who wrote, "All architecture is what you do to it when you look upon it." The visitor was looking upon life and building the book he would call *Leaves of Grass*.

WALT WHITMAN, CARE OF FOWLER
AND WELLS

· ·

VII

O<small>N</small> July 16, 1849, the thirty-year-old Walt Whitman walked into the Fowlers and Wells offices at Clinton Hall and submitted his massive head to the test of phrenology. *Leaves of Grass* would not be published for another six years. The poet, not yet known as Walt but as Walter, had followed various pursuits, among them those of printer's devil for two Long Island papers and editor of the *Brooklyn Eagle*. He had traveled south and paid what would become a legendary visit to New Orleans. With his shaggy red beard and open shirt, he had wandered much and absorbed his country long before his country would absorb him. Now in 1849, he was absorbing himself, studying his "extraordinary" impulses, and, perhaps out of some degree of terror and unease, the poet who was not yet the American bard sought at Clinton Hall a resolution of doubts, an affirmation of purposes, a direction. Emerson, who would "greet" him "at the beginning of a great career," would add that that career "yet must have had a long foreground somewhere." Whitman's phrenological examination was a significant part of that "long foreground." For Fowlers and Wells the confrontation was at the time not nearly so important. To the firm, it would bring a new editor and a new business relationship fraught with vexing problems. To Whitman, it would bring the confirmation he had sought and would play a not inconsiderable role in shaping the poet and his book.

Like *Leaves of Grass*, this phrenological examination itself had had "a long foreground." Although Whitman had traveled much about the metropolis, it was not by chance that he ventured to

99

Clinton Hall. Since the beginning of 1846 he had had some interest
in phrenology, clipping and underlining an article on the subject
from the *American Review* in January of that year. In the *Brooklyn Eagle* he had reviewed several phrenological manuals, among
them Spurzheim's *Phrenology*, which had moved him to write in
November, 1846:

> Breasting the waves of detraction, as a ship dashes sea-waves, Phre-
> nology, it must now be confessed by all men who have open eyes,
> has at last gained a position, and a firm one, among the sciences. . . .
> Perhaps no philosophic revolutionisers ever were attacked with
> more virulence—struck by more sinewy arms, or greater persever-
> ance—than Gall, Spurzheim, and the other early Phrenologists. . . .
> But the Phrenologists withstood the storm, and have gained the
> victory.[1]

A few months later, under the heading "Something about Physiology and Phrenology," the *Eagle* admitted Fowlers and Wells
to the hierarchy of "philosophic revolutionisers":

> There can be no harm, but probably much good, in pursuing the
> study of phrenology. It is easy for the superficial to ridicule the
> new, or the profound—and indeed, the fanaticism of novices is
> always fair game; but the deliberate man will not be turned aside
> from the even tenor of his course of inquiry after truth, by either
> extreme.
> Among the most persevering workers in phrenology in this
> country, must certainly be reckoned the two Fowlers and Mr.
> Wells.[2]

Having commented briefly upon Orson's *Physiology, Animal and
Mental* and *Memory and Intellectual Improvement*, Whitman
turned his attention to Lorenzo's *Marriage: Its History and Ceremonies*: "The verdant prudishness has passed away, which would
be offended at any discussion—in the plain, comprehensive, and
perfectly decorous style of this book—of the subject which it
treats on."[3]

As he continued to copy out excerpts from phrenological works, he included passages on related subjects close to the hearts of Fowlers and Wells. Although the temperance novel he had written in 1842 was a potboiler, *Franklin Evans, the Inebriate* reflected the author's personal interest in abstinence. When eventually the poet "celebrated himself," he would describe himself as "Of pure American breed, of reckless health, his body perfect . . . full-blooded, six feet high, a good feeder, never once using medicine, drinking water only . . . always dressed freely and clean in strong clothes, neck open, shirt collar flat and broad."[4] This was a sketch not only of Walt Whitman but of the model man of Fowlers and Wells—a temperance man, an antilacing man, an antimedicine man.

In 1849, the year of his phrenological examination, Whitman was actually planning "a series of lectures on diet, exercise and health," for which he may have rented a store in Granada Hall.[5] Certainly his readings in Fowlers and Wells publications and his possible attendance at Fowler lectures equipped him for such a series. Collecting articles on health and physical perfection, he was almost as deeply interested as the Fowlers in such subjects as heredity, physique, and even "Decent Homes for Working-Men." He had much in common with the proprietors of Clinton Hall, and many were the subjects upon which they might have exchanged views. One was longevity. In his *Hereditary Descent*, Orson Fowler, mentioning the "Memoirs of John Whitman and his descendants," had written, "John Whitman, called the Ancestor of the Whitman family, lived to be about 90."[6] Years later Orson would write, "One Whitman had a son when 80, who lived to be 80."[7] Perhaps through curiosity about Whitman genealogy or longevity, perhaps through interest in hydropathy or temperance or phrenology itself, Whitman crossed on the Fulton Street Ferry from Brooklyn and walked to Nassau Street. He would write in "Good-Bye My Fancy": "One of the choice places of New York to me then was the 'Phrenological Cabinet' of Fowler & Wells, Nassau Street near Beekman. Here were all the busts, examples, curios and books of that study obtainable. I went there often, and once for myself had a very elaborate and leisurely examination and 'chart of bumps' written out (I have it yet) by Nelson Fowler (or was it Sizer?) there."[8]

Actually, on that momentous July 16, 1849, it was Lorenzo Fowler whose manipulating fingers explored the skull of "W. Whitman (Age 29 [i.e. 30] Occupation Printer)."[9] At his dictation the phrenological description was written out by a copyist, followed by a listing of Whitman's characteristics and faculties with estimates of their sizes. Whitman was to quote and requote from Lorenzo's perceptive analysis, an analysis that was to exert a deep influence not only upon his character and his conception of that character but upon his work. The analysis took into account the longevity of the Whitman family and the health of the young man in the examining chair. It discerned from Whitman's head the character of one who chose "to fight with tongue and pen," of one "*too* open at times" who had not "alway[s] enough restraint in speech." It was a penetrating sketch of a man of independence who thought for himself, who could "see much that is unjust and inhuman in the present condition of society," who had but "little regard for creeds or ceremonies," of one easily moved by suffering, of one whose "considerable imagination" did not blind him to "fact or reality." Almost anticipating Whitman's own style, Lorenzo described his subject as a man who could "compare. illustrate. discriminate. and criticise." To the poet who would one day write "Myself I Sing," Lorenzo Fowler said, "You . . . are yourself at all times." On that hot summer day, as he sat in the examining room surrounded by his busts and skulls, did not Lorenzo Fowler, without once mentioning the word "poet," realize with some exuberance that here indeed was a poet in the making? In the very act of dictating his comments, he was perhaps helping to make that poet and filling in the foreground of a great career.

> You were blessed by nature with a good constitution and power to live to a good old age. You were undoubtedly descended from a long-lived family. You were not (like many) prematurely de-

veloped—did not get ripe like a hot house-plant but you can last long and grow better as you grow older if you are careful to obey the laws of health, of life and of mental and physical development. You have a large sized brain giving you much mentality as a whole. You are well calculated to enjoy social life—Few men have *all* the social feelings as strong as you have. Your love and regard for woman as such are strong and you are for elevating and ameliorating the female character. You were inclined to marry at an early age. You could not well bear to be deprived of you[r] domestic privileges and enjoyments. You are very fond of children or pets and would much desire to have your *own* intelligent and respected. You are also very fond of home and think much of having one of your own and of making it comfortable and attractive. You would like to travel and yet to go and leave family and friends would be a *task*. You are one of the most friendly men in the world and your happiness is greatly depending on your social relations. You are familiar and open in your intercourse with others but you do not by so doing lose your dignity. You would be or *are* a kind husband— an affectionate father. and a sincere friend and a feeling obliging neighbor. You can easily pass from one thing to another and you prefer short comprehensive speeches to long yarns about nothing. You have much energy when you are aroused but you are not easily moved at trifles. You would if obliged to, fight bravely for friends, woman, moral character, children and honor. You choose to fight with tongue and pen rather than with your fist. You are not quarrelsome but You mind your own business and like to see others do the same. You are cautious and look well to the future. to consequences and obstructions and are generally pretty sure you are right before you "go ahead." Your courage is probably more *moral* than *physical*. Your appetite is most *too* strong naturally and your food relishes well. You are pretty well calculated to *resist* disease and to soon *recover* if you are attacked. by it. You are no hypocrite but are plain spoken and are what you *appear* to be at all times. You are in fact most *too* open at times and have not alway[s] enough restraint in speech. You are more careful about what you *do* than you are about what you say—You are independent, not wishing to be a slave yourself or to enslave others. You have your own opinions and think for yourself. You wish to work on your own hook, and are inclined to take the lead. You are very firm in general and not easily driven from your position. Your sense of justice, of right and wrong is strong and you can see much that is unjust and inhuman in the present condition of society. You are but little inclined to the spiritual or devotional and have but little regard for creeds or ceremonies. You are not any too sanguine and generally realize as much as you hope for—You are very sympathetic and easily moved by suffering. and take much interest in those movements that are of a reformatory and philanthropic character. You are not any too fond of property but value it as a *means*—are not a penny-man, and despise narrowminded penuriousness—You have taste and considerable imagination but it does not blind you to fact or reality. You can adapt yourself to time place and company but you do not try to act out another's character but are yourself at all times. You have both reason and perception. and hence can reason well. You have a strong desire to see everything and your knowledge is practical and *available*. You have a good mechanical eye and can judge well of and recollect forms and proportions well. You have a good sense of order either *mentally* or *physically*. By practice might make a good accountant. You can locate well and have a taste for geography. You are a great reader and have a good memory of facts and events much better than their *time*. You can compare. illustrate. discriminate. and criticise with much ability. You can be sarcastic if you choose. You are a good physiognomist. You have a good command of language especially if excited.

Lorenzo followed his "Phrenological Description of W. Whitman" with "Phrenological Notes on W. Whitman," in which he calculated the size of his faculties and characteristics. On the phrenological scale of 1 to 7, where 1 stood for an undesirable very small and 7 for an undesirable very large, Whitman's ratings were those of an extraordinary man, strong in "animal will," with large Amativeness and Adhesiveness, Self-Esteem and Sublimity, Individuality and Intuitiveness. The phrenological chart which he tucked under his arm on leaving Clinton Hall was indeed the chart of a man "of pure American breed, large and lusty . . . naive, masculine, affectionate, contemplative, sensual, imperious," the representative of American democracy. It was the picture of Walt Whitman as Walt Whitman wished to see himself. It was, in phrenological terms, the image of the poet of *Leaves of Grass*. Lorenzo wrote:

> This man has a grand physical constitution, and power to live to a good old age. He is undoubtedly descended from the soundest and hardiest stock. Size of head large. Leading traits of character appear to be Friendship, Sympathy, Sublimity and Self-Esteem, and markedly among his combinations the dangerous faults of Indolence, a tendency to the pleasure of Voluptuousness and Alimentiveness, and a certain reckless swing of animal will, too unmindful, probably, of the conviction of others.
>
> Amativeness large 6, Philoprogenitiveness 6, Adhesiveness 6, Inhabitiveness 6, Concentrativeness 4, Combativeness 6, Destructiveness 5 to 6, Alimentiveness 6, Acquisitiveness 4, Secretiveness 3, Cautiousness 6, Approbativeness 4, Self-Esteem 6 to 7, Firmness 6 to 7, Conscientiousness 6, Hope 4, Marvellousness 3, Veneration 4, Benevolence 6 to 7, Constructiveness 5, Ideality 5 to 6, Sublimity 6 to 7, Imitation 5, Mirthfulness 5, Individuality 6, Form 6, Size 6, Weight 6, Color 3, Order 5, Calculation 5, Locality 6, Eventuality 6, Time 3, Tune 4, Language 5, Causality 5 to 6, Comparison 6, Suavitiveness 4, Intuitiveness, or Human Nature 6.

During the formative years of the new decade, when, fortified by Lorenzo's insight, Walt Whitman was writing and becoming his book, he was also following another trade that brought him into closer relationship with the firm of Fowlers and Wells. Although "little is known about Whitman's activities as a bookseller and stationer," in 1850 and 1851, in addition to writing newspaper articles and "doing odd jobs of printing," he did buy and sell books.[10] Among them were several Fowlers and Wells publications: Orson Fowler's *Love and Parentage, applied to the Improvement of Offspring*; a *Phrenological Guide*; and a periodical entitled *The Student: A Family Miscellany, and Monthly School-Reader*.[11] Embarking upon a new series in May, 1850, the magazine was edited by Norman Allison Calkins, the disciple of Pestalozzi, and published by Fowlers and Wells. For one dollar annually, it aimed at satisfying the tastes of a threefold audience: teachers, for whom it was advertised as the "best medium to communicate important suggestions"; children, especially "children tired of old reading-books"; and the family in general. For such readers it featured inspirational articles by Horace Mann, Horace Greeley, and Henry Ward Beecher, along with a phonographic alphabet, "Lessons in Botany by Flora Milford," and "Aunt Eliza's Stories." Eventually, when it was merged with another periodical and left the domain of Fowlers and Wells, this magazine would introduce to the world the works of Horatio Alger, Jr. At the moment it was selling well from the shelves of bookseller Walter Whitman, who received a note from the publishers: "We happen to be out of the Student at this time—Shall have a supply in a few days."[12]

The bills received by Whitman from the firm reflect his bookselling activities.[13] He seems to have sold the books in which he believed and from which he had upon occasion made extracts. Along with *Love and Parentage* he was charged for six copies of *Swimming* [*The Science of Swimming*[14]], three of Combe's *Physiology*, and five *Phrenological Journals* bound.

While Fowlers and Wells were supplying the bookseller Whitman with stock for his shelves, they were supplying the poet Whitman with a powerful impetus to get on with his own book. Through all the minor activities of journalism, printing, and bookselling, he was moving toward the climax that would come when, on May 15, 1855, he walked into the clerk's office of New York's Southern District Court and inquired about the correct wording for a copyright notice for his forthcoming book. Upon that first book and upon its author, the phrenological analysis made by Lorenzo Fowler had a profound and abiding influence.

In the "Song of the Answerer" Whitman wrote:

> The sailor and traveler underlie the maker of
> poems, the Answerer,
> The builder, geometer, chemist, anatomist,
> phrenologist, artist, all these
> underlie the maker of poems, the Answerer.[15]

106

In this category, if Whitman was the "Answerer," surely Lorenzo Fowler was the "phrenologist." Walt Whitman kept his phrenological chart to the end of his life and published it upon five different occasions: in the *Brooklyn Daily Times* of September 29, 1855, and in the first, second, and third editions of *Leaves of Grass*; the fifth reprint was made by his literary executors, to whom, in the last year of his life, he gave the chart. For forty-three years he had kept the tangible evidence of his memorable visit to the Phrenological Cabinet; he had not held it secret but had repeatedly and widely published it. Surely these reprintings were designed to give notice to the world that the maker of poems, the Answerer, the poet of democracy, the American bard, was fulfilling his phrenological potential. Moreover, by these repeated publishings he was acknowledging the truth and importance of the chart itself, which epitomized "his physiology corroborating a rugged phrenology." On his long journey from "imitative hack-writer" to "bold prophet," it had marked a signal turning point. As late as 1888, recalling the analysis to Horace Traubel, he said of phrenology, "I guess most of my friends distrust it—but then you see I am very old fashioned—I probably have not got by the phrenology stage yet."[16]

If Lorenzo's analysis had so affected the poet, Whitman's study of phrenology as deeply affected his poetry. He asked:

> Who are you indeed who would talk or sing to America?
> Have you studied out the land, its idioms and men?
> Have you learn'd the physiology, phrenology . . . of the land?[17]

Whitman had "studied out" its phrenology. Among the "Memoranda from Books and from his own Reflections," indicating his "Reading and Thought Preparatory to Writing 'Leaves of Grass,'" were comments on the temperament along with a sentence quoted from Orson Fowler. In the list of magazine and newspaper articles found among his papers and in his scrapbooks were pieces on phrenology and personal magnetism. In his preface to the first edition of *Leaves of Grass* he phrased in prose what his "Song of the Answerer" proclaimed in poetry: "Exact science and its practical movements are no checks on the greatest poet but always his encouragement and support. . . . The atomist chemist astronomer geologist phrenologist spiritualist . . . are the lawgivers of poets."

In the poems themselves lies all the inner evidence of this "greatest poet's" absorption with the theme. In a way the affirmations of *Leaves of Grass* are the affirmations of a science rooted in the doctrine of man's improvability and man's perfectibility. In poems such as the one now called "Faces," Whitman is said to have used "phrenological methods for the interpretation of character"; still others, such as "There Was a Child Went Forth," have been described as "built on a phrenological framework." In "Unfolded Out of the Folds" Whitman has been detected using Orson Fowler's theories of heredity and "primitive eugenics" to explain the "unfolding" of the poet.

Not only in his themes but in his language is the influence apparent, for phrenology, transmitted by the Fowlers, gave to the poet a new vocabulary. In poem after poem "Words of Human Phrenology" found their way: "They shall be alimentive, amative, perceptive"; "O adhesiveness! O pulse of my life!" The "Manhattanese bred" were "Voluptuous, inhabitive, combative, conscientious, alimentive, intuitive, of copious friendship, sublimity, firmness, self-esteem, comparison, individuality, form, locality, eventuality." In Whitman's crucible the terms of phrenology had undergone an alchemical change. Phrenology had become poetry.[18]

The Fowler firm had recognized the possibility of such a metamorphosis. In January, 1855, their *Journal* reported, "Literature, long seasoned with it, is almost composed of its suggestions."[19] In the months that followed, Walt Whitman, having completed a dozen poems, prepared for the press the first edition of *Leaves of Grass*. At Rome's Printing Office in Brooklyn he set some pages of the type himself. Not long afterward, a visitor

> found him revising some proof, [his] blue striped shirt, opening from a red throat. . . . His beard and hair . . . greyer than is usual with a man of thirty-six. His face and eye are interesting, and his

head rather narrow behind the eyes; but a thick brow looks as if it might have absorbed much. . . . His eye can kindle strangely; and his words are ruddy with health. He is clearly his Book.[20]

"His Book" appeared on July 4, 1855, a thin quarto volume bound in green cloth, without the name of the author-publisher, with "only his photograph as signature."[21] Some seven or eight hundred copies were printed, not all of which were immediately bound. In later copies Whitman bound in eight pages of comments and reviews, including Lorenzo Fowler's "Phrenological Notes on W. Whitman." Meanwhile, priced at two dollars a copy, *Leaves of Grass* was advertised in the *New York Tribune* on July 6 as "for sale by SWAYNE, No. 210 Fulton-st., Brooklyn, and by FOWLERS & WELLS, No. 308 Broadway, N.Y." Having recently moved to "more spacious and commodious" headquarters at 308 Broadway, the phrenologists-publishers continued to advertise the book intermittently until March 1, 1856, in brief notices that convey their own sad story of a nonselling book.[22]

Four days after the first advertisement had appeared, the name of Swayne's bookstore vanished from the *Tribune*, and between July 10 and August 4 the insertion was simply: "Walt Whitman's Poems, 'Leaves of Grass,' 1 vol. small quarto, $2. Fowlers & Wells, No. 308 Broadway, N.Y." Swayne, possibly having found the book objectionable, refused to handle it, leaving the field to the Phrenological Depot as sole agents for its sale. Inside the front cover of some copies of the first edition Fowlers and Wells pasted their label, but between August 4 and the end of September they ran no advertisements for the book. Then on September 25 they inserted a few lines that reflected two recent changes: "Walt Whitman's Poems—'Leaves Of Grass'—for sale to dealers and retail. Single copies, $1. Fowler & Wells, No. 308 Broadway."

Fowlers and Wells had been metamorphosed into Fowler and Wells with the departure from the firm of its founder Orson Fowler. Although he continued to visit the Depot, he officially dissociated himself from the company at this time. Preoccupied both by his octagon house in Fishkill and by his writings, Orson left the firm in the hands of his brother Lorenzo and his brother-in-law Samuel Wells, both of whom continued the task of selling—or attempting to sell—*Leaves of Grass*. Less than three months after its appearance they reduced the price from two dollars to one dollar. Then, toward the end of November, they altered their *Tribune* advertisement to read: "Walt Whitman's Poems—'Leaves Of Grass'—for sale wholesale and retail. Single copies, $1; paper, 75¢." Finally, in February, 1856, they made their last effort to sell the first edition by announcing: "Walt Whitman's Poems.— 'Leaves of Grass,'—This work was not stereotyped; a few copies only remain for sale, after which it will be out of print."

Although only "a few copies" remained for sale by March 1, 1856, not many of the copies that had been dispersed had been sold. Some had been distributed with the compliments of Walt Whitman; others had been sent out by Fowler and Wells for review purposes; still others had found their way to England. In each instance there would be compensation for the rebuff and rejection with which the book was generally received. One of Whitman's copies would go to Ralph Waldo Emerson; some review copies would be reviewed by Walt Whitman himself; and the Fowler and Wells London agent would play an interesting part in establishing the English reputation of an American poet.

Leaves of Grass was, for the most part, either passed over in silence or reviewed with a blend of animosity and ambivalence. According to John Burroughs,

> The only reception heard of, was such, for instance, as the use of the volume by the *attaches* of a leading daily paper in New York— collected in a swarm Saturday afternoon, waiting to be paid off— as a butt and burlesque, whose perusal aloud by one of the party, the others lounging or standing around, was equivalent to peals upon peals of ironical laughter from the whole assemblage.[23]

The first review appeared in the *Tribune*, whose critic—probably Charles A. Dana—found "much of the essential spirit of poetry beneath an uncouth and grotesque embodiment."[24] While the

New York Criterion attacked the volume, three anonymous reviews were carried away by poems that "stand for America and her times" and by the character of the "American bard" who had written them—but all three reviews were the work of that bard himself.[25]

One of those reviews, entitled "An English and an American Poet," contrasted Tennyson's *Maud, and other Poems* with Walt Whitman's *Leaves of Grass*. It was prefaced with a brief editorial comment, "We have received from a correspondent the following comparative and critical review of two poems recently published, both of which may be had at this office." "This office" was that of Whitman's booksellers, Fowler and Wells, and the "comparative and critical review" appeared in the October, 1855, issue of that firm's *American Phrenological Journal*. The review reflected Whitman's confidence both in phrenology and in himself:

> Not a borrower from other lands, but a prodigal user of his own land is Walt Whitman. Not the refined life of the drawing-room— not dancing and polish and gentility, but some powerful uneducated person, and some harsh identity of sound, and all wild free forms, are grateful to him. A thrill of his own likeness strikes him as the spotted hawk wheels noisily near his head at nightfall. . . .
>
> He is sterile in the old myths . . . but pregnant with the deductions of the geologist, the astronomer, the great antiquary, the chemist, the phrenologist, the spiritualist. . . .
>
> His is to prove either the most lamentable of failures or the most glorious of triumphs, in the known history of literature.[26]

In the same month in which the *Phrenological Journal* found room for this anonymous review, the *New-York Daily Tribune* printed a letter that was to help realize Whitman's "most glorious of triumphs." The printing of that letter has been called "perhaps an event of greater importance in the history of American literature than the printing of any other letter has ever been."[27] The letter had been written by Ralph Waldo Emerson, and it had been addressed:

Walter Whitman, Esq.
Care of Fowlers & Wells
308 Broadway
New York.

Either Whitman or the firm had sent the Concord philosopher a complimentary copy of *Leaves of Grass*. Emerson recommended it to his friends—Alcott, Thoreau, and the Unitarian minister Moncure Daniel Conway, who was to report: "I read the poem with joy. Democracy had at length its epic." But Emerson did more. On July 21, 1855, he wrote a letter to the poet that compensated for popular neglect and critical vituperation. In it he said:

> I am not blind to the worth of the wonderful gift of *Leaves of Grass*. I find it the most extraordinary piece of wit and wisdom that America has yet contributed. I am very happy in reading it, as great power makes us happy. . . . I greet you at the beginning of a great career, which yet must have had a long foreground somewhere, for such a start.

Printed at first in the *Tribune* on October 10, 1855, that letter was to be used subsequently by Whitman and Fowler and Wells entirely without consultation with Emerson. It was to be used to propel Whitman upon his "great career" and to sell copies of a second edition of his *Leaves of Grass*. By that time Fowler and Wells would be serving not only as Whitman's booksellers but, anonymously, as his publishers.

Meanwhile the firm was still engaged in efforts to sell the first edition of *Leaves of Grass*. Those efforts involved the shipping of copies to their English agents Horsell and Shirrefs, later Horsell & Co., on London's Oxford Street. One of those copies would eventually reach William Michael Rossetti, who would bring out "the edition that largely conduced to the changed position of Whitman" and aroused for the American poet "a tempest of admiration" in England. It was through Fowler and Wells and the firm's London representative that Walt Whitman was first presented to a British audience. In the story of that significant introduction William Horsell is a leading character.[28]

The Phrenological Depot had its British counterpart at 492 Oxford Street, London, where the Horsell firm of publishers offered courses of lectures on phrenology along with books on temperance, hydropathy, and vegetarianism. Indeed, William Horsell was in a small way the British alter ego of Orson Fowler. Born in 1808, a year before Orson, he studied for the ministry and, devoted to his profession, endangered his health by overwork.

> He was a laborious worker, preaching eight or ten times a week, sometimes to thousands in the open air, and his nerves had become shattered, his whole physical nature deranged ... suffering ... from a pain in his left breast, constipation, and headache.

Where Orson in similar straits had adopted the breathing cure, Horsell resorted to total abstinence and hydropathy, a combination that resulted in "his complete restoration to health and strength." During the 1840's he founded several societies, among them Nature's Beverage Society, or Independent Order of Horebites, and the Vegetarian Society. As the Fowlers published their *Phrenological Journal*, Horsell published his *Vegetarian Advocate*. While Orson was producing his phrenological manuals, Horsell wrote *The board of health and longevity: or, Hydropathy for the people*, to be followed by treatises on unbolted wheat meal and the science of cooking vegetarian food. As the New York Phrenological Depot reflected its partners' interests in reform, Horsell's firm specialized in the publication of books on water cure, abstinence, and diet—all those "progressive" reforms that would improve man's health and extend his longevity.

This was the publisher who served as Fowler and Wells' English agent. While the American editions of Horsell's books were published by the New York phrenologists, both the Horsell and the Fowler imprints appeared jointly on several health reform tracts as well as on certain copies of the 1855 *Leaves of Grass*. It was this publisher to whom Fowler and Wells habitually shipped cases with an assortment of books "for wholesale and retail," and it was the abstainer-vegetarian-hydropathist William Horsell who was initially responsible for introducing Walt Whitman to England. That introduction would culminate with William Michael Rossetti's edition of 1868, which finally brought Whitman to the excited attention of the British public. By that time William Horsell had died of fever in Lagos, and the firm for which he had acted as foreign agent had severed all connection with Walt Whitman.

However, in November, 1855, that connection was stronger than ever. The man whose character had been analyzed and whose poems had been sold by the partners of the Phrenological Depot had added a new dimension to an already remarkable relationship. Walt Whitman had become a staff writer for yet another Fowler and Wells periodical.

Life Illustrated made its first appearance in a new series on November 3, 1855, as a weekly family paper priced at $2 a year and modestly "Devoted to News, Literature, Science and the Arts . . . Entertainment, Improvement, and Progress."[29] Its publishers' purpose was "to furnish a journal, which, bound to no party, sect, or theory, embracing every human interest, and furnishing food for all the faculties of the mind, shall merit a world-wide circulation." Fowler and Wells proceeded to fulfill this purpose by presenting to the family circles of America a mélange of articles on science and agriculture, physiology and education, phonography and natural history, travel and adventure, along with "Original Essays" by a writer whose *Leaves of Grass* happened to be on sale in their office.

Since "the true mission of Life Illustrated" was "to shed a light upon every subject which interests all," nearly everything was grist for its mill. It was not a "*pictorial* paper," rather, it illustrated life by representing "human life in all its phases and aspects, moral, intellectual, and social." To this end of representing life, it employed the hydropathist Russell T. Trall as an assistant editor and, as a contributor, the spiritualist and patent agent John B. Fairbank, who, in a state of insanity induced from "close attention to spiritual rappings," was soon to commit suicide. It also employed as a staff writer the author of the recently published *Leaves of Grass*.

In the beginning, Whitman's status was merely that of "voluntary correspondent"; in the November 3, 1855, issue of *Life Illustrated*, his first contribution was listed as "Accepted" for publication. A week later, in the "General Literature" department, it appeared—a three-column article on "The Opera," in which the author invited his readers "to spend an evening with us at the opera, and listen to the music, and look at the place and people." He set the scene: "We see the rows of globe lamps outside on the balconies as we approach . . . policemen in blue frock-coats and caps . . . loungers . . . richly-dressed women . . . in their carriages . . . liveried coachmen."[30] He gave less attention perhaps to the performance of Verdi's *Ernani* than to the white-gloved hands, opera glasses, perfumes, gaslights, and crowded tiers. In much the same manner he wrote for succeeding numbers of *Life Illustrated* an article on "The Egyptian Museum"[31] and another entitled "Christmas at 'Grace,' "[32] in which he looked down his nose at New York's elegant church that dispensed expensive music for New York's elegant few. Each of these articles, although presented on the first page of the issue, bore no by-line.

Not until April, 1856, with the words "Article by Walt Whitman" did *Life Illustrated* give explicit notice that the author had become a regular staff writer. The article honored with a by-line concerned the English language—"America's Mightiest Inheritance." What is more, it was accompanied by a lengthy and perceptive editorial puff for the author and his work:

> Our readers will not overlook the article on the noble Language we inherit, written for their special delectation by the author of "Leaves of Grass;" nor will they need any assurance of ours that the article is instructive and suggestive. But as our columns may be enriched by further contributions from the same source, a word or two of introduction may not be out of place or out of taste on the present occasion.

Walt Whitman is more a DEMOCRAT than any man we ever met. He believes in American principles, American character, American tendencies, the "American Era," to a degree that renders his belief an originality. When he exclaims, in "Leaves of Grass:" "By God! I will have nothing which every one else may not have on the same terms," he expresses the very soul of democracy, and his daily walk and conversation are in accordance therewith. Emphatically and peculiarly, he is a man of the people. He is also a man of ideas, of various knowledge, of very considerable reading, and of more than considerable talent. We do by no means agree with him in all of his opinions; but the directness, the simplicity, and utter sincerity with which he announces and maintains his opinions are always delightful. Walt Whitman is not a young man, as some have supposed. He has lived long enough to have observed much, and to have reached a variety of conclusions.

We commend his writings to the friendly attention of our readers. They will not often, we think, read an article by him without drawing from it something that will encourage, stimulate, expand, or correct them.[33]

In the months that followed, at least until late August, Whitman continued to supply the columns of *Life Illustrated* with contributions embodying his "opinions" and "conclusions." In July and August a series of six of his essays was presented under the general title of "New York Dissected," in which the "DEMO-CRAT" who believed in "American tendencies" discussed such American phenomena as Fourth of July celebrations, the slave trade, Broadway, and—doubtless of special interest to Orson Fowler—"Decent Homes for Working-Men."[34] On August 30 *Life Illustrated* carried its last Whitman article, an account of Dan Rice's East Brooklyn Circus as viewed from "one of the excruciatingly narrow boards of [the] big tent."[35]

By that time the proprietors of the periodical and their staff writer were busily engaged in their most important joint venture —the publication of the second edition of *Leaves of Grass*.[36] *Life Illustrated* had long shown an almost proprietary interest in the book. In December, 1855, under the heading "Annihilation of

Walt Whitman," the paper had replied to a critical attack made by the *Criterion*:

> The editor of the *Criterion* attributes *indecency* to a book which Emerson found congenial with his own refined and delicate nature. . . . The truth is, perhaps, that the *Criterion* is in the "fogy interest," and discerns a Wat Tyler in every one that departs from the recognized forms.[37]

Leaves of Grass had been advertised in the columns of *Life Illustrated* and listed among those "New Miscellaneous Books . . . sent to any address in the United States or Canada."[38] When "Fanny Fern" offered "the cordial grasp of a woman's hand" to the poet of *Leaves of Grass*, her article was reprinted in the Fowler and Wells periodical.[39] All those puffs were designed for the first edition of the book for which the firm had served merely as bookselling agents.

Now, in August, 1856, they were prepared to announce a new edition. This new edition of *Leaves of Grass* was more than a reprinting—it was in effect an altogether different and expanded book. Fowler and Wells were its publishers, not in name but in act. Encouraged perhaps by Emerson's endorsement as well as by their own personal knowledge of the poet, they consented to publish the work but, loath to tilt openly with Dame Grundy, not to take credit for it. Hence their imprint would not appear on the title page. Nonetheless they had a vital part in the production of the second edition of *Leaves of Grass*.

The possibility of a new edition had obviously been broached as early as June, 1856, when the new staff writer was contributing to *Life Illustrated*. At that time Samuel R. Wells, chief of the firm's publishing division, was extremely reluctant to add so controversial a book to a list already heavy with unpopular reform publications on sex and health, diet and clothing. He confessed his editorial timidity in a letter to "Friend Whitman" marked "Private":

> After "duly considering," we have concluded that it is best for us

to insist on the omission of certain objectionable passages in Leaves of Grass, or, decline publishing it. We could give twenty reasons for this, but, the *fact* will be enough for *you* to know. We are not in a position, at present, to experiment. We must not *venture.*

Again, it will be *better* for *you* to have the work published by clean hands, i.e. by a House, not now committed to unpopular notions. *We* are not in favor, with the conservatism, and a more orthodox House would do better for you. Try the *Masons,* Partons publishers, (They publish Fanny Ferns works.) They are *rich* & *enterprizing,* & I *guess* would publish Leaves of Grass, on fair terms.[40]

By July, Wells' reluctance was to some extent overcome, and the decision was made. Despite the slow sales of the first edition, Whitman had written so many additional poems that a second edition would be less a new edition than a new book. Whether or not he omitted any "objectionable passages," he could supply for the publication twenty unpublished poems, so that more than half of the volume would offer "entirely new material." Probably because that "new material" included the frank paean to sex "A Woman Waits for Me," Samuel Wells had hesitated, finally reaching the compromise of offering publication without an imprimatur. Fowler and Wells would, it was agreed, make arrangements to print and sell a thousand copies of the new *Leaves of Grass.*

In the August 16, 1856, issue of *Life Illustrated,* with some degree of publisher's license, the firm announced its intentions:

Leaves of Grass.—It is evident that the American people will give a hearing to any man who has it in him to reward attention. Walt. Whitman's poems, the now famous "Leaves of Grass," would scarcely have been thought likely to become speedily popular. They came before the public unheralded, anonymous, and without the imprint of a publisher. The volume was clumsy and uninviting, the style most peculiar, the matter (some of it at least) calculated to repel the class whose favorable verdict is supposed to be necessary to literary success. Yet the "Leaves of Grass" found purchasers, appreciators, and admirers. The first edition of a thousand copies rapidly disappeared, and we have the pleasure of announcing that a second edition, with amendments and large additions, is about to be issued. The author is still his own publisher, and Messrs. Fowler and Wells will again be his agents for the sale of the work. The new edition will be a neat pocket volume of four hundred pages, price, as before, $1. It has been stereotyped. Copies will be ready about the first of September.

Walt Whitman has thus become a fixed fact. His message has been found worthy of regard. The emphatic commendation of America's greatest critic has been ratified by the public, and henceforth the "Leaves of Grass" must receive respectful mention whenever Americans are reckoning up those of their country's productions which could have sprung into existence nowhere but in America.[41]

Copyright for the new edition was recorded on September 11, 1856. Not long after, Fowler and Wells advertised in *Life Illustrated* "The New Writings of Walt Whitman . . . elegantly bound" and "Containing Thir[t]y-Two Poems."[42] For the price of one dollar purchasers could acquire at the Phrenological Depot a volume markedly unlike its predecessor. On the shelves of the publishing department the copies reposed—chunky, squat volumes bound in drab green cloth, so different from the first *Leaves of Grass* that one bibliophilic wit would eventually distinguish the two editions as "The Long and the Short of it." The "Short of it" consisted of 384 pages, a volume swollen not only with the new poems but with a section of quoted comments under the heading "Leaves-Droppings." Among those "Leaves-Droppings" were Whitman's review of himself from the *American Phrenological Journal*, Lorenzo's phrenological notes on the poet, and Emerson's laudatory letter.

Lest that letter escape notice in so modest a position, its message was emblazoned on the green cloth binding. Without Emerson's authorization or knowledge, both Whitman and his publishers had agreed to this indelicate exploitation. Stamped in gold on the backstrip of each volume appeared the triumphant words "I Greet You at the Beginning of A Great Career R W Emerson." As for the publishers, their name appeared nowhere except on one advertising leaf at the end of the volume. There they announced:

☞ The Poems of

LEAVES OF GRASS,

PUBLISHED BY THE AUTHOR,

May be ordered at any Book-Store or Newspaper Depot, or especially of

FOWLER & WELLS, 308 Broadway, New York.

Their place of business is the principal Agency for the Work, wholesale and retail. A note written to them, giving the writer's address, and enclosing $1 00, will procure a bound copy, post-paid, by return mail.

They supply Booksellers at a liberal discount.

'LEAVES OF GRASS' may also be purchased or ordered by mail, or the country-trade supplied, from the following *Agencies:*

BOSTON, . . . Fowler, Wells & Co., 142 Washington St.
PHILADELPHIA, Fowler, Wells & Co., 231 Arch street.
BALTIMORE, . . J. W. Bond & Co.
TORONTO, (Ca.,) Maclear & Co.
BUFFALO, . . . T. S. Hawks.
    "   . . . A. Burke, Jr.
CINCINNATI, . . F. Bly.
CHICAGO, . . . R. Blanchard.
ST. LOUIS . . . E. K. Woodward.
NEW ORLEANS, J. C. Morgan.
SAN FRANCISCO, George M. Bourne, M.D.

FOREIGN AGENCIES.

LONDON, . . . Horsell & Co., Oxford St.
PARIS, ... H. Bailliere & Co.
BRUSSELS, . . . William Good, Antwerp.

☞ Any communication by mail, for the author of Leaves of Grass, can be directed to him, namely, WALT WHITMAN, care of
FOWLER & WELLS, 308 Broadway, New York.

Walt Whitman, care of Fowler and Wells, a notice at the end of *Leaves of Grass* (1856)

The Poems of
LEAVES OF GRASS,
Published By The Author,
May be ordered at any Book-Store or Newspaper Depot,
or especially of
FOWLER & WELLS, 308 Broadway, New York.

Their place of business is the principal Agency for the Work,
wholesale and retail. A note written to them, giving the writer's
address, and enclosing $1 00, will procure a bound copy, post-paid,
by return mail.

They supply Booksellers at a liberal discount. . . .

Any communication by mail, for the author of Leaves of
Grass, can be directed to him, namely,

Walt Whitman, care of
FOWLER & WELLS, 308 Broadway, New York.

The volume might also, it was explained, be "purchased or ordered by mail, or the country-trade supplied, from the following
Agencies." The foreign and domestic "Agencies" listed included
those of the water-cure physician George M. Bourne in San Francisco, the health reformers Horsell & Co. in London, and two
Fowler and Wells branches recently opened in Boston and Philadelphia.

Despite this array of agents, and despite the advertisements of
the "small, thick . . . green and gold" volume, "handy for pocket,
table, or shelf" which the firm inserted in the *Tribune*[43] between
September 12 and October 11, the new *Leaves of Grass* did not
fare well. The publishers' prediction that "this book will always
be in demand" was indeed to be fulfilled—but not immediately.
At the moment, Harriet Beecher Stowe's *Dred* was attracting far
more attention than Walt Whitman's *Leaves of Grass*, and such
attention as the latter did attract was not altogether desirable from
the point of view of sales. As Whitman scholars would agree, this
second edition was "even more unfavorably received" than the
first because of its "exploitations of the sexual theme." Both "A
Woman Waits for Me" and "Spontaneous Me" shocked the mid-

nineteenth century into stunned abhorrence. As for Emerson, his "serene countenance" was darkened when he saw that a sentence from his private letter had been "wrenched from its context and . . . emblazoned" in gold letters upon the cover of the book. To Moncure Daniel Conway he commented: "If he had known his letter would be published he might have qualified his praise. 'There are parts of the book,' he said, 'where I hold my nose as I read. . . . It is all there, as if in an auctioneer's catalogue.' "[44]

Understandably, therefore, the already timid publishers of a book that aroused "every epithet of rancor and opprobrium" took fright. According to John Burroughs, the thousand bound copies "they soon sold, remunerating expenses, and then quietly asked to be excused from continuing the book any further."[45] Whitman's consequent disenchantment with the firm is also understandable. He now regarded Wells as "a shrewd Yankee,"[46] and on July 20, 1857, he wrote to a friend:

> Fowler & Wells are bad persons for me.—They retard my book very much.—It is worse than ever.—I wish now to bring out a third edition—I have now a *hundred* poems ready (the last edition had thirty-two)—and shall endeavor to make an arrangement with some publisher here to take the plates from F. & W. and make the additions needed, and so bring out the third edition.—F. & W. are very willing to give up the plates—they want the thing off their hands.—In the forthcoming Vol. I shall have, as I said, a hundred poems, and no other matter but poems (no letters to or from Emerson—no Notices, or any thing of that sort.)—I know well enough, that that must be the true Leaves of Grass—I think it (the new Vol.) has an aspect of completeness, and makes its case clearer.—The old poems are all retained.—The difference is in the new character given to the mass, by the additions.[47]

The disenchantment was obviously mutual. The third edition of *Leaves of Grass* would not be published until 1860 when Thayer and Eldridge of Boston would bring it out. By then Fowler and Wells had severed all connections with Whitman. As the years passed, it would seem indeed that they severed even their memories of Whitman, for he would never be given more than a perfunctory mention in any of their subsequent publications. When they analyzed the "Poet," the image they summoned up to represent his quintessence was that of Edgar Allan Poe and never that of the American bard who had sat for a phrenological analysis in their sanctum, who had contributed to their periodical, whose book they had published and sold.

Yet the edition of *Leaves of Grass* they had seen through the press is still "with a few older readers of Walt . . . the favorite edition," and, more important, it is the edition that laid "the foundation of future editions." They had known and understood the poet "in strong clothes, neck open, shirt collar flat and broad . . . hair like hay after it has been mowed in the field." They had seen him and worked with him during those developing years when he had become his book, and they were clearly part of the foreground that led him to his "great career." Yet for Fowler and Wells the association with Walt Whitman had been at the time only an episode in the midst of an active, many-faceted business. The "barbaric yawp" the poet had sounded had been for them less than a thunderclap dimly echoed in the phrenological rooms. Other voices called them. Like Whitman, they had their own stars to follow.

THE FIRM IN THE FIFTIES

Whitman's book had been on sale not only at the Fowler and Wells' headquarters but also at its Boston branch. It was fitting that in the city where Spurzheim had lectured and enlisted so many followers for the new science the most active and popular practical phrenologists should establish an agency. In November, 1851, their New England Depot was opened at 142 Washington Street, "near the head of School-street, two doors from the *Old South Church*."[1] Visitors to the "Athens of America" were almost as likely to include a call at No. 142 as to the Old South. The committed and the uncommitted, the curious and the scoffing climbed to the second floor of 142 to study the busts in the Phrenological Museum, sit for a character delineation, or browse among the "sterling and popular" publications with which the establishment was "fully stocked." Antitobacco and antilacing men, water-cure and teetotal friends were all welcomed there, as well as vegetarian agitators—although Sylvester Graham had recently died, his doctrine lingered on.

The men in charge of the Boston branch had naturally been selected for phrenological reasons. Some years before, while lecturing on Martha's Vineyard, the Fowlers had discovered in the skull of David P. Butler "exactly the right organization for a practical Phrenologist." Butler, then only twenty-two, had followed the suggestion, eventually gaining such skill in analysis that he was appointed examiner of the Boston branch. Assisting him was Chalkley J. Hambleton, who, like Butler, had been inspired to confidence and directed to success through a phrenological examination made by Lorenzo. A phonographic expert, Hambleton had been employed as a reporter by the firm and had exhibited such acumen in the office that he had been appointed to manage the business end of the new Boston enterprise.

The enterprise succeeded. Several Boston firms refused to employ clerks unless they showed certificates of fitness from David Butler—a point of view that led the *Liberator* to wish for the same method of choice for congressmen. Within a short time Hambleton and Butler bought out two-thirds of the Boston agency, which continued to distribute the publications of the parent house.

A few years after a branch had been started in the hub of the universe, another was established in the city of brotherly love. For this, their second Philadelphia office, the firm chose a building next to the Female Medical College of Pennsylvania, where young half sister Almira Fowler had recently studied and where she was at the moment on the faculty as "Demonstrator of Anatomy and Chemistry."[2] If the odor of sanctity was imparted to the Boston branch by the Old South Church, the odor of science was wafted to the Philadelphia agency at 231 Arch Street. Under the supervision of Nelson Sizer, this "branch office and book store" was opened in 1854 and, like the Boston annex, it was "well stocked with all of the valuable and Reformatory works published at the New-York establishment." Along with examinations, classes in practical phrenology were taught two evenings a week in which "the lady members in particular"—perhaps students of the Female Medical College taking extracurricular courses—were "evincing great zeal." Lessons in phonography rounded out the attractions of the Arch Street agency, which in 1856 was taken over by John L. Capen, who had been trained in the New York office.

The Boston and Philadelphia branches bore testimony both to the business success of the founders and to the missionary spirit that hoped to "scatter broadcast the ennobling truths of this science." In the spring of 1854, the same year that saw the establishment of the Philadelphia branch, Orson Fowler assumed the role of solo phrenological missionary by withdrawing from the firm he had founded. There were several reasons for this separation and the consequent dissolution of Fowlers and Wells, including Orson's preoccupation with his octagon house and his desire for independent travel. Another reason apparently lay in Wells' publishing timidity, which Walt Whitman was also to experience. According to Orson, "I...wrote 'Love and Parentage,' 'Maternity,' 'Manhood,' which my firm suppressed." Further, he explained, " 'Fowlers and Wells,' before I left that old firm, requested Horace Mann to prepare a work for us on ... [masturbation] which he declined on the ground that it had ruined the reputations of all who had ever broached it. For once he erred. Our firm stood alone in publishing on this subject. Yet one of its members stoutly opposed it, and we *dissolved*."[3]

On his own Orson Fowler embarked upon his independent career as itinerant lecturer on sex and apostle of nature.

> Let others help the "bears" of conservatism keep "all things as they were from the beginning," but let *me* help the "bulls" of progress lift my race out of that "old-fogy" slough in which they have been mired for ages. . . . I would proclaim *Nature's eternal edicts*. . . . Allowed to choose my own name ... it would be, *Nature's Apostle*.

By boat along the Erie Canal, on the cars of the New York and Erie Railroad, "Nature's Apostle" traveled, making phrenological sketches, advising his subjects to "wash all over every day in cold water" and "marry soon." As far north as Canada, as far west as Ohio, he spread the gospel in lectures both public and private. When he was not examining heads or gathering seeds to plant at Fishkill, he was writing "on the sexual relations." Sizer's opinion that "he has said enough on that subject already" was disregarded. By 1856, the year of Freud's birth, Orson Fowler had mapped out his life's work as sex educator to the country.

Meanwhile the flourishing New York office of the firm now known as Fowler and Wells had been re-established at 308 Broadway.[4] Broadway in the mid-1850's was still like the boy who grew up so fast he had no time to tie his shoelaces. Every spring a few

of the street's "front teeth" were "kicked out," giving it a peren-
nially unfinished appearance. Stages, omnibuses, carriages, wagons, and fancy turnouts made a constant clatter, while corner
loafers and "tooth-picking scamps" hung around hotels "staring
respectable females out of countenance." Fowler and Wells
moved to New York's busiest thoroughfare in 1854, forced out
of Clinton Hall when the building was demolished to make room
for "new marble stores." Between Duane and Pearl streets, opposite the New York Hospital, and two blocks above City Hall
Park, No. 308 was "one of the best stands" on Broadway, the
"heart's-core" of the city. The upper part of the building was
occupied by the National Daguerrean Depot of Edward Anthony.
The lower part was swiftly transformed into a "Place of Skulls."

All the busts and casts of Nassau Street, the skulls of "saint . . .
savage, and . . . sage," were moved to 308 Broadway. "All tribes,
and kindreds, and nations, and tongues, and peoples—all races,
colors, and religions—are represented in the mute eloquence of a
thousand crania arranged and labeled along the walls of the building." The museum kept up with the times, for when a murderer
was to be hanged, an agent was dispatched from Fowler and Wells
to "attend the execution and take the cast of his head." Besides
displaying skulls, the firm advertised "Human Skulls, imported
and for sale" and "Skeletons put up ready for use." Friends of
the cause sent an alligator skull from Florida and "a magnificent
skull with antlers" from Oregon. Yet, even though the "great
show window" and examining room were adorned with cranial
mementos, the firm was greedy for additional specimens, announcing in the *Phrenological Journal*:

> We have a very large collection of the skulls of murderers, who
> have been executed, and of soldiers killed on battle-fields, also of
> Indians, Africans, Egyptians, Chinese, and Cannibals, but we have
> only a few from the higher class of minds, such as Reformers,
> Statesmen, Scholars, & c. Of these we have hundreds of casts, and
> busts from living heads, but not their skulls.

What a treasure it would be, if some plan could be devised, by which these leading "types" could be preserved as specimens, for scientific purposes.[5]

Despite the withdrawal of Orson Fowler, the staff who super-intended this splendid necrological array was one happy family. Nelson Sizer, when he returned from Philadelphia, emulated Orson's incessant toil, writing for the *Journal*, managing lectures, and, with Lorenzo Fowler, examining. Assisting Samuel and Charlotte Wells in the publication office, Mary S. Rich, described in one of Sizer's lighter moments as "fat as a roach & gay as a lark & full of the dragon," helped to keep the *Journal*'s books and fill orders. John Brown, Jr., John Brown's oldest son, had been engaged a few years before as assistant, and his phrenological studies were combined with an intense belief in the efficacy of "Pure Cold Water" and a keen interest in octagonal architecture. Lecturing in Ohio, he carried the Fowler doctrine far afield and, even after his removal to Kansas in 1854, kept up his connections both with the firm and with phrenology. Edward O. Jenkins did much of the typographical work for Fowler and Wells, while William Howland, wood engraver, continued to provide book illustrations for the firm's publications from his own establishment at 229 Broadway. As Broadway expanded, the Phrenological Depot expanded. Business was brisk at No. 308.

As the 1850's rolled on, the Fowler examining room seemed to be the Mecca for famous and infamous, skeptic and believer.[6] In 1851 Nelson Sizer wrote to John Brown, Jr.: "I made 14 written descriptions in succession two or three days since. This is the longest string by more than half, that ever came off in this office without the intervention of charts or verbals."[7] Animated and direct, earnest yet "often in a high degree amusing," Sizer—though he may have lacked the subtle perspicacity of Lorenzo Fowler—imparted confidence and respect. Often those who had come to mock stayed to admire. The "telling 'hits' " of phrenology's early days were multiplied, while the wily attempts to stump the tester were repeated. The lock picker who "adjusted his long, dark hair so as to cover his forehead and face, and thus to make himself look as stupid as possible" could not conceal his cool shrewdness from the examiner, who advised him to become a locksmith. The justifiable complaint that the phrenologist overexercised his own organ of Benevolence by "exaggerating the 'capabilities' of an individual under examination" was explained with some casuistry: the individual was usually "*intellectually* capable of accomplishing more than he would be likely ever to undertake." The truth was that the phrenologist had no wish to offend in a private examination or to risk libel in a public examination. His emphasis upon the subject's assets and his disinclination to explore liabilities was in time to receive the sincerest form of flattery from modern pedagogy.

At all events, the methods practiced in the Phrenological Depot were popular. The editor of a Texas newspaper described them succinctly:

> On our annual visits to New York, we have always had occasion to call at the establishment of Fowler and Wells, in Broadway, where we have invariably been detained for an hour or two, looking over the vast collection of heads . . . all duly labeled. . . . Last summer . . . Mr. Wells . . . suggested we should have our head examined. . . . More from curiosity than any other motive, we at once agreed, and were introduced into the inner room set apart for this purpose, by Mr. Wells, who, without giving our name, profession, residence, or any clew to our identity, informed the Professor (Mr. Sizer) that we wished to undergo a phrenological examination. He commenced by taking the measure of our head, and then proceeded to give the leading features of our character, all of which was taken down in short-hand, by a very interesting young lady seated at a desk.[8]

Throughout the decade the inner room was filled with clients eager for analysis. Some, like Horace Mann—who had named his son George Combe Mann after the Scottish phrenologist and who recommended the study of phrenology to teachers—had already received renown. His head was described as a "*three-story one*"

which gave "elevation to his character, and an aspiring disposition," a description which apparently appealed to the great educator, for he wrote to Henry Barnard, "As I think more of a Phrenological exposition of character and tendencies than of any other
mode of description, I . . . send you one . . . taken at the office of
Fowler & Wells, N.Y. which I should rather be judged by, than
by any thing that can be written in any other *language*; i.e. other
than Phrenological."[9] Some of the great men of the time were
doubtless put through a phrenological analysis in absentia, through
photographs. Although the Wells manuals would include a detailed character reading of Hawthorne, for example, it is difficult
to imagine that he would have submitted his actual head to the
test.

Hawthorne's friend Herman Melville appears to have refrained
also; yet in *Moby-Dick* he did not hesitate to phrenologize his
whale.[10] On August 16, 1850, Melville wrote to Duyckinck, "A
horrible something in me tells me that you are about dipping your
head in plaster at Fowler's for your bust." While Melville never
dipped his own head in Fowler's plaster, he "Fowlerized" the head
of Queequeg as "phrenologically an excellent one. . . . It reminded
me of General Washington's head, as seen in the popular busts of
him. It had the same long regularly graded retreating slope from
above the brows, which were likewise very projecting, like two
long promontories thickly wooded on top. Queequeg was George
Washington cannibalistically developed." Although Melville
scoffed at physiognomy and phrenology, he invoked both subjects
in *Mardi* and *White-Jacket* before subjecting his Leviathan to an
examination by Ishmael, which revealed that "to the phrenologist
his brain seems that geometrical circle which it is impossible to
square," and that "phrenologically the head of this Leviathan . . .
is an entire delusion. . . . The whale . . . wears a false brow to the
common world."

Like Melville, Oliver Wendell Holmes poked fun at phrenology
but, unlike Melville, he did not balk at submitting his own brow
to an analysis.[11] Indeed, it was the analysis that immediately pre-

cipitated the literary response. On June 22, 1859, Holmes apparently purchased a copy of *The Illustrated Self-Instructor in Phrenology*, in which Whitman's analyst Lorenzo Fowler had marked the "Chart and Character of O. W. Holmes." His rating, though good, did not approach Whitman's. Granted 6 to 7 in Mental Temperament, Mirthfulness, Language, Cautiousness, and Conscientiousness, he rated only 5 in Amativeness and Parental Love, and sank to a 4 in such faculties as Continuity, Veneration, Color, and Time.

This penciled chart was elaborated on July 1 in Boston, where Lorenzo provided an analysis covering thirteen manuscript pages as reported by the phonographer Edwin R. Gardiner. There it was noted that Holmes was "constitutionally ambitious . . . excessively cautious . . . combative & fond of debate." Many things appeared to him, through his "Mirthfulness, in a ridiculous light." He was, in Lorenzo's considered opinion, "adapted to variety of thought & to some scientific or literary occupation. Your mind passes rapidly from one subject to another."

Holmes' mind passed so rapidly to the mysteries—and absurdities—of phrenology that the very next month an installment of *The Professor at the Breakfast-Table* appearing in the *Atlantic Monthly* included the following extended remarks on the subject. No contemporary reader could have failed to discern under the cloak of the Holmesian "Bumpus and Crane" the familiar names of Fowler and Wells.

Having been photographed, and stereographed, and chromatographed, or done in colors, it only remained to be phrenologized. A polite note from Messrs. Bumpus and Crane, requesting our attendance at their Physiological Emporium, was too tempting to be resisted. We repaired to that scientific Golgotha.

Messrs. Bumpus and Crane are arranged on the plan of the man and the woman in the toy called a "weather-house," both on the same wooden arm suspended on a pivot,—so that when one comes to the door, the other retires backwards, and *vice versâ*. The more particular specialty of one is to lubricate your entrance and exit,—

that of the other to polish you off phrenologically in the recesses of the establishment. Suppose yourself in a room full of casts and pictures, before a counter-full of books with taking titles. . . . Professor Bumpus is seated in front of a row of women,—horn-combers and gold-beaders . . . looking so credulous, that, if any Second-Advent Miller or Joe Smith should come along, he could string the whole lot of them on his cheapest lie, as a boy strings a dozen "shiners" on a stripped twig of willow.

The Professor (meaning ourselves) is in a hurry, as usual; let the horn-combers wait,—he shall be bumped without inspecting the antechamber.

Tape round the head,—22 inches. . . .

Feels of thorax and arm, and nuzzles round among muscles. . . .

Mild champooing [sic] of head now commences. Extraordinary revelations! Cupidiphilous, 6! Hymeniphilous, 6+! Pædiphilous, 5! Deipniphilous, 6! Gelasmiphilous, 6! Musikiphilous, 5! Uraniphilous, 5! Glossiphilous, 8!! and so on. Meant for a linguist.—Invaluable information. Will invest in grammars and dictionaries immediately. —I have nothing against the grand total of my phrenological endowments.

I never set great store by my head, and did not think Messrs. Bumpus and Crane would give me so good a lot of organs as they did, especially considering that I was a *dead*-head on that occasion. Much obliged to them for their politeness. They have been useful in their way by calling attention to important physiological facts. (This concession is due to our immense bump of Candor.)

Following this mirthful report based upon his own visit to "Golgotha," the Professor proceeded to regale the Breakfast-Table with "A short Lecture on Phrenology," in which he amused himself at the expense of the pseudo-sciences in general and phrenology in particular. Not long after, in *Elsie Venner*, Holmes would modify his opinion somewhat and find more in phrenology than a source for humor. Meanwhile, Messrs. Bumpus and Crane had provided him with food not only for thought but for the next installment. They dismissed the Autocrat's disparaging remarks with: "Yes. Prof. Fowler recently examined the little man. . . . He is one of the 'smart' little men of Boston, but he has not yet reached the top round in the ladder of all knowledge"— and turned to the other clients in their antechamber.

Along with the famous, the not so famous were analyzed: the Mathew Brady of the 1850's, the gymnastic teacher Dio Lewis, the clergyman Hosea Ballou. Allan Pinkerton, who had not yet become known to the public, had been told by Lorenzo that he "would make a capital detective; he would smell a rogue three miles." The youthful Garfield too was set in the right direction. Coming to the office, "a lean, lank boy [who] could not afford to spare the money, but did so," he was informed that "if he had as much Combativeness as Stephen A. Douglas he could achieve the position of Chief-Justice." On the other hand, John T. Trowbridge, beginning his literary career, was not altogether satisfied by an analysis which, as he put it, "made a correct map of the country, yet... failed to penetrate the life of the region."

More of the unknown than the known ventured into the Fowler "inner room" to submit their heads to the examiner's manipulations: an African girl about to teach in a mission school; a young drummer—one was never too young for an analysis; an Eskimo; a Texas merchant who "doubled his money" by following the phrenologist's advice; a Broadway saloon keeper. The notorious were examined too: the pirate-murderer Albert W. Hicks not long before his execution, and, at the other end of the scale, the handicapped and inspiring Laura Bridgman, with whom Sizer communicated through an interpreter.

Some came for repeat examinations, such as the Siamese twins Chang and Eng, who were on exhibition nearby. In this category perhaps the most interesting of the heads revisited was that of John Brown, who had been examined by Orson Fowler eleven years earlier. In 1858, on a short visit to New York, that most resolute of men sat to Nelson Sizer for a second portrait. His eyes were more than ever the eyes of an eagle, flashing or hooded; his voice was metallic; his flowing beard was white. Nelson Sizer would remember the scene vividly:

In 1858, one bright midday, I returned to the office from lunch; and, coming from the blazing light of the sun, I could hardly see the dim outline of [a man] . . . in the office waiting for me . . . who sat with his back toward me. [Asked to examine him] I . . . said carelessly, without trying to see the face, "This man has firmness and energy enough to swim up the Niagara river and tow a 74-gun ship, holding the tow-line in his teeth. He has courage enough to face anything that man may face, if he think it right, and be the last to retreat if advance be impossible."[12]

Not long after that interview Osawatomie Brown would be encamped on the Blue Ridge looking into Harpers Ferry.

Some—like Whitman and Moncure Daniel Conway—kept the tangible evidence of their phrenological examinations. Often filling seventeen quarto pages, written in longhand, the reports were placed in a loose-leaf binder tied with blue ribbon. The front cover contained woodcuts of the apostles of phrenology: Gall, Spurzheim, and Combe; the back cover was used as an advertising medium for the Fowler and Wells publishing list. Clients were advised to have their written descriptions and phrenological charts printed within "elegant gilt borders," framed, and hung in the parlor. And it is entirely possible that some, proud of their phrenological pen portraits, may have done so. Certainly the phrenological habit was catching on to such an extent that one wit advertised for a phrenologist to examine the "head" of navigation on the Mississippi.

Business was not only brisk at 308 Broadway—it was big. While Orson cultivated his Fishkill garden, Lorenzo "lectured five nights in the week, for ten months in the year, without a single break."[13] Sizer varied his sessions in the examining room with an impromptu speech on comparative cranial anatomy before "a large company of thinkers and men of science," for such was the prestige of the house that when Du Chaillu's collection of gorilla craniums was exhibited, Cyrus W. Field invited both Sizer and Wells to an "entertainment" in honor of the African explorer.[14]

Not long before that "entertainment," the firm of Fowler and

Wells had so expanded in its range of interest that it established a Patent Agency. Orson had evinced his predilection for modern improvements and mechanical devices in his Fishkill mansion, and the firm itself was cognizant that the age of steam was also the age of inventions and hence of patents. The *Phrenological Journal*, ever receptive to articles on applied science, stated, "Inventors have a most important part to act in the great cause of human reform, and whatever we can do to aid them in realizing a just remuneration for their mental acquisitions and contributions to human knowledge and improvement, we shall be ready to do." In April, 1855, the monthly explained the business of its new agency:

> There is no class of interests in our country that are assuming a more important position than those connected with the rights to mental acquisitions and labor....
>
> The rights secured by law to the inventor or discoverer of some new and useful machine, or composition of matter, has [*sic*] not unfrequently been branded as a monopoly, and by some as an unjust one. But they forget ... that our whole system of laws is founded upon similar monopolies.... The title by which the inventor holds the exclusive use of the creations of his own intellect, is of that nature which requires the utmost care in delineating....
>
> We are prepared to do all kinds of business relating to patents and patent property. Descriptions and mere rough sketches of inventions will be sufficient to enable us to judge of their patentability, or to make an application, or to file a caveat. Models ... may be forwarded to us by express....
>
> We are preparing such facilities, in addition to our own for advertising, and for disposing of patents and patent property, at an equitable and fair rate, as have never been offered to the American people. In this department of our business ... we shall accept of no interest in any patent which we do not deem of real utility; and we shall offer only such as appear really valuable to public consideration. Our agency for the sale of patent rights will not in the least interfere with our business of procuring patents for new inventions. Both will be conducted independently, and with care and fidelity.[15]

In charge of this agency, Fowler and Wells appointed John B. Fairbank, who, addicted to the lure of spiritual manifestations, was shortly to commit suicide. Before his untimely demise, he offered his knowledge as a patent attorney to the new department. As for Fowler and Wells, presumably since they were able to discern adaptation for inventiveness in men's skulls, they were also able to discern "novelty and patentability" in men's inventions. After Fairbank jumped to his death from a window in the Tremont House, his position was filled by another patent attorney, Thomas P. How of Buffalo, who had served as an examining agent in the United States Patent Office. Specializing in foreign as well as American patents and in renewing applications for rejected patents, this branch of Fowler and Wells thrived. While heads were examined in one room, inventions were examined in another—a concurrence of activity that led to the publication of a new book by a rival house: *The Patent Hat: Designed to promote the growth of certain undeveloped bumps, and thereby increase the thinking, reasoning and acting powers of the wearer.*

Fowler and Wells were well prepared to handle this new business. The pages of their journals were emblazoned with pictures of the age's new inventions; advertisements were solicited for successful patents; and some of the machines and instruments were actually on sale at the Phrenological Depot itself. Along with "beautiful Skeletons," "Separated Heads," and manikins imported from Paris and priced at a thousand dollars, such diverse wonders of the decade were offered as Dr. Briggs' Patent Suspenders and Woodruff's Patent Self-Acting Gate, sewing machines and Vermont windmills, corn planters and improved handmills "for Farmers and Emigrants." Thanks to Orson's interest in agriculture, and perhaps to his overplanting of certain varieties, flowers, seeds, berries, and fruits were sold at attractive prices—ten dollars a bushel for apple seeds, two dollars a dozen for strawberry plants, and twenty-five cents a dozen for Honolulu squash seeds. "With the hope of encouraging and facilitating the cultivation of flowers in all parts of our country, and thereby promoting the happiness, refinement and elevation of the people," the Phrenological Depot sent packets of seeds to any part of the United States.

There were few whose needs could not be met at 308 Broadway. For hydropathists, syringes, bathing fixtures, and thermometers were available at all times, the firm making the somewhat startling pronunciamento that "Proprietors of Hydropathic Establishments, School Committees, Sextons of Churches, Janitors of Lecture-rooms, Housekeepers, and every body that has a room, be it a palatial residence or an attic bedroom, should have a Thermometer." Obstetricians and prospective mothers could be supplied with obstetric plates, improved breast pumps, and nipple shields; students could obtain Prince's Protean fountain pens and symbolical self-sealing envelopes.

The work of the Patent Agency went hand in hand with the sale of new appliances. As business flourished, it also increased in range until Fowler and Wells supplied "every variety of merchandise and produce" from dry goods and groceries to musical instruments and "Rare Books at Half Price." Announcing their "New York Wholesale Agency," they listed among the articles available agricultural implements, mechanics' tools, surgical and dental instruments, jewelry, stationery, books, and artists' materials.[16]

As purveyors of artists' supplies, they added by the end of the decade still another department to their many-faceted business, their "American and Foreign Stereoscopic Emporium."[17] This division of Fowler and Wells offered an assortment of "American and Foreign Views and Groups," while among the requisites for lecturers supplied by the firm were crayon, oil, and watercolor heads as well as oil paintings on rollers—a Greek slave or a Hercules for twelve dollars, a fashionable woman or a deformed woman for ten dollars. For the general public, portraits of the presidential candidates were supplied in "fine electrotyped engravings" at three dollars each.

Stereotyping and book and job printing completed the sidelines of the house.[18] For the most part, however, the new Fowler and

Wells power presses, "propelled" like the age "by the power of steam," were used to keep pace with the ever increasing output of the firm's own publishing department.

By the mid-fifties the periodicals bearing the Fowler and Wells imprint formed a small empire of their own ruled over by the *Phrenological Journal*.[19] The bulk of its burden was carried by Sizer and Wells, who complacently agreed that "if the Fowlers should die today . . . [Wells] would not announce the fact in the Journal, nor would they be missed from it."[20] Issued in a new dress with a larger format, the *Journal* offered "a wider range of general subjects" and, with a circulation of over fifty thousand copies, gave every evidence that it would fulfill the firm's "earnest desire" of surviving "long after our bones are laid in the dust." While the management was "not in favor of the various gambling schemes by which unprincipled publishers set traps, bated with poor jewelry, to catch dimes," it did offer attractive club rates, prizes, and premiums to satisfied subscribers. Contributors were less easily pleased, one captious recipient of a rejection complaining about a returned manuscript, "You should have said outright and promptly—'It is not adapted to the Journal,' and not, after keeping it a year, find out that it is too '*melancholy*.' "[21]

Under the new aegis, the monthly offered—or claimed to offer —a broader approach to phrenology, seeking "to analyze man's complicated nature; to develop the philosophy of his mind." This the *Journal* strove to achieve by carrying articles on ethnology, octagonal architecture, and women's rights, along with the customary character analyses. Although no advertisements of patent medicines, rum, or tobacco darkened its pages, matrimonial advertisements at twenty-five cents a line were still available to the "middle-aged bachelor" possessed of a peaceable disposition and three thousand dollars who sought an alliance with a lady of "congenial spirit" and congenial pocketbook.

The pages of the *Journal* also reflected the passage of time, recording the deaths of various Fowler and Wells co-workers: the bitterly lampooned Sylvester Graham; the "late lamented pioneer of Hydropathy" Joel Shew; the first American phrenologist Charles Caldwell, who had embraced the science "when bigots called it infidelity."

For survivors who espoused such causes, the Fowler and Wells periodicals supplied appropriate reading matter. The *Water-Cure Journal* continued to sprinkle its special audience with "Drippings from a Wet-Sheet," announcing unabashedly that what had begun as a "little bubbling . . . spring" had become a "Niagara . . . sousing and washing . . . millions of poor drugged, dirty, dying humans!" To accomplish the "physical regeneration of the race," it offered to the general cold-water-minded public articles on beards, bloomer dresses, and the "prevention of pregnancy." For professional hydropathists, still another magazine was launched—the short-lived *Illustrated Hydropathic Review*, a quarterly edited by Russell Trall.

Life Illustrated continued its weekly appearances after Whitman's departure from the premises, supplying "Entertainment, Improvement, and Progress" to the families of America in return for two dollars a year. With the *Phrenological Almanac*, the *Water-Cure Almanac*, and for a short time even a *Mechanics' and Engineers' Pocket Almanac* compiled chiefly from back numbers of their magazines, the Fowler and Wells serials reached a large reading public.

While the Boston and Philadelphia branches were stocked with the periodicals, the West was kept *au courant* with the latest in phrenology and water cure by authorized agents who traveled "with *engraved certificates*" especially "after Harvest . . . always a good time to sell books in the country."[22] Women, particularly those qualified to make phrenological examinations, were sought after as agents. George M. Bourne carried on, furnishing journals for the California and Oregon market. With the increased activity of Fowler and Wells agents came the nuisance—and flattery—of imitators, from the author of an "Improved Phreno-Chart" to "his Royal Highness, Prince Luximon Roy, M.D.," creator of the "Grand Hindoo Poetical Phrenological Chart." Despite detractors, who still classified phrenology as a delusion, the Fowler and Wells periodicals circulated in the tens of thousands throughout the fifties, and the Fowler and Wells coffers reaped their reward not merely in the coin of the realm but in English shillings, Spanish quarters, and gold dust.

The firm's books paralleled the success of their magazines. Fowler and Wells sent their publications "by Express, or as Freight, by Railroad, Steamships, Sailing Vessels, by Stage, or Canal, to any City, Town, or Village, in the United States, the Canadas, to Europe, or any place on the Globe." At mid-century they boasted that "no publishing house in New York sends so large a number of books and periodicals through the mail as the firm of Fowler and Wells." They waxed almost poetic in describing the route of their publications, from their "great Metropolitan Emporium" along the "iron tracks of the locomotive and the watery pathways of the steamer," "in wagons and buggies, and on horse-back . . . into every . . . corner of the continent."[23] A California miner, armed with his pick and his Fowler, recorded in his diary his debt to the firm's publications: "Was[h]ed fifty buckets in the fore noon; made three dollars and sixty cents. Read Fowler on Self Cultur[e] or perfection of character in the afternoon; very much edified."[24] A team of phrenologists had developed into one of New York's largest mail-order houses.

The Fowler and Wells publishing list strengthened and expanded to meet the needs of the decade.[25] Popular interest in health was keen during an era of overeating and national dyspepsia. Practical answers to practical questions were sought by practical Americans. For a public eager to learn, in a few easy home lessons, how best to live and how to make the most out of life, Wells supplied the answers. He had not read his medicine in vain. Without benefit of diploma he still made a knowledgeable physician, for his hand was ever on the public pulse.

Wells specialized during the fifties in manuals for the masses, small, cheap, useful handbooks that taught his readers *How to Write* and *How to Talk*, *How to Behave* and *How to Do Business*.

Compiled by himself or by Daniel Harrison Jacques, these "Hand-Books for Home Improvement" were designed for "popularizing and widely diffusing the various branches of useful knowledge." Studious readers could learn from them how to use "The Right Word in The Right Place" and "how to breed and rear The Various Tenants of the Barn-Yard," "How to Build Country Houses," and "How to Cultivate All the Field Crops." For bee-keeping and practical horticulture, for debating and writing for the press, the Fowler and Wells publications provided handy shortcuts. In addition, these manuals gave the firm the opportunity for considerable gratuitous advertising. A rural manual on *The House* could, in a discussion of the circle and the octagon, refer would-be architects to Orson Fowler's *A Home for All*. A hand-book on *How to Write* could include specimen business letters ordering huge quantities of Fowler publications from Fowler and Wells. This hidden or subliminal advertising paid off, for it helped sell the firm's books at the same time that it padded the firm's manuals.

One manual in particular seemed to epitomize the publishing designs of Samuel Wells. *How to Behave* was subtitled *A Pocket Manual of Republican Etiquette, and Guide to Correct Personal Habits . . . Good Manners . . . Care of the Person, Eating, Drinking, Exercise. . . Dress . . . Dinners, Evening Parties . . . Funerals . . . with . . . A Chapter on Love and Courtship*. It incorporated most of the Fowler health maxims, from "bathe frequently" to "nature makes no mistakes." It championed unbolted wheat flour while it attacked tobacco, hot biscuits, and "slavish uniformity in dress." It aimed at "usefulness rather than originality," and it was eminently American, "desiring to make our readers something better than mere imitators of foreign manners." As an earnest little etiquette book, it reflected both the age for which it was written and the character of its publisher. Wells was indeed well aware of the requirements for a successful publisher. In his *How to Do Business* he listed these requirements, doubtless basing his ideal portrait upon the publisher he knew best—himself:

To be a successful book-publisher one requires a rare combination of qualifications. A spirit of enterprise, tact, discrimination, a knowledge of human nature, a careful and continual study of the public tastes and wants, and a general knowledge of modern literature, are indispensable. A mistaken judgment in reference to a single work may lead to serious loss, and even to pecuniary ruin. . . . The publisher, who is generally also a seller of books, should have *a thorough knowledge of the wares in which he deals.*[26]

Most of the Fowler and Wells publications issued under Wells' direction aimed at increasing the physical health of readers en masse. "The true philosophy of reform must be based on physiological science. . . . The whole man should be developed harmoniously; and we should be as careful to learn and obey the physiological as the moral and intellectual laws of our being."[27] For this purpose he provided variations on the old antitobacco and antialcohol themes of Orson Fowler, publishing prize essays against the weed; for this purpose too he reprinted George Combe's *Constitution of Man* in its twentieth American edition along with *Outlines of Phrenology* "By Fowler and Wells." Books on water cure continued to roll from the press, from Trall's *New Hydropathic Cook-Book* to Balbirnie's *Philosophy of the Water-Cure.* The goal was physical perfection, as D. H. Jacques indicated in his *Hints toward Physical Perfection.* To realize that goal Samuel R. Wells published such diverse health books as Gregg's *Fruit Culture for the Million* and Wark's *Prevention and Cure of Consumption by the Swedish Movement-Cure.*

For the same purpose he published, as he wrote to Walt Whitman, the books that gave his firm the unorthodox reputation of a house "committed to unpopular notions." Love, as Jacques put it, was "Nature's grand cosmetic." As believers in nature's laws, Fowler and Wells therefore published a variety of manuals on the subject of love and sex education, from Orson Fowler's *Matrimony* to George S. Weaver's *Hopes and Helps for the Young of both Sexes,* from *Passional Zoology* to M. Edgeworth Lazarus' turgid and ambitious treatise *The Human Trinity; or Three As-*

pects of Life: The Passional, The Intellectual, The Practical Sphere.

Wells' publishing list, concerned as it was with the harmoniously developed man, was devoted to those "three aspects of life." His how-to manuals covered the practical; his tomes on sex, the passional, and a wide range of unusual books on the psyche, the so-called intellectual sphere. Psychology, vaguely interpreted as the science of the soul, was a subject that included the animal magnetism that had fascinated Poe and the Fowlers in the forties, the spiritualism that became popular in the fifties, and what has been somewhat ponderously called the "interregnum between mesmerism and spiritualism."

As Fowler and Wells put it in advertising their "Library of Mesmerism and Psychology": "It is but a few years, comparatively, since these subjects were brought conspicuously before the public. . . . Mesmerism is now . . . a *fixed fact*, invulnerable alike to the attacks of ignorant bigotry and learned sophistry, and challenging the most searching examination and the most thorough investigation." As phrenologists, they were especially fascinated by "investigations relating to the Human Mind"; as publishers, they responded to "the increasing demand for works on Psychology . . . Magnetism, and other kindred subjects."[28]

Psychology, as the Fowler and Wells house understood it, had a host of "kindred subjects," all more or less related. Hence, along with their health manuals, phrenological tomes, and practical how-to books, the firm expanded their list with a tremendous array of volumes on mental alchemy and spiritualism, clairvoyance and electrical psychology. William Fishbough's *The Macrocosm and Microcosm* appeared under their imprint, along with Alfred Smee's *Electro-Biology, or The Voltaic Mechanism of Man.* Andrew Jackson Davis, the slim, black-haired clairvoyant, having enjoyed his "psychic flights through space," wrote his *Philosophy of Spiritual Intercourse*, which was published by the firm, and announced that all worldly communications should be addressed to him in their care. The Phrenological Depot was becoming more and more receptive to psychical investigations. Indeed, when a volume of *Spiritual Instructions* was announced as published, not by a flesh-and-blood publisher but simply "by direction of the Spirits," it was guaranteed a sale at phrenological headquarters.

Along with advertisements of pianofortes and sewing machines, the *Phrenological Journal* touted the benefits of electromagnetic remedies and offered "Practical Instruction in Animal Magnetism." Promising to explore this new field in the "empire of the mind," the *Journal* introduced a regular department devoted to "Psychology," explaining:

> Within the last five or six years the world has been made extensively acquainted with an interesting class of phenomena . . . known under the general title of "electro-psychology," or "electro-biology." They consist of vivid fantastic impressions produced upon the minds of certain susceptible persons, generally by the authoritative declarations and commands of an operator.[29]

The *Phrenological Journal* knew whereof it spoke. Its publishers had by this time heard the "declarations and commands" of a younger generation of Fowlers, one of whom had traveled much in the far-flung empire of the mind. Among the Fowlers themselves—from the seeds of Horace Fowler's second marriage—an "operator" had sprouted who played a strange if short-lived role as trance medium to the family.

THE YOUNGER FOWLERS

. . . .

IX

Tʜᴇ animal magnetism of the forties had gradually led into new bypaths which were fairly well defined by 1850. One path, charted by those absorbed in "the creative phenomena of the mesmerized patient," would lead eventually, through hypnotism and suggestion, to psychoanalysis. The other, to which the spiritualists flocked, would point the way, through clairvoyance, somnambulism, and thought transference, to extrasensory perception. At mid-century, both paths attracted the susceptible and the gullible, the scientific and the merely curious.[1]

Both paths enticed such seers as Andrew Jackson Davis, the "first medium to claim divine inspiration,"[2] as well as the Fox sisters, who explored them profitably. Famous for their "Rochester Knockings," the Fox girls were holding daily séances in the parlor of Barnum's Hotel in New York City, to which the public was admitted at one dollar each.[3] Many, like Horace Greeley, were impressed by the revelations of the mediums; others, like young Edward Fowler, were moved to join them.

Edward Payson Fowler was the youngest of the second group of children sired by Horace.[4] Born in Cohocton in November, 1834, after Orson's graduation from Amherst, he had been brought up in Michigan, seeing his older half brothers and half sister only during their intermittent visits and lecture tours. Endowed with a keenly perceptive mind, he shared the family interest in mental science. By 1850, having decided to become a physician, he had come east with his brother Samuel, prepared to enroll in New York Medical College. The Lorenzo Fowlers and the Wellses shared a fine mansion at 233 East Broadway. Lorenzo's second daughter Loretta having made her appearance, there was apparently no space available there for the two young brothers. Samuel and Edward therefore lodged in Brooklyn with the Baner family, printers to the phrenologists-publishers. Both homes were to provide the setting for a mesmeric melodrama with cosmic—and comic—overtones.

It soon became clear that not just Edward and Samuel but the spirits themselves had "arrived & taken up lodging." Having been present at various séances, public and private, young Edward had apparently been so affected by spirit lights and spirit sound effects, so imbued with the magnetic fluid that permeated the universe, that he vibrated in harmony with the ghostly spheres. "Green cucumber" though he was, he exhibited a strong affinity for somnambulism and thought transference, automatic writing and electrical emanations. And such was his power of falling into the trance condition that he gave promise of extraordinary success as a medium. The Fowler family watched with fascination the flowering of their home-grown exotic.

Edward Fowler's spiritualistic experiences were recorded by historians of the phenomenon; the room in which they occurred was diagrammed; and his authenticity was attested by one of New York's greatest scholars.[5] His utterances in trance were recorded at almost tedious length, and his trafficking with the spirits impressed not merely the members of his family but one or two of the strongest minds of the day. Varying his medical studies with his flights into the empyrean, Edward Fowler was perhaps the busiest of all the busy Fowlers.

He was especially busy at night. Edward's nocturnal interviews with the spirits were to occupy considerable space when his communications were published in a two-volume compendium on *Spiritualism.* The general pattern of those interviews remained the same. Retiring at midnight, he would within five minutes see lights, hear footsteps, and watch in a state of paralyzed horror while a group of men—some in "ancient costume" and one, resembling Benjamin Franklin, bearing a box of electrical apparatus —entered through his bedroom window and conferred for hours. In the morning the results of their handiwork were visible—a written message often in Hebrew, Sanskrit, Arabic, Malay, or Chinese—languages unknown to Edward. Upon at least one occasion the message was signed by "some fifty spirits," including the signers of the Declaration of Independence and Edgar A. Poe. Upon another, Edward was "aroused from his slumbers by the Spirits, and requested to write what they should dictate"—in this instance, a rather elaborate diagram of "The Four Periods of Human Life." Although Edward's spirits apparently used either pen or pencil, they also seem to have used a galvanic battery carried by the shade of Benjamin Franklin which bore close resemblance to a gilding and plating electromagnetic machine described in the *Phrenological Journal* and sold at the Phrenological Depot.

Edward Fowler's "Spirit-Writings" were by no means confined to the privacy of his bedroom. Many a spiritual circle or conference witnessed his remarkable powers and saw the results of his automatic writing. Emma Hardinge Britten, noted spiritualist, trance medium, and messenger for the Rosicrucians, later recorded:

> Amongst the most remarkable manifestations which were preserved in the archives of the New York Conference, none are more interesting than those which relate to the mediumship of Mr. Edward Fowler . . . medical student. . . .
>
> Besides the faculty of seeing and conversing intelligently with spirits, Mr. Fowler's mind, being of a scientific cast, was frequently instructed through vivid pictorial imagery or direct communications with the methods adopted by spirits to effect their communion with mortals by means of raps, movements of bodies, entrancement, etc. Languages of the most unfamiliar nature, hieroglyphical figures, and Oriental writings, were constantly found in his chamber inscribed on scraps of paper, vases, and other objects, under circumstances that rendered the action of human agency impossible.
>
> Many . . . descriptions of spirit-life . . . [were] written or spoken by him in trance condition.[6]

Edward Fowler's "trance condition" was observed not merely by the Fowlers and the Baners but by the spiritualist Judge Edmonds, by Horace Greeley (who questioned the spirits about the value of Association), and by the orientalist and Swedenborgian George Bush. The tall, spare Dr. Bush, who had been professor of Hebrew at New York University, translated the "Mystical Manuscripts" that clustered in Edward's wake and vouched for their authenticity. Bush, who occupied a study near the firm's Nassau Street office, had the skill of " 'seeing darkly' . . . beyond the limits of the old doctrines."[7] He also had the skill of identifying young Edward's communications "in Hebrew, Arabic, Bengalee, &c.," of which he remarked:

> They come proximately from the hands of Mr. E. P. Fowler, a young gentleman with whom I had previously no acquaintance, but who, since I have become acquainted with him, does not at all impress me as one who would knowingly practice deception upon others, however he might, by possibility, be imposed upon himself. He certainly has no knowledge of the above languages, nor do I think it likely that he is leagued in collusion with any one who has. . . . It must, indeed, be admitted to be possible that Mr. Fowler may himself have copied the extracts from printed books, but I can only say for myself that, from the internal evidence, and from a multitude of collateral circumstances I am perfectly satisfied that he never did it. . . . In the present case, the only alternative solution that occurs to me is, that it was either an unconscious feat of somnambulism, or that it was the veritable work of spirits, effected by some spiritual-natural dynamics.[8]

The "dynamics" were especially impressive during séances presided over by Edward as medium. Although Lydia Fowler was noncommittal on the subject, feeling it "still veiled in mystery,"[9] and Samuel Wells dismissed it as "consummate charlatanism & deception,"[10] his wife hung upon Edward's every word, going so far as to record her young half brother's communications with the spheres beyond. Charlotte Wells' report occupies fifty quarto pages and begins with an account of a séance on November 28, 1850, which established the procedure generally followed:[11]

> Being asked if they—the spirits—had any directions to give for our guidance during the evening they rapped for the alphabet, and spelled, "Put out the light," which being put in the Hall they expressed satisfaction, and we seated ourselves around the table and joined hands, keeping perfectly quiet, when . . . in the course of a few minutes . . . Edward passed to the superior condition. . . . He was at first, spasmodically effected, then became perfectly rigid, after which, he rose, opened the folding doors and went in the other parlor where it was dark, closed the doors, and went out and laid himself on the sofa for a short time, and awoke while in that room. After a short time, other members of the family came in the room, when we formed another circle and he soon passed to the superior condition when, after a few minutes, he said, "The past is an *atom* to what is before us. . . ."
>
> After conversing with the spirits of some of his old friends, and receiving directions for the next Wed. evening, he joined hands with us, and after apparently watching the departure of spirits as they soared aloft, he awoke, and knew nothing of what had passed until we told him.

It was indeed amazing that such communications were received at those weekly spiritual conferences by a boy still in his teens. To the question, "Do you know Edgar A. Poe, the Poet? . . . In what sphere is he?" the reply was, "He is in [what I consider] the third society, second sphere." Having found Poe, Edward proceeded upon another occasion to pinpoint the origin of all creation, enunciating a pre-Darwinian view of evolution from his "superior condition." "The mineral or inanimate—earthy—creation," he explained, "was formed first and tended to develop vegetable nature, and that, again, to form the lowest order of animal creation, and from that to the creation of man." There was presumably little that he could not discuss in trance, from the Millerites to "fraternal harmony," from the "Cost Principle" of the American anarchist Josiah Warren to utopia, from the Negro to telepathy. "Adam," he announced, "the first man—was a coloured man. He was black." As for thought transference, that too he explained. "I can now see the reason that some persons receive an impression from others, although far separated—where there is an attachment between them. It forms a connecting cord—a sort of universal telegraph."

Charlotte, recording with meticulous zeal her young half brother's communications from beyond, doubtless found him as stimulating when he was unconscious as when he was conscious. So too did the members of what was called the New York Circle or Conference, who, on August 1, 1851, banded together to make "careful observations concerning modern Spiritual phenomena." The group, among them a number of homeopathic physicians, concluded that Edward Fowler's "statement . . . relative to the occurrences in his room have, on numerous occasions and in various ways, been fully confirmed by the spirits that are wont to visit our circle."

Although those spirits confirmed the young medical student's veracity, and although *The Shekinah*, a magazine devoted to "inquiry into the Laws of the Spiritual Universe," publicized their confirmation, not everyone accepted Edward's messages as authentic and genuine. B. W. Richmond, co-author of *A Discussion of The Facts and Philosophy of Ancient and Modern Spiritualism*, called the mystical writings into question; testimony was gathered from believers until the whole affair gave signs of becoming a *cause célèbre*, in the spirit world at least. As one commentator put it in *Spirit Rapping Unveiled!*:

> The idea of seeing the spirit of Benj. Franklin with a *galvanic battery* under his arm, as described by Mr. Fowler, is extra "spiritual."
> . . . Although Mr. Fowler is the brother of the phrenologists, who publish the "Supernal Theology" and other ghost-books, it is more probable that he is merely the dupe of the "New York Circle" than a wilful deceiver. His seeing Franklin, however, with his galvanic battery under his arm, is a strong symptom of incipient insanity, if not of something worse.

The firm itself was divided on the subject of Edward and the spirits. "All hands at the house hear the knockings," it was said, except Samuel Wells, for "the spirits will not communicate in his presence." While Orson was at work on what Wells continued to call his "mud house," "our women," the publisher deprecated, "are running after the knockers."[12] In a lengthy letter Rodney Wells, a relative, confided that Edward had faked the role of medium, moving beds, chairs, pillows, and books about when he thought everyone else was asleep—a playful deception to which, according to Rodney, the so-called medium had confessed under pressure.[13] Nelson Sizer took a detached and amused view of the goings-on: "The Spirits favor our folks at the house. They have some rich times tho it has never been my good fortune to be present." Yet he concluded, "If the spirits don't know more in the next life than their reports indicate we shall be little wiser for their communications, or by going there ourselves." As for Edward, Sizer was highly skeptical:

> I have questioned whether he was honest in the matter & whether such a green cucumber *could* deceive, & more than this, whether a Spirit of sense would choose such a medium except on the principle that "the weak things of this world are chosen to confound the wise." . . . If true it will, like beer or new cider, work itself clear. If false it will die of its own rottenness.[14]

By 1855, when Edward Payson Fowler received the degree of Doctor of Medicine from New York Medical College, his spiritualistic furor was over and the tempest in the witch's caldron subsided. Entering into partnership with two homeopathic physicians who had been members of the New York Circle or Conference, he began a practice that was to last well into the twentieth century.[15] Dr. Fowler would in due course explore the phenomena of mind and display no little skill in translating the scientific writings of medical pioneers. Thus the polyglot experience vouchsafed to him on his spiritual Tower of Babel stood him in good stead. While the oldest Fowler was lecturing on good health in his Fishkill octagon, the youngest Fowler was dispensing it in such fashion as may or may not have been prescribed by spiritual ukase. Like all the Fowler clan, both Orson and Edward were bent upon improving the world.

Still another member of the family was developing his blueprint for reform—a blueprint that had, indeed, been adumbrated in the course of one of brother Edward's trance communications. Samuel Theron Fowler, the eldest product of Horace's second marriage, had been born in 1821 and so was chronologically the central link between the two groups of children.[16] About midway in age between his half brother Orson and his full brother Edward, he was exposed equally to the work of the older generation and to the vagaries of the younger. At fourteen he had begun the study of phrenology, and at sixteen he had investigated the mysteries of mesmerism along with the revelations of Scripture. Upon three different occasions he had been stricken with grave illness, and each time he had announced that he would not die until his work was done. The exact nature of his work was not manifested to him until, obeying a clairvoyant communication from Charlotte, he left Michigan for the East, at first visiting his half brother Orson in Fishkill and later living in Brooklyn with Edward.

While Edward was alternating between medical studies and mesmeric trances, Samuel was distributing handbills for Fowler lectures and studying the nature of New York. In the course of his wanderings through the city's slums he "discovered the existence of a degree of poverty, misery and crime that he [had] never dreamed . . . possible."

> So wrought up was he by this discovery that he then and there declared "These evils need not be, and they shall not continue," and decided to devote his life to discovering the cause and a cure for the evil. From that day to the day of his death . . . his life [would be] . . . devoted chiefly to this object, though it compelled him and his family to live in poverty.[17]

It was in the course of his war against evil and poverty that Samuel Fowler gained a reputation for "being odd." Impelled toward reform both by his observations and by mesmeric communications, he developed a system for the reconstruction of society by means of what he called "genetive analogies." Using a vocabulary borrowed partly from Swedenborg, partly from phrenology, and only infrequently from the dictionary, he spent his life elaborating a plan of social reform that is no more comprehensible today than it was when Samuel first projected it. "The processes of nature," he believed, "were generative, and not creative . . . without space nothing else could exist . . . the unlimitedness (the on-and-on-itiveness) of space rendered it negative . . . the negative condition, wherever it dominates, endows with mattine sexuality . . . the limitedness of matter renders it positive, and . . . [therefore endowed] with maline sexuality."[18]

Out of this apparently meaningless verbiage, Samuel Fowler arrived at the concept that space was the primitive mother, matter the primitive father, and everything was continuously generated from those two prime factors. Existence, he believed, was divided into four worlds: the star, or structural, world; the plant, or organic, world; the zo-onic, or machine, world; and the societary, or social, world—worlds succeeding each other and analogous to each other. It was obviously the fourth world that preoccupied Samuel after his visit to the New York slums. In an effort to reconstruct that societary world, he eventually organized a "Home on an industrial basis"—a "Home of Industry and Exchange," to which he called "All Lovers of Human Well-Being" and for which he indited a Constitution, which he named "the Industrial Public."

Samuel Fowler's peculiar views formed the subject of one of Edward's communications from the "superior condition":

> Society may and will yet arrive, at some future period, at that point where your conceptions shall be more than fully realized, although not in a manner which you now anticipate. The principles which you now sustain are not those which are destined to revolutionize the world of society. You are vainly striving to ascend to the summit of the edifice at one stride. . . .

153

The greatest good which you can now do, is not to try, prematurely to perfect society . . . but to clear the ground. . . . Look
back to the various and systematic changes which society has thus
far undergone, and you will at once see your true position.[19]

Although Samuel Fowler never quite clarified that "true position," he never ceased his laborious and turgid attempts to do so.
In this respect he was not unlike other social reformers who at
mid-century were also experimenting with more or less obscure
ideas designed to improve man's relations with man. Their concepts, like Samuel's, provided conversation pieces for Edward
Fowler in trance. A lengthy session, at which the eccentric reformer Stephen Pearl Andrews was present, considered in detail
the "Cost Principle" enunciated by the first American anarchist,
Josiah Warren, and publicized by Andrews in his book *The Science
of Society*.[20] It almost seemed as if the world could be equally divided between those who needed the benefits of reform and those
who, trending toward utopia, offered their panaceas and remedies
for society's evils.

The Phrenological Depot, all embracing as it was, provided a
kind of headquarters for those intellectual reformers; as it lent its
imprint to works on mesmerism, so it published the tracts for the
times indited by the Fourierists and anarchists, by all who sought
to create social harmony out of social chaos. As the *Phrenological
Journal* announced, "PHRENOLOGY . . . will revolutionize the
world. Philosophy and religion have a new interpreter, and heaven
is thereby made more accessible."[21] To make heaven more accessible, the Fowler firm published the works of those apostles of
utopia who preached the approach of a golden age.[22]

Their list included Stephen Pearl Andrews' most lucid work, *The
Science of Society*, in which he explained Josiah Warren's "Cost
Principle" and outlined his own concept of "The True Constitution of Government in the Sovereignty of the Individual." Andrews lectured at the Depot on the economics of a new age, and
the columns of *Life Illustrated* eventually found space for comments upon his utopian Long Island community "Modern Times,"

where Warren's "Cost Principle" was put into operation. Warren himself was among the Fowler authors, the firm publishing his *Practical Details in Equitable Commerce*, which elaborated upon the principle that cost should be the limit of price in a world where the greatest evil was profit.

Profit nonetheless must have played some part, however small, in the selection of manuscripts, for the firm continued to publish works on what they called "Social Harmony," from Albert Brisbane's *Social Destiny* to Parke Godwin's *Popular View of the Theory of Charles Fourier*, from Robert Dale Owen's *Labor* to Adin Ballou's *Practical Christian Socialism*, a plea for "uncompromising Non-Resistance and non-participation in sword-sustained governments." Along with works on sexual freedom, these books presenting unpopular prescriptions for reform were surely among those that Samuel Wells had in mind when he suggested a more orthodox publisher for Walt Whitman. Social reform occupied an important position in a list that included Horace Greeley's *Hints toward Reforms*, Kossuth's lecture on *The Future of Nations*, and Hurlbut's *Essays on Human Rights and Their Political Guarantees*. For a short time too the Fowler imprint appeared upon *The Spirit of the Age*, successor to Brook Farm's organ *The Harbinger*, a weekly edited by William Henry Channing and proposing to turn mankind from competitive to co-operative industry.

The spirit of the age was clearly reflected in the Phrenological Rooms, where the doctrines of Saint-Simon and the attractive industry of Fourier, the correspondences of Swedenborg and the societary abracadabra of Samuel Fowler found a forum. The personal preoccupations of the younger generation of Fowlers not only were part of that spirit of the age but they apparently bore some influence upon the firm's publishing program. With Edward's devotion to mesmerism—whether genuine or spurious— came an increase in the firm's publications on that subject, and with Samuel's groping efforts at societary reconstruction came an expansion of their "Social Harmony" list. In the same way the activities of two other younger Fowlers seem to have intensified the firm's already strong interest in the improvement of physical man and physical woman.

Almira Fowler matriculated at the Female Medical College in Philadelphia after her precocious younger brother Edward had entered New York Medical College.[23] Having graduated from Jackson Academy in Michigan, she pursued a year's study in anatomy and physiology, obstetrics and materia medica at the pioneer college which introduced women to the field of eclectic medicine, a field bound by no restrictions but open to all medical roads and medical, or even pseudo-medical, bypaths. Located next door to the firm's Philadelphia branch, the Female Medical College on Arch Street offered the advantages of a "commodious Dissecting Room" as well as proximity to the Fowler house of skulls. Since Almira's thesis concerned the "relations of body and mind," this was indeed a happy concatenation of sites. In 1853, at the age of twenty-six, Almira was one of nine ladies upon whom the degree of doctor of medicine was conferred. Thereupon she joined the faculty of her alma mater as demonstrator of anatomy and chemistry, and shortly thereafter moved to New York, where she put out her shingle on East Twenty-first Street, using *Life Illustrated* as a medium for advertising her availability. After office hours Almira studied homeopathy and took time to sit for a phrenological examination, which revealed to her that she was not only "capable of becoming interested in intellectual pursuits" but that she had "quite a reformitory [*sic*] mind . . . fond of new ideas."

Many of the "new ideas" in medicine explored by Almira had been introduced to her by her half brother Lorenzo's wife. Though Lydia Folger Fowler belonged by marriage to the older set of Fowlers, she was chronologically closer to the younger generation, being a year younger than Samuel and only four years older than Almira. Despite her youth, she had by the mid-1850's not only exerted an influence upon the interests and publications of her husband's firm but made a niche for herself in the history of American medicine.

Lydia Folger Fowler was indeed a remarkable woman—more

remarkable even than Lorenzo's phrenological analysis had indicated.[24] Between the births of her first two daughters—Amelia in
1846 and Loretta in 1850—Mrs. Fowler successfully pursued the
study of medicine. Although Elizabeth Blackwell, who received
her medical degree in 1849, achieved the honor of being "the first
woman doctor of medicine of modern times," Lydia was close
upon her heels, becoming the second woman to graduate from an
American medical college. Both Lydia and her half sister-in-law
Almira were clearly in the vanguard of American women medical students. At a time when, according to most, even "the phrenology of woman proved her unsuited for the medical profession,"
the Fowler women, exercising their faculties of Firmness and Individuality, stormed the field.[25] Lydia especially combined a vital,
robust practicality and a sense of dedication to the science, believing that "there can be nothing repulsive . . . in the study of the
laws of life . . . for every bone and muscle is an unwritten poem
of beauty."[26]

In 1849, at the age of twenty-seven, already the mother of a
young daughter, she began the formal study of those "laws of
life." The newly opened Central Medical College in Syracuse was
not only a coeducational institution but an eclectic school "aiming
to investigate fully and freely the various medical practices of the
day, selecting from each liberally . . . and adopting only the Safest
and Best agencies for the treatment and removal of disease."[27]
There, with two or three other women and a full contingent of
men, Lydia studied with enthusiasm all those "agencies," from
practical anatomy and dissection to obstetrics and hydropathy.
One of the so-called peculiarities of the school was that it authorized the use of "no remedial agents or means that may tend to
diminish or impair conservative power in removing diseased conditions"—a peculiarity that pointed, with Lydia's full approval,
toward homeopathy. While Lorenzo lectured in New York State,
his wife continued her eclectic studies. In 1850, when, because of
dissension among the faculty, the school was moved to Rochester,
where it was reorganized, Lydia moved with it. In June of that

year, twenty-one students received the degree of doctor of medicine: twenty men and one woman. Lydia Folger Fowler, M.D., had become the second accredited woman physician in the country. Two months later she gave birth to her second child, Loretta.

Thanks not only to the encouragement and understanding of her husband but to the help of John Brown, Jr.'s wife, who was engaged to supervise the Fowler housekeeping, Lydia was freed not only to study medicine but to teach it. In this field her priority remains unchallenged, for she became the first woman professor of medicine in America. In 1850 Lydia was named principal of the female department of her alma mater as well as demonstrator of anatomy for female students. *The Eclectic Medical and Surgical Journal* announced the appointment:

> In consequence of the number of ladies in attendance on the last course of lectures: and at the request of a number of others who propose attending the next session, the Board of Trustees have concluded to establish a female department, and have placed it under the charge of Mrs. L. N. Fowler, M.D., who from her spirit of investigation, and scientific and medical acquirements, has obtained a wide spread and merited popularity. . . .
>
> For the convenience of the ladies attending the school, a dissecting room will be exclusively appropriated to their use, and will be under the charge of Mrs. L. N. Fowler.
>
> The Principal of the Female Department, Will instruct the Ladies belonging to the class, in those portions of the profession that propriety dictates. The female dissecting room will be under her charge, and she will render her pupils every assistance they may wish in attaining a thorough knowledge of anatomy.[28]

Lydia's writings—her trilogy of *Familiar Lessons* in *Physiology*, *Astronomy*, and *Phrenology*—as well as her lectures on the "Physical Education of Woman" had helped lay the groundwork for her new assignment. Teaching anatomy and midwifery, "such portions as propriety dictates," she conducted experiments, made dissections, and, using "models, wet specimens, plates, drawings,

[and] diagrams," taught with such skill that in 1851 she was appointed professor of midwifery and diseases of women and children at Central Medical College. Western New York, credited with giving birth to the Anti-Masonic and Liberty parties, could now be credited with providing a proving ground not merely for women physicians but for women professors of medicine.

The medicine dispensed by Professor Lydia Fowler was of course eclectic, accepting the best of the homeopathic and even a modicum of the drug-ridden allopathic system, holding for the most part that disease was a "mere functional weakness."[29] To the wits who had the homeopath say, "If you take me you'll die of the disease," and the allopath rejoin, "If you take me you'll die of the cure," Lydia could reply that there was some good in both, though far more good in homeopathy, which eschewed drugs, than in allopathy, which insisted upon them.[30] With the water-cure physicians, she rejected nothing in the whole materia medica except "putting *poison* into the system and taking *blood* out."[31] Nature's materia medica, it went without saying, was infallible. Lydia's general credo was based upon the trinity of temperance, hydropathy, and the complete, unrestrained development of the whole woman.

In her introductory address at Central Medical College, Professor Fowler exhorted women to awake from their "mental and physical coma" and "be developed physically and mentally." Her address on obstetrics before the New York State Eclectic Medical Society was followed by an essay on "Hydropathy for Females," in which she wrote, "This is truly an eclectic age."

Upholding the benefits of hygiene, hydropathy, and friction, Dr. Lydia Fowler went forth after her professorship at Rochester to teach the gospel of nature. With her husband Lorenzo, who lectured on phrenology, she toured the western cities, lecturing to ladies on "Physiology and the diseases of women and children." In Chicago she discoursed on "Physiology as applied to health and disease"; in Indiana she enlarged upon the temperance doctrine; in New York State she unfolded "the laws of life." Her lectures were enlivened by "extensive apparatus," including skeletons and models, drawings and a French manikin doubtless borrowed from the Phrenological Depot. Everywhere she established an immediate rapport with her audience, her round, ruddy face glowing with the enthusiasm she hoped to kindle in her listeners. Sizer reported to John Brown, Jr.: "L. N.'s wife has had a brilliant triumph . . . at Rochester. She has recently given a course of lectures in Newark. She has a new manakin [*sic*] and is destined to 'make a handsome sum of money.' " Equally handsome were the resolutions proposed at the close of at least one of her lectures, "That we consider Mrs. Fowler a true benefactress, who, by her knowledge and skill in the medical profession, is accomplishing woman's highest mission—that of relieving the woes of the suffering."

Lydia relieved those woes not only by lecturing but by her private practice. Besides supervising her young daughters, providing a home for Lorenzo, and tossing off a temperance tale entitled *Nora, The Lost and Redeemed*, she had daily office hours from 9 A.M. to 2 P.M. at 50 Morton Street, between Hudson and Bleecker, and also from 4 to 5 P.M. in the Phrenological Rooms at 308 Broadway. Presumably, besides examining heads and registering patents, serving as wholesale agency, offering a forum to social reformers and trance mediums, and publishing handbooks to perfect mankind, the Phrenological Depot provided the ladies with facilities for gynecological examinations between 4 and 5 P.M., Dr. Lydia Fowler in attendance.

Any leisure moments Lydia may have had were spent at a newly organized institution called the Metropolitan Medical College, a "physiopathic" school at 63 East Broadway.[32] There, on the first Tuesday in April, 1854, and continuing for eight weeks, Mrs. Fowler, M.D., in return for fourteen dollars gave a course of "private medical lectures to . . . ladies wishing to qualify as nurses, and . . . to pursue medicine as a profession." Armed with her diagrams, manikins, and dissections, she reviewed for those ladies anatomy and physiology, hygiene and practical medicine.

To round out her professional life, Lydia, an honorary member of the American Hygienic and Hydropathic Association, took a profound professional interest in the New York Hydropathic and Physiological School opened by Dr. Russell T. Trall, Fowler author, in October, 1853.[33] Located at 15 Laight Street in New York City, the institute offered not only instruction in the "Healing Art" but hydropathic home practice and electrochemical baths, graham bread, calisthenics, and a full line of Fowler and Wells hydropathic publications. It offered also a faculty that included Lorenzo Fowler, lecturer on phrenology and mental science, and Lydia Fowler, lecturer on midwifery and female diseases.

Lydia's life, like her professional credo, was eclectic, embracing with lively enthusiasm the best of the many worlds in which she lived. By 1855, the word "eclectic" had, in its medical connotations at least, come to be synonymous with reform. As Dr. Henry A. Archer explained in a lecture at the Metropolitan Medical College: "As far . . . as a name can be given to the present age, the most common and appropriate is 'The Age of Reforms.' . . . Strange revelations are taking place. . . . Liberty of thought goes hand in hand with liberty of conscience. . . . The *Spirit of Reform has entered the field of Medicine.* . . . The principles of true medical science are not pathological, but physiological."[34] This medical credo, to which Dr. Lydia Folger Fowler fully subscribed, was also the credo of the Phrenological Depot. Publishers of the eclectic, hydropathic, and homeopathic manuals of the day, the firm itself became the herald of a health reform movement whose god was nature and whose name was literally writ in water.

As the *Water-Cure Journal* put it: "The time *has* come for America to lead the world onward and upward to a higher destiny. We can *feed* the world, and we can *clothe* the world; we can also transport the world cheaper and quicker, either with steam or sail, than any other nation. We shall soon *teach* the world." The teaching of Fowler and Wells postulated that only through the "Physical Regeneration of the Race [could] the Intellectual and Moral Elevation of our fellow men [be promoted.] Health of Body and Health of Mind and Heart are so intimately connected . . . that, while the former is wanting, we despair of the latter."[35]

In their efforts to instruct the nation in the laws of hygiene, Fowler and Wells became a potent force in the health reform movement.[36] Members of the American Health Reform Society were instructed to send their remittances to the firm whose publishing division seemed devoted to the complete development of the whole man. From its presses rolled books against swill milk and tobacco; Edward Youmans' *Alcohol and the Constitution of Man*; *Delia's Doctors*, a novel in which Hannah Gardner Creamer exposed her heroine to all the medical sects of the day from allopathy to homeopathy, from mesmerism and phrenology to hydropathy.

The Fowler firm was staunch in the support of homeopathy, whose pellets, as Orson held, might not cure but would not kill. They subscribed to the oath of their own *Water-Cure Journal*, "We have sworn eternal hostility to Druggery and Quackery in all their forms." The *Journal* was expanded in an effort to annihilate the mounting pharmaceutical horrors of the day, from cod liver oil to expectorants, from pills and "slops" to "mixed up fixings." Advertisements for such remedies were refused. "We have been offered $100 to advertise a . . . *Compound Patent Medicine*, in the Water-Cure Journal. We politely informed the distinguished chap, that it would cost him more than he was worth, ($100,000, which he had filched from the pockets of suffering invalids,) to obtain the desired space." Interpreting Oliver Wendell Holmes' address on the "Currents and Counter Currents in Medical Science" as an exposé of the "Horrors of Druggery," Fowler and Wells offered to furnish copies at twenty-five cents each, despite the doctor's antagonism to "Homœopathy and Its Kindred Delusions." No equivocation was needed for the firm's endorsement of William Cullen Bryant. As president of the first Homeopathic Society of New York Physicians, the poet stood squarely in their camp. While Dr. Lydia Folger Fowler may have dispensed considerable advice in her consultations at the Phreno-logical Depot, it is certain she dispensed no allopathic drugs in that fortress of health.

Although the firm insisted that they had "no pecuniary interest whatever in *any* Water-Cure Establishment," they supported those establishments with a crusading ardor. Advertisements of water cures dotted the pages of the *Water-Cure Journal*, and further information regarding their facilities or their sale could always be had from Fowler and Wells. *Life Illustrated* published a directory of water-cure establishments; and when Dr. Eli Peck Miller began his Turkish baths, it may be taken for granted that the Fowlers were among his first customers. Editor Russell T. Trall's Hydropathic School boasted an executive committee that included Dr. Eli P. Miller as corresponding secretary and Fowler and Wells as treasurers. With or without "pecuniary interest," the firm certainly dabbled in the watery affairs of the day. Their imprint appeared upon Sir Edward Lytton Bulwer's *Confessions*, in which the author reported that "water . . . skilfully administered is in itself a wonderful excitement." When Joel Shew advocated the "Hunger-Cure" as "a useful adjunct of water treatment" in chronic disease, the firm published his findings, just as they pub-lished the *Experience in Water-Cure* of Mary S. Gove Nichols, who believed that "persons who sleep on a feather bed are not as willing to get up in season and take a bath, as those who sleep on a mattress, but they need the bath much more."

Motivated perhaps by the medical ambitions of Lydia and Al-mira Fowler, the members of the Phrenological Depot took a special interest in the trials and accomplishments of pioneer women physicians. Harriot K. Hunt, for whom George Combe's lectures had "opened . . . the labyrinth of life," had entered that labyrinth in Boston as a physician without benefit of diploma but with benefit of the Fowler combination of hygiene and hydro-therapy, temperance and phrenology. To her own natural com-mon sense and animation she added the psychological insight that made her a successful physician, especially for neurasthenic women. Miss Hunt was a good friend of all the Fowlers but especially of Charlotte Wells, with whom upon one occasion she paid a visit to the traveler from Scandinavia Fredrika Bremer, who noted in her diary:

> This morning I had a charming visit from a little lady doctor, that is to say, a lady who practices the healing art, a Miss Hunt, "female physician," as she calls herself, from Boston, who . . . was . . . so full of animation and so irresistibly merry that we . . . burst into one peal of laughter after another. There was besides so much that was excellent and really sensible in what she said, and I felt that there was so much heart in the zealous little creature, that I could not help liking her. . . . With her was another lady, as quiet as she was active, a female professor of phrenology, who wished to get hold of my head.[37]

This "little lady doctor" Miss Hunt was refused admission to Harvard Medical School in 1847 and again in 1850. Her cause was naturally espoused by the phrenologizing Fowlers, to whom Miss Hunt sent the correspondence regarding her case—her request to Dr. Oliver Wendell Holmes, and President Walker's rejection. The *Phrenological Journal* became a forum on behalf not merely of Harriot K. Hunt but of all "female physicians." "In the Athens of America," the *Journal* fulminated, "the temple of science is forbidden to a woman, Because She Is A Woman!" The city of brotherly love turned out to be less reactionary than the Athens of America, and it must have been particularly gratifying to the Fowlers when, at the same commencement at which Almira received her degree from the Female Medical College of Pennsylvania, the "honorary degree of M.D. was conferred on Harriet [*sic*] K. Hunt."

Not Miss Hunt alone but most women pioneers in medicine, especially those who undertook nursing and "the *ordinary* duties of a family physician," were championed by the phrenologists. As they explained in 1856, "Women are beginning to study medicine, and we doubt not, this will do much to popularize the study of human nature."[38] Women physicians, in their turn—practitioners like Miss Hunt and Mrs. Clemence Lozier, who had studied at Lydia's school in Rochester—flocked to the Fowler standard, endorsing the virtues of cold water and hard mattresses, graham bread and homeopathic pellets.

Nonprofessional women too followed the Fowler ways to health. Neurasthenic sufferers responded to the benison of water; mothers were grateful for the mild homeopathic remedies that their children accepted without a struggle. Most women were attracted by the temperance doctrine. If Almira and Lydia Fowler were emulated by prospective women physicians, Charlotte, carrying out much of the business in the Fowler and Wells office, pointed the way that all emancipated women could go. There was a strong rapport between the firm and women in general, who looked to the Fowlers for advice on marriage, sex education, maternity, child guidance, and health. For their part, the members of the Phrenological Depot applauded the "Water-Cure Bloomer, who believes in the Equal Rights of Men and Women to Help Themselves and Each Other, and who thinks it Respectable, if not Genteel, to be Well!"[39]

The bridge was short between the rights of women to water cure, dress reform, and health, and the rights of women to extended employment, equal pay for equal work, and full suffrage. Now, with Charlotte in the vanguard, the Fowlers crossed that bridge.

RADICALS OF REFORM

THE FOWLERS crossed the bridge to woman's rights not through overt political activity—by and large they were politically non-partisan—but through the books they published and the friends they chose, through the advice they dispensed in their Cabinet and the views they aired in their journals. Those views were based upon the phrenological concept of woman as a human being in her own right endowed with many, if not all, human potentials. In one of his lectures Lorenzo described his abstract woman:

> Phrenologically, a woman has large Approbativeness and Benevolence, which give a desire to please and make others happy. . . . she has the qualities to keep a shop, stationery and book-store, to sell goods, to take care of property, to make wearing apparel, to design, engrave, draw, to copy law-papers, to write prose and poetry, to report, set and distribute type, sing, teach, entertain company, practice the healing art among women and children, nurse the sick, and take care of her house and family. She possesses the negative and passive qualities. Having large Veneration, and not as large Combativeness and Destructiveness, she desires to look up to man as her protector. . . . Physiologically . . . she is organized on a high key, is ardent, intense, susceptible, warm-hearted, impulsive, and excitable. Physiognomically, she has sloping shoulders, rotund face and form, penetrating eyes, a kind, anxious, affectionate expression. . . . She has 140 cubic inches of brain.[1]

If, as seems probable, it was Lydia who sat to her husband for this portrait, an even bolder woman of the future was envisioned by Orson when he wrote:

Women's Sphere of Industry should . . . be enlarged till it equals that of men. . . . Printing, architecture, drawing, engraving, all the arts, all kinds of storekeeping and manufacturing, all departments of literature, telegraphy, law, legislation, public offices and clerk-ships . . . should be shared and filled equally by both. . . . In teaching and doctoring, women are naturally men's superiors. All the avenues of industry should be opened to her. They have as "inalien-able" a right to vote as men. . . . What but "female suffrage" can save our republic? Women's wages should equal men's for the same work.[2]

Being a woman who had fully exercised her own inalienable right to work, Charlotte Wells went further than either of her brothers in her concept of woman as the medium through whose influence the millennium would eventually be achieved.

While the *Illustrated Phrenological Almanac* promised to agitate the subject of woman's rights "until woman shall merit equal-ity with man, so far as nature's gifts will allow," the *Phrenological Journal* ran discussions of "Reform in the Condition of Woman."[3] In the House of Skulls, suggestions and advice for women fol-lowed manipulations and examinations. Early crusaders against tight lacing naturally applauded dress reform in general and the Bloomer costume in particular. Energetic gentlemen who be-lieved in the stimulating effects of brisk walking and deep breath-ing for themselves sponsored exercise and home gymnastics for loosely garbed members of the distaff side.

In the same way, publishers who had themselves written on marriage and maternity were the obvious choice for an omnibus volume on *Sexual Diseases*, which included Trall's *Home-Treat-ment for Sexual Abuses* and Newman's *Philosophy of Generation*. Advocates of hydropathy for women, Fowlers and Wells were the logical publishers for Dr. James C. Jackson's *Hints on the Reproductive Organs: Their Diseases, Causes, and Cure on Hy-dropathic Principles*. Dr. M. Edgeworth Lazarus' utterances on conjugal harmonies and Mrs. Hugo Reid's *Woman, Her Educa-tion and Influence* were issued by the firm, whose imprint appeared also upon a variety of books designed to free the oppressed "Isabellas" of the country—from *Woman and Her Wishes* by Thomas Wentworth Higginson to *Woman and Her Needs* by Elizabeth Oakes Smith.[4]

Of all the books by women published by the phrenologists, perhaps the most important were those written by that redoubtable New England bluestocking Margaret Fuller, who years before had sat for a phrenological analysis by Orson Fowler. Friend of Emerson and Thoreau, writer, lecturer, citizen of the world, Margaret Fuller had labored all her life for woman's rights to intellectual and personal freedom and to political action. By 1850, at the time of her tragic death by shipwreck, she seemed to many to personify those rights. Among those who regarded her in this light were certainly the partners of the Phrenological Depot, who between 1852 and 1856 reprinted her *Papers on Literature and Art*, issued a new edition of her revolutionary tract for the times *Woman in the Nineteenth Century*, and, shortly before undertaking Whitman's *Leaves of Grass*, published her *At Home and Abroad; or, Things and Thoughts in America and Europe*. Even in their manual *How to Write*, the firm inserted among the specimen letters several penned by Margaret Fuller, including her last, sent to her mother from Italy.[5]

The year of Margaret Fuller's death, a woman whom she had known and who had also undergone phrenological analysis ventured to California, armed with most of the Fowler views on life. Eliza Farnham, whom the Fowlers had once joined in the work of penal reform, decided to substitute for the prisons of the East the open spaces of the West.[6] Her attempt to organize a brideship of women eligible for phrenologically approved unions in California had failed, but after her husband's death Eliza herself had made the journey and by 1850 had settled in Santa Cruz with her young friend Georgiana Bruce. Clad in their Turkish or Albanian trousers and tunics—variants of the Bloomer costume—the ladies divided their hours between farming and reading, also taking time to send accounts of local activities to their friends at the Phrenological Depot. Those letters must have been read with intense interest, for they informed the recipients that, like the gold-seekers, the new reforms of the day had broken down frontiers and arrived in El Dorado—hydropathy and spiritualism, magnetism and mesmerism, temperance and the Fowler laws of health. Besides printing a description of Mrs. Farnham's head in the pages of the *Phrenological Journal* and publicizing her lectures in the Golden State, the firm would eventually publish an extraordinary book on heredity by Georgiana Bruce, entitled *Transmission; or, Variation of Character through The Mother*.

Meanwhile another lecturer was advancing the cause in a different western state. In 1853, Lydia Folger Fowler traveled through Wisconsin, where she instructed her audience on the "physiological effects of alcoholic drinks," and by her very presence increased the world's respect for woman's independence. As one of her colleagues reported, "Mrs. F.'s company was . . . a happy insurance against pot-house witlings on the alert to impale upon the world's dread laugh, any woman who, to accomplish some public good, should venture for a space to cut loose from the marital 'buttons' and go out into the world alone!"[7]

While Lydia served as secretary of various woman's rights conventions and offered homeopathically phrased resolutions on behalf of her sex,[8] her sister-in-law Charlotte supported the cause both directly and indirectly. By mid-century her devotion to woman's rights on the phrenological principles enunciated by her brothers was so well known that the New England Brahmin William Henry Channing, nephew of the great Dr. William Ellery Channing, came to her for advice on the subject.[9]

Channing, who had dedicated himself to "spread the reign of love among mankind" and had edited *The Spirit of the Age* published by Fowlers and Wells, had been invited to speak before the Second National Woman's Rights Convention at Worcester, Massachusetts, in 1851 on the topic of "Woman in Her Social Relations." Eager to explore such pertinent subjects as the dignity of single women and the prevention and dissolution of unsuitable marriages, the statistics of licentiousness and the "promiscuous association of youth of both sexes in workshops . . . such as bookbinderies, cap or shoe factories," he turned for guidance to Charlotte Fowler Wells. In a series of interesting letters, he asked for and received information on his subject, incidentally alluding to the *Memoirs of Margaret Fuller*, upon which he was hard at work. So apparently helpful were Charlotte's replies that Channing's discourse occupied "nearly an hour and a half in delivery." Although Fowlers and Wells published the *Proceedings* of the convention, Charlotte, as a member of the convention's committee on publication, agreed that it was best to defer publication of Channing's all but interminable contribution to the crusade for the emancipation of women.

Most of the women leaders in that crusade were personally known to the Fowlers as members of their circle or as visitors to their examining room. The phrenological character of Paulina Wright Davis, who established the first woman's rights paper in the country, appeared in the *Phrenological Journal*.[10] Susan B. Anthony, a friend of the Fowlers, had submitted to a phrenological examination.[11] Antoinette Blackwell used the services of the phrenological office for forwarding her mail and invited Charlotte for cherry pie and tea.[12] In Albany, Lydia and Amelia Bloomer attended a mass temperance meeting together, and when the personification of dress reform visited New York she was a guest of the Lorenzo Fowlers.[13]

Amelia Bloomer descended upon New York in February, 1853, for the purpose of attending the Woman's Grand Temperance Demonstration at Metropolitan Hall, where Jenny Lind had made her debut.[14] The audience of three thousand was almost as large and "fully as respectable" as it had been for the Swedish Nightingale, and it too witnessed a debut. As presiding officer, Lydia Folger Fowler became the first woman to deliver a public speech from the Metropolitan's platform. Since the adoption of the Maine Liquor Law in 1851, the "Temperance Reformation" had made great strides. The Phrenological Depot, original subscribers to the Maine Law Statistical Society, were about to publish a series of Whole World's Temperance Tracts, by Horace Greeley, P. T. Barnum, and others, aimed at ending the traffic in liquor. Now, at Metropolitan Hall, Lydia shared the stage not only with Greeley, who looked like a rustic philosopher, but with Susan B. Anthony in Bloomer costume and with Amelia Bloomer herself, who sported a "suit of brown satin cut in the most approved style of her own costume." Lydia, in more conservative attire—"a sky-blue delaine . . . open corsage"—introduced the topic of the evening, thus exercising woman's right to be heard on the subject of temperance and indeed upon any subject. The meeting, opened by Lydia Fowler, closed with a vegetarian banquet graced by graham bread and corn blanc mange, molded wheaten grits and pumpkin pies. The rally thus managed to combine in one way or another such causes of the day as woman's rights and temperance, dress reform and vegetarianism.

The Phrenological Depot itself was soon to support a movement that formed a microcosm of many related reforms, from vegetarianism to octagonal architecture and the rights of emigrants. On their many-headed hobby horse, the firm was about to ride—in spirit at least—to Kansas.

Samuel Wells especially had long had a keen interest in the West, an interest reflected in the books he published. N. Howe Parker's *Iowa As It Is in 1855* was, at $1.75, a useful handbook for emigrants, and this was followed by Frederic Gerhard's *Illinois As It Is in 1856* and J. Wesley Bond's *Minnesota As It Is in 1856*. In addition to their agencies for patents and wholesale merchandise, the firm opened a pension agency to "procure and forward to applicants" not merely pensions but bounty land warrants. While settlers prepared to make the overland trek, the Phrenological Depot at 308 Broadway did a brisk business in providing them with information. In 1855 the *Journal* announced:

Bounty Land.—Any person wishing information in relation to obtaining bounty lands or pension, may have it without charge, by addressing Fowlers and Wells, No. 308 Broadway, N.Y., . . . We are also prepared to make application for Bounty Lands, or prosecute any other claims at the Pension Office, which may be required. . . . Our charge for making an application, is five dollars in all cases.[15]

For the purpose of establishing a colony of socialists in the state of Texas, an organization was formed under the pretentious title of the Europeo-American Colonization Society of Texas.[16] Its committee of direction was represented by the Fowler staff writer Daniel Harrison Jacques, who used the phrenological office as his headquarters for dispensing information about the venture. Two years before, in 1853, Albert Brisbane and the French Fourierist Victor Considérant had visited Texas "with a view to the ultimate location there of a colony of European and American Socialists." A joint stock company with a reputed capital of a million dollars was finally organized, and by 1855 D. H. Jacques was prepared to provide full details about the colony from his desk at 308 Broadway. While phrenological examinations were taking place in one room, applications for bounty lands were made out in another, and in his corner Jacques discussed the "New Social Order" with colonists eager to plant the doctrines of mutualism and co-operative association in the soil of Dallas County.

The westward push was spurred on by the work of the phrenological office and by the policy of its journals.[17] When the publishers and booksellers paid a mass visit to the western explorer and Republican nominee John Charles Frémont, *Life Illustrated* ran a full account of the event. Its business columns discussed the "Gold Crop of California," while its features included a prophetic article entitled "Is a Pacific Railroad Possible?" The publication of the *Wisconsin Mirror* in an oak forest filled with deer and partridges inspired the Fowler editors to run an exuberant account of "Printing in the Woods." The suggestion of a female emigrant society to increase the population of California was applauded, and "See Your Own Country" was the Fowler injunction to all "educated Americans."

To a small handful of Americans the Fowler injunction was

Seal of the Fowler and Wells Patent
Agency Department

From *American Phrenological Journal*,
Vol. XXIII (1856)

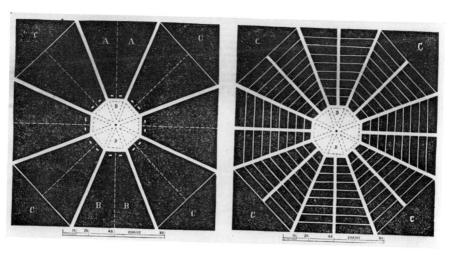

Plans of the Octagon Settlement in Kansas

From *American Phrenological Journal*,
Vol. XXIII (1856)

Examination in silhouette, O. S. Fowler, *Synopsis of Phrenology; and the Phrenological Developments . . . of John C. Hoadley as given by L. N. Fowler June 24, 1845 (New York, n.d.).*

Nelson Sizer in consultation

Fowler Family Papers, Collection of
Regional History, Cornell University

The octagon house near Fishkill

From O. S. Fowler, *A Home for All*
(New York, 1854)

Phrenology.

1st boy.—SAY, BILL, LET'S GO IN AND HAVE OUR HEADS EXAMINED.
2d boy.—THEY CAN'T FIND ANYTHING NEW, COS I HAD MINE EXAMINED
TWICE YESTERDAY!

Phrenological humor

From *Yankee Notions*, Vol. VI (July, 1857)
The New-York Historical Society

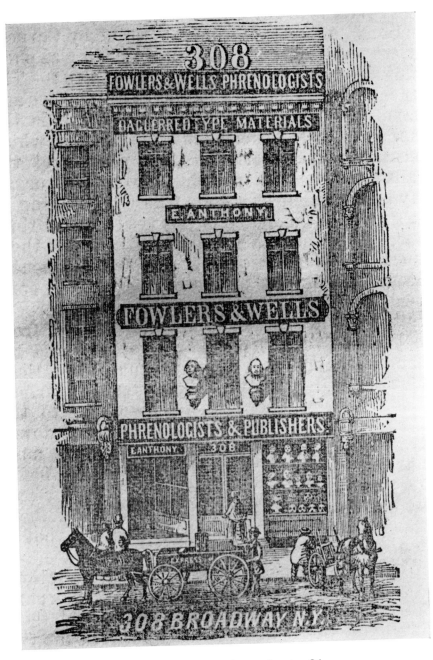

The Fowler office from 1854 to 1865

From *American Phrenological Journal,*
Vol. XX (1854)

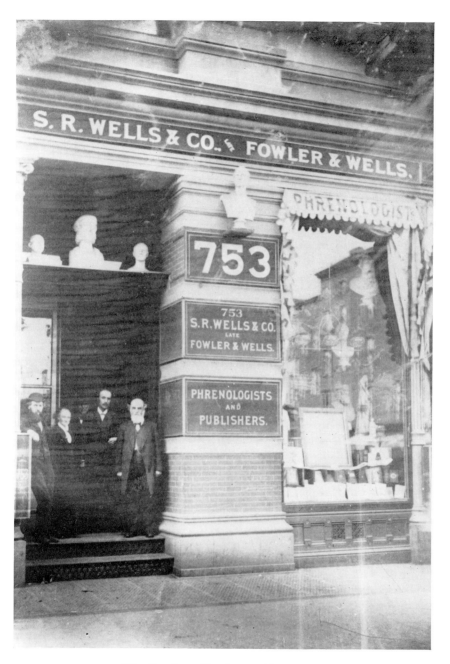

The Fowler office from 1880 to 1887

Fowler Family Papers, Collection of
Regional History, Cornell University

A group of early phrenologists including, clockwise from the top, Combe, Orson Fowler, Charlotte F. Wells, Samuel R. Wells, Nelson Sizer, Lydia F. Fowler, Lorenzo Fowler, and Spurzheim. Gall is in the center.

"See Your Own Country" in general but see Kansas in particular. Although the firm was nonpartisan on principle, it could have no other view on the Kansas-Nebraska Bill than that of the free-soil press everywhere. The concentration of southern proslavery and northern antislavery men in Kansas prompted both sides to send settlers there, taking their stand for or against a free Kansas. Henry Ward Beecher urged that Sharpe's rifles—"Beecher's Bibles"—be dispatched to the territory. The Fowler assistant and disciple John Brown, Jr., moved to Kansas with his brothers to fight the battle for free soil. The Fowler firm, in the same camp as Beecher and John Brown, Jr., endorsed still another plan to save Kansas for the side of freedom. True to their basic tenets, they would dispatch to the territory not merely antislavery men but antislavery men who were also vegetarians.

Years before, on May 15, 1850, the American Vegetarian Society had been organized at the Fowler office in Clinton Hall. Now, when the fate of the country seemed to hinge upon the fate of Kansas, the secretary of the Vegetarian Society, Henry S. Clubb, conceived the extraordinary plan of creating a Vegetarian Settlement Company in Kansas.[18] Like Walt Whitman and like the Europeo-American Colonization Society of Texas, this company too was to be addressed care of Fowler and Wells, 308 Broadway.

Among the many birds of strange plumage who congregated at the phrenological office, none sang more persistently than Rev. Henry Stephen Clubb. Born in England, he had opened a Phonographic Institute in London and contributed articles to the *Vegetarian Advocate*, published by the Fowler British agent William Horsell. Clubb's interest in "humane diet" had absorbed him from the age of nine, and when he arrived in New York he naturally gravitated to the Fowler and Wells office, where the skulls of so many vegetarians presided over repasts of apples and unbolted bread.

Under Clubb's direction and with Fowler and Wells' full accord, the Vegetarian Settlement Company was formed not merely to save the vegetarians for Kansas but to save Kansas for the vegetarians. With the Alcoholics Anonymous of a later century, Clubb held that if the vegetarians were not banded together in a permanent home, they might, "solitary and alone in their vegetarian practice . . . sink into flesh-eating habits." On May 16, 1855, a meeting was held, the joint stock principle was adopted, and an advance scout—the water-cure physician John McLauren—was sent ahead to select a location in Kansas. An assessment was levied to establish a fund for tents and provisions, sawmill and gristmill. All moneys were collected at Fowler and Wells, the office from which all operations were also directed. By September a group of pioneers had gone forth to eat vegetables on the bank of the Neosho River, and their progress was ecstatically reported in the pages of *Life Illustrated*:

> The pioneers sent out by this Company in September last have reported in favor of a location in Southern Kanzas [*sic*], within a day's walk of Fort Scott, on a rapid part of the Neosha [*sic*] River. . . .
>
> Springs of pure water are interspersed throughout a fine rolling prairie. The soil is composed of rich vegetable mold and loam. . . .
>
> The stock already taken in the Company amounts to $23,000, in shares of $5 each. . . .
>
> It is a movement which must, from the elements which it has called together, take an important and novel position among the reformatory undertakings of this country. United for the purpose of carrying out a favorite principle, there is a bond of union among the members not usually enjoyed by new settlements; and, from the character of that principle, it necessarily draws together persons of good moral character, who are generally sincere and earnest reformers in every department of social progress.
>
> We have had pleasure in aiding this movement thus far, and we shall watch its progress with great interest, reporting, from time to time, the measures taken and the success which attends them. The Vegetarian Settlement will be a place for physical and moral education such as can not be found in any other part of the world.[19]

The Vegetarian Settlement was joined a few months later by an even more extraordinary Kansas settlement close to the heart

174

and the pronunciamentos of Orson Fowler. Following the injunctions laid down in his *Home for All*, the new settlement—called the Vegetarian Kansas Emigration Company—added to the vegetarian principle the octagon principle. The new band of settlers went one step further than those who had simply laid vegetarianism upon the altar of a free Kansas. The second wave of pioneers extolled the free territory over vegetables nibbled in a paradise octagonal in shape. Still another group, who styled themselves the Octagon Settlement Company, waived the vegetarian restriction but insisted upon the octagonal architecture.

The plans for Kansas' Octagon City were grandiose. It was to include an agricultural college and a hydropathic establishment, a scientific institute and a museum of curiosities—each octagonal in shape. In a village four miles square each farmhouse, octagonal in shape, was to face a central octagon, from which would radiate eight avenues. Every family would thus be within easy and equal distance of the common or central octagon, where they could agitate against slavery and for temperance. Like the Vegetarian Settlement Company, the octagon settlements had their headquarters in the Fowler and Wells office and, under the influence of Orson Fowler, enjoyed the Fowler and Wells special endorsement. As the *Phrenological Journal* explained: "On the ordinary plan of settlement, on square farms, settlers become isolated. . . . On the best plan . . . the Octagon plan, all the farm-houses would be placed in proximity to each other." Designed for sixty-four families (eight squared), the octagonal community was begun with the laying out of Neosho City on the Neosho River opposite the Vegetarian Settlement Company. For a time the sound of the ax echoed smartly through the Kansas woods. A delegation of Osage Indians visited the settlement, and a vegetarian blacksmith moved in. Specimens of Kansas minerals were sent to the Fowler and Wells Museum for exhibition, and the firm publicized the experiment in octagonal living, vegetarian eating, and antislavery thinking in a variety of tracts and pamphlets. *The Illustrated Vegetarian Almanac for 1855*, edited by Henry S. Clubb and published by the firm, explained the ideals of the Vegetarian Kansas Emigration Company, which had been "established for the purpose of enabling Vegetarians who are desirous of promoting freedom in Kansas by going to live there, to become acquainted; to coöperate with each other . . . to promote the growth of fruits, vegetables and grain; to select a suitable locality . . . where they can live in proximity to each other, where they can adopt such regulations as will secure at least One Tract of Land on this fair earth free from the stain of habitual bloodshed."

The *Kansas Emigration Almanac and Guide for 1855*, priced at six and a quarter cents a copy, was designed to forward "the great and determined movement which is now going on among the people of this country to secure to those Territories [Kansas and Nebraska] the common rights of humanity." At the phrenological office Redfield's *Guide to Kansas* and Reed's *Guide to the Kansas Gold Region* were sold; from the phrenological press emerged a pamphlet entitled *The Octagon Settlement Company, Kansas*, published for the company by Fowler and Wells, and Max Greene's *The Kanzas Region*, with its map of the territory and suggestions as to route, pioneer's outfit, and localities for settlement.

Part of the larger stream of emigration from the free states, part of the abolition movement, the Kansas Vegetarian and Octagon Settlements had been advanced by the phrenologist publishers, who, though they held themselves apart from politics, still believed, as Nelson Sizer phrased it, that the "Fugitive Slave Bill is the . . . roughest bill that a legal Turkey buzzard ever held a piece of human carrion in."[20] Yet, almost while the Fowler pamphlets were being published, the settlements themselves started to peter out. Orson Fowler, lecturing on phrenology in Kansas, must have been disheartened by the outcome of the strange experiments in communal living, octagonal architecture, and vegetarian dining that had been attempted in the territory. No Octagon City had towered above the plains, only a log cabin "mudded between the logs on the inside" without door or window. No agricultural college dotted the landscape, only a single plow. Even the saw-mill and gristmill failed to materialize. Weeds, vegetables, and fruit had apparently not been strong enough fodder for the pioneer families, who, camping in tents, had succumbed to the plague of chills and fever. The "spring of pure water" dried up, and the crops were raided by Indians. Many settlers, broken in health, deserted; others died. By the spring of 1857 there was scarcely a trace of the settlements and but one reminder of the experiment—a stream called Vegetarian Creek.

The year 1857 was an ill-fated one, not merely for the Kansas pioneers but for the entire nation. In this panic year banks suspended payments and factories closed down, farmers could not sell their crops and unemployment mounted. Few were untouched by the disaster, which Fowler and Wells characteristically regarded from the phrenological or psychological standpoint, finding its causes in the predatory nature of man. In an unusually candid editorial statement they presented their views to their readers and begged for more subscribers:

> Who expected so sudden and so violent a monetary whirlwind? Nor was there any need of it. It was brought about mainly by fear. It was over-cautiousness—pure, sheer *panic*—beginning in over-trading, and aggravated by distrust and a grab-game selfishness, which set each to tearing the flesh and sucking the blood of his debtor, while those he owed did the same. This brought about and still keeps up this crisis. . . . We calculate that no one shall lose a dollar by us pecuniarily. . . .
>
> We have *published too cheaply*. We have kept neither "fast horses" nor fast company, have dressed and lived plainly, have worked hard, yet spent little on our own selves personally—the main cause of our difficulty is that we have given too much for too little. . . . We have furnished a portion of our reading matter below its actual cost, and it has taken large drafts from our professional services to make up the deficit of our publishing department.[21]

Both the nation and the Fowlers survived the panic, but it left its marks. Orson Fowler leased his Fishkill octagon, initiating a series of catastrophes for the house of his dreams. While the firm was—temporarily at least—dogged by financial problems, the family suffered the loss of their father. On May 26, 1859, Horace Fowler died in his seventy-eighth year—the patriarch who had founded one of America's most colorful dynasties.[22]

Meanwhile the members of that family had begun somewhat to change the pattern of their lives. The youngest of Lydia's three daughters, Jessie Allen Fowler, had been born in 1856.[23] Two years later, in company with Samuel Wells, the Lorenzo Fowlers began an extensive tour through the United States and Canada.[24] Leaving the office in the competent charge of Nelson Sizer, they set forth to sell phrenology to a younger generation of Americans.

For Lorenzo the journey must often have recaptured the past as he revisited the South and Middle West, lecturing on scientific character reading or the application of phrenology to the choice of occupation, on social relations or the education of children. While Lydia grasped every opportunity to discourse on physiology and temperance, her husband, with the "polished and agreeable" Samuel Wells, spread the phrenologic doctrine. In New Orleans and Mobile they examined and lectured in private parlor or in public hall. Once again Lorenzo manipulated the heads of prisoners, detecting in a polygamist a "desire to cohabit . . . stronger than his desire to caress." In Boston, where phrenology had first taken hold, Lorenzo's lectures gave "a new impetus to phrenological investigation." With enormous relish Samuel Wells savored the pleasures of overland travel to the Middle West, convinced that since an Atlantic cable was soon to materialize the times were ripe to "canvass for a railway to the Pacific." Between 1858 and 1860 they traveled through the chief cities of the country and in Canada, covering "upward of 30,000 miles by rail, river and sea from New York to New Orleans, through the Southwestern States, to the great lakes in the north, and on to Newfoundland."

Then in 1860, their appetite for wandering fired by what it had fed on, they climaxed their journey with a voyage to England.

The tide had turned. The phrenological theory expounded in America two decades before by the British George Combe had undergone a metamorphosis. Now, in its applied and practical form, Lorenzo Fowler and Samuel Wells would carry phrenology back to England. The phrenologists were armed not only with their experience and their enthusiasm but with a letter from Horace Greeley:

> Messrs Fowler & Wells for twenty years known and honored as publishers in our City, and as theoretical and practical Phrenologists throughout our country and the Canadas, start for England soon, on a tour in which they hope to unite business with pleasure. I commend them to your kind regards and to that of the British Press and Public as gentlemen of liberal attainments and solid practical worth.[25]

Phrenology, Yankee style, was on its way to Albion.

CITIZENS OF LONDON, BOSTON,
AND THE WORLD

. . . .

XI

In August, 1860, with a lecture in Liverpool, Lorenzo Fowler embarked upon what would be a new life in Britain. He came with a strong reputation to a country where, although "Phrenology . . . had a great vogue," it gave signs of languishing for want of adequate practitioners. As one observer noted: "Phrenology in England is not so prominent as it was, but it is exercising a most potent influence: it is a leaven which is permeating all branches of morality and of intellectualism and of those practical matters in relation to human society growing out of these. In America you seem to have more intensity, more prominence, and thus keep the matter more actively before the public mind."[1] Except for James De Ville and Cornelius Donovan of London, there were, according to Lorenzo, only "a few obscure smatterers going from house to house to *examine*." There was, he discovered, a demand for the new twist he gave to his subject "by dwelling on the temperaments" and uniting "physiology to phrenology." More important to him personally, there was a demand for Lorenzo Fowler, whose stirring lectures left in their wake an ardent zest for exploring the skull and analyzing the character. A later colleague would astutely observe that Lorenzo "possessed a very observant, thoughtful mind. Human Nature was one of the largest mental organs he possessed . . . the key-note of the whole of his character and intellect. As a phrenological practitioner he was accounted a most shrewd, apt and penetrative delineator of character. With this strong intuitive characteristic, he had quite a subtle sense of humour, and as a lecturer and character delineator he attracted a very large following."[2]

Without displaying any apparent enthusiasm himself, Lorenzo had the knack of kindling enthusiasm in others. In Liverpool and Newcastle, Perth and Edinburgh, "crowds flocked . . . night after night" for public lectures or "private delineations." The travelers remained in each town from one week to three weeks, hiring a large hall, where they hung a "well-selected gallery of painted portraits" (probably the set of reproductions used by Fowler and Wells "to illustrate lectures on phrenology"). In 1862 they came to London during the International Exhibition, lecturing in various halls and renting offices in the Strand. While Samuel Wells explained the "knotty points of the science," Lorenzo topped the lectures with a practical American phrenological examination, reading off characters with dispatch and perspicacity—among them that of the American eccentric George Francis Train.[3]

While the men were proselytizing for the science in Britain, Lydia was dividing her days between lecturing and taking care of her daughters. She found time too for a trip to Italy, a winter of medical study in Paris, and a three-months' stint in charge of the obstetrical department of a London hospital.[4]

In August, 1862, the trio returned to the States—Wells to take his place as the head of the firm, Lydia to resume her medical practice and her teaching of midwifery in Trall's Hygeio-Therapeutic College, and Lorenzo to reconsider his way of life. The man who had analyzed so many characters now examined his own and, at the age of fifty-two, determined to uproot himself and his family from America and live out his life in England. The Civil War, which had broken out during his absence, may have played some part in this decision. To Lorenzo, by nature and phrenology apolitical and nonresistant, by profession above politics, the war probably seemed a violent and unhappy intrusion upon the serene pursuit of his career. Perhaps too in the course of his travels he had come to feel less allegiance to a single country than to the world, of which he was fast becoming a citizen. Actually, because of the family's indefatigable traveling the last few years, the uprooting was less an act of sudden deracination than a gradual resettling. They had liked what they had seen of England—its countryside and its receptive people, the pace and steadiness of London after the swift changes of New York. Once established there, Lorenzo could work out a lucrative business arrangement with Wells, in time setting up an English publishing agency while he supplied the demand for phrenology in Britain.

In 1863, therefore, the Lorenzo Fowlers carried their lares and penates to England, and the Fowler family could now boast a British branch. On London's Fleet Street, near Ludgate Circus and New Bridge Street, in Cook's Buildings at Number 107, Lorenzo Fowler eventually put out his shingle. Thomas Cook himself was an admirer not only of phrenology but of hydropathy, and had much in common with the well-traveled professor. Having substituted Fleet Street for Broadway, Lorenzo now received in his office, besides the English devotees of the science, aliens who, passing through London, often gravitated to the headquarters of the American phrenologist. Mazzini, the dark Italian revolutionary brooding over his country's fate, submitted to the test and went off with an analysis that declared him "remarkable for a high degree of the nervous temperament. . . . He is more of a poet, philosopher, schemer—a man capable of devising ways and means for others than one remarkable for available, practical intellect. He has talent, but not tact." "When examining his head," Lorenzo recalled, "I told him that I had never seen but one man who had such a large organ of Language, and that man was Kossuth."[5]

Others, among them the son of the future king of Corsica, bared their heads to the wizard fingers, and many an American on tour stopped by eventually, as did Julia Ward Howe and her husband Dr. Samuel Gridley Howe for a chat on their way through London.[6]

Of those Americans none was more celebrated in reputation

or more complicated in character than Mark Twain. Remembering the itinerant phrenologists of his Hannibal days, he was attracted by the Fowler name in London and decided to make what he called "a small test of phrenology for my better information." This test consisted in Twain's making two visits to the phrenologist, spaced three months apart, the first under an assumed name, the second under his famous nom de plume. The humorist claimed to have received conflicting analyses from the professor, and went away disenchanted not only with Fowler but with his science. Practicing deception, he did little more than deceive himself, for Lorenzo, authority on mnemonics, could never have forgotten Mark Twain's unmistakable features in a matter of three months. The author who came, pretending to test phrenology, was doubtless far more concerned with being tested, for Twain's interests ranged "through every subject from protoplasm to infinity," and not the least of his interests was, and would continue to be, the mind of man. The charts made out for Mark Twain unfortunately have not survived, but, twisting the truth for his own, perhaps humorous, purposes and stressing "bumps" and "cavities," which were rarely part of the Fowler phrenological vocabulary, Twain left a remarkable record of his sessions at the Golgotha of Fleet Street:

> In London . . . I made a small test of phrenology for my better information. I went to Fowler under an assumed name and he examined my elevations and depressions and gave me a chart which I carried home to the Langham Hotel and studied with great interest and amusement—the same interest and amusement which I should have found in the chart of an impostor who had been passing himself off for me and who did not resemble me in a single sharply defined detail. I waited three months and went to Mr. Fowler again, heralding my arrival with a card bearing both my name and my nom de guerre. Again I carried away an elaborate chart. It contained several sharply defined details of my character, but it bore no recognizable resemblance to the earlier chart. These experiences gave me a prejudice against phrenology which has lasted until now.

I am aware that the prejudice should have been against Fowler, instead of against the art; but I am human and that is not the way that prejudices act. . . .

When I encountered Fowler's advertisements in London . . . I went to him under a fictitious name. . . . I found Fowler on duty, in the midst of the impressive symbols of his trade. On brackets, on tables, on shelves, all about the room, stood marble-white busts, hairless, every inch of the skull occupied by a shallow bump, and every bump labeled with its imposing name, in black letters.

Fowler received me with indifference, fingered my head in an uninterested way and named and estimated my qualities in a bored and monotonous voice. He said I possessed amazing courage, an abnormal spirit of daring, a pluck, a stern will, a fearlessness that were without limit. I was astonished at this, and gratified, too; I had not suspected it before; but then he foraged over on the other side of my skull and found a hump there which he called "caution." This hump was so tall, so mountainous, that it reduced my courage-bump to a mere hillock by comparison, although the courage-bump had been so prominent up to that time—according to his description of it—that it ought to have been a capable thing to hang my hat on; but it amounted to nothing, now, in the presence of that Matterhorn which he called my Caution. He explained that if that Matterhorn had been left out of my scheme of character I would have been one of the bravest men that ever lived—possibly the bravest—but that my cautiousness was so prodigiously superior to it that it abolished my courage and made me almost spectacularly timid. He continued his discoveries, with the result that I came out safe and sound, at the end, with a hundred great and shining qualities; but which lost their value and amounted to nothing because each of the hundred was coupled up with an opposing defect which took the effectiveness all out of it.

However, he found a *cavity*, in one place; a cavity where a bump would have been in anybody else's skull. That cavity, he said, was all alone, all by itself, occupying a solitude, and had no opposing bump, however slight in elevation, to modify and ameliorate its perfect completeness and isolation. He startled me by saying that that cavity represented the total absence of the sense of humor! He now became almost interested. Some of his indifference disap-

184

peared. He almost grew eloquent over this America which he had discovered. He said he often found bumps of humor which were so small that they were hardly noticeable, but that in his long experience this was the first time he had ever come across a *cavity* where that bump ought to be.

I was hurt, humiliated, resentful, but I kept these feelings to myself; at bottom I believed his diagnosis was wrong, but I was not certain. In order to make sure, I thought I would wait until he should have forgotten my face and the peculiarities of my skull, and then come back and try again and see if he had really known what he had been talking about, or had only been guessing. After three months I went to him again, but under my own name this time. Once more he made a striking discovery—the cavity was gone, and in its place was a Mount Everest—figuratively speaking— 31,000 feet high, the loftiest bump of humor he had ever encountered in his life-long experience! I went from his presence prejudiced against phrenology, but it may be . . . that I ought to have conferred the prejudice upon Fowler and not upon the art which he was exploiting.[7]

Yet Mark Twain was not so prejudiced against phrenology that he would not at least once more in a later decade submit his skull to its probing test. Surely there is more of Mark Twain than of Lorenzo Fowler in the author's recollections. The Lorenzo Fowler who examined Walt Whitman with such perceptive skill and such profound influence turns into a mountebank devoid of sight and all but devoid of sense. And Mark Twain here reveals himself as one more interested in poking fun at a pseudo-science than in understanding it. Like a cat with a mouse, he worries his subject and, ashamed perhaps of its attractions for him, belittles the analyst along with the analysis.

The analyst himself was a busy man. Lecturing on "Self-Made Men" and "Perfection of Character," "How to Train Up A Child" and "How to Succeed in the World," he continued to attract followers by his quiet, professional, matter-of-fact manner. The intensely practical Yankee succeeded in England where a more flamboyant enthusiast might have failed. John Bull welcomed Brother Jonathan as "the prince of phrenological delineators." When published, his *Lectures on Man* sold, at a penny each, in the tens of thousands.[8]

Early in his London life, before establishing his own permanent headquarters, Lorenzo formed a publishing connection with William Tweedie of the Strand, who issued the *Lectures* verbatim and sold the standard works published by the New York office. Taking the place of William Horsell as English agent for Fowler and Wells, Tweedie was, like his predecessor, a temperance man and author of such high-minded pamphlets as *Temperance and High Wages* and *The Philosophy of Drinking and Drunkenness*. He provided readers of the *American Phrenological Journal* with a "London Letter Box" and Lorenzo with an address while on tour.[9]

Although he had taken the British Isles as his adopted country, Lorenzo was not one to remain very long in any one place. His work was punctuated, if not interrupted, by his travels, and he enjoyed recounting them to his audience:

> I have sat in the seats of emperors, kings, and princes; have been in the birthplace of Burns and Shakespeare; have visited the ashes of Byron; have sat at the desk and in the chair where Walter Scott wrote his wonderful tales; visited the tombs of Hugh Miller, John Knox, and the Scotch Martyrs . . . have wandered in the lands which have been the scenes of the labours of Luther, Melancthon, Zwingli, Goethe, Richter, Kepler, and Humboldt. I have been on many battle-fields, seen the monuments of heroes and statesmen.

Later, Lorenzo wandered still farther afield, taking a journey to the East and visiting Greece and Turkey, Egypt and Palestine. In the course of his travels he never forgot the needs of his Phrenological Cabinet, for everywhere he went he found "something to carry home—a stone . . . shell, mineral, pressed leaves or flowers."[10]

Lydia shared his travels as she shared his work. Her strong constitution seemed to become stronger, her presence more majestic as she moved through the long day's labors in London. Between establishing a home and raising her daughters, assisting her husband in his office and continuing with her lectures to ladies on "How to Preserve a Healthy Skin" or "How to Dress a Child," she somehow found time to give lessons in calisthenics, serve with the British Women's Temperance Association, and write. Her lectures were published under the title of *The Pet of the Household*, and her poems in a volume entitled *Heart-Melodies*. Her medical work took the form of social service—a natural consequence perhaps of a brain "strongly developed in the superior region, which gave to her character a decidedly moral and beneficent tendency." This tendency she cultivated by becoming district visitor for the City Temple on High Holborn. As she herself put it, "the body . . . cannot be separated from its mental influences," and Lydia's vigorous body certainly responded to the bidding of her determined mind.[11] Her marriage too applied her own standard of "equality" or "perfect adaptation" of man and woman. Lorenzo and Lydia conferred together and worked together as his business expanded.

James Burns of London, phrenologist, spiritualist, and later managing representative of the Progressive Library and Spiritual Institution, joined Lorenzo for a time as agent and manager. Lorenzo's phrenological busts in china or plaster appeared on the stately mantelpieces of Great Britain. His colleagues, such as the Scottish David George Goyder, who concluded phrenological lectures with prayers and the singing of psalms, cogitated over Lorenzo's latest discoveries. The prince of phrenologists had localized Human Nature in the "superior frontal convolution, below Benevolence and above Comparison." He had also somehow localized Repose, although his own Repose was small indeed. Between lectures and character delineations, he took his family to Paris to show the girls Dr. Gall's Anthropological Institute in the Jardin des Plantes. Conferences with Tweedie or Burns about publications or the sale of books from the New York office were interspersed with private examinations. Lorenzo added to his col-

lection of busts, skulls, and portraits until the London headquarters became a small-scale replica of the Broadway firm.

Through the 1870's Professor and Mrs. Lorenzo Niles Fowler, "phrenologists, physiologists and lecturers," could be found
at 107 Fleet Street teaching man to know himself. Their youngest
daughter Jessie, who had inherited her father's perceptive powers noted that he was developing "wrinkles under the eye as do
persons who study the interests of the masses." Those interests
were indeed his. His conviction that he had the science and the
power to instruct and improve had suffered no sea-change by
crossing the Atlantic. Lorenzo was as calmly sure of himself
and his skill when he manipulated the skull of Mark Twain in
London as when he had phrenologized Walt Whitman in New
York. He had taken not all knowledge but all mankind for his
province, merely substituting for the American genus the English
variety. At the end of a lecture on self-knowledge Lorenzo advised his audience: "Write your own epitaphs in legible characters
on a slip of paper; make them as flattering and eulogistic as possible. Then spend the remainder of your lives, endeavouring not
only to reach the standard . . . you have raised, but to go far
beyond it."[12] As a British import, Lorenzo Fowler practiced what
he preached.

So too, but in a vastly different way and with vastly different
results, did his older brother Orson. If Lorenzo, with his emphasis
upon practical ethics, vaguely foreshadowed the pragmatist William James, Orson, with his close concentration upon sex, boldly
prefigured the giant Sigmund Freud.

For some time after his retirement from the firm he had founded,
Orson spent about ten months of every year lecturing through
the South and West. After exploring the "whole slope" of California, he came to the peculiar conclusion that the "active gender
is Nature's great beautifier."[13] After crossing the Bay of Fundy
he contracted "Typhoid Pneumonia . . . by the striking in of the
perspiration incident to sea-sickness."[14] Orson recovered from his
illness and collected his more or less enigmatic maxims for future

publication. Meanwhile, in 1863, he set out his own independent shingle in Boston, at the same time taking up residence in Manchester, Massachusetts, the "first of the 'cape towns.' " A place of sandy beaches and rocky bluffs, Manchester was dedicated to the manufacture of cabinet furniture and to "cosy summer residences." Some years later Orson would build a house there that boasted an octagonal dining room in memory of the Fishkill venture.[15] Shortly after his move to Massachusetts, he lost his first wife Eliza, whom he replaced the next year with the widowed Mrs. Mary Poole, daughter of a Gloucesterman, William Aiken.[16]

Now in his fifties, the indefatigable Orson Fowler took the twenty-five-mile trip from Manchester to Boston and opened a new business on his own. At 514 Tremont Street, opposite the Clarendon, he was available for phrenological examinations, opinions, and advice. No longer connected with the New York firm but actually a competitor, he announced that he could be "consulted, never in the New York, but only at his new *Boston* establishment. . . . Let those who prefer an examination by Wells . . . or by his employés, pay their money *understandingly*, while those who prefer one having the *genuine* O. S. Fowler *ring* in its metal, can obtain it at his Boston residence, 514 Tremont Street, where he has purchased, and located for life."[17]

Between writing and examining, Orson filled the hours. His plans were more grandiose than ever. He would present to the world his "Complete Revised WORKS ON MAN," including tomes on all the sciences—physiological, phrenological, sexual, religious, and intellectual—in a "complete series of exhaustive volumes" that embodied "all his former writings, revised, condensed, systematized, enlarged, illustrated, and . . . improved."[18] His exercise now consisted mainly in kneading his bowels, a practice that "rendered him as antic as a colt . . . as lively and happy as the lark."[19] "My usual day's routine," he confided, "was, in summer, to rise before the sun, write till after ten, breakfast, wait on professional calls, read proof, answer correspondence, and rest till seven P.M., then write with all steam on till eleven; but in

AT MUSIC HALL

TUESDAY EVE.,—FREE.

CHILDREN,

THEIR

HEALTH, GROWTH, TRAINING & SCHOOLING,

AS TAUGHT BY PHRENOLOGY AND PHYSIOLOGY,

By Professor O. S. FOWLER

FORMERLY OF NEW YORK, BUT NOW OF 514 TREMONT STREET, BOSTON, MASS.,

To conclude with a public Description of noted persons nominated.

. FINE CHILDREN—healthy, talented, and good—are their parents' most precious earthly treasures. Yet how many—over one-half—die prematurely! How many more, lovely and rosy at four, become ailing or ugly before twelve, and worse before twenty! How many "turn out badly," because spoiled by well-meant, but misguided management, whom a "good bringing-up" would have rendered the pride of parents and a blessing to society! And how incomparably better all would become if "trained up" in the best possible manner! Parents, do you feel fully competent to execute your eventful task ? Then, learn in this lecture, what FIRST PRINCIPLES should guide their development from birth to marriage. There is a RIGHT, a SCIENTIFIC educational system, which Phrenology expounds, even in detail.

SYNOPSIS.

GOOD CHILDREN vs. POOR. Children rendered either by parental conditions. Hereditary entailments. All might be borne much better than now. Parental responsibility. A right and wrong education.

Their physical regimen. Why 300,000 die annually. Parents can not afford the loss. Its prevention. Food. Clothing. Air. Exercise. Sleep. Play. Work. Special treatment at various ages. Schooling. When. How. Moral training. Love the great governmental instrumentality.

Flogging barbarous. Scolding bad. Affection vs. Force. Christ vs. Solomon. Conscience vs. Fear. Inducing them to will right vs. conquering their wills. Sweet vs. cross mothers. Home influences. Example vs. precept. How they learn to deceive. Fulfilling promises. Mothers moulding their characters from every-day incidents. Cultivating and restraining their faculties. Different training for different dispositions. All children can become good. Maternal vs. hireling education. Instructing them by stories and experiments, &c., &c.

INTELLECT, MEMORY, THEIR CULTURE, SELF-EDUCATION, &c.

How much is a powerful intellect and a retentive memory worth over a poor one ? How much "rent" could a lawyer or literati well afford to be enabled to recall all he ever knew, always speak eloquently, and reason profoundly ? How many dollars do most business men lose per annum through forgetfulness, the failure of imperfectly laid plans, &c. ? What means of re-improving yourselves or the race at all compares with cultivating intellect ? Then learn in this Lecture how to attain ends thus glorious,— become learned, and redouble your every intellectual capacity every year. "Minstrels," "Concerts," &c., only amuse for the time, whereas these Lectures instruct and improve FOR LIFE.

☞As Prof. F. is settled in Boston (514 Tremont St.) and travels little, and as his brother L. N. remains in England, this is your Last Chance to get a FOWLER'S Phrenological Examinations, Charts and Advice, as to Health, Self-Culture, best Business, Managing Children, Choosing a Wife or Husband, &c., &c.

Those, therefore, who would know all about themselves or children, ABSOLUTELY MUST call at his suit of rooms, between 8 A. M. and 10 P. M., at the

CITY HOTEL,

Before TUESDAY, P. M., June 23.

Handbill for a Fowler lecture in the 1870's

cold weather, to rise at eight, and write from seven P.M., to two A.M."[20]

Both in summer and in winter throughout the 1860's, while the Civil War was uppermost in the thoughts of most of his countrymen, Orson was dominated by a single purpose, driven to the point of eccentricity by one consuming desire. His long-standing credo, "Study and follow Nature," he applied to only one aspect of nature. In 1870 he wrote, "God in Nature has interested the author for fifty years." The "God in Nature" to whom he paid obeisance was sex, and the remainder of his long life would be devoted to the sexual guidance of all who bared their heads to the *"genuine"* Boston Fowler.[21]

His practice, he boasted, increased yearly, the children and grandchildren of those who had patronized him years before consulting him now "by thousands," awaiting their turn as they sat in the Tremont Street office. The advice he gave them was concerned largely with what Orson called "Right Sexuality." "I never examine any person, not even a child, professionally, without describing the one to whom they are adapted in marriage, and telling them whom they must not marry." Sexual guidance was implicit in his marriage counseling. Both in his phrenological analyses and in his writings Orson devoted himself to "this art of arts" which, he prophesied, would "some day . . . be studied." In the 1860's and early 1870's on Boston's Tremont Street, when Sigmund Freud was a boy barely in his teens, this "art of arts" was studied. Without many apologies to his ideological descendant, the Boston Fowler can be described today as the Freudian Fowler, for he used only one lever to move his world—the lever of sex.

In everything about him, Orson saw a sexual—a loving or creating—agent. The voice, the walk, the handwriting, the blood itself indicated and were affected by "sexual states." Even "the rap at the door," he said, "is sexed." Orson regarded himself as an authority on the subject of estimating "sexual states." "The pleasure . . . is really inexpressible of being able to read with absolute cer-

191

tainty at a glance the existing amount of gender, and all its states, in all we meet. . . . The author claims to be 'expert' here." The author claimed to be expert too in the advice he offered after he had ascertained the amount of sexuality with which an individual was charged. Celibacy he regarded as outraging nature. Sexuality was the cornerstone of the world. Hence he proclaimed, "Let no sun set without a full, hearty, soul-inspiring love-feast. Not a few days of courtship or honeymoon Love, but its completest life-long exercise alone should suffice." Orson did not shrink from describing the details of that exercise:

> This Love making, this incessant delicious agitation of this nervous pith in each, by the sexual electricity of the other, explains that *modus operandi* by means of which the action of all the physical and mental functions are thus wrought up, excited, exhilarated, intoxicated, disciplined, mobilized, thrilled in both.[22]

Not lust, not free love, he insisted, but simply "enjoyment"—enjoyment by both participants—was nature's test of her laws. "Intercourse," he noted, "summons all the organs and parts of the system to its love-feast, *compels* their attendance, and then lashes up their action to the very highest possible pitch. . . . The non-participant female . . . is a natural abomination."

Women especially needed and appreciated the knowledge the expert in sex could supply. He regretted the years when in his lectures to women he had been too modest and afraid of offending. Actually, he discovered, women "thirst for this particular kind of knowledge." Orson slaked their thirst in his books and in his analyses. As he explained:

> My profession furnishes rare opportunities for ascertaining the state of the affections of the married; the vast majority of whom are seriously dissatisfied. Tens of thousands consult about conjugal differences. . . .
> Deep, dark, heart secrets of untold thousands, lie below and behind all, impenetrably closed against all confessions. . . . A wife came twelve miles in a terrible snow-storm solely to express her

overflowing gratitude for having been reconciled to her husband thus: Three years before, at a professional consultation, she told a most pitiable story of their incessant wranglings. I saw and showed her that she was in that soured, hating, awful, ugly *mood* created by Love reversed, which could not live in peace with an angel unless it was converted, but could then; because she was well sexed, and both retained its animal aspect—powerful lever of reform— meanwhile telling her how to proceed. She left pledged to try; found him equally willing to help; and succeeded in rendering both so superlatively happy that she had to face this storm to thank me.[23]

In his tome of 1,052 pages entitled *Creative and Sexual Science,* Orson Fowler distilled his views on sex and sexuality, producing a work which, he claimed, 100,000 women rated "next to their Bibles." Copyrighted in 1870—when Freud was fourteen years old —it was an extraordinary volume. Its purpose was to provide sexual education and guidance to the ultimate end of increased sexual enjoyment in marriage and improved offspring. Striking a blow against the evil of Anglo-Saxon civilization that fostered "female weakliness . . . due chiefly to fashions and education," Orson frankly championed "full breasts," a "large and well formed pubis," and "*summum bonum* enjoyment" in coition. At the same time he cautioned against such "marital errors" as haste or promiscuity, embarrassment or nonparticipation. Sexual ailments, he believed, were caused by "interrupted love" or "self-pollution." His purpose was to convert sexual sufferings into sexual enjoyments, and that purpose was the purpose of the philanthropist. In fulfilling it, he wrote a book that reads today like a combination of *What Every Wife/Husband Should Know* and Freud on sexuality. Amazingly frank for its day, it was neither salacious nor pornographic. Opposed to free love, it aspired to teach the married "how to love *scientifically.*" Like its author, it was well in advance of its time. It is filled with so many quotable passages that it could well bear reprinting in all its thousand pages.

An expansion of his earlier tracts on *Maternity, Matrimony, Love and Parentage,* and *Hereditary Descent, Creative and Sexual*

Science was enriched by "all the Author's subsequent observations, aided by all those *heart* experiences readers were inspired to communicate." As a result it included such observations as, "The unhappy marriages of these degenerate days are due chiefly to sexual degeneracies . . . and can be cured not by divorce, but by sexual *hygiene*." "Sexual knowledge," Orson proclaimed, "is sexual salvation." That knowledge he supplied, beginning naturally with the phrenology and physiognomy of love:

Phrenology locates Love in the back and lower part of the brain. . . . It lies just above and on each side of the nape of the neck, and is the organ lowest down and farthest back in the head. . . .

Its Natural Language . . . cants the head directly back upon the nape of the neck. All lovers can tell by this sign whether and how much they are beloved. Note that affectionate or backward reclining or drooping of the heads of all loving brides during their honeymoon. . . . This language is still more apparent in its ultimate exercise.

Its facial Pole is in the lips, near their middle portions. . . . love always kisses . . . only with the middle of the lips; while Friendship and Platonic Love kiss about half way between the corners of the mouth and middle of the lips, and Parental Love with one corner of the mouth.[24]

Orson's investigations in sexual conduct led him to some rather astounding observations: "Men undersized, but highly electric, are far better than those large, yet stag-like." "Homely men take best with women, because prominent, outlandish features signify a powerful organism." "Well-sexed women set their breasts forward . . . by carrying their shoulders clear back as far as possible. Beaux 'pop questions' to girls who carry themselves thus, much sooner than to those who lotch forward."

The Boston Fowler did not confine his sexual study to the outward man. He concerned himself with such details as the "male breast-loving instinct" and the odors emitted by "all sexual states." He was not reticent about the act of love, which he described with some candor. He offered such homely advice as: "Love must be fed, or starve to death. Then why not nurture it at a stated *hour* each day?" Among the directions he gave for "attaining sexual vigor" was one he had himself been quick to follow: "Form a second Love just as soon as your first is dead." The "womb was made for Love, just as the stomach . . . for appetite, and for nothing else." Orson did not hold with mechanical contraceptive devices. Pessaries, he cautioned, "necessarily injure." In spite of endorsing some old wives' remedies, among them "squaw-vine tea for miscarriages," the author was far ahead of his day. He believed that all schools should be coeducational and that sex should be taught in all schools. His own purpose was "to teach all," and his book was an extension of himself. As he himself described it: "This Book Nails Its Flag Fast. It may be killed, but it don't surrender. It proffers sexual knowledge to old and young, married and single, maidens included, and defies all its opponents to their teeth."[25]

To broaden his influence in the field, Orson Fowler hoped to establish a "judiciously conducted matrimonial intelligence office [which] would fill precisely the same want in the affectional world, which stores, advertisements, markets, bazaars, &c., do in the commercial." Barring this, he suggested a "conjugal post-office" through which wives and husbands might register their needs and complaints. Neither suggestion seems to have material-ized, although there is little doubt that Orson's practice in Boston was concerned primarily with the sex education of his clients.

Orson did not devote himself exclusively to sexual guidance. Books on other subjects too were adapted from his earlier manuals, among them *Human Science or Phrenology*, based upon his phrenological examination "of a *quarter of a million*, of all ages and of both sexes"—a work which he extravagantly described as "the first attempt ever made to embody *all* branches of Anthro-pology into one collective *whole*."[26] A tome on *Religious Science* continued his series on life. If it was true that "hot foreheads will almost always be found" in those "who overwork their intellec-tual Faculties," Orson's forehead must have been hot indeed. His forehead, along with his other features, was offered to readers of *Human Science*, who found on page 1,199 a "Picture of Prof. O. S. Fowler" with a complacent self-analysis:

> A Likeness of its Author may please some readers, and enable all to see how far his "developments" correspond with his productions. It at least shows that desire to do good is its largest organ, and . . . it certainly evinces that high, long, and narrow form of head which indicates a predominance of the moral, intellectual, and good over the animal and selfish; while its Temperament is precisely such a one as the work itself gives as a model of the thought-writing organism. Let its moral, its affectional, its intellectual lobes speak for themselves, and the likeness as a whole say what must needs be the character and the talents of one having this phrenological organism.

Neither the Boston fire nor the panic of 1873 interfered with the activity of Orson's "intellectual lobes." His consumption of paper vied with and surpassed his phrenological practice. He projected his own periodical *Fowler's Journal of Life, Health, Man, and Phrenology*, and took time off in 1874 for a lecture tour in Arkansas. The professor may have journeyed farther west to Dodge City, Kansas, where a delegation led by Bat Masterson invited a phrenologist whose "fame had preceded him" to analyze the heads of suspected cattle rustlers and horse thieves. The anonymous lecturer of Dodge was greeted by a full house, in which "the hip of every man supported a sharp-shooter." Although the meeting, presided over by Bat, ended ignominiously with the shooting out of lights and the professor taking a rear exit, it is tempting to identify Orson with this venturesome phrenologist on the frontier.[27]

At this time he was materially aided by his son-in-law Eugene W. Austin, whom his daughter Charlotte had married in the early 1860's.[28] The two men traveled together, and Austin worked as agent for his father-in-law's books, which were "sold only by subscription." Although Orson threatened to "retire from practice to write," he managed to combine both departments of his profession. The older he became the more imposing were his plans:

If I can yet do the *travelling* requisite, I think to inspect the *phrenologies* of all the nations and peoples of earth's teeming millions, and put their phrenologies and customs side by side . . . orientals and occidentals, Islanders and continentals, Tartars, Parsees, Japanese, Chinese . . . Kamtschatkans, Kalmucks, Hottentots and Siamese, Cape Horners and Bushmen.[29]

Orson's ambitious program in comparative anthropology was not to be realized. Yet he traveled widely in Boston. He was as much a pioneer in sex education as he had been in domestic architecture, and the amateur builder who foreshadowed Frank Lloyd Wright was also the amateur psychiatrist who foreshadowed Sigmund Freud.

If Orson was a healer without benefit of diploma, other members of his family made up for that deficiency. His half sister Almira Fowler, who in 1871 became Almira Ormsbee, practiced as a homeopathic physician in Orange, New Jersey.[30] In New York, Orson's half brother, the erstwhile medium Edward, served as visiting physician at Ward's Island and Hahnemann Hospital and later became an editor of *The Homœopathic Times*.[31]

The Fowlers were still bent upon perfecting the world. While Almira and Edward fought disease with their homeopathic pellets, while Lorenzo examined heads in London, and Orson dispensed sexual advice in Boston, their other half brother Samuel was testing his socialistic theories at Ancora in New Jersey's Camden County. There, under his aegis, a small group of reformers established the "Ancora Productive Union of the Industrial Public." The union unfortunately proved neither productive nor industrial nor public, and, after a few years of farming and exchanging manual labor for the use of a horse or plow, its members, bankrupted by the panic of 1873, abandoned the community.[32]

If the panic brought about the end of Samuel's Ancora Union, the Civil War had resulted in the founding of an institution in which several Fowlers took an active interest—the New York Medical College for Women. In 1863, when the war was causing an excess in the country's female population, the need for women

physicians was both "wide-spread" and "imperative." To meet
that need, the college was founded. Its staff included Almira
Fowler, M.D., censor; Edward Fowler, M.D., member of the
faculty; and Charlotte Fowler Wells, incorporator and corresponding secretary.[33]

Charlotte Wells had found time to advance the cause of women
while she sustained much of the work of the New York Phrenological Depot. The Philadelphia branch, which had been taken
over years before by John L. Capen, was still run by him as the
Phrenological Museum, Book Store & Office.[34] The Boston
agency, with which Orson had no connection and which had been
managed by David P. Butler, had been discontinued when Butler
started his Lifting Cure, a new health exercise.[35] In the New York
premises now the only Fowler on hand was Charlotte; her husband Samuel Wells, after his return from England, became sole
proprietor of the establishment.[36] Tall and graceful, he was still in
his forties "polite and modest in his bearing"; although he stood his
ground, he disarmed by gentleness rather than by force. Like the
Fowlers, he was bent upon "the improvement of the human race,"
but this proclivity in no way interfered with his interest in good
business. Indeed, the more Wells did to improve the human race,
the brisker his business became. Through war and panic, fire and
flood, the Phrenological Depot endured, a Broadway showplace,
a reforming agency, a thriving emporium.

WAR AND PANIC, FIRE
AND FLOOD

· ·

XII

E ARLY in 1861 the firm's printing plant burned; late in 1868 the premises were flooded as the result of a conflagration next door.[1] Between those catastrophes, which the New York Golgotha survived, the office was characterized by change and newness. It was as if, especially after his return from abroad, Samuel Wells were trying to quicken the pace of his business, modernize it, relate it to the war and postwar years. Old staff members were replaced by younger men. William Howland, for many years the firm's wood engraver, joined the Seventh Regiment as captain. Daniel Harrison Jacques became engrossed during the sixties in the development of the South, moving at first to the Pine Hills of Georgia and later to Florida, which he boosted as "a winter resort and as a home." In their place, new employees were recruited— Albert Turner from New York's Cayuga County, who began a long-term connection with the firm as "general assistant and boy of all work"; Samuel Barrows, who, on his way to becoming a renowned penologist and editor, spent enough time as phonographic reporter with Fowler and Wells to describe their office as "not only a place of skulls, but a place of brains and kind hearts." Under Nelson Sizer's tutelage, over fifty young phonographers were trained by the early seventies—testimony to the popularity of that "place of skulls."[2]

In 1864 Golgotha was moved from the east to the west side of Broadway, four blocks farther north, to number 389, and the firm name soon became simply S. R. Wells.[3] Although the premises were "not quite so large as the old store," they were "more pleasantly situated" and easier of access by the city railway at Canal Street. Wells had not escaped the pandemonium of Broadway by the move; visitors still heard the rattle of carts and coaches, the clatter of hoofs, the scream of the newsboy—all the "noisy gimcracks devised by Yankee ingenuity." But once past the showcase filled with skulls that stood in front of the door, visitors were admitted to another world. That world was described in some detail by a lady who spent "An Afternoon at '389.' ":

> The street window is filled with casts and engravings. At the right hand of the door inside are bright-colored ethnological pictures; beyond are rows of shelves filled with the publications of the house; and opposite . . . skulls of Greenlanders, Indians, Kaffirs, Australians, idiots . . . and casts of heads of men and women who were either very good or very bad. . . .
>
> Perhaps while you sit on the sofa looking about you at these records . . . you hear some one reading rapidly. Looking up, you find that it is from a page of Nature's imprint, and that . . . the reader does it by the sense of touch. Standing beside a young girl, with his hands upon her head, forthwith that head under his deft manipulation turns tell-tale . . . betraying her idiosyncrasies. Its revelations are recorded by some one at the desk, to be elaborated into a description of her characteristics. . . .
>
> Before you leave the first floor, you may take an awe-stricken survey of the "Examining Room," and peep into the Editor's den . . . with its books and busts and pictures. . . .
>
> Away up stairs there is a place where wood-cuts and electro-types are stored, and a room for packing the books sold. On a lower floor is . . . the room where the thousand exchanges . . . are looked over, culled, and scissored.
>
> As you go down to the room you first entered . . . Don't overlook . . . the "Subscription Desk."[4]

As the firm later announced: "We have an Exhibition Hall of our own, at 389 Broadway . . . open the *year round*, and always *free to visitors*. It is a good place to rest an hour or two, and study heads, every head being a history and a text-book." They needed an exhibition hall to display their specimens, for the Phrenological

Cabinet was constantly being enlarged. Wells habitually solicited friends of phrenology to "remember the . . . Cabinet . . . and permit us to place your name on record as the donor of valuable . . . specimens." From the battlefields of Mexico he received skulls with gunshot wounds or saber marks; skulls of Eskimos and casts of reptiles, pottery fragments and flint weapons—all found their way to the Cabinet. "During the past twenty-five years," the *Phrenological Journal* revealed in 1864, "we have paid for busts, casts, and skulls . . . not less than $30,000."[5]

The stepped-up activity under Wells' aegis was marked by daily lectures in the "handsome lecture-room" on the second floor, where the collection was housed—lectures on "the training of the mind and the body for health, usefulness, and success," lectures designed to "Put The Right Man in the Right Place."[6]

This also remained the basic purpose of the phrenological examinations conducted at 389. Phrenology was, as Wells put it, "the camera through which we may look at ourselves."[7] It was a highly popular camera, and in the 1860's examinations at number 389 were as much a feature of New York life as ever. Many visitors who came to the city to see Charlotte Cushman or Edwin Booth, to attend a Beecher sermon, a Dickens reading, or a debate in Cooper Union dropped in at 389 either to observe or to be observed. Both private examinations and public examinations for parties and families were available. Private examinations were offered in four varieties: with a mere oral statement, with a chart, with a written statement and chart, with a full and complete written description taken down in shorthand and suitable for publication.[8]

For obvious reasons the last of these was the most satisfactory. As Wells explained:

> In a printed delineation, [that is, a chart] we can only approximate to the real character. No two persons, even though they be twins, are exactly alike. The almost numberless combinations of which the temperaments and mental faculties (to say nothing of the ever-varying physiological conditions involved) are susceptible, result in phases and shades of character as numerous as the individuals

of the human race. To bring these out in a fully satisfactory manner requires a *carefully written* analysis.

All those "shades of character," all sorts and degrees of mankind passed through the door of number 389 and sat to the Wellses, to Nelson Sizer, or to an assistant for their portraits, for the reading of their "soul through the dim rough exterior."[9]

Sizer was almost as perceptive a character analyst as Lorenzo Fowler. Starting with the temperament and physical fitness of his client, he proceeded to the faculties and the advice consequent upon their degree of development. "Some men's minds," he considered, "are like great broad-axes; not very sharp, but they have a tremendous amount of power and breadth; another mind is like the lynx,—pointed & keen; another mind is like a corkscrew more than it is like an augur [*sic*]." Still another mind was "like the circular saw—that is keen—and walks through its work with all its might."[10] With all those minds both Sizer and the Wellses were familiar, and, although many scientists and laymen continued to look down their noses at the entire process, the firm's analyses were widely endorsed. The relative of one satisfied customer wrote, "I mean to have every faculty thouroughly [*sic*] trained, that she may make a perfect woman whatever business she may undertake."[11] Another declared, "I could have gotten a position on the U.P.R.R. through Dr Wells' letter, for $130 per month."[12] Still another wished to have his published analysis mailed to every member of Congress.[13] A student at Harvard Law School sent the following astounding letter to Wells:

> I have some prospects of an opening in the Oil Region of Pa. as the assistant buyer & seller of a well-to-do oil shipping firm. On the supposition that it is to be a paying thing would you advise me to drop the law & take it or to continue on here at the school? Would or *could* I make a first class lawyer doing the very best that is in me, and would I make & could I make a business man of the very first water?

Such was the young man's confidence in the firm's judgment that he "declined an offer such as does not come more than once or twice in a lifetime . . . for you . . . advised me so strongly to stick to the law, I concluded to do so." The same young man confided that he "would like to develop my moral, mental & physical natures harmoniously, and, if the thing is possible, each to a scale of 7 on your list."[14] He was not the only man of law who subscribed wholeheartedly to the firm's phrenological readings. The attorney of the eccentric George Francis Train later expressed a desire to put Samuel Wells on the stand and use his phrenological evidence in a court trial.[15]

Other professions too submitted with confidence to the analyses of 389 Broadway. The young medical student John Ward[16] sat for five phrenological readings between 1868 and 1871; the future psychologist G. Stanley Hall paid five dollars for a session.[17] Editors and journalists, endowed with large Curiosity, were amenable models for phrenological portraits, among them Horace Greeley and Kate Field.[18] Shortly before her death Lola Montez appeared at the Cabinet "disguised by an unfashionable and we might say an untidy dress, with a view . . . of impressing us with the idea that she was uncultivated, and . . . filling some menial station."[19] Bowery boys and Broadway swells gravitated to the Depot. Rev. Jacob S. Harden, "The Youthful Wife-Poisoner," was analyzed.[20] Stammerers received sound advice, and stock speculators learned that their baldness had been caused by the rubbing of their overactive organs of Acquisitiveness. Grave young men were advised to expand their lungs, perfect their digestion, and—as always—take a wife. One not so grave young gentleman informed Wells he had had his "hair cut because my Veneration and Benevolence were getting bald—especially the Benevolence—the Veneration, with its concavity looking Heavenward, was not so noticeable."[21]

Many of the phrenological analyses made at 389 Broadway appeared in due course in the columns of the *Phrenological Journal*. The most popular of these during the early 1860's were the phrenological characters and biographies of Civil War notables. Based upon daguerreotypes or photographs, they were by and large scissors-and-paste thumbnail sketches, but occasionally they provided penetrating analyses of their subjects. George Gordon Meade and Ulysses S. Grant, Benjamin F. Butler and George B. McClellan, Abraham Lincoln and his assassin—all eventually looked forth from the pages of the *Journal,* so that readers could almost chart the progress of the war and the history of their country from the personages selected for analysis.[22] Indeed, phrenology was proving—at least to the firm's satisfaction—that it had its wartime as well as its peacetime uses.

As early as 1850, after the capture and return of a fugitive slave, Nelson Sizer had written to John Brown, Jr.: "I am glad Hamlet was siezed [*sic*] here & carried away in chains and that our people had to raise $800 dollars to get him back, but didn't we have a time of it in the Park when he returned! I say I am glad because it brought the damning disgrace to an optical & auracular demonstration. . . . I am ripe for the rupture & the whole East, West & North are on fire."[23] Although Lorenzo removed himself from the field—his antislavery leanings tinged perhaps with pacifism—the rest of his family was still, in thought at least, "ripe for the rupture" a decade later, after the firing on Sumter. Orson placed his opinions squarely on the line, regarding states' rights as "but another phase of isolated action" resolving society "back to its primal state." "God," he stated—and, he might have added, phrenology—"wrote co-operative, not isolated action, into the human constitution." In phrenological terms, he described Hope as very large in the South before the war but after it "pitiably small."[24]

During the Civil War the firm made some feeble attempts to apply their science to the understanding of white and black. Today their ethnological statements would be scorned as racist, for their view of the phrenology and physiology of the Negro was not high. "We find," they blandly announced in August, 1863, "in the uncultured classes of the white the protrusive mouth (jaws and teeth) and the retreating forehead, such as commonly appear in the negro."[25] Nonetheless, the firm believed in union and freedom, and, though its chief members fought the war from their desks, they lent the facilities of their office for the cause. The firm's wood engraver William Howland used the Phrenological Depot as a headquarters for raising four companies of volunteers; the 127th Regiment was mustered in, leaving for Virginia in October, 1862.[26] To Major General Banks in New Orleans, who applied for "a competent phonographer," the Phrenological Cabinet dispatched James Andem, who had been trained there. In return, Andem sent back a detailed letter about life at the front and about the application of shorthand to the war:

> Yesterday morning the General dictated several letters to me, and on my presenting them to him a short time afterward, he said that the plan of dictating letters and having them written in that manner, pleased him more than anything he had ever before seen, and thought it would save him an immense amount of time and labor. ... We have about 25,000 men, including cavalry, and several large batteries of artillery. We have captured immense quantities of sugar, & some cotton, ... The negroes are in a sad state. Their masters have left them to take care of themselves, and our troops are somewhat unmerciful to them. I fear their sufferings will be greatly increased by our occupation of the country. Most of them are making their way to New Orleans, and on the road we met men, women and children travelling, not knowing where, but supposing they were going to a land of freedom.[27]

The post boxes of the firm were filled with letters from correspondents in the field, sending news of bribery and vote selling in the South, of military advances and setbacks. Henry Clubb, who had organized the Kansas Vegetarian Settlement, was wounded at Corinth and served under Grant at Vicksburg.[28] For soldiers reported dying of dysentery and typhoid, pneumonia and measles, the publishers supplied *The True Healing Art*, by the hydropathist Russell Trall. Corinth and Shiloh, Antietam and Fredericksburg, Chancellorsville, Chickamauga and Gettysburg—all were transfigured, no longer unfamiliar geographical names but places of death and sometimes places of triumph. At last Appomattox was joined to the names, and the *Phrenological Journal*, edited by Samuel Wells, printed for its subscribers a roseate editorial entitled "Our Country":

> Let us wipe out all dividing lines which separate us. . . . With blockades removed, ports thrown open, trade revived, and free intercourse renewed among the people, we shall soon come to a better understanding and a more perfect agreement. There will be in sentiment no North, no South, but we shall be one in rights and privileges, in education, politics, and religion.
>
> The condition of the freed-men will rapidly improve, and this will re-act on the white man, stimulating him to "hold his own" in the grand march of material, intellectual, and moral improvement. We leave the question of differences in race for other times and places. . . . If the white be superior to the black, there can be no danger of their changing situations. But if the black be equal to the white, he will make it manifest, and that is the whole matter in a nut-shell. . . . Each may help the other for the good of each.[29]

To speed the renewal of "free intercourse . . . among the people" and especially to revive trade, Wells injected a get-ahead spirit, an *élan*, a newness into his business at the end of the war. New enticements were offered for agents, new advertisements appeared in the annuals and journals, and grander premiums were presented to subscribers, from Steinway pianos and Mason organs to Wheeler and Wilson's sewing machines and washing machines. Even the terrestrial globe listed among the premiums was "new." And since there were "no sexes in heaven," new lady canvassers were employed to make up clubs for trial subscriptions.[30]

What was not new in the firm's activity was intensified. Pictorial posters and oil paintings, symbolical heads and human skeletons, calipers, tape measures, and a new instrument for measuring heads were sold wholesale to lecturers, physicians, and examiners. To the phrenological bust were added busts of Psyche and Sabina, Apollo and Homer, Shakespeare and Franklin. The old merchandising agency was renamed the American Advertising and Purchasing Agency, and its range was enlarged until it was "prepared to receive orders for anything and everything to be had in New York." The largest orders filled by the firm came from pioneers in the West, although trade with Europe was also "becoming extensive."[31]

Especially as a publisher, Samuel Wells tried to reach "the masses of the people" and to train them to "think for themselves." Occasionally he accepted for publication a book with limited audience appeal or one "in advance of public sentiment" that had been declined by other, wealthier publishers. But on the whole, when offered a manuscript he asked two questions only: "Will it be useful?" and "Can I afford it?"[32] To continue the cure of a nation of dyspeptics, he kept on his list the hydropathic effusions of Drs. Trall and Gully, along with books on the Swedish Movement Cure, affections of the nerves, and his own pamphlet on *Father Mathew, The Temperance Apostle*. The line of how-to manuals was expanded with: *The Invalid's Library*, which enabled every man to be his own doctor; and *Notes on Beauty, Vigor, and Development; or, How to Acquire Plumpness of Form, Strength of Limb, and Beauty of Complexion . . . with Additions . . . By Handsome Charles, the Magnet*. For the medical profession, Wells provided *A Special List of the Best Private Medical Works* designed for "private, professional and confidential use." For the general dyspeptic, pill-swallowing public, he provided a *New Illustrated Health Almanac*, announcing:

> The land is flooded with falsities, shams, swindles, humbugs, in the name of health. Every extensive nostrum monger sends out his advertising almanacs every year by the ton. . . . He steals the livery of heaven to sell the devil of avarice in. We have nothing to advertise but ideas; nothing to sell but knowledge. . . . We destroy our own business as fast as we make it; for as soon as our customers become intelligent, they are independent of us.

Over 50,000 copies of the *Almanac* were distributed among the firm's subscribers and circulated by their agents to counteract the trade in "powders, pills, plasters, bitters, and other poisonous preparations or slops . . . vile compounds."

Having provided sustenance for the body, the publisher proceeded to food for the mind. More boldly than his predecessors in the firm, Wells struck out in the literary field, applying phrenology to the great writings of the past. In his edition of Pope's *Essay on Man* in 1867, he added original designs and notes that interpreted the poem phrenologically. The same procedure was carried out in other editions of such "gems of literature" as Aesop's *Fables*, Goldsmith's *The Traveller* and *The Deserted Village*, Coleridge's *Rime of the Ancient Mariner*, and Milton's *Comus*. These cheap illustrated editions, known as the People's Editions, had a wide sale, supplying the masses with "reading matter of a high class," phrenologically interpreted, at low cost. To insure endorsement, Wells continued the practice of sending gift copies to readers in high places who might express suitable and sometimes printable acknowledgment. Between his books on health reform and his books on literature, it was probably only a mild exaggeration to boast, as the *Phrenological Journal* did, that "every hamlet and many a cabin receives light for the mind and guidance for the body" from the publications of his house.

As a publisher, Wells kept abreast of the times with a pamphlet on capital punishment, a memoir of a poet-soldier "who fell in the service of his country," and a soldier's edition of his *Annual* of phrenology. With his appeal to women, he was, like the Fowlers, in advance of his times. His own book on *Wedlock; or, The Right Relations of the Sexes* applied science to "conjugal selection." Emma May Buckingham dedicated her *Self-Made Woman; or, Mary Idyl's Trials and Triumphs* to her publisher Samuel R. Wells; the well-known editor Jennie June Croly informed him that it was "one of the dearest wishes of her heart" to write a book on the "physical life of woman" with Wells as publisher.[33]

Even more markedly than his book publications, the Wells periodicals reflected the newness of the war and postwar years.[34]

SHOULD WE MARRY?

Are We

Well

Mated?

The most important question in connection with marriage should be in regard to mutual adaptation, physically, mentally and morally. Phrenology explains this, and therefore should be consulted. There are many works on the subject that can be read profitably by all, but the best work relating to this specially is

WEDLOCK; OR, THE RIGHT RELATION OF THE SEXES.

A Scientific Treatise Disclosing the Laws of Conjugal Selection and Prenatal Influences, also Showing Who Ought and Who Ought Not to Marry. By Samuel R. Wells, author of "New Physiognomy," "How to Read Character," etc. Price, $1.50; in fancy gilt, $2.

To show something of the character of this work, we copy the following from the table of **CONTENTS :**

Qualifications for Matrimony; The Right Age to Marry; Motives for Marrying; Marriages of Consanguinity—of Cousins—when Justifiable; Affinities ; Courtship – Long or Short; Duty of Parents; Ethics of Marriage; Second Marriages—are they Admissible; Jealousy—Its Causes and Cure; Grounds for Separation and Divorce; Celibacy--Ancient and Modern; Polgamy and Pantagamy; Love Signs in the Features, and How to Read Them by Physiognomy; Sensible Love Letters--Illustrious Examples; The Model Husband and the Model Wife—their Mutual Obligations, Privileges and Duties; What Constitutes a True Marriage; The Poetry of Love, Courtship and Marriage; Development and Renewal of the Social Affections; Inordinate Affection; Function of Adhesiveness and Amativeness; Admiration not Love; Addresses Declined, How to Do It; Matrimonial Bargains; True Beauty; Celibacy and Health; Law of Conjugal Selection; Conjugal Harmony; Conjugal Resemblances of Husbands and Wives; Pleasure of Courtship; Confidence in Love; Woman's Constancy; Laws and Remedy for Divorce; Etiquette of Long Engagements; Falling in Love; Whom Great Men Marry; Girls of the Period; Housekeeping; Good Habits Essential; How to Win Love; Honeymoon; Mutual Help; Conjugal Harmony; Hotel and Club Life; Inhabitiveness; Terrible Effects of Morbid Jealousy; Juliet's Confession; Kisses; Parental Love; How to Win it, Declamations of Love; Romantic Love; Second Love; Is Love Unchangeable? Should Parents Interfere? Love-Letters; Love Song; Early Marriage among the Ancients; Motives for it; Marriage Customs; Marriage Defined; Its Legal Aspects; Marriage Ceremonies; Health and Marriage; Hasty Marriages; Marriage Maxims; Morganatic Marriages; Marrying for a Home, for Money, for Love, for Beauty; Right Motive for Marrying; Advice to the Married; Matrimonial Fidelity; Matrimonial Politeness; Legal Rights of Married Women; The Mormon System; Man's Requirements; The Maiden's Choice; Letters of Napoleon; When to Pop the Question; Meddling Relatives; Step-Mothers; The Shakers; Singleness; Temptations of the Unmarried; Hereditary Taints; Temperaments; May Women Make Love ; Lesson for Wives; Wedding Gifts; Plain Talk with a Young Man ; Soliloquy of a Young Lady, and much more, covering the whole ground of Marriage.

The Work being a Practical Guide to all the Relations of a Happy Wedlock, and it should be read by all, and especially those contemplating Marriage. Is handsomely printed and beautifully bound. Copies will be sent, postpaid on receipt of price, $1.50; full Gilt edges, $2.00.

Address, **FOWLER & WELLS CO., Publishers,**

775 Broadway, New York.

Should they marry?

FROM NELSON SIZER, *Heads and Faces*
(New York, 1888)

In place of the *Water-Cure Journal*, whose publication was taken over in 1863 by its editor Dr. Trall, the firm eventually offered a new monthly, *The Science of Health*, in which "Nature's Remedial Agencies" were extolled. Between 1872 and 1876 that periodical aimed at restoring and preserving the national health by monthly discussions of Turkish baths and the lifting cure, dress reform and hygienic medication. During the panic of 1873, when a "deranged currency" was the target of general attack, Samuel Wells directed his most pointed barbs against "Doctors, Drugs, and Death," "Compound Extract of Humbug" and "Rum [that] rules the roost."

Like many magazines discontinued by the firm, *The Science of Health* was not terminated but merged with the seemingly indestructible *Phrenological Journal*. This had been the fate of *Life Illustrated* as well as of *Packard's Monthly*. As a result, the *Phrenological Journal* underwent not only a series of changes in subtitle but metamorphoses in size and appearance. Through the years it adopted several new covers, one of the most eye-catching being a symbolical phrenological head surrounded by the heads of bishop and bully, philosopher and fool, Florence Nightingale and Miss Fury, the Princess of Wales and Sally Muggins.

The *Phrenological Journal* would enjoy a life span of more than seventy years. In a century that saw the rise and fall of so many family papers and of so many publishing empires, it is certainly a matter for reflection and investigation that a specialized journal devoted to a borderline science should have survived so long, weathering war and the scarcity of paper, panic and the scarcity of funds. The editor, Wells held, "should understand human nature physiologically, phrenologically, and theologically . . . he should study . . . the inner life of humanity." Avoiding partisanship, the *Journal* stood on the party platform of humanity, especially American humanity. Although its mission was "to reach, impress, and improve all mankind," it distrusted old-fogyism, "polished with pharisaical piety—long-faced and long-prayered," that was nothing but a "stumbling-block to true reform." In gathering information for its articles, the editors took pains to unearth the truth, writing to authorities for answers to questions about the brains of idiots or sages and returning contributions to writers for the correction of "errors of doctrine & of fact." The *Journal* had a surprisingly respectable reputation among the *cognoscenti* of the day. At one time the actress-writer Anna Cora Mowatt offered to be its London correspondent, and the historian-educator Moses Coit Tyler humbly requested a "favorable notice" for a new lecture.

Perhaps the principal reason for the monthly's survival was the fact that despite its advocacy of a specialized cause it did indeed reflect the times. In 1867 it announced that "The Spirit of the Age is *'electricity* and *steam.'* " From the electricity and steam that were the newness of the sixties to the newnesses of other decades, it viewed events and ideas through a phrenological spectrum. In its pages the history of the country was mirrored, not as history but as fascinating vagaries of the human mind.

As a result, in studying the 1860's and the 1870's, a scholar might do well to turn the pages of the *Phrenological Journal*, where the life of the times lives on. A civil service system based upon merit makes its tentative appearance in these columns. The women of the country petition for universal suffrage. The labor problem is destined for solution in "a millennial reign of peace and prosperity," for the editor's faith "is ingrained in the very structure of the human mind." The servant question is debated, along with the possible control of man's dreams and the "Psychology of the Sexes." Dio Lewis and his New Gymnastics find a place here, as does Charles Darwin. John Neal of Portland writes a "Phantasmagoria" for the monthly, and the woman preacher Phoebe Hanaford offers a picture of "Lady Ministers." The degeneration of some water cures into cheap boarding houses is viewed with dismay, while Dr. Charles H. Sheppard's Turkish bath and Dr. E. P. Miller's Home of Health receive editorial endorsement along with graham flour and Hecker's grits. The peculiarities of Jews and Italians are studied ethnologically, and the career of the early

Hebrew-American publisher Henry Frank of New York is outlined. The importance of phrenology to artists is pointed out, and rapid reading by the line and paragraph method is adumbrated. Emerson is quoted in support of universal amateur phrenology: "The gross lines are legible to the dull; the cabman is a phrenologist so far—he looks in your face to see if his shilling is sure." Still, the *Phrenological Journal* was more than a journal devoted to phrenology. Through a glass phrenologically, it viewed the country. Now that a century has passed, there is perhaps more of the country than of phrenology in its pages.

One kindred subject elaborated in its columns from time to time was physiognomy, a subject that especially interested Samuel Wells. In his own *New Physiognomy*, the publisher announced that physiognomy, physiology, and phrenology were "three . . . parts of one great whole—anthropology—the science of man." On the basis of so-called scientific principles, he offered new classifications and combinations of old temperaments, proving conclusively that "the mouth tells tales" though the tongue be silent and that the ears of leading reformers are large.[35]

Somehow, between publishing books and editing a periodical, running a merchandising agency and enlarging his Cabinet, Wells found time for a tome on physiognomy. Nelson Sizer, when he was not giving examinations, was compiling his *What To Do and Why*, a study of the phrenological endowments necessary for different occupations, trades, and professions. Despite the constant bustle of activity at 389 Broadway, the firm members were able to add still another department to their many-faceted enterprise. By 1866 they felt that although they had succeeded in popularizing phrenology and demonstrating its relation to life, they had not found the means to perpetuate themselves as popularizers. More phrenologists would be needed for the future. To insure the supply of competent analysts to the third and fourth generations, the Phrenological Depot therefore decided to establish a formal teaching branch. The Broadway Cabinet was about to become the home of the American Institute of Phrenology.

In April, 1866, the institute was incorporated under a charter from the New York State legislature. It started off with the blessings of the press, the bar, and the state, for among its incorporators were Horace Greeley, the eminent lawyer Amos Dean, and the future New York mayor A. Oakey Hall, an illustrious trio joined by the firm members—Wells, Sizer, and Lester A. Roberts—as well as by Wells' physician brother-in-law Edward Fowler. An outgrowth of the phrenological societies scattered across the country, the institute announced as its purposes the "promoting [of] Phrenological Science, and instruction" and the "collecting and preserving Crania, Casts, Busts . . . of the different Races, Tribes, and Families of men."[36] Six-week courses in theoretical and practical phrenology were offered, and a certificate or diploma was granted to graduates. Eventually the course of instruction, provided by a faculty of eight—still a Fowler magic number—consisted of over a hundred lectures given each morning, midday, and afternoon of the term. On paper at least, the topics covered were grandiose, ranging from anatomy, physiology, and brain dissection to elocution and "The Natural Language of the Faculties," from ethnology to heredity, from psychology, mesmerism, and clairvoyance to insanity and idiocy, from the choice of occupations to matrimony—the last covering such problems as "Who may and may not intermarry" and the "proper developments of body and brain for a true and happy union." At its height the institute was a combined premedical and charm school from which students, having majored in applied psychology, matrimonial guidance, or public relations, could emerge as accredited phrenologists.

The class of 1866 numbered eight students, each of them receiving a certificate. The next year it was claimed that one member of the class of 1867 had "learned enough before the class was half finished to save his firm from trusting a villain to the extent of three hundred dollars."

There is no doubt that the institute filled what the firm regarded as an urgent need. In 1864 the *Journal* had advertised:

"Wanted, Immediately, one hundred honest, enterprising, intelligent, and capable Practical Phrenologists, to engage in public lecturing, in teaching."[37] According to Samuel Wells, "Letters are received almost daily at this office requesting information as when we can visit this or that city, or send a suitable person to give public lectures, private lessons, and phrenological delineations of character. We have 'calls' from the chief cities in all the States, the Canadas, . . . and from many towns in the Old World."[38] The teaching arm of Wells' establishment answered these "calls."

Phrenology had, by the mid-1860's, filtered deeply into the common life of the country. Its vocabulary was used by writers and speakers; its analytic methods were occasionally applied in the courtroom. As the *Annual of Phrenology* for 1868 summed up:

> One of the most certain indications of the advancing influence of Phrenology is the adoption by writers and speakers of the phrenological terms and nomenclature relative to character. This is observed in the court-house in the trial of causes—in the selection of juries—in the estimate placed upon witnesses, or of persons accused of crime; we observe it in the pulpit. . . . In the lecture-room, the lyceum, and the debating club, character is analyzed and referred to in a manner indicating that Phrenology is made, consciously or unconsciously, the basis of the analysis. . . . it is respectfully and kindly regarded by clergymen, statesmen, and even by many physicians, and by the great majority of literary men.[39]

Often without knowing precisely what they were saying, people spoke phrenology in the 1860's as they would speak psychiatry in the 1930's and existentialism in the 1960's. For the very reason that phrenological words and concepts had become so interwoven in current speech and thought, the demand for trained phrenologists had increased. For many years the Phrenological Depot had taught laymen the advantages and the methods of phrenological analysis; now it directed its instruction to the training of professionals. It would never lose its missionary character or cease to regard itself as the center from which new generations of phrenologists could go forth to finger the skulls of the world. "It is our desire," Wells proclaimed, "when we retire from the field, to leave in it a thousand honest, intelligent men imbued with a missionary spirit, and fully qualified to carry on and carry upward this great work."[40]

In order to fulfill this purpose, the institute emphasized not only its first aim of "promoting Phrenological Science" but its second aim of "collecting and preserving Crania, Casts, Busts." As the *Annual of Phrenology* put it with unconscious humor, "the person [who studies phrenology] should possess a good phrenological bust."[41] The making of plaster casts was explained at the institute:

> To Take the Cast of a Head.—Let the subject be laid down on the back, and cloths brought around the head at the ears. . . . Fill the hair and eyebrows and lashes with a paste made of rye flour and cold water, and lay the hair in smooth folds or masses; then oil it, and with a spoon, beginning at the forehead, pour the plaster on, and let it flow down till it strikes the cloths that surround the head.[42]

The results of such trying procedures surrounded the students, for the collection assembled by the Fowlers and by Wells had been donated to the institute as a "nucleus around which may be gathered one of the richest museums in America." Over the years the firm would plead for donations with which to establish "a large fire-proof building with lecture-room, museum or exhibition hall" where the crania and casts, the paintings and busts could be adequately housed. This, with their proposal of a phrenological convention to meet in Philadelphia at the time of the Centennial celebration, would come to nothing. Nonetheless, like the *Phrenological Journal*, the American Phrenological Institute endured for decades, instructing students from Maine and Alabama, Iowa and Indiana, Europe and New Zealand, and sending forth, after appropriate closing exercises, masters of the science of the mind.

A number of Wells' graduates made their way to California, whence, having manipulated the skulls of pioneers, they sent back to the Phrenological Museum mementos of the West. After phrenology, perhaps the publisher's most abiding interest had been the breaking down of the country's frontiers—an interest long reflected in the pages of the *Phrenological Journal*. There he had published articles on the brideships, proposed by Eliza Farnham and others for carrying eastern spinsters to western bachelors, as well as pleas for the development of the West and Southwest by means of extended trunk railways. During the seventies Wells found space in the columns of the *Journal* for accounts of the "Rocky Mountain Scenery around Colorado Springs" and "The Rocky Mountain Printer"—William N. Byers, who had taken his printing press to Pikes Peak and printed the first newspaper there.[43] Under Wells' influence, *The Science of Health* had initiated a "Pacific Department," written by the corresponding editor and woman physician Dr. C. F. Young.

Perhaps the most interesting articles on western life that appeared in the *Phrenological Journal* were those that concerned neither Rocky Mountain scenery nor a Rocky Mountain printer but a Rocky Mountain bookstore. Actually a combination bookstore and art and photography establishment, the Rocky Mountain Bookstore was in Salt Lake City. Its proprietors—Charles R. Savage and George M. Ottinger—established productive relations with the Phrenological Depot. Savage, who became one of the outstanding photographers of the West, and Ottinger, a pioneer artist, had both been converted to Mormonism, crossed the plains to Utah, and formed a partnership. Ever on the alert for paintings to add to his Phrenological Galleries, Wells entered into a business arrangement with the firm of Savage and Ottinger, an arrangement described in the May, 1868, issue of the *Phrenological Journal*, where an engraving of the Utah "book store and photographic art emporium" also appeared:

> Besides supplying the "Saints" and the "Gentiles" with the best literature of the Old World and the New, they produce good pictures—we may safely say some of the best we have ever seen. Portraits of the "saints" and "sinners" . . . Indians, pictures of trees, mountains, water-falls . . . and some of the most sublime scenery in the world.

These gentlemen are artists! They combine business with art, and supply school books, phrenological books, and every variety of *useful* books. . . .

Here is a store . . . three thousand miles west from New York, in the center of a vast Territory teeming with life, enterprise, education, and MORMONISM! A hundred thousand hardy people now have their homes in these mountains. . . . Look now on one of its first book stores.[44]

The Salt Lake City emporium served as an agency for the sale of Wells' publications, while Ottinger supplied the phrenologist-publisher of New York with canyon views and paintings of the West, among them a landscape of "City Creek Falls," which was sold to Vice-President Schuyler Colfax. The phrenology, portrait, and biography of "The Utah Artist" George M. Ottinger enriched the pages of the *Phrenological Journal* in due time, as did a series of colorful articles on the Mormon reform movement and life in Utah.

Wells' interest in the West was widely known. The publisher of Meeker's *Life in the West; or, Stories of the Mississippi Valley* received letters from correspondents who offered him a manuscript that would "turn the tide toward Nebraska" and a novel of the Yosemite Valley, "The Daughters of Ah-wah-nee."[45] The Samuel Wells who in 1869 exclaimed, "Clear the track, for the locomotive is on its way to Salt Lake City," was no armchair traveler. Both before and after the completion of the transcontinental railway, he traveled the rails of the country, covering by 1873 "more than 50,000 miles" of track, yet ever "hungering for more."[46]

Among Wells' most memorable journeys had been the Union Pacific Railway excursion of 1866, when, with a group of congressmen, including future President Rutherford B. Hayes, he had celebrated the opening of the line "to the hundredth parallel of latitude" and collected both mental images and landscape paintings of the West. He had perhaps been more impressed as a traveler than impressive as a phrenologist, for, after studying

Wells' phrenological estimate of his law partner R. P. Buckland, Hayes had written to his uncle:

> I send you a rather curious phrenological estimate of the Congressmen on the Pacific Railroad excursion (Buck[land] and myself included) with portraits. It is curious as showing that Mr. [Samuel R.] Wells, who is a respectable person, and who *professes* to judge people on the principles of what he calls the sciences of phrenology and physiology, really gets his impressions just as you and I do, from their manners, conduct, and conversation. He is evidently not influenced a particle by temperament or head and features. He is singularly and laughably wrong in Buck's case. The only interest in the whole thing is that it shows the impression that a tolerably good observer gets on a short acquaintance with us.[47]

Perhaps Mormons made better phrenological subjects than congressmen, for the "tolerably good observer" was more successful four years later, when on a visit to Salt Lake City he "examined the heads of hundreds" of their "representative men and women." Salt Lake City, regularly laid out in blocks with wide streets and large mansions, appealed to the publisher as he walked past the office of Wells Fargo and the Salt Lake Hotel, paying his respects to his friends Savage and Ottinger. Camping out and climbing in the Rockies, Wells came to the exuberant conclusion that "the West is a 'great country.' "[48]

His conclusion was confirmed in the summer of 1873, when, accompanied by his wife, he climaxed all his railway excursions with a six-week grand tour that covered eight thousand miles and led to the Pacific Coast.[49] This time his party consisted not of congressmen but of editors, among them: the organizer of the trip, Henry T. Williams of the *Independent*; Samuel Bowles, Jr., of the *Springfield Republican*; artists and writers from *Harper's Weekly*, *Rural World*, and *Country Gentleman*. Armed with "pen, pencil, and paper, hammer and chisel," the group of about thirty boarded at New York a special complimentary train that took them southwest. "Taking notes, making sketches, pumping strangers," they rode the steamer down the Ohio River to

218

Cincinnati, enjoyed the luxury of a Pullman Palace Car as they passed through Indian Territory and rolled on through Texas and California. They talked with all they saw—the dramatis personae of the frontier: railwaymen and agents for land grants, governors and bishops, miners and explorers, hunters and soldiers, Indians and cattle herders, missionaries, Chinese and Japanese. When they were not taking notes, they were uprooting specimen plants or gathering minerals and skulls—memorabilia of the great West.

The journey led them everywhere, through Kansas and the Arkansas valley, through buffalo country and the Rockies. Encamped in a valley at the base of the mountains, Wells enlivened the camp meeting with phrenological analyses, earning for himself the title of "*Great Bump Analyzer*" who told "us how good we are, and says he will tell us how bad we are for $5 more to a crowded audience." Professor Wells, the editors quipped, was "First for a speech, next for the heads of his countrymen." How far his fame had preceded him was brought strikingly close when he saw a Fowler symbolical head on the wall of a lonely loghouse in the Rockies. Back through the plains to Cheyenne and Salt Lake City, through the canyons and the Platte valley, Charlotte and Samuel Wells returned with notes for their *Journal*, specimens for their Cabinet, and a renewed exhilaration for their work and their country.

The year of the excursion had been ushered in with another "terrible fire," which had consumed the firm's bindery.[50] It was to be ushered out with the panic of 1873, an economic debacle that Wells viewed as "senseless," an explosion produced by "defaulting cashiers, speculating bank presidents, and excessive importations, together with new, non-paying railways."[51] Despite these calamities, Wells summed up his year's work with exuberance:

> Besides the Phrenological Journal and the *Science of Health* . . . we have published and republished during the present year more than 75 different books . . . relating directly or indirectly to the

Science of Man. . . . We have given more than a hundred lectures
. . . have delineated the characters of several hundred persons. . . .
We have visited convicts in prisons, lectured in insane asylums . . .
before temperance societies, and have instructed a class. . . .

We are now sending our publications to . . . China, Japan, Africa,
New Zealand, Australia. . . . We have 2000 local agencies in
America. . . .

We also supply Phrenological societies and lecturers with cabinets of busts, skulls, manikins, skeletons, portraits—size of life—in
sets, mounted on canvas, and in sheets.[52]

For all of Wells' confidence, the panic of 1873 cast a long
shadow that loomed well into the years that followed. Most busi-
nesses were affected, and by 1875 the building at 389 Broadway
which had housed the Phrenological Depot for more than a decade
was taken over by what Wells called "money changers" who
"secured the property . . . compelling modest dealers to seek quarters elsewhere."[53] One of the last analyses made by Nelson Sizer
at the old stand was a delineation of the character of New York's
Governor Samuel J. Tilden.[54] Following the upward trend along
Broadway, Wells found a new location a mile or more above the
old place at No. 737—"a number," he wrote, "which all who once
look attentively will remember, like the name Hannah, which
spells the same both ways." Two or three blocks below Union
Square and facing Astor Place, the new phrenological headquarters was close to the Mercantile and Astor libraries, Cooper Institute and the Bible House, and "within pistol shot of A. T. Stewart's great bazaar." It was in a neighborhood where the great
publishers clustered—Scribner and Dutton, Wiley, and Dodd and
Mead. "Our office," Wells boasted, "is . . . in the very centre of
mental culture and of business activity."

Unfortunately Samuel Wells never enjoyed the rarefied atmosphere of his new place of business. In March, 1875, the move had
been made—an enormous undertaking, involving the transfer of
the firm's huge collections, the skulls and busts, the paintings and
minerals of the museum, memorabilia of nearly forty years of col-

lecting, from the earliest plaster casts to the latest western souvenirs. To the artifacts had been added the large stock of books, the "materials used in the preparation of the . . . magazines," and all the "property and effects relating to the professional and publishing departments of his business." By the end of the month Wells was hard at work in the new store, supervising its "fitting up" and decoration, superintending carpenters, painters, and upholsterers. Never robust, he had caught a cold which, thanks to exhausting labor and insufficient sleep, developed into pneumonia. On April 2 he took to his bed and, on the morning of April 13, died.

The New York papers, their columns nearly filled with titillating details of the Beecher-Tilton scandal trial, found space for tribute to the phrenologist-publisher. The May issue of the *Phrenological Journal*, prepared well in advance of its dateline, announced the firm's move "Up Broadway." The June issue, its articles bordered in black, announced the death of the fifty-five-year-old "Late Publisher," Samuel R. Wells, who had "literally fallen at his post." It recalled the career of the self-made man who had "disarmed by gentleness" and had ever been "ready to shake hands with new truths."[55]

Though most of the articles in the June issue looked to the past, one looked to the future, describing the arrangements by which his work and "the work of his office" would go on. That article was entitled "To Our Friends," and it was written by Samuel Wells' widow.[56] Having announced Henry S. Drayton's appointment as editor of the *Journal* and chief examiner Sizer's continuance in charge of the Cabinet, Charlotte explained that the firm name of S. R. Wells would now be altered to S. R. Wells and Company, "indicative of the purpose to carry on the work in the spirit of enterprise and humanity which has characterized it." Then she concluded:

In accordance with an understanding which had long existed between Mr. Wells and myself, to the effect that I should continue the business should any event occur to prevent his personal super-

intendence of it, I am warranted in making the above announcement, and would invite a continuance of the favor shown us in the
past by the friends of mental and moral progress.

For nearly forty years Charlotte Wells had been associated with
the work of the Phrenological Depot, but always as assistant or
adviser, never as chief. Now suddenly she had lost the man who
had been both husband and co-worker and gained, as dubious
compensation for that loss, her independence and her responsibility. She saw herself for what she was—not yet old but far from
young, a woman in a world where women's rights were still de-
rided or deplored, alone in a business that had always been dominated by a brother or a husband. The tapestry of her life and of
her work had changed. Now, at the age of sixty, Charlotte Fowler Wells must weave a pattern of her own within the framework
of the future.

TO THE *FIN DE SIÈCLE*

· ·

XIII

Aᴄᴛᴇʀ her husband's death Charlotte Fowler Wells was the dynamo that activated the Fowler domain for the next generation. Small, compact, and strong, logical and alert, she vibrated from room to room, overseeing all departments of her phrenological factory. Living in New Jersey with her half brother Samuel's daughters, she traveled daily to Broadway to superintend a business now almost equally divided between phrenologizing and publishing.[1] One of the first analyses made under Charlotte's regime was of General Custer, who dropped in incognito and was informed that he was "like an express train" that goes "faster, and . . . wants the track kept clear."[2]

In this respect, Charlotte Wells had much in common with the general. She too could take the role of express train, rejoicing in an age of modernity, to which she paid obeisance by introducing the typewriter into her business. She met the hard times of 1878 by investing boldly in the future, endorsing not only Holbrook's Turkish Baths but the newer Health Food Company and any home exercisers that filled the needs of physical culture faddists. In 1880 she moved her business farther uptown to number 753 Broadway at the corner of Eighth Street, "near various lines of horse cars and stations on the elevated roads."[3] At the same time, the firm name was changed to Fowler and Wells with the brief reentry of Orson, along with his son-in-law Eugene Austin, into the company.[4] But it was Charlotte who dominated the action.

She took her hints from the age in which she lived.[5] Even her advertising techniques were modern. She distributed free phrenological calendars. "Take This Home," she headed her leaflets and fliers, one of which promised a free hundred-dollar accident policy for a "Fatal R. R. Accident [payable by the Automatic Box Advertising Card Co.] to the taker of only one of these cards." Below this announcement appeared the statement: "The above Company insures against Railway Accidents as stated, but EVERY MAN [by means of a phrenological examination] may secure for himself all reasonable INSURANCE OF SUCCESS in following the pursuit or avocation for which he is best adapted." With all the modern devices available to her, Charlotte Fowler Wells was pushing a product no longer modern—a product that was indeed fast declining, in the view of many, from pseudo-science to charlatanry.

Still she persisted. From her emporium went forth plates of the human brain "enlarged and mounted on muslin," and charts of the human body were designed for "elementary instruction in physiology and hygiene." Anything that emphasized the scientific aspects of phrenology as well as its applications to the new decades was stressed. Charlotte seemed to value newness as highly as she valued phrenology. The anatomical manikins sold at her office were "new," and premiums for subscribers included such advanced products of the eighties as the Bissell carpet sweeper.

Charlotte Fowler Wells poured the old wine of phrenology into the new bottles of the *fin de siècle*. She offered "Lessons By Mail," and she hoped to attract not only capital but capitalists to the glories of mental science. For the ladies she established a pattern department and an employment bureau for household help. The New York Vegetarian Society, meeting at the Fowler and Wells office, now pondered not the colonization of Kansas but a pure food bill. Charlotte had no difficulty relating herself to her times. Modernizing her product was more difficult.

The analyses of the eighties and nineties included perhaps more medical advice than those of earlier years.[6] Sizer, still chief examiner, did not hesitate to dispense dietary counsel along with suggestions for eliminating "nervous exhaustion and dyspepsia." Occasionally the phrenologists even hazarded opinions in cases of what they termed "psychological disease" to aid the doctor in making diagnoses. An elaborate analysis was available, "intended especially for those who are broken down in health by over-work, over-study, wrong habits of diet, or otherwise." After an extended two-hour analysis, the examiner "explained to the subject his condition, and how he reached it, and how to recover from it, and thus how to avoid it in the future." So the phrenologist ventured not merely into medicine but into preventive medicine.

Under Charlotte's aegis, the scope and purpose of the examination were enlarged wherever possible. Advice was given on the adoption of children who had been subjected to analysis and, in at least one instance, to a clergyman on the question of the removal of his congregation. To increase business, examinations from photographs were widely encouraged by means of a leaflet entitled *The Head and Face: A Mirror of the Mind.* On the basis of photographs, head measurements, and related information, advice on marriage and business was dispatched to "English settlers at the Cape of Good Hope," to residents of New Zealand and Australia, the West Indies and Europe. After studying their photographs, the firm provided avid readers with character estimates of such newsworthy figures as Garfield's assassin Charles Guiteau and the enigmatic lady of Fall River, Massachusetts, Lizzie Borden.

By and large, the examination itself and the technique of giving it had not changed. The descendants of those who had submitted to Orson and Lorenzo Fowler's manipulations listened now to Professor Sizer's rich, anecdotal characterizations. Seated in his inner sanctum, he exuded strength and confidence, with his broad shoulders, his short, thick neck, his large, prominent head. By the mid-nineties he could boast over 300,000 delineations. As the years passed, his fingers probed the skulls of the sculptress Harriet Hosmer, the editors Cyrus Curtis and Edward Bok, the prolific and soulful Ella Wheeler Wilcox, and the eccentric George Francis Train. When the temperance reformer Frances E. Willard visited the Cabinet, Sizer was as much the observed as the observer, for Miss Willard recorded her own graphic characterization of the professor:

> I . . . let him know who I was when we dropped in one day to look at the collection of casts, whereupon he proceeded to give me the benefit of his life-long studies of the "bumps." I told him that mother always had a kind side for phrenology, one of her earliest and most oft-repeated remarks to me having been this: "You have combativeness largely developed, my child." . . . Nelson Sizer is the talker among ten thousand. He seems to be endowed with the balanced, or "tempered temperament." . . . His vocabulary is boundless, its pictorial quality exhaustless, and his anecdotes many and apt. A skilled stenographer with a little stenographic type-writing machine sat near him; and as he walked back and forth, between making his cranial observations, Mr. Sizer had only to speak his mind and the swift click of the machine did all the rest.[7]

The paradox was marked as modern machinery came to the aid of phrenology, and Sizer could be likened to an alchemist using a Bunsen burner.

The firm's publishing department lent itself more readily to modernization than did its phrenological division.[8] Charlotte, reviving the search for Spurzheim's preserved brain at Harvard and preparing a catalogue of the Phrenological Cabinet, found that her husband's mantle rested securely on her shoulders. Like Samuel Wells, she was perceptive of the public interest, and she catered to it with an expanded publishing list aptly entitled "From the Cradle to the Grave." A good portion of her list was given over to health books—manuals on physical, mental, and emotional health. In this field she had inherited a strong backlist of books on hygiene and physiology, sex and marriage, temperance and temperament, and she did not hesitate to reprint or keep in print the works of George Combe and Orson Fowler, Daniel Jacques and Russell Trall.

To support the health cult, she published or republished the works of the physical culture pioneer Dio Lewis and of the health reformer M. L. Holbrook. Mrs. Poole on *Fruits* and Mrs. Dodds on *Health in the Household* looked back to the joys of vegetarianism and forward to the importance of nutrition. For the new generation of gymnast addicts, Charlotte supplied not only the manual of D. L. Dowd, "Prof. of Physical Culture" but his "Home Exerciser," including apparatus with ropes and pulleys. Along with the latest in dumbbell exercises, customers could find on the premises a "Health and Muscle Roller," invented to bring the benefits of massage within the reach of all, with which of course went treatises on massage and massotherapy. For the grandchildren of antilacing women Charlotte provided books on Delsartean physical culture along with Helen Ecob's *The Well-Dressed Woman: A Study in the Practical Application to Dress of the laws of Health, Art, and Morals.* All the splendors of health were epitomized in one book issued by the house, *The Man Wonderful in the House Beautiful* by the Drs. Allen, an allegory in which the house was the symbol of the body, its foundations the bones, its walls the muscles, its kitchen the stomach, and its laundry the lungs.

Although Charlotte Wells was very much of this world, she had not abandoned her interest in the world of spirits, an interest that was reflected in her publications. During the eighties and nineties she issued books that were perhaps the descendants of the old Fowler "Library of Mesmerism," books on mental suggestion and hypnotism, ghostism and "Psychology . . . applied to the Solution of Occult Psychic Phenomena." Swinburne may have superseded Poe as the embodiment of the poetic temperament, but Poe's spirit had not altogether abandoned the Phrenological Depot.

The how-to books of earlier decades also had their counterparts in Charlotte's list. A "Self-Culture Library" was issued monthly in paperback for forty cents, in cloth for seventy-five cents, and the firm's "Practical Hand-Books" covered such subjects as *How to Succeed as a Stenographer* and *How to Keep a Store, How to be Weather-Wise*, and even *How to Live.* The latter-day Fowler and Wells still clung to the motto "Self-Made or Never Made," and still provided short cuts to the proper study of mankind. There was little that subscribers to their publications could not learn, from *How to Educate the Feelings* to *How to Strengthen the Memory*.

Many of the firm's how-to books were aimed at a female audience. As a result of her abiding interest in the struggle for women's rights, as well as of her own economic necessity, Charlotte Fowler Wells was induced to publish a line of mediocre books by scribbling females in what were called "Author's Letter-Press Editions." These included the effusions in verse and prose of ladies with middle names, a strong urge to write, and some connection with psychic societies or Chautauqua circles. To Charlotte's credit, her firm also published a far more substantial work —the American edition of *Three Visits to America* by the English woman publisher and philanthropist Emily Faithfull. The American publishers inserted a preface explaining their methods and their motives:

> In entering into a definite agreement with Miss Faithfull . . . three points of importance were considered: *First*, that Miss Faithfull was well known in England and America as a lady of superior practical judgment, who united good business capabilities to excellent mental culture.
>
> *Second*, that she had been engaged for many years in works combining philanthropy and industry for the improvement of the condition of English women. Over twenty years ago an acquaintance was formed with her by the late Mr. Samuel R. Wells while he was visiting London, and when she was absorbed in the multifarious duties of her publishing business . . . "The Victoria Press." . . .
>
> The *third* point is that the book . . . is the conscientious opinion of a woman of matured intelligence, who . . . has visited America *three* times. . . .
>
> In the outset of their negotiations with Miss Faithfull, which were made before the volume was prepared, the publishers believed that Miss Faithfull had things to say to the American people that would . . . be welcome and helpful to women in the industrial

callings and out of them, and instructive to society at large, and that in making a liberal pecuniary advance to the author for the privilege of publishing the American editions they were warranted by the expectation of meeting a wide demand that should arise from the announcement of the book from their press.[9]

From the early fifties, when Charlotte had collaborated with William Henry Channing, Fowler and Wells had had a reputation for boldness in undertaking books on women's rights. The militant Susan B. Anthony was well aware of that reputation. In 1876, writing to Mrs. Wells for permission to include Charlotte's biography in *Johnson's Universal Cyclopædia*, she added, "I am spending a few weeks . . . with Mrs Stanton—& together we are working to gather up the broken and scattered threads of our woman's rights work to weave into a history."[10] Susan Anthony was referring to what was to become the foundation stone in the history of women's rights, the multivolume *History of Woman Suffrage*, originally edited by Susan B. Anthony, Elizabeth Cady Stanton, and Matilda Joslyn Gage. In January, 1877, Mrs. Anthony journeyed to New York to find a publisher for the projected history. The Fowler and Wells Company, she knew, "had made considerable profit out of publications on a controversial subject and were less timid than most publishers in this respect. The women of the family had been firm supporters of woman suffrage for many years. Furthermore, the firm was known as a reputable and reliable concern." She did not add that "none of the [other] publishing firms of New York would consent . . . to take the book." In short order, arrangements with Fowler and Wells were agreed upon: "The authors were to pay for typesetting, printing, and engravings; the publishers, for the paper, presswork, binding, and advertising. The authors were to receive 12 ½ per cent royalty on the sales. . . . In any case, the contract assured the authors of actual publication and stimulated them . . . to go promptly to work."

Each chapter was printed as soon as it had been written. Volume I was completed by May, 1881, Volume II a year later. Both volumes were said to have enjoyed success, and there was "nothing to indicate that Fowler and Wells had not done well by them." Prompted by the profits of the venture and believing also that she "could publish for less money than the publishers were charging her," Susan B. Anthony bought out the rights from Fowler and Wells and contracted with a printer in Rochester, New York, to produce the third volume. Although further participation by Fowler and Wells in the publication of this basic history was no longer invited, it was the phrenological publishers who had launched the work, and their imprint on the first two volumes bears testimony to Charlotte Wells' identification with the cause.

Other publications reflected her interest in other causes and other ideologies. Under her direction the firm issued an unusual study of creative evolution, *A New Theory of the Origin of Species*; a perceptive analysis of political economy, *The Fallacies in "Progress and Poverty"*; and a contribution to communal living, *Peacemaker Grange*. In 1887, under the editorship of Sizer and Drayton, Fowler and Wells launched still another publishing enterprise, the Human Nature Library. This consisted of ten-cent paperback publications issued quarterly and distinguishable by only one feature from the numerous cheap serial lines or "libraries" of books published during the period. Each number of the Human Nature Library was complete in itself. However, unlike its competitors, all numbers were loosely related to the general topic of "What most concerns Body and Mind." As the publishers boasted, "As distinguished from the Fiction Libraries of the day it has an elevating tendency and much of utility." The first number, written by Sizer, was entitled "Self-Reliance"; subsequent numbers covered phrenology, the choice of occupation, who should marry, resemblance to parents, and even the servant question. By 1895 the Human Nature Library reached its thirtieth number, a long line of new bottles that stored old wine.

The present incumbents of Fowler and Wells were as pedagogically inclined as their predecessors, and Charlotte believed as strongly in the application of phrenology to teaching as had her brothers. Her firm issued U. J. Hoffman's *The Science of the Mind Applied to Teaching*, introduced a Child Culture Department, and in 1886 first published the monthly magazine *The American Kindergarten and Primary Teacher*, described as the "leading exponent of the most advanced thought on *Child Culture*." Premiums—boxes of "toy money"—were offered to children who induced their parents to subscribe; sets of blank books designed for do-it-yourself pasting were advertised, along with such "Gems for the Kindergarten" as materials for weaving, embroidery, and color alphabets.

Charlotte Wells, alert though aging, constantly strove to add the touch of newness to the publications of her house, no easy task for one who viewed modern man through a phrenological telescope. To some extent she succeeded, dressing the old bones of her ideas in the garb of a new age. Basically, however, for all her dedicated effort, her publishing list was a continuation rather than a new departure.

The same charge may be leveled against the *Phrenological Journal*, whose columns presented new interpretations of old ideas and traditional phrenological analyses of heads and faces lately come to fame. "It is the editor's business," the *Journal* announced in 1882, "to have a perfectly harmonious temperament and a splendidly balanced organization, with a very conspicuous development of Benevolence and Suavity. Of course it is unnecessary to say that his intellect should be A 1, and his memory as tenacious as a spring bear-trap."[11] It is doubtful that any of the editors—from Drayton and Sizer in the eighties to Edgar Beall and Martin Luther Holbrook in the nineties—fulfilled this grandiose concept. Nonetheless the *Journal* had Vitativeness to the seventh degree, and, despite a certain monotony in style and content, it adopted enough of the newness of the times to attract readers in the South and East and as far off as New Zealand and Tasmania.

Indeed, one young woman from the prairies was said to have sold her hair to pay for a subscription. Through all the changing decades the *Journal* survived.

It survived primarily because it attempted to relate phrenology to those changing decades. It analyzed the mental characteristics of presidential candidates, and its views were "scrutinized and criticised and quoted by leading newspapers." It offered articles whose titles were almost prophetic in their applicability to the future: "Alcoholism Treated Phrenologically," "The Pollution and Purification of Our Rivers and Harbors," "Offensive Breath." During the seventies it discussed "Mr. Edison's Supposed New Force" and that "sensation of the day" the telephone; during the eighties it turned to the work of Henry George, "Alaska's Promise," and the problem of strikes; during the nineties it considered "Hypnotism in Medicine," "Photographing Thought," and automatic "Brain Registration."

Side by side with the timely was the nostalgic. The methods and the friends of Fowlerism were welcomed to the columns of the *Journal*. The deaths of old associates and supporters were recorded; Charlotte invited Nahum Capen to write his reminiscences of Spurzheim; autobiographical recollections were supplied by Orson, Sizer, and Charlotte herself. Yet on one or two occasions, when their reminiscences would have been of singular interest, the editors betrayed a complete lapse of memory. In analyzing the character of Clara Barton, "The American Apostle of the Red Cross," the *Journal* made no mention of Lorenzo Fowler's early and important influence upon her; and in announcing the death of the "good, gray poet," it made not a single reference to Walt Whitman's phrenological analysis or his connection with the firm.

For the most part, the contributors to the *Journal* were undistinguished. They came from the ranks of women temperance workers, diet reformers, historians of spiritualism, writers on mental science, and genteel bluestockings. Of them all, the most interesting was the prolific Elizabeth Oakes Smith, who provided serials, articles, and "Recollections of Prominent Americans." Obviously the appeal of the *Journal* did not stem from any flaunting of great names. Yet the appeal, however limited, continued. In 1876 the *Science of Health* was incorporated with the *Phrenological Journal*; a dozen years later the periodical's price was lowered; and in 1896, after having sported a larger format, it returned to the octavo size. It offered ten dollars for the "best true story of a hit made by a phrenologist in giving a delineation of character," and it sponsored a prize essay contest. Its departments included the "Science of Health," "Child Culture," and "Phrenological Society and Field Notes."

Certainly the hard core of the *Journal* remained its section on character readings. The editors, Edgar C. Beall and Henry S. Drayton, developed slight variations on the old phrenological theme, the former dubbing his analyses "phrenographs," a "shorter term for 'Written Delineation and Analysis of Character and Talents,' " the latter preferring the word "phrenotypes." Neither phrenograph nor phrenotype, as recorded in the *Journal*, was as detailed or as candid as the description given in private consultation. It was a "violation of professional ethics" to emphasize a subject's worst faults, and, as the magazine put it, "if we must err, we prefer to err upon the side of charity." Charitable phrenographs were therefore offered after personal examinations of such newsworthy personages as Paderewski and Walter Damrosch, Emma Goldman and Sarah Bernhardt, while the list of phrenotypes served up by the *Journal* boasted such diverse subjects as Edward Bellamy and Helen Keller, Alfred Dreyfus and Hetty Green.[12]

The *Journal* survived the strikes and panics that provided subject matter for its columns. So too did the firm. In February, 1884, the Fowler and Wells Company was incorporated, with Charlotte as president, Sizer as vice-president, Drayton as secretary, and Albert Turner as treasurer and business manager.[13] They made an effective as well as an indefatigable board. Charlotte, beaming with a sense of accomplishment, dignified and now almost queenly, had been elected to the American Association for the Advancement of Science. She celebrated her seventieth birthday in 1884, and would continue an active member of the firm for more than another decade. Her interests, as recorded by the American Association for the Advancement of Science, included "Anthropology, Biology, Economic Science & Statistics, Mechanical Science & Engineering, and Physics."[14] To this list she might have added gardening and interior decoration—interests reflected in her home in West Orange, New Jersey—and of course the all-embracing science of the mind, phrenology.

When Charlotte's aides were not editing or examining, they were busy producing books concerned principally with the interrelations of body and mind. Drayton, slight, with fine, dark brown hair, exercised "more than common mental activity," and knew how to say no calmly. He looked and talked and sometimes wrote "like a philosopher," and had produced a phrenological novel, which occasionally resorted to Irish brogue, as well as a study on human magnetism.[15]

As for Sizer, his years sat venerably upon his stalwart shoulders, and his life was punctuated by the books that climaxed a succession of phrenological examinations. After his one hundred thousandth analysis, he produced *How to Teach*, followed in due course by *Forty Years in Phrenology*, *The Royal Road to Wealth*, *Heads and Faces*, *Choice of Pursuits*, and *How to Study Strangers*, a sequel to *Heads and Faces* which appeared in 1895.[16] Indeed, it seemed that in the office of the Fowler and Wells Company the sequels and the sequels to sequels would go on forever.

Though the company gave little indication of changing, its location did. After seven years at 753 Broadway, they moved to larger quarters at 775 in 1887.[17] At that time they announced a reduction in the price of "Remnant Editions," offering ten pounds of reading matter for $1.50. Their reason for selling retail books and periodicals at wholesale prices was a bit specious: "We do this for the purpose of closing out remnants of editions and books bearing our present address, that we may open with a new and fresh stock, with new imprints."[18]

After five years at 775, another move was made uptown to 27 East Twenty-first Street, near Broadway, a four-story and basement brownstone with "handsome business offices and spacious editorial rooms, lecture-rooms and phrenological parlors."[19] The Golgotha that had endured for nearly sixty years on Broadway had moved slightly off Broadway, but the Golgotha continued. So too did that offspring of Golgotha, itself twenty-five years old, the Phrenological Institute.

Under Charlotte's determined leadership, the American Phrenological Institute struggled on.[20] Its treasury never matched its ambitious purposes, which included the study of race origins, the human body and brain, psychology and education. Yet for a college devoted to phrenology merely to survive in the New York of the eighties and nineties was in itself no inconsiderable tribute to phrenology's so-called mother in Israel, Charlotte Fowler Wells, and her colleagues Sizer and Drayton. The students of the institute were, like the contributors to the *Phrenological Journal*, undistinguished. They included a large number from the West, some from New England, and occasional travelers from Europe and Australia. By 1894 the institute had graduated over six hundred students, who had presumably paid the required fifty dollars for a full course, among them firm and family members: Albert Turner's wife, Orson Fowler's son-in-law, Alice P. Vanderbilt, and one Byron Trawatha, a five-year-old boy who attended a session with his father and mother. Having listened to lectures on anatomy and physiology, magnetism, psychology and clairvoyance, the annual classes enjoyed annual dinners and closing exercises, at which students offered lavish praise to the teachers in addresses subsequently printed in the pages of the *Phrenological Journal* or the Human Nature Library. A "Sizer Scientific Society" was organized by the more advanced students. The semicentennial of Spurzheim's death was commemorated appropriately at the institute in 1882 when "Mrs. Wells distributed a number of small floral paintings on wood, cut in the form of an artist's palette, the design being the letter S intertwined with flowers of memorial significance and appropriate lettering." Three years later another semicentennial jubilee celebrated the anniversary of the beginning of the Fowlers' missionary work. Indeed, the American Phrenological Institute often deserved another name—Mutual Admiration Society. At alumni banquets and institute dinners, graduates respectfully listened to Charlotte's phrenological reminiscences, requesting her to prepare for publication historical sketches on the progress of phrenology in America. This was her forte. Her short, compact figure still exuded vitality as she approached her eightieth year. Her hair was now completely white; yet she still read without glasses, regaling her disciples with her recollections of the early days of phrenology. As Edgar Beall put it in a phrenograph prepared for her eightieth birthday, "Mrs. Wells would attract attention in any company, although she might remain seated in silence with folded hands."[21]

Another of Charlotte's specialties was the Cabinet of nearly two thousand busts, crania, and portraits assembled through the years. In 1884 she gave a large collection to the institute, repeating at the time her deep desire to establish a permanent building to house the specimens. Through the years she solicited funds for such a building. In 1892 Nelson Sizer presented to the Ithaca merchant, Henry W. Sage, Charlotte's project:

> It has long been the burden of Mrs. Wells' life to have a home established for Phrenology. . . .
>
> The Alumni for several years have agitated the subject of a home for their Alma Mater, and have made some provisional subscriptions as a donation when a place could be selected. One aged man and wife who have practiced Phrenology have made each a will donating their savings, about $7,000 to the American Institute of Phrenology. . . .
>
> Many men acknowledge that our advice to them as to occupa-

Edward P. Fowler, M.D.

From *The National Magazine*, Vol. XIX
(February–March, 1894)

The interior of the Fowler and Wells phrenological museum at 308 Broadway

From the *New-York Illustrated News*, Vol. 1 (February 18, 1860)

Examining room at the Fowler and Wells phrenological museum at 308 Broadway

From the *New-York Illustrated News*, Vol. 1 (February 18, 1860)

Samuel T. Fowler
"*The distinguishing marks of character in this portrait of Mr. Fowler, are Delicate Quality, a highly developed Mental temperament, with the Vital and Motive relatively subordinate, a strong infusion of the Electric, endowing him with considerable Endurance. There is a very strong subjective intellect and much Dignity with very moderate Alimentiveness and Acquisitiveness.*"

From William Windsor, *Phrenology*
(Big Rapids, Mich., 1921)

The Fowler office from 1892 to 1902

From *King's Photographic Views of
New York* (Boston, 1895)

Nelson Sizer

From William Windsor, *Phrenology*
(Big Rapids, Mich., 1921)

Edgar C. Beall, M.D.

From William Windsor, *Phrenology*
(Big Rapids, Mich., 1921)

Students and faculty of the American Institute of Phrenology about 1895. Charlotte Wells is seated at the extreme right, and Nelson Sizer is standing behind her.

Fowler Family Papers, Collection of Regional History, Cornell University

An Analysis of Four Prominent Presidents of the United States.

By Jessie A. Fowler.

THE WORLD, MAY 8, 1898.

Jessie Fowler analyzes the presidents

tion has made their fortune, and such men will aid in this work if a proper opportunity can be afforded to them.[22]

Despite his interest in mental science, Henry Sage did not advance the suggested eighteen thousand dollars, and eventually the collection of busts and crania was dispersed or destroyed. Although the institute and the firm weathered the panic of the early nineties, phrenology was still marching through enemy country—a fact that never dismayed Charlotte Wells. She had faced with equanimity the struggles of phrenology's beginnings as she would face the struggles of its latter days. She had faced changes too, changes not only in her firm but in her family.

After her husband's death, during the late 1870's when Charlotte was taking her place as head of the New York firm, her brother Lorenzo was basking in his position as *doyen* of phrenology in England. Tending toward plumpness now, moving "in society with a quiet amiability," he still captivated his audiences. As a lecturer, he was likened to an auger cutting steadily through solid timber. As an examiner, he was noted for the deceptive ease with which he eyed a man and seemed merely to stroke his hair before arriving at an astute analysis. Between his office on Fleet Street and his home in Camden Square, his days were full. He varied his professional activities with his travels, and his life was rounded by the intellectual companionship of his wife and the gratifying development of his daughters.[23]

Then, in 1879, Lorenzo suffered the shattering loss of his wife. Both he and Lydia were members of Dr. Parker's church in London's City Temple, and, in addition to her collaborations with her husband, Lydia had taken on the duties of district visitor of the church. In the course of her visits among London's poor, she contracted a disease which swiftly developed into pleuropneumonia. On January 26, 1879, Lydia Folger Fowler, fifty-six years old, died at her home in England.[24] She had come a long way from Nantucket Island, this woman who had been one of America's first women physicians and the first woman professor of medicine in the country. The empty place she left in Lorenzo's office was easier to fill than the emptiness in his life. His daughters rallied round, Jessie especially taking over the work her mother had done before her, studying brain dissection in London's Medical School for Women, and becoming an associate in her father's Fleet Street office.[25]

In 1879, after Lydia's death, Lorenzo paid a brief visit to the United States to see his family and renew old acquaintances.[26] Charlotte promptly arranged with him for a special agency for Fowler books in London. Upon his return to England, Lorenzo, with the aid of his daughters, set up offices in the Imperial Buildings, Ludgate Circus, and launched the *Phrenological Magazine*. The approach of his own seventieth birthday did not deflect him from marching along new avenues in his work. Others might be cut off—Samuel Wells and Lydia, Daniel Harrison Jacques and Dr. Trall—but the Fowlers, it seemed, must go on forever.

The year of Lydia's death had seen the appearance of an important work by one of those Fowlers. Indeed, the 1870's had been especially productive for Lorenzo's half brother Edward.[27] The teen-age boy who had astonished the less skeptical members of his family with his mesmeric revelations had become an established physician, a "man of genial manners and benevolent disposition," the father of two children, and a liberal rather than an exclusive homeopathist who championed "the oneness of science universal." In 1878, Dr. Edward Fowler had helped found the New York Medico-Chirurgical Society for the purpose of collecting "a body of workers . . . untrammelled by the theories or prejudices of the hour . . . able and willing to investigate life in all its phases . . . who possessed the courage of their convictions."

As part of his own effort "to investigate life in all its phases," Edward Fowler became the first American translator of three renowned students of the brain. Although he never practiced phrenology, he was, like all the Fowlers, intrigued by the mysteries of the human mind, and as a result of his explorations and studies, Edward Fowler presented to the country the first translations of Charcot, Richet, and Benedikt. The very title of his translation of Charcot seemed to strike accord with the phrenological camp: *Lectures on Localization in Diseases of the Brain*. Appearing in 1878, it apparently upheld the phrenologists' view that the brain was not "a homogeneous organ . . . but rather . . . a confederation . . . of diverse organs" to each of which "belong certain distinct physiological properties and faculties." Unlike the phrenologists, however, Charcot was an objective scientist, a clinical observer, and a pathologist. At the Salpêtrière in Paris his experiments in the phenomena of hypnotism, which he was applying to the treatment of mental disturbances, were already under way. In 1885 a Viennese physician would seek instruction from Charcot, and ten years later, with the publication of Freud's *Studies on Hysteria*, psychoanalysis would be launched. Meanwhile it was a mesmerist turned physician, half brother of a team of practical phrenologists, who had introduced Charcot's work on cerebral localization to America.

In 1879, Edward followed up his pioneer work with his translation of Richet's *Physiology and Histology of the Cerebral Convolutions*, a study which he regarded as "a natural complement to Charcot's." A year later he translated from the German the work of the Viennese professor Moriz Benedikt, *Anatomical Studies upon Brains of Criminals*, a work that seemed to corroborate the view of the early reforming phrenologists that crime was "the outcome of anatomical deformity" and that prisons were savage relics of a primitive age. Edward Fowler's linguistic skill—perhaps a gift from those many-tongued spirits with whom he had been in communication as a boy—had been put to good use. Besides introducing to this country the work of a trio of pioneer students of the brain, his translations were interpreted, by the phrenologists at least, as incontestable scientific corroboration of their views.

The work of still another member of the Fowler family was more difficult to interpret. Like brother Edward's translations, Samuel Fowler's writings involved a language problem. The founder of the Ancora Productive Union of the Industrial Public had formulated a vast new system of thought and learning which he termed genetics, but—until 11 A.M., February 22, 1876—he had lacked words in which to couch it. At that fateful moment when Samuel solved his dilemma, he was "moved to make a plain capital letter . . . and upon that to place another, and another, until all the capitals were comprised in one monogram."[28] The resulting *"diagram* of astronomical knowledge" became, in the author's mind at least, a "key to many mysteries." Samuel's key appears to have been lost, although the mysteries remain in a volume which he published in 1882, *Genetics, A New System of Learning based on the Analogies comprised in a complete abstract of the requirements of Genitive Law as they apply to the origin and production, or to the source and genesis of the star, plant, zo-onic and societary worlds.* Although one thousand copies of this tome were printed, only two hundred were bound, the balance of the edition being destroyed in a fire at the bindery. Hence Samuel T. Fowler's *Genetics* is as rare as it is rarefied. Still absorbed in the genesis of things, the author made his exodus in 1883, the year after the publication of *Genetics.*

Samuel was the first of the immediate family to depart the earthly sphere. The next would be Charlotte's oldest brother, Orson. From a post office box in Boston he continued for a time to fill the "imperious mandate" of nature.[29] His so-called "Revised Works"—a rehash of the effusions of his tireless pen—were offered by subscription to all who wished to study *Life, Health, and Self-Culture, as Taught by Phrenology.* The professor, still tall and erect despite the white hair and beard, continued to exalt nature's laws of mating, the joys of vibration, electricity, and parental pleasure, holding that *"a wrong Love* is the trunk cause, and right the cure, of most human degeneracies, diseases, and miseries." He continued to practice his own preachments. In 1882, at the age of seventy-two, he married for the third time. His bride, the former Abbie L. Ayres of Wisconsin, became in time his publisher and, in her own right, a lecturing phrenologist. She also became the mother of his children, three of whom arrived to crown his declining but still virile years.

The crown had its thorns. During his later years Orson was plagued by debts—doubtless the result of family expenses and perhaps too of building expenses for his house in Manchester, Massachusetts. His plans remained grandiose. In 1880, having rejoined Charlotte's firm for a short time, he announced that the "special feature of my future work, aside from condensing all my writings into one comprehensive volume, will be to visit foreign countries —Australia, New Zealand, India, Asia, and Europe," for the purpose of making studies in comparative phrenology.

Instead of venturing so far afield, Orson moved with his bride to Sharon Station in New York's Dutchess County. Not far from the great octagon he had built, he revisited the abandoned house of his dreams, where he was once observed running up the outer stairway "like a cat." Harassed by his creditors, he still lectured for the benefit of the village improvement fund. Harassed by his accusers, he still followed the ukases of nature and the dictates of his phrenological faculties.

Orson Fowler, pioneer American phrenologist, had been dubbed with a less savory epithet. Charged with licentiousness, he had been described in the public prints as *The Foulest Man On Earth*. In 1878, while still in Boston, Orson had committed to print his *Private Lectures on Perfect Men, Women and Children, in Happy Families*, a work that undertook to analyze such subjects as "Just how Love-Making should be Conducted," "The Sexual Embrace," and "Male and Female Electricity." That candid and informative treatise had been published by Fowler and Max Bachert, Orson's business manager during the late 1870's. It was this associate who turned against Orson, accusing him of immorality not only in word but in deed. "His private lectures to ladies," Bachert claimed, "were of an immoral character, and often grossly obscene in action and speech, and his correspondence and books contained indelicate and unchaste suggestions, which . . . were continually involving their author in private troubles." In addition to "sexual intrigues" and the pursuit of "a libidinous course by mail," Bachert charged his erstwhile associate with "sustaining the most disreputable relationship with certain female quacks, and . . . writing to them grossly immoral letters, which actually undertook to systematize sexual vice. . . . The correspondence which fell into my hands is so sickening in its sensuality, so infamously lecherous and vile . . . that even the ordinary men of the world, and criminal lawyers themselves, stand aghast at it."

In a world where Anthony Comstock upheld the laws of Dame Grundy, Orson Fowler was finding it all but impossible to uphold the laws of nature as he interpreted them. In June, 1881, the attacks against him reached the *Chicago Tribune*, in which the headlines read: "Fowler, the Phrenologist, Likely to Run Afoul of Anthony Comstock. Under the Cloak of Science He Disseminates the Seeds of Vice." Orson Fowler was described as a "bird of prey" who has "debauched the minds of young females," and "More Concerning the Vile Humbuggery of Prof. Fowler" was promised. In this crisis Charlotte Fowler Wells printed and published a circular vindicating her brother and her house from the charges of immoral practices. Max Bachert replied to that circular in a brochure entitled *Is Prof. O. S. Fowler The Foulest Man On Earth?*—a question which, for Bachert, remained rhetorical.

With this stain upon his scutcheon, Orson Fowler lived out his few remaining years until on August 18, 1887, he died at Sharon. The death of America's pioneer practical phrenologist, reformer in diverse fields, architect, publisher, and founder of a firm that would long survive him occasioned perhaps briefer notices than the immorality with which he had been charged. After the funeral services his remains were taken to Woodlawn Cemetery, in the Bronx, where he was buried on a hillside in an unmarked grave. By this act of omission at the end, Orson Fowler was repudiated by the family whose fortunes he had launched half a century before.

Any conflicting emotions that may have plagued Charlotte for her brother's sake were eventually overshadowed by the demands of her firm and her own approaching infirmity. The productiveness of the 1880's gave little sign of diminishing during the 1890's.

242

Although science continued to look down its nose at phrenology, the journals and books rolled from the press of the Fowler and Wells Company, examinations were given in the inner sanctum on Twenty-first Street, and students continued to gather at the institute. There was still a demand for the wares of Golgotha, and, with an industriousness almost compulsive in nature, the firm supplied them. In the early months of 1896 the controlling stock of the company was purchased by Edgar Beall, editor of the *Phrenological Journal*, and an associate, N. W. Fitz-Gerald.[30] Nonetheless, Charlotte made her interest and her presence felt. For the phrenological celebration of 1896 commemorating the centennial of Gall's lectures in Vienna, a program was planned and the Twenty-first Street hall was repainted and refurnished. Then the same year, when she was eighty-five, Charlotte sustained a serious fall that deprived her of the sight of one eye but not of her Vitativeness; despite her incapacity, she was able to deliver two lecture courses before the institute.[31] A year later she was deprived of perhaps more, for the patriarchal Nelson Sizer, her chief examiner, who had shared and to some extent influenced the fortunes of the firm since 1849, died.[32]

Yet Charlotte was not alone. In addition to her staff she had found help from abroad in the shape of her niece, Lorenzo's daughter Jessie. In the early 1860's America had sent to Albion its first successful practical phrenologist. Now Albion was returning the favor. The forty-year-old Jessie Allen Fowler, having served as apprentice and journeyman in the cause of phrenology, was becoming a master. The London office had trained her well, and she in turn had given the touch of a new generation to the mental science she purveyed. Her touch was apparent even in the vases of flowers that made of Lorenzo's sanctum in Ludgate Circus a "charming little gem of an office." By the eighties and early nineties the Fowler Phrenological Institute in London boasted its own large circulating and reference library and a museum of skulls and casts. It offered not only weekly classes and private tuition but "lessons by post." It offered a London version of the *Phreno-*

243

logical Journal—the *Phrenological Magazine*, of which Jessie assumed charge in 1883. Examinations in Ludgate Circus were made either by Lorenzo himself, an associate, D. T. Elliott, or Jessie Fowler, who analyzed from "personal observation" such notables as Herbert Spencer and Conan Doyle. Besides circulating books published by the New York firm, the institute presented to the British public the various collaborations of father and daughter— a *Phrenological Dictionary* and a *Phrenological Annual*—as well as Jessie's own writings, *Men and Women Compared*, *Life of Dr. Gall*, and *Manual of Mental Science for Teachers and Students*. Jessie was especially interested in the phrenology of children, keeping a diary of her nephew's growth for the first five years of his life.

As indefatigable as her mother had been, she was honorary secretary of the British Women's Temperance Association, treasurer of the British Phrenological Association, and fellow of the Anthropological Institute in London. Her lecture tours took her as far afield as Australia, where in 1888 she examined "men of all classes, from miners to statesmen."[33]

Yet it was not until some years later that Jessie began to overshadow her father—still "old-man-eloquent" in his lectures, still the "prince of mental scientists" to his imitators, still the recipient of highly charged, emotional letters from former subjects recalling, as Clara Barton did, the Lorenzo of a half-century earlier, whose "heart had in it the essence of kindness and broad humanity, with chords atuned to human needs."[34] Although Lorenzo Fowler suffered a paralytic stroke in 1893, he was able three years later to accept a model of Gall's skull at the Phrenological Centenary in Queen's Hall during a program enlivened by the Aeolian Ladies' Orchestra and the blindfold examination of a head by his daughter Jessie.[35]

In the late summer of 1896 the aged and infirm Lorenzo returned to America with his daughter to spend some time in New Jersey with Charlotte. Though the two octogenarians had so many memories to share, they had but little time to recollect the early days on the Cohocton farm, the phrenological furor of the 1830's, the exhilarating beginnings when a new mental science was first touted, spread-eagle Yankee style, in America. Little more than a week after his return, Lorenzo sustained another stroke, and on September 2, 1896, he died. Both *Times* and *Tribune* were generous in allotting space to his obituary, mentioning his lecturing style, his work in England, the famous heads the eighty-five-year-old phrenologist had examined—a list from which the name of Walt Whitman was conspicuously absent.[36]

Lorenzo was buried in New Jersey's Rosedale Cemetery, and the second of the pioneer phrenological Fowlers passed from the picture. But neither phrenology nor the family had made its final gesture. In the office on Twenty-first Street Jessie Fowler gradually found her place, becoming editor of the *Phrenological Journal*, for which she analyzed famous American presidents, lecturing to students of the institute (class of 1896), contributing to the Human Nature Library a brochure on *Phrenology. Its Use in Business Life*. As busy as Charlotte had ever been, the new incumbent opened discussions at the Social Culture Club, spoke before the Theosophical Society, and by the turn of the century even found time to attend the Women's Congress in London. By then it was clear that the Fowler family had become a dynasty and that the New York firm had an heiress apparent.[37]

Nonetheless, for the forty-year-old woman phrenologist from London the closing years of the century paralleled in a way the decline of the family. In 1897, Orson Fowler's great octagonal mansion was razed, an event that heralded other finales.[38] Jessie's aunt Almira, who had studied medicine in Philadelphia and subsequently lived in England with her second husband Edward Breakspear, died at Charlotte's home and joined her half brother Lorenzo in Rosedale Cemetery.[39] In 1900, Jessie's sister Loretta Piercy died in her forty-ninth year.[40] A year later, on June 4, 1901, the seemingly indestructible Charlotte finally succumbed two months before her eighty-seventh birthday.[41] She herself had written, "The last spark goes out at the top,"[42] an observation that would have made a fitting epitaph for the oldest phrenological Fowler. Now, except for Jessie's uncle Edward who had no part in the conduct of the firm, the older generation was gone with the opening of the new century.

Paradoxically, while the climate of the times was uncongenial for phrenology—except perhaps as a source of humor in, for example, George Ade's *Fables in Slang*—hope for the so-called science of the mind seemed to come from unlikely sources. The progress of pure science and inductive medicine had enchanted the country with the glories of the laboratory and at the same time disenchanted it with the pseudo-sciences and the deductive methods of "Fowler's favorite phantasy." The objection that the relation of the frontal sinus to the brain made accurate phrenological diagnoses impossible was hauled forth repeatedly by physicians.[43] Yet, as Emerson had put it in his *Historic Notes of Life and Letters in New England*, though phrenology was "coarse and odious to scientific men," it "had a certain truth in it; it felt connection where the professors denied it, and was a leading to a truth which had not yet been announced."[44] One medical man, the Autocrat of the Breakfast Table, who had mocked phrenology with venomous delight, had modified his views, declaring: "It has melted the world's conscience in its crucible, and cast it in a new mold with features less those of Moloch and more like those of humanity. If it has failed to demonstrate its system of correspondence, it has proved that there are fixed relations between organization and mind and character."[45] Like Holmes, William James expressed a genial and sympathetic ambivalence: "Phrenology . . . may still be, in the hands of intelligent practitioners, a useful help in the art of reading character. . . . But the brain . . . need no more be the *organ* of the signified faculty than the jaw is the organ of the will. These correlations between mind and body are, however, so frequent that the 'characters' given by phrenologists are often remarkable for knowingness and insight."[46] Indeed, at one eastern university a department of psychology was established by a wealthy believer in the phrenological science of mind.[47]

Support came from abroad too—from Herbert Spencer, who stated that "localization of function is the law of all organization";[48] from the neuropathologist David Ferrier; from the criminologist Lombroso, who labeled craniology the "precursor of Criminal Anthropology."[49] As the nineteenth century rolled on, confirmation of the validity of the pseudo-science came from an area where it was least expected—from science itself. The effect of a galvanic current upon a portion of the brain was observed to produce expressions of joy exactly in the area where the organ of Hope had been located. The empirical theory of the phrenologists that every portion of the brain had its own distinct function was finding some support now from the laboratory scientists themselves. As the *New York Sun* succinctly put it, "It is a curious fact that modern research appears about to establish a firm scientific basis for some of the teachings of phrenology just at the time when that doctrine has passed almost entirely out of vogue."[50]

The phrenological millennium, for which the older generation of Fowlers had struggled, seemed close at hand. In 1899 the scientist Alfred Russel Wallace, whose work on natural selection had coincided with Darwin's, wrote a book entitled *The Wonderful Century*, in which he devoted a chapter to "The Neglect of Phrenology." In those pages he voiced his belief that phrenology was a "purely inductive science, founded step by step on the observation and comparison of facts, confirmed and checked in every conceivable way, and subjected to the most rigid tests." Wallace looked into the future confidently: "In the coming century Phrenology will assuredly attain general acceptance. It will prove itself to be the true science of mind. Its practical uses in education, in self-discipline, in the reformatory treatment of criminals, and in the remedial treatment of the insane, will give it one of the highest places in the hierarchy of the sciences."[51]

For Jessie Fowler, age forty-five, heir to the firm of Fowler and Wells, "The Wonderful Century" began.

"THE WONDERFUL CENTURY"

ALMOST from the beginning Jessie Allen Fowler, who had been "born with the instinct of INTUITION," seems to have sensed that, despite Alfred Wallace, "The Wonderful Century" would be something less than wonderful for phrenology.[1] Had she faced this intuitive knowledge squarely, she might have abandoned its practice in favor of some other profession. In 1901 she had completed a course in the woman's law class of New York University. Like her uncle Orson, she was a facile writer; her major work *Brain Roofs and Porticos. A Psychological Study of Mind and Character* was to reveal interesting insights into modern experimental psychology. As a lecturer she had Orson's dash and magnetism, and upon at least one occasion she was described as "a genius . . . a seer and a prophetess, a harmonizer of men." As woman lawyer, writer or lecturer, perhaps even as prophetess, Jessie Fowler might have attained success—but such success would not have gratified her. By family background, by training, and by inclination, she was committed to the pursuit of phrenology.

This commitment in "The Wonderful Century" became almost desperate. Using every old device the firm had ever developed and adding a few new techniques, Jessie Fowler strove to sell her outmoded product to an increasingly indifferent public.[2] Correspondence lessons in phrenology were offered along with "casts of the brain in plaster of paris" and "steel measures to measure the circumference of the head." Fowler's Friction Soap was advertised as well as the newest in colored busts—an elaborate affair by one Eulogio Prieto of Cuba, who used a different color for each group of faculties. At a woman's suffrage bazaar a phrenological booth was presided over by Miss Fowler; the science of life was taught at the Scientific Christian League; and a phrenological game was available entitled "The Perfect Man." An evening course of instruction was geared to businessmen and women, for whom also a National Vocation Bureau was formed. For the care of nervous troubles, "The New Physical and Mental Culture" was especially applicable—a "new system . . . to train the body in order to control the faculties of the mind." Under Jessie's influence, the firm went so far as to enter deliberately into the entertainment business. As the *Phrenological Journal* explained in 1904:

> In view of the remarkable interest shown in our recent public lectures and the concentrated attention with which people listen to the reading of the heads of volunteers given to demonstrate Phrenology, we have arranged a bright lecture entertainment for Y.M.C.A.'s, churches, Sunday-schools, Y.P.S.C.E.'s, Epworth Leagues, lodges, fraternities, orders, clubs, and societies, hoping thereby to arouse even more latent interest in the study of human nature. . . .
>
> The exhibition is a strictly high-class entertainment . . . astonishing, mirthful, unique, instructive, and calculated to please both old and young.
>
> We are also prepared to entertain receptions or house parties with brief circle readings which would tell the leading points for each person and greatly interest all as a practical demonstration of Phrenology. The fee, $10.00.[3]

The Fowler firm now had an Entertainment Bureau, and the head of the firm was beginning to bear strong resemblances to the barker at a side show.

The Fowler publications too catered less to the scientific and technological concerns of the twentieth century than to the meretricious interests of the ignorant and the gullible. Jessie Fowler saw the need for cheap literature in wholesale quantities, writing in *Phrenology. Its Use in Business Life:*

Publishing to-day is a very different business to what it was some years ago. The consolidation of some of the principal publishing houses in America as well as in England, have unified the interests of booksellers considerably, and cheapened the literature of the present age considerably, and compelling any profit to be made out of the publication of books to come from the result of selling large quantities only. Hence the need has been created for more business shrewdness in not producing or placing on the market anything that will not warrant the confidence of the public.[4]

What Jessie Fowler placed on the market was cheap not only in price but in content.[5] As modern psychotherapy, she offered a popular manual entitled *How to Acquire and Strengthen Will-Power*, which prescribed for neurasthenia and insomnia, nightmare and stage fright a combination of herb tea and sympathetic suggestion. Like her forebears she had a fancy for series—the "New Self-Help Series," the "Self and Sex Series," the "Natural Treatment Series." The old "Library of Mesmerism" suffered a time change, reappearing in the guise of books on thought transference, telepathy, hypnotism, somnambulism, and psychic phenomena. *Modern Ghost Studies* adorned her list along with popular investigations into the mysteries of cheirognomy and graphology. The works of O Hashnu Hara on practical theosophy and reincarnation, karma, the astral body and personal magnetism were especially delectable. Under the aegis of the last of the family, the Fowler list degenerated steadily into the occult and the sensational.

The *Phrenological Journal* followed suit.[6] While it recognized the more serious preoccupations of "The Wonderful Century" in essays on Lombroso, Nordau, and William James, it highlighted fact less than fancy and truth less than the perversions of truth. During the first decade of the new century the faithful could read in its pages intriguing speculations on graphology and "biophilism," articles on the latest food fad of Fletcherizing and on that "Dean of Hygiene" Dr. James H. Kellogg of Battle Creek, advertisements of osteopaths and naturopaths. Side by side in its final issue of January, 1911, the *Journal* ran an editorial on aviation and the characteristics of aviators and an advertisement for the Portland School of Astrology—a paradoxical though characteristic swan song for the country's longest-lived phrenological magazine.

The Phrenological Institute was not yet ready to give up the ghost.[7] It continued to graduate students annually until at least the 1920's. For a time Rev. Thomas A. Hyde, Harvard graduate and Long Island Episcopalian minister, served as president, aided by

Human Being meets Learned Phrenologist

FROM GEORGE ADE, *Fables in Slang*
(Chicago and New York, 1900)

Henry S. Drayton and Jessie's brother-in-law Michael H. Piercy. By the 1916–17 season, when courses were offered in heredity and public speaking, Drayton had become "Associate Emeritus" and Jessie Fowler "Consulting Phrenologist" and vice-president. At the centenary celebration of Orson Fowler's birth a gentleman who had been examined as a boy by the "Pioneer Phrenologist . . . Health Culturist and Physiologist" was re-examined by Jessie. The two examinations not only accorded but testified to the continuity of the institute's appeal. This offbeat college now offered a postgraduate course in psychology, hypnotism, animal magnetism, and therapeutics, as well as a library containing the "choicest selection of phrenological reading" and such "Life-like Casts" as remained from the once extensive collection. Though it attracted a decidedly limited audience, it did attract, and students from Yale, Harvard, Princeton, Cornell, and Columbia were said to have come to the institute for phrenological examinations.

Somehow, in spite of the advances of experimental and clinical psychology, in spite of the incipient Freudian revolution, the phrenological analysis still had its adherents, not all of whom were visitors to a fun fair. Twentieth-century examinations were performed either by Jessie herself or by Edgar C. Beall, who regarded phrenology as the modern substitute for Christianity and himself as a practical phreno-physicist.[8] By 1907, Beall had personally examined Mrs. Frank Leslie and Susan B. Anthony, Henry Ward Beecher and Oscar Hammerstein, and was well equipped to analyze from actual head or photograph the characters of later twentieth-century subjects. Under Jessie's direction, analyses lasted anywhere from one to three hours and prices ranged from three dollars to fifty dollars. Until the demise of the *Phrenological Journal* examinations made from life or from likeness were recorded in its pages. There subscribers might study the temperaments of Winston Spencer Churchill and Theodore Roosevelt, John D. Rockefeller and Judge Ben Lindsey. As they had once read analyses of Bryant and Poe, they now considered those of Stephen Crane and Frank Stockton, Bret Harte and Joaquin

Miller. In 1902, Edwin Markham, acclaimed as the poet of labor, the laureate of the hoe, appeared personally at the institute and bared his head for a phrenograph that revealed his major strengths and his one major weakness—a deficiency in the faculty of Time.

The year before, a more interesting meeting had taken place between a writer and a phrenologist. The illustrious author of *Tom Sawyer* had recently published his scathing article "To the Person Sitting in Darkness," and in their veteran fun-maker the public was beginning to discern a crusading, reforming spirit. Mark Twain was becoming "Huck Finn with a gun," the preacher of the "new Gospel of St. Mark." At this period of his life, remembering with amused nostalgia the itinerant character limners of Hannibal and the Lorenzo Fowler of London whose "bumpology" he had twice tested and scorned, Mark Twain actually underwent, for at least the third time, a phrenological examination. His notebook for 1901 mentions an appointment at 10:30 on March 7, with Jessie A. Fowler. His examiner rose to perceptive heights upon this occasion. With no allusions whatsoever to bumps or cavities, Jessie Fowler made her measurements and read off the dispositions and talents indicated by Mark Twain's cranial developments as easily as if she had been reading *Tom Sawyer*. The writer's Conscientiousness and Benevolence, his Hope and Veneration, his Ideality and Vitativeness were charted, and in the April, 1901, issue of the *Phrenological Journal* the results were published:

MARK TWAIN—THE WORLD'S GREATEST HUMORIST.
TWENTY REASONS WHY WE SAY SO.
From a Personal Examination.
If all the doubters of the truth of Phrenology had accompanied us the other day when we had the great privilege of examining Mr. Clemens's head, they would, I think, have realized why there can never be a second Mark Twain, and would have agreed with us that there are reasons why he has made an indelible impression upon the public and, further, why other men who are equally humorous and funny will never be as great as he.

The "observations from his head" that followed included a succession of discerning comments:

> Mark Twain is really a very serious man. . . . He says the most serious things in a way which is humorous. . . . He does not write to make you laugh, but to make you think, and uses humor as a vehicle. . . . His popularity is not due to the humor of his writings, but to the undercurrent of serious thought to which the subordinating humor gives expression. . . . His moral brain largely dominates over the remainder of his faculties, hence he is capable of suffering acutely through the influence of his Benevolence and Conscientiousness, while Hope and Veneration are the least developed faculties in this group. . . . There is remarkable fullness around the upper portion of the forehead, and a little on the lateral portion, which we do not always find. Jefferson has a square forehead, and is humorous . . . but Mark Twain, though he has a similar development of Mirthfulness, shows a deeper, more intellectual force of mind, literary criticism, and an ethical sentiment in his writings which we do not find in others who have written in the same vein. . . . His sympathies are very strong, and he must have suffered considerably by and through their expression. He is a believer in humanity, and is tender toward those who are oppressed; he is a reformer at heart, and many of his remarks have been aimed against abuses and snobbishness. . . . The key-note of his character is his Conscientiousness. His ability to act as a citizen for other citizens—as every citizen should act for his neighbor.[9]

Jessie Fowler's phrenograph of Mark Twain was certainly extraordinary. In her emphasis upon the serious, reforming character of the citizen who acts "for other citizens," in her stress less upon Mirthfulness than upon Conscientiousness—the "key-note of his character"—the analyst presented an early view of the "funmaker's" "tragic character" which later critics would confirm. Yet, as extraordinary as the analysis was Mark Twain's reaction, or lack of reaction, to it. For, although he later recalled his phrenological experiences, he made no reference to the published phrenograph of 1901. In 1906, Mark Twain was invited, along with Francis Galton and Max Nordau, G. K. Chesterton and George

Bernard Shaw, to contribute to a symposium on "Bumps and Brains: The Old Phrenology and the New," to be published in the London *Daily Graphic*.[10] Although his recollections extended back decades to Hannibal and London days, they made no mention of his far more recent experience in the phrenological examining room. Perhaps the analysis had been too telling, the hint at his "tragic character" too disturbing. Perhaps too Mark Twain balked at disclosing his abiding fascination with the pseudoscience he had scoffed but whose persistent lure he could not resist.

Unlike their distinguished subject, the Fowler firm boasted of the "privileged interview" with the "veteran writer," and when he died in 1910 the *Phrenological Journal* recalled with pride the day when the topography of Mark Twain's skull had been charted by a phrenological explorer:

He was a wonderful combination of the elements of seriousness and humor, and told us that he considered his serious works his best productions, and that he only wrote in a humorous way to make people sit up and take notice of what he wanted to tell them, and he knew they would not pay the same attention to him if he was always serious.[11]

By 1910, when the *Journal* carried its reminiscences of "The Late Mark Twain (Samuel L. Clemens)," Jessie Fowler was managing, between her own examinations and her consultations with Beall, to live almost as many lives as her forebears. A committee woman par excellence, she was a member of the Woman's Press Club and the New York Legislative League, chairman of the Portia Club's legislative committee and of the Committee for Legal Aid to Women Writers. Her own writing all but matched her uncle Orson's in volume and often in viewpoint. Her articles on "The Psychology of Arkansas" and "Phreno-Psychology" illumined the *Journal* while her books and pamphlets flowed in a steady stream. In *Brain Roofs and Porticos* Jessie recommended that food be selected according to the shape of the head and, in a style reminiscent of her uncle's, announced that "broad-headed people should eat wheat, oatmeal, hard crackers." Even as she cited Havelock Ellis on mixed marriages, she declared, à la Orson Fowler, that the "tall man is generally generous but does not look out for a rainy day," while the "short man is penurious but looks out for a rainy day." Capitalizing upon the police department's use of the Bertillon system of detecting criminals by the shape of ear or nose, Jessie wrote her *Practical Physiognomy: A Psychological Study of the Face*—a twentieth-century variant of Samuel Wells' tome on the same subject. In a series of twelve booklets character analysis was applied to ear and forehead, nose and hand, voice and walk. She developed her own charts of *Character Types* and of *Brain Centers*.[12]

Yet, for all her concentrated devotion and ceaseless activity, Jessie Allen Fowler, phrenologist, lecturer, writer, could not stave off the tides that were about to engulf her cherished philosophy of mind. Although Jessie studied experimental psychology, she still believed that "a phrenologist sees all that a psychologist does, and much more besides."[13] She appears to have been impervious to, or unimpressed by, the probings of Freud, who was soon to deliver almost single-handed the coup de grace to Gall and Spurzheim, Combe and Fowler. Despite the strong intuition with which she was endowed, she did not sense the approaching displacement of phrenoanalysis by psychoanalysis. Yet she could not help sensing in the very air of the twentieth century the ending to much she had known. With the passing of time came change. A finale had been written in the skies.

Even as she labored for phrenology, Jessie Fowler must have read the portents of its end. The signs were everywhere. In 1902 she moved the firm one block north to 24 East Twenty-second Street, where "modern conveniences, such as electric light, steam heat, and elevator service" were available.[14] There under her supervision the Fowler and Wells Company of phrenologists and publishers placed its last advertisement in *Publishers' Weekly* on January 2, 1904,[15] its last listing in the *Publishers' Trade List Annual* the following year, and in January, 1911, issued the final number of the *Phrenological Journal*, which had endured almost seventy-three years.

For a while the New York firm continued its old connections with the London office of L. N. Fowler and Company and the Fowler Institute, London. In time, however, Lorenzo's mantle fell upon Stackpool E. O'Dell, the leading English practitioner, who with his wife offered phrenological consultations in "an oasis of philosophic calm" on Ludgate Circus. As for L. N. Fowler and Company, that firm of publishers, booksellers, and wholesalers persists into the 1970's, but under a directorship "in no way connected with the Fowler family."[16]

Of that once large family, few were left. In 1913, Jessie's second sister Amelia died,[17] and the following year her uncle Edward Payson Fowler, aged seventy-nine, died of pneumonia at his home in Pelham Manor.[18] The last and youngest of the older generation, mesmerist, homeopathist, translator of pioneer medical writings, had joined his brothers.

For a few more years Jessie continued her work, lecturing, reading skulls, analyzing temperaments. Then, in 1916, doubtless in an attempt to survive through division of labor, her firm was split. Fowler and Wells was moved to 27 East Twenty-second Street and placed under the charge of Jessie's brother-in-law Michael H. Piercy. The American Institute of Phrenology, with which Jessie remained directly associated, was relocated in the Sheridan Building at 1358 Broadway. There, with a trio of aides —Messrs. Singleton, McGuire, and Coffin—Jessie Fowler specialized in what she described as the "Study of Human Nature and Vocational Guidance." The institute's motto, "Self-Knowledge is the Key that Unlocks All Doors of the Mind," was designed to attract all varieties of men to the door of 1358 Broadway at the corner of Thirty-sixth Street, "easily reached by tube, subway, surface car and ferry." For a fee of fifty dollars the doors of the mind could presumably be unlocked by lectures on heredity and sessions with Miss Fowler, "famous Character Analyst."[19]

The American Institute of Phrenology managed to survive the

First World War, although its changing addresses bear evidence of its financial difficulties. From the Sheridan Building it moved in 1922 to 125 West Forty-second Street, and in 1925 farther west to 239 West Forty-second Street. Three years later, Jessie A. Fowler, phrenologist, appeared in the New York directories at 135 West 119 Street—a far cry from Clinton Hall, where, nearly a century before, two brothers had staked their claim to the new science of the mind that promised to liberate humanity.

The Fowler brand of phrenology, which had withstood the panics of the nineteenth century, the Civil War, and even the First World War, could survive neither the great depression nor the growing inclination of mankind to be liberated by a newer philosophy of the mind. Wall Street and Freud together broke the back of the American Institute of Phrenology.

From its bare and ruined rafters the cry "Self-Made or Never Made" was a hollow echo lost in the winds of a changing society. The mandate of the Delphic oracle, "Know Thyself," was heeded no longer in the inner sanctum of Golgotha but on the couches of Freudian analysts. Jessie Allen Fowler, inheritor of a philosophy of mind attuned to a vanished century, had already lived too long. On October 15, 1932, she remedied the fault, dying of endocarditis at the age of seventy-six in her New York home on West 179 Street.[20]

The press, whose headlines bore the plight of the banks and President Hoover's appeal for the needy, still found space for the obituary of a woman phrenologist whose father had been a "noted expert" in the subject and whose mother had been one of the first American women to receive a medical degree. The obituary did not state that Jessie Allen Fowler had chosen a remarkably appropriate season in which to die. Almost to the day a century earlier, Johann Spurzheim had delivered in Boston those lectures that had unfolded to the country a new philosophy of mind, that had fired Orson Fowler to his mission, that had started the whole phrenological frenzy in America. There would be some desultory reading of heads and faces in later decades, but with Jessie's death the frenzy and the commitment were largely over. The last of the phrenological Fowlers was gone and with her the science of the mind that one hundred years before had promised emancipation from "the despotism of Error," the perfectibility of everyman, and a practical answer to the riddle of the Sphinx.

APPRAISALS

For a century the Fowler family had devoted itself to the advancement of an idea now discarded as erroneous. The extraordinary progress of pure science in the late nineteenth and early twentieth centuries provided an uncongenial climate for the progress of a borderline science. The marvels emerging almost on schedule from scientific and technological research centers provided sufficient intoxication for the modern world. In spite of Alfred Wallace, the thinking man of the "Wonderful Century" has placed his burnt offerings on the altar of the laboratory table, poured his libations into the test tube, and, with seeming finality, shattered that nineteenth-century image of man—the phrenological head.[1]

Yet for those with eyes to see the past recur in the present, that head emerges now and again whole, unbroken, with all its faculties marked, bearing its implicit message of perfectibility, pointing the way to reform. The work of the Fowler brothers lingers on, albeit intermittently and in strange places.

For those who are bridge builders, there are analogues everywhere. In 1900, Ernest Loomis of Chicago reprinted Lorenzo Fowler's study of love, courtship, and marriage as a "special chapter" in an anonymous work, *Should Woman Obey?*[2] Fifty years later, a former governor of Oklahoma, William H. Murray, published a rehash of Orson Fowler's *Science of Life* in a volume entitled *Christian Mothers*, which, according to the author, "if followed will redeem and enoble [*sic*] the Race."[3]

Another governor—Woodbridge N. Ferris of Michigan—

avowed that "through the reading of Fowler I was ushered into a new world."[4] William Windsor, "LL.B., Ph.D. A Member of the Bar of the Supreme Courts of Wisconsin, Kentucky and Texas, and of the Supreme Court of the United States," reaffirmed in 1921 the doctrines not only of Orson Fowler but of his half brother Samuel. In his own study on *The Science of Character*, Windsor announced that Samuel Fowler's "remarkable book entitled 'Genetics,' in which he explained the phenomena of Existence upon an entirely new theory . . . is a masterpiece of abstract reasoning and his conclusions are so consistent with observed facts that the author of this work has adopted the fundamental principles of Fowler's Genetics in . . . his [own] system of philosophy."[5] In the same year that Windsor's curious treatise made its bow, Samuel Fowler's son Horace published a book entitled *The Industrial Public*, applying his father's societary innovations to the social reconstruction of the twentieth century.[6]

William Windsor, author of *How to Become Rich*, founder of a system called Vitosophy, vendor of purified sand for table use, and latter-day American phrenologist, demanded twenty-five dollars for a reading as opposed to the twenty-five cents charged by his Coney Island colleague. Both had more in common with the quacks and fakers who read the past from tea leaves and the future from a deck of cards than with the Fowler family; yet they bore testimony to the continuing if sporadic appeal of a discredited pseudo-science which in the 1930's was taught in a phrenology school in Ohio and as late as the 1950's had its practitioners, "especially on the West Coast."[7] Indeed, if business firms resort, as they are said to do, "to handwriting analysis before hiring" and if a "college credit course in handwriting analysis" has been offered at the New School for Social Research, why should corporations not resort to head analysis and why should educational institutions not provide instruction in phrenology?[8] Though not entirely analogous, both methods judge inner man from outward signs.

There has been other, more significant, testimony than the activities of a William Windsor or a Coney Island head reader to the current manifestations of the nineteenth-century science of the mind. If the Coptic Fellowship of America develops a "Brain Lobe Index," which is nothing but the old phrenological chart in Hollywood makeup, no one but a faddist is impressed.[9] If, however, prefrontal lobotomy releases a patient from anxiety, apprehension, and mental anguish, the phrenological chart that localized the mental faculties becomes a little less ludicrous and psychosurgery appears to have connections, however slight and tentative, with phrenology. As early as 1901, in a study provocatively entitled *The Revival of Phrenology*, Dr. Bernard Hollander reported that his clinical and pathological investigations of brain localizations confirmed those of the discoverer of phrenology.[10] In 1929, in his *History of Experimental Psychology*, Dr. Edwin G. Boring admitted that "the word *function* in the sense of 'mental function' . . . was derived by psychologists from phrenology. . . . Even the psychologists who opposed phrenology could gain from it the notion of an analysis of the total personality into functions."[11]

Once again, as in the time of Alfred Wallace, confirmations of some aspects of the phrenological system seem to come from science. The phrenological hypothesis that the mind can be analyzed from a study of the skull, that the exterior is a guide to the interior—so long denied by physicians and scientists—crops up in a most unlikely place. When George Bernard Shaw wrote, "To feel a man's head with the object of finding out something about him is obviously as scientific a proceeding as feeling his pulse, or listening to his heart, or taking a print from his finger-tip,"[12] the remark might be dismissed as a not too logical Shavian extravagance. But who can dismiss the scientific statement in the April, 1969, issue of the University of Illinois *Engineering Outlook*: "Measurement of the human body for medical purposes can be accomplished swiftly with stereometric cameras. Studies of an apparent correlation between a child's body shape and his mental condition have been made with the aid of the cameras."[13] When we read in Dr. Robert S. Morison's review of the current *Biological Time Bomb* that, according to the author, "man is already able to . . . develop his intelligence, and even change his own mood,"[14] are we not receiving support from the scientists for the phrenological view that by exercising his mental functions man can develop or restrain them?

Does not the so-called matchmaking computer of the age of electronics recall Orson Fowler's marital charts and his efforts at scientific mating in the age of steam?[15] Does not the current search for the "memory molecule" bear some comparison with the Fowler investigations of mnemonics?[16]

If phrenology bequeathed more to functional psychology than to the mental science that displaced it, "amateur psychoanalysis" is still regarded as "our current substitute for phrenology."[17] While Mesmer is said to have led indirectly to Freud, Freud's methods were, like Gall's, "empirical." It is somehow suitable that the first public recognition received by Freud in this country came with an invitation to lecture extended by G. Stanley Hall, the psychologist who had once undergone a phrenological analysis at the Fowler emporium.[18]

Dr. Karl M. Dallenbach has pointed out, in an extraordinarily stimulating article, the correlations between phrenology and psychoanalysis: "Despite their separation in time of 100 years, they are so similar that Psychoanalysis is almost a case of history repeating itself . . . for though the voice and the words are new— the structure, form, and development of the refrain are those of Phrenology."[19] Another medical historian had added a timely admonition, warning us that their endings may also be identical: "Our modern theories, based on the concept of the unconscious, are no less hypothetical than their predecessors and are bound to become obsolete."[20] And, indeed, when we learn that traditional concepts of the brain and its diseases are continually being revised and disproved, we are left amid all the uncertainties with but one certainty—the still uncomprehended relationship that does exist between body and mind, between exterior and interior, a relationship that lies at the core of phrenology.

Not phrenology alone but the various related aspects of Fowlerism linger on, often assuming strange disguises. Claude Lévi-Strauss, the distinguished French ethnologist and "father of structuralism," uses in *The Savage Mind* illustrations reminiscent of the comparative physiognomy profiles that adorn the Fowler textbooks.[21] A sociologist scanning Karl Menninger's *The Crime of Punishment* might well be reminded of the similar and earlier indictment of our penal system agitated by a firm of phrenologists-publishers.[22] Riffling through the Hammacher Schlemmer catalogue of *Mid-Winter Specialties*, a shopper attracted by the turbojet or the nonelectric whirl-a-bath might harken back to those worshipers of cold water who followed the Fowler brand of hydropathy.[23] A historian reading in Graham Greene's *The Comedians* that "vegetarianism and conscientious objection . . . go together"[24] might well recall the devotees of bran bread who assembled at Fowler headquarters and launched an ill-fated settlement in Kansas. An occasional visitor to the duodecagon House of Tomorrow at the Chicago World's Fair of 1933 might have been reminded of an octagonal house of yesterday built by an amateur architect named Orson Fowler whose work foreshadowed that of Louis Sullivan, Frank Lloyd Wright, and Buckminster Fuller.[25]

The work of the Fowlers has been caught in yet another net—the net of the collector. The Fowler edition of Walt Whitman has become a highly valuable property, and the firm's phrenological publications are in demand among antiquarians. The phrenological heads they manufactured adorn the show windows of antique dealers and have become expensive conversation pieces on the coffee tables of connoisseurs. Modern imitations, available for thirty-five dollars from the Pentone Company, makers of "handcrafted originals," are used for advertising displays.[26]

The family that cried in the nineteenth-century wilderness for vocational guidance and sex education, penal reform and the understanding of the insane, the rights of women and the rights of children, have come at last into their own. Even the Cohocton annual Fall Foliage Festival now honors its sons by including among its attractions a Fowler Dinner.[27] In their native place the prophets of reform have been honored. There are modern analogues of Fowlerism in today's liberal thinking; their ideas have filtered into the stream of progress.

Still disdained by most scientists as erroneous, the Fowler version of phrenology nevertheless sustains a creative function. Dr. Iago Galdston has described as "a theme worthy of the medical historians . . . *the creative function of the erroneous idea.*"[28] Phrenology's creative uses have been to enunciate the localization of function in the brain, to stimulate the study of the brain as the organ of the mind, to free science for the investigation of physiological psychology.[29]

But the discarded nineteenth-century science of mind has still another, less scientific but perhaps more vital, creative function. No idea ever survives in a vacuum. Phrenology, like every other medical sect or pseudo-medical fad, is inextricably related to the age in which it flowered. Those who wave it aside as a fad or an eccentricity should be referred to Oscar Handlin's pregnant observation:

> The quacks and cultists dealt with important issues of life and death, sex and family, knowledge and tradition, and the proper order of society. Their garbled messages answered genuine questions in a mobile and disorderly society which lacked firm roots and which suffered from the shocks of change in science and economic organization. In some ways their strivings for meaning came closer to the truth as we now see it than did the staid answers of more conventional men.[30]

To understand thoroughly the nineteenth century, sociologist and historian, philosopher and literary critic must also understand phrenology, for that philosophy of mind is interwoven with the society, the thought, and the literature of a vanished era. To understand its literary giants—Poe, Whitman, and even, though to a lesser degree, Mark Twain—we must understand the allusions of phrenology. To appreciate fully certain nineteenth-century cartoons and newspaper reports, we must comprehend the vocabulary of phrenology, for it enriched the language of that century. To trace with intelligence the multitudinous reforms of the age, we must go to the phrenological source of those reforms. In the final analysis, no other single philosophy encompasses so well the motive force of that exhilarating time when man was a sovereign individual who could cross all frontiers, the molder of his own mind who could attain perfectibility. For its documentary importance alone, the study of phrenology becomes a productive pursuit, opening the mind of twentieth-century man to the spirit of the age that went before.[31]

Otherwise that spirit is all but lost to us, for we have become disenchanted. We have shed our belief in the perfectibility of everyman, and our disillusionment with phrenology is, in the end, our disillusionment with ourselves.

NOTES ON SOURCES

. . . .

INTRODUCTION

1. Arthur M. Schlesinger, *New Viewpoints in American History* (New York, [1961]), 215, citing James Russell Lowell in his essay on Thoreau (1865).

2. Charles Caldwell, *Autobiography* (Philadelphia, 1855), 201 f.; Orson S. Fowler, *Physiology, Animal and Mental* (New York, 1847), *Education and Self-Improvement*, I, 112.

3. A. Boardman, *A Defence of Phrenology* (New York, 1855), 23f.; Eric T. Carlson, "The Influence of Phrenology on Early American Psychiatric Thought," Department of Psychiatry, Cornell University Medical College Center, 2.

4. Robert E. Riegel, "Early Phrenology in the United States," *Medical Life*, Vol. XXXVII, No. 7 (July, 1930), 361–76; J. Collins Warren, "The Collection of the Boston Phrenological Society—A Retrospect," *Annals of Medical History*, Vol. III, No. 1 (Spring, 1921), 1–11.

5. *The American Phrenological Journal and Miscellany* (hereinafter *Phrenological Journal*), Vol. III, No. 4 (January 1, 1841), 186; B. H. Coates, *Biographical Notice of Charles Caldwell, M.D.* (Philadelphia, 1855), 3 and *passim*; R. W. Haskins, *History and Progress of Phrenology* (Buffalo, 1839), 105; Riegel, "Early Phrenology in the United States," *loc. cit.*, 365.

6. Frances Trollope, *Domestic Manners of the Americans* (London and New York, 1832), 71. For an early American satire of phrenology, see [James Kirke Paulding], *The Merry Tales of the Three Wise Men of Gotham* (New York, 1826), in which Dr. Gallgotha is lampooned.

7. Nahum Capen, *Reminiscences of Dr. Spurzheim and George Combe* (New York, 1881), 8, 25, and *passim*; J. G. Spurzheim, *Phrenology in connexion with the Study of Physiognomy* (Boston, 1833), *passim*.

8. Andrew Carmichael, *A Memoir of the Life and Philosophy of Spurzheim* (Boston, 1833), v.

9. George Combe, *An Address delivered at the Anniversary Celebration of the Birth of Spurzheim* (Boston, 1840), 4; George Combe, *Elements of Phrenology* (Boston, 1835), iii; L. N. Fowler, *Synopsis of Phrenology and Physiology* (Boston, 1845), back cover; O. S. and L. N. Fowler, *The Illustrated Self-Instructor in Phrenology and Physiology* (New York, n.d.), 10f.

10. O. S. and L. N. Fowler assisted by Samuel Kirkham, *Phrenology Proved, Illustrated, and Applied* (New York, 1837), 251; Samuel R. Wells, *New Physiognomy, or Signs of Character* (New York, 1875), 601.

11. Nelson Sizer and Henry S. Drayton, *Heads and Faces, and How To Study Them* (New York, 1892), 118.

12. Harriet Martineau, *Retrospect of Western Travel* (London, 1838), III, 201.

13. Carmichael, *op. cit.*, v.

14. T. L. Nichols, *Forty Years of American Life* (London, 1874), 32.

CHAPTER I

The Family

1. W. W. Clayton, *History of Steuben County, New York* (Philadelphia, 1879), 238; Orson S. Fowler, *Creative and Sexual Science* (n.p., n.d.), 776.

2. Orson S. Fowler, *Hereditary Descent* (published at end of *Phrenological Journal*, Vol. V, 1843), 446 and *passim*; Adolf Growoll Collection, American Book Trade History (courtesy R. R. Bowker Co.), XIII, 30; Clyde Ray Jones, "Orson Squire Fowler Practical Phrenologist 1809–1887," Master's Thesis, State University of New York College at Oneonta, at its Cooperstown Graduate Programs, 1965, p. 13.

3. O. S. Fowler, *Creative and Sexual Science*, 70; O. S. Fowler,

Hereditary Descent, loc. cit., 450; O. S. Fowler, *Human Science or Phrenology* (n.p., n.d.), 617.

4. Clayton, *op. cit.*, 243; O. S. Fowler, *Creative and Sexual Science*, 895; O. S. Fowler, *Hereditary Descent, loc. cit.*, 566; *Phrenological Journal*, Vol. 78, No. 3 (March, 1884), 175.

5. Lorenzo N. Fowler, "Thinkers, Authors, Speakers," [*Lectures*] (London, n.d.), 16; O. S. Fowler, *Creative and Sexual Science*, 776; O. S. Fowler, *A Home For All or The Gravel Wall and Octagon Mode of Building* (New York, 1854), 189f. (hereinafter Fowler, *Home*; all subsequent page references in notes are to this revised edition); O. S. Fowler, *Self-Culture and Perfection of Character* (New York, 1847), *Education and Self-Improvement*, II, 179f., 309; Millard Roberts, *Historical Gazetteer of Steuben County, New York* (Syracuse, 1891), 238; Information from Esther Bower Snyder, Cohocton, N.Y.

6. Hamilton Child, *Gazetteer and Business Directory of Steuben County, N.Y., for 1868-9* (Syracuse, 1868), 91 f.; Clayton, *op. cit.*, 237f., 240f.; Jones, *op. cit.*, 12.

7. O. S. Fowler, *Human Science*, 615.

8. O. S. Fowler, *Creative and Sexual Science*, 631; O. S. Fowler, *Self-Culture*, 82.

9. O. S. Fowler, *Creative and Sexual Science*, 835f.

10. *Amherst College Biographical Record of the Graduates and Non-Graduates* (Amherst, Mass., 1939), # 368, 30; Walter A. Dyer, "The Amazing Career of Orson Fowler," *Amherst Graduates' Quarterly*, Vol. XXXIV, No. 1 (November, 1944), 2; Spencer Miller, Jr., *Rev. Moses Miller of Heath, Massachusetts* [South Orange, N.Y., 1932], 2-7.

11. Clayton, *op. cit.*, 243.

12. O. S. Fowler, *Hereditary Descent, loc. cit.*, 458.

13. *Ibid.*, 567; *Temperance Recorder*, Vol. III, No. 8 (October, 1834), 60f.

14. Horace N. Fowler, *The Industrial Public* (Los Angeles, 1921), 65f.; "New York Physicians. Edward Payson Fowler, M.D.," *The National Magazine*, Vol. XIX, Nos. 4-5 (February–March, 1894), 315; *Phrenological Journal*, Vol. 109, No. 2 (February, 1900), 46.

15. Carl Carmer, "That Was New York: The Fowlers, Practical Phrenologists," *The New Yorker*, Vol. XII (February 13, 1937), 26; *Phrenological Journal*, Vol. 122, No. 12 (December, 1909), 399.

16. Orson S. Fowler, *Fowler's Practical Phrenology* (New York, n.d.), 29f.

17. [Samuel Hopkins Emery], *The Life of Samuel Hopkins Emery Begun as an Autobiography Completed by Ralph Davol* (Taunton, Mass., 1901), 34; "Heman Humphrey," *DAB*; Alice M. Walker, *Historic Homes of Amherst* (Amherst, Mass., 1905), 92 (courtesy Miss Rena Durkan, Curatrix, Edward Hitchcock Memorial Room, Amherst College).

18. O. S. Fowler, *Human Science*, 615f.; O. S. Fowler, *Physiology, Animal and Mental*, 235; Jones, *op. cit.*, 17.

19. O. S. Fowler and L. N. Fowler assisted by S. Kirkham, *op. cit.*, 256.

20. "Charles Baker Adams," *DAB*; [George R. Cutting], *Student* [Emery], *op. cit.*, 23f., 26; Edward Hitchcock, *Reminiscences of Life at Amherst College* (Amherst, Mass., 1871), 13f., 25f., 57f., 135; *Amherst College* (Northampton, Mass., 1863), 74.

21. Harriet Beecher Stowe, *Men of Our Times* (Hartford, 1868), 529ff.

22. William C. Beecher and Rev. Samuel Scoville, *A Biography of Rev. Henry Ward Beecher* (New York, 1888), 130; [Cutting], *op. cit.*, 59; John D. Davies, *Phrenology Fad and Science: A 19th-Century American Crusade* (New Haven, 1955), 31; Walter Dyer, "Henry Ward Beecher in College," *Amherst Graduates' Quarterly*, Vol. XXIII, No. 3 (May, 1934), 188f. (courtesy Miss Rena Durkan, Amherst College); Claude Moore Fuess, *Amherst: The Story of a New England College* (Boston, 1935), 113; Paxton Hibben, *Henry Ward Beecher: An American Portrait* (New York, [1927]), 58; *Phrenological Journal*, Vol. 47, No. 6 (June, 1868), 211, Vol. 84, No. 5 (May, 1887), 240, Vol. 92, No. 5 (November, 1891), 200; Nelson Sizer, *Forty Years in Phrenology* (New York, 1888), 12f.; Samuel R. Wells, *The Illustrated Annuals of Phrenology and Physiognomy for the Years 1865–[187]3* (New York, n.d.) [1871], 22.

23. Henry Ward Beecher, *Yale Lectures on Preaching* (New York, 1881), I, 94; L. N. Fowler, "How to Succeed in the World," *Lectures on Man, as explained by Phrenology, Physiology, Physiognomy, and Ethnology* (London, 1864), 11; O. S. Fowler, *Human Science*, 213f.; *Phrenological Journal*, Vol. XI, No. 4 (April, 1849), 137ff. The suggestion made by James R. Newhall in *The Legacy of an Octogen-*

arian (Lynn, Mass., 1897), 49, that Fowler may have attended a lecture by Dr. Charles Caldwell as early as 1828 is probably erroneous.

24. O. S. Fowler, *Love and Parentage, applied to the Improvement of Offspring* (n.p., [1844]), 16n.; *Phrenological Journal*, Vol. IV, No. 1 (January 1, 1842), 3, Vol. V, No. 4 (April, 1843), 229.

25. John C. Holbrook, *Recollections of a Nonagenarian* (Boston and Chicago, [1897]), 47; information from Mr. Barrows Mussey, Duesseldorf, Germany.

26. "Fifty Years of Phrenology. A Review of Our Past and Our Work," *Phrenological Journal*, Vol. 80, No. 1 (January, 1885), 10; L. N. Fowler, "How to Live," [*Lectures*] (London, [1866]), 1; *Professor L. N. Fowler. A Sketch* (London, [1886]), 3; *Phrenological Journal*, Vol. 68, No. 1 (January, 1879), 9f.; Sizer and Drayton, *op. cit.*, advertisement at end.

27. H. N. Fowler, *The Industrial Public*, 67.

28. "Fifty Years of Phrenology," *loc. cit.*, 13; *Phrenological Journal*, Vol. 96, No. 4 (April, 1893), 167, Vol. 99, No. 2 (February, 1895), 145, Vol. 112, No. 1 (July, 1901), 1f.

29. "Institute Extra," No. 16 (March, 1887), *Phrenological Journal*, Vol. 84, No. 2 (February, 1887), 1f.

30. H. W. Beecher, *op. cit.*, I, 96.

31. O. S. Fowler, "Temptation—Its influence on guilt," For the Commencement at Amherst College, August 27, 1834, MS (courtesy Miss Rena Durkan, Amherst College).

32. O. S. Fowler, *Human Science*, 897.

CHAPTER II
O. S. and L. N. Fowler

1. O. S. Fowler, *Human Science*, 213f.
2. Davies, *op. cit.*, 33.
3. Riegel, "Early Phrenology in the United States," *loc. cit.*, 365.
4. For the method of giving a phrenological analysis, see L. N. Fowler, "How to Read Character," *Lectures on Man*, 13ff.; L. N. Fowler, *The Principles of Phrenology and Physiology applied to Man's Social Relations* (New York and Boston, 1842), 73ff., 76; O. S. Fowler, *Fowler's Practical Phrenology*, 253f.; O. S. Fowler, *Human Science*, 205f., 291; O. S. and L. N. Fowler, *The Illustrated*

Self-Instructor in Phrenology, passim; [O. S. and L. N. Fowler], *New Illustrated Self-Instructor in Phrenology and Physiology* (New York, 1877), 168ff.; O. S. Fowler, *Phrenological Chart* (Baltimore, 1836), *passim*; *A Phrenological Guide, designed for Students of Their Own Character* (New York, 1845), *passim*; *Phrenological Journal*, Vol. IV, No. 1 (January 1, 1842), 14f., 18, Vol. IV, No. 5 (May, 1842), 128f., Vol. V, No. 8 (August, 1843), 356f.; Sizer and Drayton, *op. cit.*, 9, 20–30, 89f., 152, 154f., 178; [Samuel R. Wells], *How To Read Character* (New York, 1871), iii, 37f., 120–29; Wells, *New Physiognomy*, 564f. A typical early reading is that in L. N. Fowler, "Phrenological Character of Mr —— Nov. 30th 1838" (MS, Harvard College Library).

5. "Institute Extra," *loc. cit.*, 2f.

6. *Uncle Sam's Letters on Phrenology to His Millions of Friends in America* (New York and London, 1896), 23.

7. Boardman, *op. cit.*, 75f.; *Phrenological Journal*, Vol. V, No. 1 (January, 1843), 31.

8. *Phrenological Journal*, Vol. V, No. 8 (August, 1843), 354.

9. L. N. Fowler, "Tact and Talent," [*Lectures*], 2; *Phrenological Journal*, Vol. 96, No. 2 (August, 1893), 107.

10. L. N. Fowler, "Objections to Phrenology Considered and Answered," *Lectures on Man*, 1; L. N. Fowler, "Perfection of Character," [*Lectures*], 1; O. S. Fowler, *Fowler's Practical Phrenology*, 409f.; O. S. Fowler, *Phrenological Chart*, 2n.; O. S. Fowler, *Phrenological Controversy. Answer to Vindex* (Baltimore, 1835), *passim*.

11. Margaret Fuller to her mother, Margaret Crane Fuller, Providence, November 18, 1837 (Houghton Library, Harvard University); Madeleine B. Stern, *The Life of Margaret Fuller* (New York, 1942), 160.

12. Elizabeth Ruth Hosmer, "Science and Pseudo-Science in the Writings of Nathaniel Hawthorne," Ph.D. Dissertation, University of Illinois, 1948, 36.

13. Charles Neider (ed.), *The Autobiography of Mark Twain* (New York, [1959]), 64.

14. For details regarding these itinerant phrenologists, see Davies, *op. cit.*, 37; L. N. Fowler, *The Illustrated Phrenological Almanac For 1850* (New York, [1850]), 24, 33; L. N. Fowler, *The Phrenological Almanac for 1842* (New York, [1842]), 10, 42; O. S. Fowler, *Fowler's*

Practical Phrenology, 322, 324f., 343; O. S. Fowler, *Human Science*, 511, 1086; [H. R. Howard], *Pictorial Life and Adventures of John A. Murrell* (Philadelphia, 186?), iii f.; Thomas Huston Macbride, *In Cabins and Sod-Houses* (Iowa City, 1928), 42f.; Ross Phares, *Reverend Devil: A Biography of John A. Murrell* (New Orleans, [1941]), 196, 256; *Phrenological Journal*, Vol. III, No. 9 (June 1, 1841), 407, 430f., Vol. III, No. 12 (September 1, 1841), 547ff., Vol. IV, No. 8 (August, 1842), 205ff., Vol. 65, No. 4 (October, 1877), 268; James Harvey Young, *The Toadstool Millionaires* (Princeton, 1961), 44.

15. Clara Barton, *The Story of My Childhood* (New York, 1907), 110–15. See also "Clara Barton," *DAB*; William E. Barton, *The Life of Clara Barton* (Boston and New York, 1922), I, 46–50; Percy H. Epler, *The Life of Clara Barton* (New York, 1932), 18.

16. H. N. Fowler, *The Industrial Public*, 66; information from Mr. Paul J. Howe, Ridgewood, New Jersey.

17. Jones, *op. cit.*, 23.

18. J. Millott Severn, *The Life Story and Experiences of a Phrenologist* (Brighton, Eng., 1929), 105. For Orson's manner, see also *Phrenological Journal*, Vol. V, No. 8 (August, 1843), 355, Vol. 122, No. 11 (November, 1909), 368.

19. O. S. Fowler, *Human Science*, 222; Thomas Sewall, *An Examination of Phrenology* (Washington, D.C., 1837), 66.

20. For Orson's work in Washington, see O. S. Fowler, *Fowler's Practical Phrenology*, 30, 297f.; *Phrenological Journal*, Vol. IV, No. 8 (August, 1842), 201f.

21. O. S. Fowler, *Fowler's Practical Phrenology*, 29.

22. Grace Adams and Edward Hutter, *The Mad Forties* (New York and London, [1942]), 74f.; James O'Donnell Bennett and Everett L. Millard, *The Mask of Fame The Heritage of Historical Life Masks Made by John Browere, 1825 to 1833* (n.p., [1938]), *passim*; *Catalogue of Portraits, Busts, and Casts, in the Cabinet of The American Institute of Phrenology* (New York, 1879), 4; L. N. Fowler, *The Phrenological Developments and Characters of J. V. Stout, the Sculptor, and Fanny Elssler, the Actress* (New York, 1841), iii; O. S. Fowler, *Human Science*, 1043n.; O. S. Fowler, *Self-Culture*, 283n.; Orson S. Fowler to J. G. Percival, New Haven, August 10, 1838 (Beinecke Library, Yale University); Charles Henry Hart, *Browere's Life Masks of Great Americans* (New York, 1898), *passim*; Charles

Henry Hart, "Unknown Life Masks of Great Americans, *McClure's Magazine*, Vol. IX, No. 6 (October, 1897), 1053–61; *Phrenological Chart; presenting a Synopsis of the Science* [New York, 1840]; *Phrenological Journal*, Vol. III, No. 4 (January 1, 1841), 189.

23. For Brevoort and the Philadelphia office, see *The Boston Medical and Surgical Journal*, Vol. XXII, No. 22 (July 8, 1840), 353; George Combe, *Notes on the United States of North America* (Edinburgh, 1841), II, 238; O. S. Fowler, *Synopsis of Phrenology* (Philadelphia, [1838]), *passim*; O. S. Fowler to J. G. Percival, August 10, 1838; Jones, *op. cit.*, 24f.; Philadelphia directories 1839, 1840; *Phrenological Journal*, Vol. II, No. 12 (September 1, 1840), 544, Vol. 122, No. 11 (November, 1909), 366.

24. Nathan Allen, *An Essay on the Connection of Mental Philosophy with Medicine* (Philadelphia, 1841), 4; "Nathan Allen," *DAB*; Davies, *op. cit.*, 58; "Fifty Years of Phrenology," *loc. cit.*, 19ff.; Adolf Growoll Collection, American Book Trade History, VI, 28; "History of Phrenology," incomplete typescript, Fowler Family Papers, Collection of Regional History, Cornell University; Jones, *op. cit.*, 41; Frank Luther Mott, *A History of American Magazines, 1741–1850* (Cambridge, Mass., 1957), 447f.; D. N. Patterson, "Life and Character of Nathan Allen, M.D., LL.D.," *Contributions of The Old Residents' Historical Association, Lowell, Mass.*, Vol. IV, No. 2 (August, 1889), 151–63; *Phrenological Journal*, Vol. I, No. 1 (October 1, 1838), prospectus of Vol. I, Vol. III, No. 12 (September 1, 1841), 576, Vol. IV, No. 1 (January 1, 1842), 1ff., Vol. V, No. 8 (August, 1843), 355f., Vol. 37, No. 1 (January, 1863), 17, Vol. 66, No. 3 (March, 1878), 121ff. At the beginning, the Reverend J. A. Warne was employed as editor "at a salary of $1000 per year, or $2000 if it cleared that sum." Orson adds [*Phrenological Journal*, Vol. IV, No. 10 (October, 1842), 314f.]: "I was then persuaded to change my original plan of 48 duodecimo pages per month, at $1,00 to that of 32 *octavo* pages per month, and $2,00 per year. . . . Wishing the Journal to stand on its own merits, so that the public might not be influenced either way by my connexion with it, I gave the publisher, A. Waldie, $500 per vol. for his *name alone*, as publisher. My brother soon joined me as part proprietor . . . .

"30,000 copies of the prospectus, and 5,000 extra copies of No. 1, were circulated gratis at an enormous expense, and nearly $1000 was paid to *writers* for the first volume, besides the salaries of the Editor and Publisher, and the stereotyping, paper, and printing.

"As soon as the first No. was issued, Mr. Warne resigned, leaving the Journal committed to the public, but without an editor."

25. *Phrenological Journal*, Vol. IV, No. 10 (October, 1842), 314ff.

26. *Ibid.*, Vol. V, No. 6 (June, 1843), 278f., Vol. V, No. 7 (July, 1843), 303f., Vol. V, No. 8 (August, 1843), 354, Vol. 96, No. 5 (November, 1893), 248f.

27. Jones, *op. cit.*, 30; Amy Pearce Ver Nooy, "More About Orson Fowler," *Dutchess County Historical Society Year Book*, Vol. 34 (1949), 101.

28. "Fifty Years of Phrenology," *loc. cit.*, 13; Adolf Growoll Collection, American Book Trade History, XIII, 30; *Phrenological Journal*, Vol. IV, No. 10 (October, 1842), 315f.

29. O. S. Fowler, *Creative and Sexual Science*, 1037; O. S. Fowler, *Human Science*, 383.

30. George Combe, *An Address delivered at the Anniversary Celebration of the Birth of Spurzheim*, 3; George Combe, *Lectures on Phrenology* (New York, 1839), v.

31. *Phrenological Journal*, Vol. 91, No. 6 (June, 1891), 256f., Vol. 96, No. 1 (July, 1893), 55, Vol. 100, No. 6 (December, 1895), 294.

32. Sizer, *Forty Years*, 181.

33. Gilbert H. Barnes and Dwight L. Dumond (eds.), *Letters of Theodore Dwight Weld, Angelina Grimké Weld, and Sarah Grimké, 1822–1844* (New York and London, [1934]), II, 529; Boardman, *op. cit.*, 55; Julia Ward Howe, *Reminiscences 1819–1899* (Boston, 1900), 132f.; John Morley, *The Life of Richard Cobden* (London, 1881), I, 121 and *passim*; *Phrenological Journal*, Vol. III, No. 10 (July 1, 1841), 480; Harold Schwartz, *Samuel Gridley Howe, Social Reformer, 1801–1876* (Cambridge, Mass., 1956), 93; S. R. Wells to Dr. [Samuel Gridley] Howe, New York, March 30, 1849 (S. G. Howe Papers, Houghton Library, Harvard University).

34. Boardman, *op. cit.*, 46, 48, and *passim*.

35. *Phrenological Journal*, Vol. IV, No. 1 (January 1, 1842), 1f., 5.

36. *The Boston Medical and Surgical Journal*, Vol. XVI, No. 21 (June 28, 1837), 355; Card, "New-York Phrenological Rooms 286 Broadway" (Landauer Collection, New York Historical Society); "Institute Extra," *loc. cit.*, 2; [*New York*] *Evening Post* (January 2, 1838), [2].

37. *Bulletin of the Mercantile Library of New York*, Vol. IV, No. 26 (March, 1967), 359; Davies, *op. cit.*, 47; "Fifty Years of Phrenology," *loc. cit.*, 30; O. S. Fowler, *Fowler's Practical Phrenology*, 255n.; "Institute Extra," *loc. cit.*, 2; Mercantile Library Association MS Reports, July 10, 1846; New York City directories 1837, 1839–40;*Phrenological Journal*, Vol. XIX, No. 3 (March, 1854), 72; Wells, *The Illustrated Annuals of Phrenology* [1871], 22.

38. O. S. Fowler, *Fowler's Practical Phrenology*, 368ff.

39. James Freeman Clarke, *Autobiography, Diary, and Correspondence* (Boston and New York, 1899), 49.

40. *Phrenological Journal*, Vol. IV, No. 1 (January 1, 1842), 7.

CHAPTER III

Phrenological Panaceas

1. O. S. Fowler, *Self-Culture*, 85; *Phrenological Journal*, Vol. 122, No. 11 (November, 1909), 366.

2. *Phrenological Journal*, Vol. VI (1844), "Miscellany," 23.

3. Wells, *New Physiognomy*, iii.

4. *Phrenological Journal*, Vol. XI (1849), "The American Phrenological Journal for 1849," 12.

5. O. S. Fowler, *Self-Culture*, iii, 118.

6. O. S. Fowler, *Fowler on Memory: or, Phrenology Applied to the Cultivation of Memory* (New York, 1842), 29 and *passim*; O. S. Fowler, *Human Science*, 1054; O. S. Fowler, *Memory and Intellectual Improvement* (New York, 1846), *Education and Self-Improvement*, III, 88, 90; O. S. Fowler, *Phrenological Journal Extra. Fowler on Memory* (New York, 1842), preliminary page; O. S. Fowler, *Phrenology and Physiology applied to the Cultivation of Memory* [New York, 1842], *passim*; O. S. Fowler, *Phrenology and Physiology explained and applied to Education and Self-Improvement* (New York, 1842), 107.

7. Merle Curti, *The Social Ideas of American Educators* (New York, [1935]), 111, 122; L. N. Fowler, "Education," [*Lectures*], 1; L. N. Fowler, "How to Train Up A Child," *Lectures on Man*, 12, 19; L. N. Fowler, *The Illustrated Phrenological Almanac For 1850*, 20; L. N. Fowler, *The Illustrated Phrenological Almanac 1855* (New York, [1855]), 22; O. S. Fowler, *Memory and Intellectual Improve-*

ment, 45; O. S. Fowler, *Self-Culture*, 301; *The New-York Institute for the Physical and Mental Training of Imbecile, Idiotic, Backward . . . Children* [New York, 185?], *passim* (courtesy Miss Gertrude L. Annan, former Librarian, New York Academy of Medicine); *Phrenological Journal*, Vol. VII, No. 6 (June, 1845), 183, Vol. VIII, No. 4 (April, 1846), 124f., Vol. XXXIII, No. 1 (January, 1861), 13; Sizer and Drayton, *op. cit.*, 121; Wells, *The Illustrated Annuals of Phrenology* [*1867*], 41.

8. L. N. Fowler, *The Illustrated Phrenological Almanac 1855*, 45; L. N. Fowler, "Thinkers, Authors, Speakers," [*Lectures*], 16; L. N. Fowler, *Phrenological Almanac 1860* (New York, [1860]), 26; O. S. and L. N. Fowler, *New Illustrated Self-Instructor in Phrenology and Physiology* (New York, [1859]), 176, advertisement at end; O. S. Fowler, *Self-Culture*, 115; *Phrenological Journal*, Vol. XV, No. 2 (February, 1852), 42; Sizer and Drayton, *op. cit.*, 187; [Nelson Sizer], *My Right Place in Life, and How To Find It* (New York, 1888), 2; Charlotte Fowler Wells, Lecture on Phrenology at New Brighton, MS, Fowler Family Papers, Collection of Regional History, Cornell University.

9. Charles Bray, *How to Educate the Feelings or Affections* (New York, 1883), 7f.; Davies, *op. cit.*, 93f., 102; L. N. Fowler, "Tact and Talent," [*Lectures*], 2; *Phrenological Journal*, Vol. I, No. 5 (February 1, 1839), 155f.; Gilbert Seldes, *The Stammering Century* (New York, [1965]), 311.

10. L. N. Fowler to John Bigelow, New York, June 2, 1846, John Bigelow Papers, State Prisons, 1836–55, MS Division, New York Public Library.

11. John Bigelow to C. H. Halsey, August 12, 1846, John Bigelow Papers, New York Public Library; George Combe, *Capital Punishment: or, the Proper Treatment of Criminals* (New York, 1873), iv and *passim;* Rev. Charles H. Halsey to Mrs. E. W. Farnham, Sing Sing, August 3, 1846, John Bigelow Papers, New York Public Library; Dr. Leiter to Rev. Mr. Morse, New York City, August 4, 1846, John Bigelow Papers, New York Public Library; W. Davis Lewis, *From Newgate To Dannemora: The Rise of the Penitentiary in New York, 1796–1848* (Ithaca, 1965), 233–50; *Phrenological Journal*, Vol. IV, No. 10 (October, 1842), 314; *The Phrenological and Physiological Almanac for 1849* (New York, [1849]), 31; *The Prisoners' Friend: A Monthly*

Magazine, Vols. I–II (1849–50); M. B. Sampson, *Criminal Jurisprudence considered in Relation to Mental Organization* (London, 1841), *passim*; M. B. Sampson, *Rationale of Crime* (New York, 1846), xx; Madeleine B. Stern, "Two Letters from the Sophisticates of Santa Cruz," *The Book Club of California Quarterly News-Letter*, Vol. XXXIII, No. 3 (Summer, 1968), 51–62.

12. Andrew Combe, *Observations on Mental Derangement* (Boston, 1834), *passim*; Davies, *op. cit.*, 93; Pliny Earle, *Memoirs*, ed. by F. B. Sanborn (Boston, 1898), 150 and n.; L. N. Fowler, *The Illustrated Phrenological Almanac 1855*, 21; O. S. Fowler, *Physiology, Animal and Mental*, 43; *Phrenological Journal*, Vol. I, No. 5 (February 1, 1839), 155ff.; Sizer and Drayton, *op. cit.*, 16f.

13. O. S. Fowler, *Fowler on Memory*, 78f.; [Samuel R. Wells], *How To Read Character*, vii.

14. Sidney Ditzion, *Marriage Morals and Sex in America* (New York, [1953]), 339f.; L. N. Fowler, "Love, Courtship, and Marriage," *Lectures on Man*, 4, 17; L. N. Fowler, *Marriage: Its History and Ceremonies* (New York, 1847), 196 and *passim*; L. N. Fowler, *The Principles of Phrenology and Physiology applied to Man's Social Relations*, 69, 72f., 86, 88, 95f., and *passim*; L. N. Fowler, "Tact and Talent," [*Lectures*], 5; L. N. Fowler, "Utility of Phrenology," *Lectures on Man*, 2; O. S. Fowler, *Amativeness: or Evils and Remedies of Excessive and Perverted Sexuality* (New York, 1848), *passim*; O. S. Fowler, *Creative and Sexual Science*, 441, 449, 452; O. S. Fowler, *Fowler on Matrimony* (New York, 1842), 77 and *passim*; O. S. Fowler, *Love and Parentage*, 1, 26, 35, and *passim*; O. S. Fowler, *Matrimony; or Phrenology and Physiology applied to the selection of Companions for Life* (London, 1843), 50, 54, and *passim*; O. S. Fowler, *Memory and Intellectual Improvement*, 151n.; Jesse W. Goodrich, *The Phrenological Organs: The Phrenological Character: (as marked, and given by Prof. O. S. Fowler,) together with . . . Occasional Poems, and Prose Writings* (n.p., 1855), *passim*; *Phrenological Journal*, Vol. VI (1844), 112, Vol. VII, No. 11 (November, 1845), 374ff., Vol. VIII, No. 9 (September, 1846), 289, Vol. X (1848), 262, Vol. XVIII, No. 6 (December, 1853), 137, Vol. 37, No. 1 (January, 1863), 22; Sizer and Drayton, *op. cit.*, 180; Wells, *New Physiognomy*, 568.

15. For these beliefs as well as the general Fowler attitude toward reform, see L. N. Fowler, *The Principles of Phrenology*, 39f., 84f.;

Phrenological Journal, Vol. IV, No. 1 (January 1, 1842), 7, Vol. IV, No. 2 (February 1, 1842), 41–44, Vol. IV, No. 6 (June, 1842), 150, Vol. IV, No. 8 (August, 1842), 197, Vol. IV, No. 10 (October, 1842), 281, Vol. VI (1844), "Miscellany," 23 and 112, Vol. XI (1849), "The American Phrenological Journal for 1849," 10ff.; *The Water-Cure Journal*, Vols. XI–XII (1851), title verso.

16. L. N. Fowler, *The Principles of Phrenology*, 81, 104f., 107–15, 121–24; O. S. Fowler, *The Evils of Tight Lacing* (n.p., n.d.), *passim*; O. S. Fowler, *Matrimony*, vii, 38; O. S. Fowler, *Phrenology and Physiology explained and applied to Matrimony* (New York, [1842]), "The Evils of Tight Lacing," *passim*; O. S. Fowler, *Physiology, Animal and Mental*, 206f.; O. S. Fowler, *Tight-Lacing, or the Evils of Compressing the Organs of Animal Life* (n.p., [1849]), *passim*; *Phrenological Journal*, Vol. V, No. 2 (February, 1843), 49; *Water-Cure Journal*, Vol. IX, No. 5 (May, 1850), 137.

17. *Water-Cure Journal*, Vol. VII, No. 4 (April, 1849), 120; *Works on Tobacco . . . by Several Distinguished Writers* (New York, [1849]), *passim*.

18. L. N. Fowler, *The Principles of Phrenology*, 57; O. S. Fowler, *Phrenology* versus *Intemperance. A Lecture* (Philadelphia, 1841), [3], 32, and *passim*; O. S. Fowler, *Temperance, Founded on Phrenology and Physiology* (New York, 1842) and (n.p., [1849]), *passim*; O. S. Fowler, *Temperance and a Prohibitory Law as Enforced by Phrenology and Physiology* (New York, [185?]), 5 and *passim*; J. C. Furnas, *The Life and Times of The Late Demon Rum* (London, 1965), 82f.; *Phrenological Journal*, Vol. III, No. 5 (February 1, 1841), 239.

19. William A. Alcott, *A System of Vegetable Diet* (New York, 1850), 111f., 193f., 285, and *passim*; *The Boston Medical and Surgical Journal*, Vol. XLV, No. 15 (November 12, 1851), 316f.; Gerald Carson, *Cornflake Crusade* (New York and Toronto, [1957]), 49f.; Davies, *op. cit.*, 109; "Fifty Years of Phrenology," *loc. cit.*, 26f.; "Sylvester Graham," *DAB*; Russell Hickman, "The Vegetarian and Octagon Settlement Companies," *The Kansas Historical Quarterly*, Vol. II, No. 4 (November, 1933), 377f.; *The Illustrated Vegetarian Almanac for 1855* (New York, 1855), *passim*; Nichols, *op. cit.*, 34; *Phrenological Journal*, Vol. VII, No. 2 (February, 1845), 62; Richard H. Shryock, "Sylvester Graham and the Popular Health Movement, 1830–1870,"

The Mississippi Valley Historical Review, Vol. XVIII, No. 2 (September, 1931), *passim*; John Smith, *Fruits and Farinacea* (New York, 1854), *passim*; *Water-Cure Journal*, Vol. IX, No. 5 (May, 1850), 157, Vol. X, No. 1 (July, 1850), 5f., Vol. XII, No. 5 (November, 1851), 110f., Vol. XVII, No. 3 (March, 1854), 59.

20. O. S. Fowler, *Physiology, Animal and Mental*, 91 ff.

21. Adams and Hutter, *op. cit.*, 31, 37, 41; Davies, *op. cit.*, 110, 112f.; "Fifty Years of Phrenology," *loc. cit.*, 24ff.; L. N. Fowler, "Thinkers, Authors, Speakers," [*Lectures*], 8; *Fowlers and Wells' Water-Cure Library . . . in Seven Volumes* (New York, 1850–[1851]), *passim*; *The Illustrated Water-Cure Almanac for 1854* (New York, [1854]), 22 and *passim, for 1857* (New York, [1857]), *passim*; Jones, *op. cit.*, 71f.; *The Knickerbocker*, Vol. XXXV, No. 1 (January, 1850), 76f.; Mott, *A History of American Magazines 1741–1850*, 441; Nichols, *op. cit.*, 34; [H. F. Phinney (ed.)], *The Water-Cure in America* (New York, 1852), *passim*; *Phrenological Journal*, Vol. VII, No. 12 (December, 1845), 409, Vol. X (1848), 199, Vol. XXII, No. 5 (November, 1855), 100f., Vol. 65, No. 6 (December, 1877), 394ff.; J. H. Rausse, *The Water-Cure applied to Every Known Disease* (New York, 1851), *passim*; Joel Shew, *The Cholera, Its Causes, Prevention, and Cure* (New York, 1849), [5]; Joel Shew, *The Hydropathic Family Physician* (New York, [1854]), *passim*; R. T. Trall, *The Bath: Its History and Uses in Health and Disease* (New York, 1876), *passim*; *Water-Cure Journal*, Vols. VII–XXII, XXIX–XXX (1849–56, 1860), *passim* (courtesy Mr. Harold Celnick, New York) [see especially Vol. VIII, No. 1 (July, 1849), 18, Vol. VIII, No. 4 (October, 1849), 113, Vol. IX, No. 1 (January, 1850), 24, Vol. IX, No. 5 (May, 1850), 157, Vol. X, No. 1 (July, 1850), 30, Vol. X, No. 2 (August, 1850), 71, Vol. X, No. 3 (September, 1850), 130]; Harry B. Weiss and Howard R. Kemble, *The Great American Water-Cure Craze* (Trenton, New Jersey, 1967), *passim*; James Wilson and James Manby Gully, *The Practice of the Water-Cure* (New York, 1852), *passim*.

CHAPTER IV
"Self-Made or Never Made"

1. Appletons' *Cyclopædia of American Biography*, VI, 431; George W. Bungay, *Traits of Representative Men* (New York, [1882]),

196f., 201; "Fifty Years of Phrenology," *loc. cit.*, 13ff.; *New-York Daily Tribune* (April 14, 1875), 7; *Phrenological Journal*, Vol. 60, No. 6 (June, 1875), 352; *The Science of Health*, Vol. VII, No. 37 (July, 1875), 6f.; Sizer and Drayton, *op. cit.*, advertisement at end; Albert Welles, *History of the Welles Family* (New York, 1876), 170–73; S. R. Wells, *The Illustrated Annual of Phrenology and Physiognomy 1871* (New York, [1871]), 22f.; "Samuel Roberts Wells," *DAB*.

2. O. S. and L. N. Fowler, *The Phrenological Almanac and Physiological Guide, for . . . 1845* (New York, [1845]), 39–44; Will Gardner, *The Clock That Talks and What It Tells: A Portrait Story of the Maker: Hon. Walter Folger, Jr.* (Nantucket Island, Mass., [1954]), *passim.*

3. *Professor L. N. Fowler. A Sketch,* 10f.; Mrs. L. N. Fowler, *Familiar Lessons on Astronomy* (New York, 1850), iv and *passim*; O. S. Fowler, *Hereditary Descent, loc. cit.*, 435, 569f.; Gardner, *op. cit.*, 121; Kate Campbell Hurd-Mead, *Medical Women of America* (New York, 1933), 41; *New-York Times* (February 10, 1879), 3; *Phrenological Journal*, Vol. 68, No. 3 (March, 1879), 159; Nelson Sizer, *How to Study Strangers by Temperament, Face, and Head* (New York, 1895), 148ff.; *Vital Records of Nantucket, Massachusetts, to the Year 1850* (Boston, 1925–27), I, 490; Frederick C. Waite, "Dr. Lydia Folger Fowler," *Annals of Medical History*, N.S. Vol. IV, No. 3 (May, 1932), 293f., 297; Wells, *New Physiognomy*, 560.

4. *Phrenological Journal*, Vol. 68, No. 6 (June, 1879), 288–92.

5. *Vital Records of Nantucket*, III, 479.

6. *Phrenological Journal*, Vol. VII, No. 12 (December, 1845), 405f. See also *ibid.*, Vol. VIII, No. 1 (January, 1846), 31f., Vol. VIII, No. 12 (December, 1846), 388ff., Vol. 60, No. 6 (June, 1875), 352f.; Wells, *The Illustrated Annual of Phrenology*, [*1871*], 23.

7. L. N. Fowler, "How to Succeed in the World," *Lectures on Man*, 16.

8. *Phrenological Journal*, Vol. XXVI, No. 6 (December, 1857), 118.

9. Jones, *op. cit.*, 26, 44; New York City directories 1842–50; *Phrenological Journal*, Vol. IV, No. 5 (May, 1842), 137.

10. For the Cabinet, see *The Boston Medical and Surgical Journal*, Vol. XXX, No. 12 (April 24, 1844), 247; *Catalogue of Portraits, Busts, and Casts*, 1 and *passim*; Davies, *op. cit.*, 48–51; L. N. Fowler, "Proofs

of Phrenology," *Lectures on Man*, 13; O. S. Fowler, *Memory and Intellectual Improvement*, 193; New York City directory 1847–48, advertisement opp. p. 154; *Phrenological Journal*, Vol. V, No. 6 (June, 1843), 284, Vol. IX (1847), 39, Vol. X (1848), 129f., 260; Sizer, *Forty Years*, 291.

11. *Catalogue of Portraits, Busts, and Casts*, prelim. page.

12. *New-York Daily Tribune* (September 18, 1849), [2]; *Phrenological Journal*, Vol. V, No. 6 (June, 1843), 283ff., Vol. X (1848), 134.

13. Adams and Hutter, *op. cit.*, 142f.; Karl M. Dallenbach, "Phrenology versus Psychoanalysis," *The American Journal of Psychology*, Vol. LXVIII, No. 4 (December, 1955), 518; Ditzion, *op. cit.*, 338f.; L. N. Fowler, *The Principles of Phrenology*, 33; O. S. Fowler, *Matrimony*, 17; R. B. D. Wells, *A New Illustrated Hand-Book of Phrenology Physiology and Physiognomy* (London, n.d.), 161.

14. L. N. Fowler, *Synopsis of Phrenology and Physiology*, 10. See also O. S. and L. N. Fowler, *The Phrenological and Physiological Almanac for 1846* (New York, [1846]), advertisement.

15. Alcott, *op. cit.*, advertisement at end; Davies, *op. cit.*, 48; L. N. Fowler, *Phrenological Almanac 1860* (New York, [1860]), 28; New York City directory 1847–48, advertisement; J. Smith, *op. cit.*, advertisement at end.

16. For details of the Fowler analyses, charts, and subjects examined, see Davies, *op. cit.*, 47f.; L. N. Fowler, *The Phrenological Developments . . . of J. V. Stout, . . . and Fanny Elssler, passim*; L. N. Fowler, *The Phrenological and Physiological Almanac for 1847* (New York, [1847]), 26ff.; *Professor L. N. Fowler. A Sketch*, 8; O. S. Fowler, *Human Science*, 276f., 1108; [O. S. and L. N. Fowler], *New Illustrated Self-Instructor in Phrenology, passim*; O. S. and L. N. Fowler, *The Phrenological and Physiological Almanac for 1846*, advertisement; O. S. Fowler, *Synopsis of Phrenology* (New York, 1849), *passim*; *Phrenological Journal*, Vol. V, No. 8 (August, 1843), 357, Vol. IX (1847), 269, 351, 361–65, Vol. 96, No. 1 (January, 1893), 11, Vol. 101, No. 1 (January, 1896), 18f.; Sizer and Drayton, *op. cit.*, 164.

17. O. S. Fowler, Phrenological Description of John Brown, New York, Feb. 27th, 1847 (John Brown, Jr., Papers, The Ohio Historical Society, Columbus, Ohio).

18. Besides the books themselves, see Andrew Combe, *The Princi-*

ples of Physiology Applied to the Preservation of Health ... to which is added, Notes and Observations, By O. S. Fowler (New York, 1844), xf.; O. S. Fowler, *Hereditary Descent, loc. cit.*, 567; O. S. Fowler, *Human Science*, 617; O. S. Fowler, *Matrimony*, xif.; O. S. Fowler, *Physiology, Animal and Mental*, iii; *Phrenological Journal*, Vol. VI (1844), "Miscellany," 112.

19. O. S. Fowler, *Hereditary Descent, loc. cit.*, 566.

20. *American Journal of Insanity*, Vol. V (January, 1849), 280f.; Waite, "Dr. Lydia Folger Fowler," *loc. cit.*, 294.

21. Fowler, *Hereditary Descent, loc. cit.*, 450. For further details regarding the Fowlers' full days, see Dutchess County Court House, Liber 78, 377–78 (Indenture between Joseph H. Jackson and Eliza Fowler, October 8, 1842); L. N. Fowler, *The Illustrated Phrenological Almanac for 1854* (New York, [1854]), [21]; O. S. Fowler, *Human Science*, 849; O. S. Fowler, *Memory and Intellectual Improvement*, 194; Jones, *op. cit.*, 25–28, 30; New York City directory 1847–48, advertisement; *Phrenological Journal*, Vol. IV, No. 10 (October, 1842), 299, Vol. V, No. 4 (April, 1843), 229, Vol. V, No. 7 (July, 1843), 336, Vol. V, No. 8 (August, 1843), 356, Vol. VI (1844), "Miscellany," 23, 112, Vol. VII, No. 1 (January, 1845), 25, Vol. VII, No. 3 (March, 1845), 93, Vol. VII, No. 12 (December, 1845), 405, Vol. VIII, No. 1 (January, 1846), 31, Vol. XII, No. 6 (June, 1850), 195f., Vol. 66, No. 6 (June, 1878), 285n.

22. Besides the publications themselves, see Alcott, *op. cit.*, advertisement at end; *The Boston Medical and Surgical Journal*, Vol. XXXV, No. 23 (January 6, 1847), 482; A. Combe, *The Principles of Physiology*, xi; George Combe, Robert Cox, and Others, *Moral and Intellectual Science: applied to the Elevation of Society* (New York, 1848), iv; Davies, *op. cit.*, 55; Ditzion, *op. cit.*, 341; Milton Drake, *Almanacs of the United States* (New York, 1962), *passim*; L. N. Fowler, *The Phrenological and Physiological Almanac for 1847*, cover; *Phrenological Journal*, Vol. VIII, No. 1 (January, 1846), 30, Vol. X (1848), 260, Vol. XVII, No. 4 (April, 1853), 95.

23. *Phrenological Journal*, Vol. IV, No. 2 (February 1, 1842), 41, Vol. IV, No. 10 (October, 1842), 318f., Vol. VII, No. 3 (March, 1845), 94, Vol. VIII, No. 1 (January, 1846), 30, Vol. VIII, No. 4 (April, 1846), 125, Vol. VIII, No. 12 (December, 1846), 388ff., Vol. IX (1847), 39, Vol. X (1848), 40.

CHAPTER V

Poe and the Glory That Was Clinton Hall

1. Otto L. Bettmann, *A Pictorial History of Medicine* (Springfield, Ill., [1956]), 215; Charles Caldwell, *Facts in Mesmerism* (Louisville, 1842), xxi; H. S. Drayton, *Human Magnetism* (New York, 1889), *passim*; "Mesmerism," *Ciba Symposia*, Vol. IX, No. 11 (March–April, 1948), 841, 851, and *passim*.

2. Pliny Earle, *Memoirs*, 59n.; *The Magnet*, Vol. I, No. 1 (June, 1842), *passim*; Harriet Martineau, *Miss Martineau's Letters on Mesmerism* (New York, 1845), 4, 27; T. L. Nichols, *op. cit.*, 32f.; *Spiritual Philosopher*, Vol. I, No. 1 (July, 1850), *passim*; Taylor Stoehr, "Hawthorne and Mesmerism" (1968), *passim*, Typescript, courtesy Mr. Taylor Stoehr, State University of New York at Buffalo.

3. O. S. Fowler, *Human Science*, 600.

4. L. N. Fowler, *Facts About Mesmerism* (London, [1886], 11–16; *Phrenological Journal*, Vol. IV, No. 7 (July, 1842), 185, Vol. IV, No. 8 (August, 1842), 215, Vol. V, No. 2 (February, 1843), 67ff., Vol. VII, No. 8 (August, 1845), 288.

5. Robert H. Collyer, *Lights and Shadows of American Life* (Boston, [1838?]), 17; Robert H. Collyer, Psychography (New York, [1843]), *passim*; Drayton, *Human Magnetism*, 120, 122; O. S. Fowler, *Human Science*, 204f.; *Phrenological Journal*, Vol. IV, No. 3 (March 1, 1842), 81, Vol. IV, No. 4 (April 1, 1842), 118, Vol. IV, No. 7 (July, 1842), 185, Vol. IV, No. 8 (August, 1842), 215ff., Vol. IV, No. 10 (October, 1842), 316f., Vol. V, No. 1 (January, 1843), 23n., Vol. VIII, No. 4 (April, 1846), 126; Robert E. Riegel, *Young America, 1830–1840* (Norman, [1949]), 333f.; Seldes, *op. cit.*, 313f.

6. Quoted in *Phrenological Journal*, Vol. V, No. 6 (June, 1843), 276.

7. George Combe, *A System of Phrenology* (New York, 1876), 363f.; Robert Macnish, *The Philosophy of Sleep* (New York, 1835), *passim*; *Phrenological Journal*, Vol. V, No. 7 (July, 1843), 336, Vol. 51, No. 4 (October, 1870), 249; Sizer and Drayton, *op. cit.*, 17.

8. Justus Liebig, *Chemistry, and its Application to Physiology, Agriculture, and Commerce* (New York, 1847), back cover.

9. L. N. Fowler, *The Illustrated Phrenological Almanac* 1855, 34; L. N. Fowler, *Mental Science, as explained by Phrenology* (London,

1896), 13; O. S. Fowler, *Memory and Intellectual Improvement*, 223; *Phrenological Journal*, Vol. XI (1849), 14, Vol. XI, No. 11 (November, 1849), 337–40; Sizer and Drayton, *op. cit.*, 188.

10. Madeleine B. Stern, "Poe: 'The Mental Temperament' for Phrenologists," *American Literature*, Vol. XL, No. 2 (May, 1968), 155–63.

11. *Library of Mesmerism and Psychology. Comprising Philosophy of Mesmerism, Electrical Psychology, on Fascination, the Macrocosm, Science of the Soul* (New York, [1885]), *passim*.

12. Davies, *op. cit.*, 130; *Phrenological Journal*, Vol. IV, No. 7 (July, 1842), 187, Vol. XI, No. 5 (May, 1849), 151.

13. *Phrenological Journal*, Vol. VII, No. 9 (September, 1845), 304, 306–11.

14. *Ibid.*, Vol. VII, No. 10 (October, 1845), 345; Stern, "Poe: 'The Mental Temperament' for Phrenologists," *loc. cit.*, 162f.

15. Edward Hungerford, "Poe and Phrenology," *American Literature*, Vol. II, No. 3 (March, 1931), 211–31; Sidney E. Lind, "Poe and Mesmerism," *Publications of the Modern Language Association*, Vol. LXII, No. 4 (December, 1947), 1077–94; Stern, "Poe: 'The Mental Temperament' for Phrenologists," *loc. cit.*, 155f.

16. L. N. Fowler, *The Illustrated Phrenological Almanac for 1851* (New York, [1851]), 24f.

17. *Phrenological Journal*, Vol. XII, No. 3 (March, 1850), 87f., Vol. XIII, No. 2 (February, 1851), 34.

18. L. N. Fowler, "Tact and Talent," [*Lectures*], 10; Sizer, *How to Study Strangers*, 83; Nelson Sizer, *The Royal Road to Wealth* (New York and San Francisco, 1883), 314; Wells, *New Physiognomy*, 524f., 527.

19. *Catalogue of Portraits, Busts, and Casts*, 26.

20. P. L. Buell and N. Sizer, *A Guide to Phrenology* (Woodstock, Vt., 1842), *passim*; "Fifty Years of Phrenology," *loc. cit.*, 17ff.; Lillian Hubbard Holch, *Sizer Genealogy* (Brooklyn, 1941), 231, 240; *New-York Daily Tribune* (October 19, 1897), 7; *New York Times* (October 19, 1897), 7; *Phrenological Journal*, Vol. IV, No. 10 (October, 1842), 318, Vol. VII, No. 11 (November, 1845), 374ff., Vol. XXXVIII, No. 6 (December, 1863), 164ff., Vol. 43, No. 6 (June, 1866), 173f., Vol. 67, No. 3 (September, 1878), 166f., Vol. 75, No. 1 (July, 1882), 16–19, Vol. 93, No. 6 (June, 1892), 259–62, Vol. 96,

No. 6 (June, 1893), 298, Vol. 98, No. 5 (November, 1894), 217–20, Vol. 104, No. 6 (December, 1897), 251–53, Vol. 105, No. 5 (May, 1898), 162; Nelson Sizer, *Cupid's Eyes Opened, and Mirror of Matrimony* (Hartford, 1848), iii; Sizer, *Forty Years*, 181f., and *passim*; Sizer, *How to Study Strangers*, 75; "Nelson Sizer," *DAB*; *Vital Records of Chester Massachusetts to the Year 1850* (Boston, 1911), 89.

21. *Phrenological Journal*, Vol. 101, No. 6 (June, 1896), 49f., Vol. 104, No. 2 (August, 1897), 87.

22. *Ibid.*, Vol. 97, No. 3 (March, 1894), 136.

23. *Appletons', Cyclopædia of American Biography* III, 396; "Fifty Years of Phrenology," *loc. cit.*, 23f., 27f.; John W. Moore, *Moore's Historical, Biographical, and Miscellaneous Gatherings . . . relative to Printers* (Concord, N.H., 1886), 552f.; *Phrenological Journal*, Vol. 91, No. 5 (May, 1891), 200f.

24. D. H. Jacques, *The Temperaments* (New York, 1878), 191f. and plate opp. p. 192.

25. *A Complete Catalogue of Works for Shorthand Writers and Typewriters* (New York, n.d.), *passim*; "Fifty Years of Phrenology," *loc. cit.*, 30; L. N. Fowler, *The Illustrated Phrenological Almanac 1855*, 21; *Phrenological Journal*, Vol. VII, No. 11 (November, 1845), 381, Vol. VIII, No. 1 (January, 1846), 61, Vol. VIII, No. 7 (July, 1846), 218, Vol. IX (1847), 178f., Vol. XII, No. 1 (January, 1850), 35, Vol. 103, No. 3 (March, 1897), 112; *The Universal Phonographer*, Vol. I, No. 3 (March, 1852), *passim*; E. Webster, *The Phonographic Teacher* (New York, 1854), advertisement at beginning.

26. For details regarding the spread and acceptance of phrenology, see H. W. Beecher, *Yale Lectures*, I, 93–96; *The Boston Medical and Surgical Journal*, Vol. XXXV, No. 23 (January 6, 1847), 482; J. G. Buckley, *An Epitome of Phrenology* (Springfield, Ohio, 1848), *passim*; Merle Curti, *The Growth of American Thought* (New York, [1964]), 332f.; Davies, *op. cit.*, 52f.; Ditzion *op. cit.*, 339; Carl Russell Fish, *The Rise of the Common Man* (New York, 1927), 245; L. N. Fowler, *The Illustrated Phrenological Almanac for 1850*, 46; Denton Offutt, *A New and Complete System of Teaching the Horse. On Phrenological Principles* (Cincinnati, 1848), cited in *Charles Hamilton Auction Catalogue* No. 22 (New York, October 25, 1967), Item 15; *Phrenological Journal*, Vol. VII, No. 6 (June, 1845), 183, Vol. X (1848), 380, 387, 392, Vol. XI (1849), 70, 191, 193, 232, 263,

Vol. XII, No. 1 (January, 1850), 35, Vol. XII, No. 6 (June, 1850), 195, Vol. XIV, No. 6 (December, 1851), 134, Vol. XXI, No. 6 (June, 1855), 121, Vol. 84, No. 5 (May, 1887), 240; R. C. Rutherford, *A Synopsis of Phrenology* (Conneaut, Ohio, 1848), *passim*; Seldes, *op. cit.*, 315; Sizer, *Forty Years*, 229, 231, 241f., 348; Nelson Sizer to John Brown, Jr., New York, July 18, 1851 (Ohio Historical Society, Columbus, Ohio); Stowe, *op. cit.*, 532; [Samuel Roberts Wells], *Hand-Book for Home Improvement, How to Do Business* (New York, 1875), 137.

27. For details of the continued scorn of and hostility to phrenology, see Boardman, *op. cit.*, *passim*; Collyer, *op. cit.*, *passim*; Walter Edgerton, *A Brief Review of Certain Phrenological Works of O. S. Fowler* (Newport, Iowa, 1848), [3] and *passim*; O. S. Fowler, *The Christian Phrenologist* (Cazenovia, N.Y., 1843), *passim*; O. S. Fowler, *Human Science*, 224n., 225; O. S. Fowler, *Phrenology Defended: or Answer to Dr. Frank H. Hamilton's Attack upon Phrenology* (New York, 1842), *passim*; O. S. Fowler, *Religion; Natural and Revealed* (New York, 1844), 15; Frank H. Hamilton, *Lecture on Phrenology* (Rochester, 1841), 29 and *passim*; *The Ladies' Repository*, Vol. VII, No. 1 (January, 1847), 30; *Phrenological Journal*, Vol. IV, No. 10 (October, 1842), 298, Vol. V, No. 7 (July, 1843), 331f., Vol. VII, No. 3 (March, 1845), 95, Vol. VIII , No. 4 (April, 1846), 126, Vol. X (1848), 163; David Meredith Reese, *Humbugs of New-York* (New York, 1838), 77f.; Nathan L. Rice, *Phrenology Examined* (New York, 1849), 19f. and *passim*; Robert E. Riegel, "The Introduction of Phrenology to the United States," *The American Historical Review*, Vol. XXXIX, No. 1 (October, 1933), 78; Riegel, *Young America*, 333; Seldes, *op. cit.*, 316.

28. *Phrenological Journal*, Vol. XI (1849), 323; Phrenology. Broadside poster for Dr. J. Haynes cited in *Swann Galleries, Inc. Sale Catalogue No. 697 (American Posters and Broadsides)*, New York, March 3, 1966, Item 225.

29. For details of the Fowlers' success, see Davies, *op. cit.*, 55f.; Fowler, *Hereditary Descent, loc. cit.*, 567; *New-York Times* (August 20, 1887), 5; *Phrenological Journal*, Vol. VIII, No. 1 (January, 1846), 30, Vol. XI (1849), 385, Vol. XVIII, No. 1 (July, 1853), 19; *Water-Cure Journal*, Vol. IX, No. 4 (April, 1850), 128.

30. O. S. Fowler, *A Home For All*, iii; Sizer, *Forty Years*, 229f.

CHAPTER VI

The Octagon House

1. Dutchess County Court House, Liber 78, 377f.; Jones, *op. cit.*, 29, 75f.; Amy Pearce Ver Nooy, " 'Fowler's Folly,' and Its Builder," *Dutchess County Historical Society Year Book*, Vol. 33 (1948), 50, 66. For Fishkill, see [T. Van Wyck Brinckerhoff], *Historical Sketch and Directory of the Town of Fishkill* (Fishkill Landing, N.Y., 1866), *passim*; *Peekskill, Fishkill . . . Their Representative Business Men, and Points of Interest* (Newark, 1892), 44.

2. O. S. Fowler, *Home*, iii.

3. *Phrenological Journal*, Vol. XII, No. 8 (August, 1850), 252.

4. Andrew Jackson Davis, *Memoranda of Persons, Places, and Events* (Boston and New York, 1868), 42.

5. Walter Creese, "Fowler and the Domestic Octagon," *The Art Bulletin*, Vol. XXVIII, No. 2 (June, 1946), 89; Davies, *op. cit.*, 117 and n. 21; Henry-Russell Hitchcock, *American Architectural Books* (Minneapolis, 1946), No. 465 (later editions are cited in Nos. 466–72); *Holden's Dollar Magazine*, Vol. I, No. 5 (May, 1848), 307.

6. Fowler, *Home*, iii.

7. *Ibid.*, 138.

8. *Godey's Lady's Book*, Vol. 49 (October, 1854), 337. For other descriptions of the house, contemporary and later, see Turpin C. Bannister, "The Architecture of the Octagon in New York State," *New York History*, Vol. XXVI, No. 1 (January, 1945), 48; John Bullock, *The American Cottage Builder* (New York, 1854), 192; Carl Carmer, *The Hudson* (New York and Toronto, [1939]), 272–79; Carmer, "That Was New York: The Fowlers," *The New Yorker*, Vol. XII (February 13, 1937), 26; Davies, *op. cit.*, 115ff.; Stewart H. Holbrook, *Dreamers of the American Dream* (Garden City, N.Y., 1957), 46f.; Clay Lancaster, *Architectural Follies in America* (Rutland, Vt. [1960]), 134, 137, 139; *Poughkeepsie Sunday Courier* (August 21, 1887 and May 27, 1894); Ver Nooy, " 'Fowler's Folly,' " *loc. cit.*, 50–82.

9. Fowler, *Home*, 10, 12.

10. Nelson Sizer to John Brown, Jr., New York, July 18, 1851 (Ohio Historical Society).

11. Fowler, *Home*, 13.

12. *Ibid.*, 65.

13. Jones, *op. cit.*, 29ff.; United States Federal Census, Fishkill Township, Dutchess County, New York, August 16, 1850, Fowler Family #1433, House #1038 (National Archives), Roll 496, p. 96 R.

14. Carl F. Schmidt, *The Octagon Fad* (Scottsville, N.Y., 1958), 3.

15. Carl Carmer, "The Octagonal Home," *Town & Country*, Vol. 94, No. 4199 (April, 1939), 68ff.; Creese, *op. cit.*, 92, 96, 99; Davies, *op. cit.*, 115 n. 20; Dyer "The Amazing Career of Orson Fowler," *loc. cit.*, 7f.; Fanny Hale Gardiner, "The Octagon House," *Country Life in America*, Vol. XXIII, No. 5 (March, 1913), 79f.; Clay Lancaster, "Some Octagonal Forms in Southern Architecture," *The Art Bulletin*, Vol. XXVIII, No. 2 (June, 1946), 108, 111; Frank J. Metcalf, "Octagon Houses of Washington and Elsewhere," *Records of the Columbia Historical Society*, Vol. 26 (1924), 91, 93.

16. Fowler, *Home*, iv, 82, 88.

17. For Goodrich, his building material, and Fowler's use of it, see Harry Ellsworth Cole, *Stagecoach and Tavern Tales of the Old Northwest*, ed. by Louise Phelps Kellogg (Cleveland, 1930), 126ff.; Charles P. Dwyer, *The Economic Cottage Builder* (Buffalo, 1856), 44; Fowler, *Home*, 16–26 and *passim*; *Phrenological Journal*, Vol. XII, No. 8 (August, 1850), 248ff.; W. A. Titus, "The First Concrete Building in the United States," *The Wisconsin Magazine of History*, Vol. XXIV, No. 2 (December, 1940), 183–88.

18. Fowler, *Home*, 16, 20.

19. *Ibid.*, 52f.

20. *Phrenological Journal*, Vol. XII, No. 12 (December, 1850), 383.

21. Fowler, *Home*, 55.

22. For this and other modern conveniences, see Creese, *op. cit.*, 98; Fowler, *Home*, 136f., 149, 151; Jones, *op. cit.*, 83; Lancaster, *op. cit.*, 139; Bertha Kitchell Whyte, *Wisconsin Heritage* (Boston, [1954]), 107.

23. For the various activities, visitors, lectures at Fowler's residence, see Creese, *op. cit.*, 101; Davies, *op. cit.*, 116f.; *Fishkill Journal* (August 5, 1854), [3]; Fowler, *Home*, 125; O. S. Fowler, *Human Science*, 776; Jones, *op. cit.*, 31; "Lectures on Phrenology and Physiology by O. S. Fowler," 4-page brochure, Landauer Collection, New York Historical Society; *Phrenological Journal*, Vol. XVIII, No. 1 (July, 1853), 22; Ver Nooy, " 'Fowler's Folly,' " *loc. cit.*, 53, 64; Weiss and Kemble, *op. cit.*, 82.

24. For the influence of his book and the octagon fad, see Wayne Andrews, *Architecture, Ambition, and Americans* (New York, [1955]), 124f.; Z. Baker, *The Cottage Builder's Manual* (Worcester, 1856), 165f.; Carl Carmer, "Fowler Was Right," *New York History*, Vol. XXXIII, No. 2 (April, 1952), 211–20; *The Harbinger*, Vol. VIII, No. 2 (November 11, 1848), 14; Holbrook, *op. cit.*, 47f.; D. H. Jacques, *The House: A Manual of Rural Architecture* (New York, 1867), v; *Life Illustrated*, Vol. I, No. 7 (December 15, 1855), 53, Vol. VIII, No. 10 (July 2, 1859), 77, Vol. IX, No. 14 (January 28, 1860), 107; "New York Home of Mark Twain," *International Herald Tribune* (May 25, 1967), 16; "New York's Octagons," *North Country Life*, Vol. VII, No. 1 (Winter, 1953), 4, 9; *Phrenological Journal*, Vol. XII, No. 9 (September, 1850), 292, Vol. XIX, No. 4 (April, 1854), 96, Vol. XXI, No. 3 (March, 1855), 67, Vol. XXI, No. 5 (May, 1855), 110f., 116; Frank J. Roos, Jr., *Writings on Early American Architecture* (Columbus, 1943), 15, 19; Ruby M. Rounds, *Octagon Buildings in New York State* (Cooperstown, N.Y., 1954), 3; Schmidt, *op. cit., passim.*

25. *Phrenological Journal*, Vol. XIX, No. 4 (April, 1854), 96.

26. Fowler, *Home*, 109; Nelson Sizer to John Brown, Jr., New York, September 6, 1852 (Ohio Historical Society); Ver Nooy, " 'Fowler's Folly,' " *loc. cit.*, 78. If this chapter has any special forcefulness it is owing to the fact that it was written in an octagonal shaped study.

27. For the later history and end of the house, see Bannister, *op. cit.*, 49; Carmer, *The Hudson*, 278f.; Carmer, "That Was New York," *loc. cit.*, 27; Creese, *op. cit.*, 100f.; Davies, *op. cit.*, 56, 174; Dutchess County Court House, Liber 110, 230–32 (Indenture between Orson S. Fowler and William A. Riker, September 14, 1857); *Fishkill Standard* (August 14, 1897), 2 (courtesy G. Marion Davies, Librarian, The Howland Circulating Library Company, Beacon, N.Y.); *Fishkill Weekly Times* (April 2, 1890, September 16, 1896, August 11, 1897), courtesy Mr. Clyde Ray Jones, Cooperstown, N.Y.; Jones, *op. cit.*, 31, 85ff.; *Poughkeepsie Daily Eagle* (June 26, 1862); *Poughkeepsie Sunday Courier* (May 27, 1894); Schmidt, *op. cit.*, 65; Ver Nooy, " 'Fowler's Folly,' " *loc. cit.*, 76f., 80f.

28. *Fishkill Weekly Times* (April 2, 1890).

CHAPTER VII

Walt Whitman, Care of Fowler and Wells

1. *Brooklyn Daily Eagle* (November 16, 1846), 2. For further details of Whitman's early interest in phrenology, see Gay Wilson Allen, *The Solitary Singer* (New York, 1955), 81, 103; Newton Arvin, *Whitman* (New York, 1938), 156; information from Professor Harold Aspiz, Department of English, California State College at Long Beach; William L. Finkel, "Sources of Walt Whitman's Manuscript Notes on Physique," *American Literature*, Vol. XXII, No. 3 (November, 1950), 308–31; Edward F. Grier, "Walt Whitman's Earliest Known Notebook," *Publications of the Modern Language Association*, Vol. 83, No. 5 (October, 1968), 1455f.; Edward Hungerford, "Walt Whitman and His Chart of Bumps," *American Literature*, Vol. II, No. 4 (May, 1931), 357ff.; Walt Whitman, *The Gathering of the Forces* (New York and London, 1920), II, 304; Walt Whitman, *The Uncollected Poetry and Prose* (New York, 1932), I, 127f., n. 2.

2. *Brooklyn Daily Eagle* (March 10, 1847), 1.

3. *Ibid.*, (March 12, 1847), 2.

4. [Walt Whitman], *Leaves of Grass* (Brooklyn, 1855, Facsimile Edition), comments and reviews at end.

5. Charles E. Feinberg, "A Whitman Collector Destroys a Whitman Myth," *The Papers of the Bibliographical Society of America*, Vol. 52, No. 2 (1958), 80.

6. O. S. Fowler, *Hereditary Descent, loc. cit.*, 552 and n.

7. O. S. Fowler, *Creative and Sexual Science*, 70; *Phrenological Journal*, Vol. X (1848), 81.

8. Walt Whitman, *The Complete Writings* (New York and London, [1902]), VII, 54 ("Good-Bye My Fancy"). See also Emory Holloway, *Whitman* (New York and London, 1926), 25; Frederik Schyberg, *Walt Whitman* (New York, 1951), 49.

9. [Richard Maurice Bucke]. *Manuscripts, Autograph Letters, First Editions, and Portraits of Walt Whitman Formerly the Property of the Late Dr. Richard Maurice Bucke . . . Sale Number 4251*, American Art Association, Anderson Galleries, Inc. (New York, 1936), 5, # 12; Ellen Frances Frey, *Catalogue of the Whitman Collection in the Duke University Library . . . Trent Collection* (Dur-

ham, N.C., 1945), 66f., # 24; Clarence Gohdes and Rollo G. Silver (eds.), *Faint Clews & Indirections: Manuscripts of Walt Whitman and His Family* (Durham, N.C., 1949), [233]–36; Hungerford, "Walt Whitman," *loc. cit.*, 363 and *passim*. See also Henry Bryan Binns, *A Life of Walt Whitman* (London, [1905]), 67f.; Holloway, *op. cit.*, 25f.; Horace L. Traubel, Richard Maurice Bucke, Thomas B. Harned (eds.), *In Re Walt Whitman* (Philadelphia, 1893), 25 and n.; "Walt Whitman," *DAB*. The chart of Whitman's faculties as given here, cited from Hungerford, differs slightly from the list of forty-nine characteristics and faculties printed at the end of the phrenological description in *Faint Clews & Indirections*. Did Whitman possibly alter the text?

10. Feinberg, *op. cit.*, 81 ff.

11. Mott, *A History of American Magazines 1850–1865*, 100 f.; *Phrenological Journal*, Vol. XIV, No. 5 (November, 1851), 119; *The Student: A Family Miscellany and Monthly School-Reader*, Vols. I–VI (1850–53), *passim*; R. T. Trall, *The New Hydropathic Cook-Book* (New York, 1854), advertisement for *The Student* at end; *Water-Cure Journal*, Vol. IX, No. 5 (May, 1850), 156.

12. Feinberg, *op. cit.*, 82; notation at foot of bill to Walter Whitman from Fowlers & Wells, New York, August 30, 1851 (courtesy Mr. Charles E. Feinberg, Detroit, Michigan).

13. *Ibid.*; bill to W. Whitman from Fowlers & Wells, June 27, 1851 (courtesy Mr. Charles E. Feinberg).

14. According to Professor Harold Aspiz, this is merely "a mini-pamphlet . . . incorporated in toto within Dr. Trall's *The Hydropathic Encyclopedia*."

15. Walt Whitman, *Leaves of Grass* (Garden City, N.Y., 1928), 143.

16. [Bucke]. *op. cit.*, 5, # 12; Hungerford, "Walt Whitman," *loc. cit.*, 363 n. 39, 366; Thayer and Eldridge, *Leaves of Grass Imprints* (Boston, 1860), 32; Horace Traubel, *With Walt Whitman in Camden (March 28–July 14, 1888)* (Boston, 1906), I, 385.

17. Whitman, *Leaves of Grass* (1928 ed.), 293 ("By Blue Ontario's Shore").

18. Harold Aspiz, "Educating the Kosmos: 'There Was a Child Went Forth,'" *American Quarterly*, Vol. XVIII, No. 4 (Winter, 1966), 655–66; Harold Aspiz, "Unfolding the Folds," *Walt Whit-*

man Review, Vol. XII, No. 4 (December, 1966), 81–87; Richard Maurice Bucke (ed.), *Notes and Fragments: Left by Walt Whitman* (n.p., 1899), 81f., 205ff.; Emory Holloway, "Walt Whitman's Love Affairs," *The Dial*, Vol. LXIX (November, 1920), 473–83; Hungerford, "Walt Whitman," *loc. cit.*, 367f. and *passim*; Walt Whitman, *An American Primer* (Boston, 1904), 27; Whitman, *Leaves of Grass*, (1928 ed.), 100 ("Not Heaving From My Ribb'd Breast Only"), 399 ("Mediums"), 497 (preface to 1855 edition), 617 (Variorum Readings).

19. *Phrenological Journal*, Vol. XXI, No. 1 (January, 1855), 1.

20. Moncure Daniel Conway, *Autobiography Memories and Experiences* (Boston and New York, 1904), I, 215f.

21. Holloway, *op. cit.*, 117.

22. *New-York Daily Tribune* (July 6, 1855–August 4, 1855, September 25, 1855–November 24, 1855, February 18, 1856–March 1, 1856), 1. For further details regarding the sale of the first edition, see Ralph Adimari, "Leaves of Grass—First Edition," *The American Book Collector*, Vol. V, Nos. 5–6 (May–June, 1934), 150f.; Allen, *op. cit.*, 149, 151; *First Books by American Authors, 1765–1964* (New York, Seven Gables Bookshop, 1965), Item # 304; Hungerford, "Walt Whitman," *loc. cit.*, 355f., 366, 368 n. 59; Honor McCusker, "Leaves of Grass First Editions and Manuscripts in the Whitman Collection," *More Books*, Vol. XIII, No. 5 (May, 1938), 180f.; Frank Luther Mott, *Golden Multitudes* (New York, 1947), 110f.; Horace Traubel, *With Walt Whitman in Camden January 21 to April 7, 1889* (Philadelphia, 1953), IV, 152; Walt Whitman, *Leaves of Grass, Reproduced from the First Edition (1855), with an introduction by Clifton Joseph Furness* (New York, 1939), vif., xi, xiii.

23. John Burroughs, *Notes on Walt Whitman, as Poet and Person* (New York, 1867), 15f.

24. *New-York Daily Tribune* (July 23, 1855), 3.

25. Whitman reviewed himself in "Walt Whitman and His Poems," *The United States Review*, Vol. 36 (September, 1855), 205–12. As Hungerford points out ("Walt Whitman," *loc. cit.*, 368f.), Whitman printed his "chart of bumps" in his own anonymous review in the *Brooklyn Daily Times* (September 29, 1855). See also Walt Whitman, *New York Dissected* (New York, 1936), 6.

26. *Phrenological Journal*, Vol. XXII, No. 4 (October, 1855), 90f.

27. Ralph L. Rusk (ed.), *The Letters of Ralph Waldo Emerson* (New York, 1939), IV, 520. For details regarding Emerson's letter, see Jacob Blanck, *Bibliography of American Literature* (New Haven, 1959), III, # 5225; Conway, *op. cit.*, I, 215ff.; Charles E. Feinberg, *Walt Whitman: A Selection of the Manuscripts, Books, and Association Items Gathered by Charles E. Feinberg. Catalogue of an Exhibition held at the Detroit Public Library* (Detroit, 1955), 48, Item 144; *New-York Daily Tribune* (October 10, 1855), 7; Bliss Perry, *Walt Whitman* (Boston and New York, [1908]), 115; Walt Whitman, *An 1855–56 Notebook Toward the Second Edition of Leaves of Grass* (Carbondale, Ill., [1959]), 31.

28. For Horsell and the introduction of Whitman into England, see Allen, *op. cit.*, 176; Harold Blodgett, *Walt Whitman in England* (Ithaca, 1934), 14–17; Frederic Boase, *Modern English Biography* (Truro, England, 1912), V, 704f. (courtesy Mr. D. N. Jervis, Department of Printed Books, British Museum); information regarding the *Vegetarian Advocate* from Mrs. Laura B. Hawke, Reference Librarian, Medical Center Library, University of Michigan; William Horsell, *Hydropathy for the People* (New York, [1850]), iii, 187 [Vol. III of *Fowlers and Wells' Water-Cure Library*]; W. Horsell, *Respectable Man-Killers! Oberlin Tracts No. 21* (London, n.d.), 2 pp.; *Phrenological Journal*, Vol. XXI, No. 2 (February, 1855), 27, Vol. 118, No. 12 (December, 1905), 382; William Bell Scott, *Autobiographical Notes* (New York, 1892), II, 33, 267f.; *Water-Cure Journal*, Vol. XVIII, No. 2 (August, 1854), 41, Vol. XIX, No. 6 (June, 1855), 131; P. T. Winskill, *The Temperance Movement and Its Workers* (London, 1892), II, 150.

29. For *Life Illustrated* and Whitman's work on it, see Boardman, *op. cit.*, advertisement at end; Frey, *op. cit.*, 101f.; *Life Illustrated*, N.S., Vol. I, No. 1 (November 3, 1855)–Vol. III, No. 6 (December 6, 1856), *passim*; Mott, *A History of American Magazines 1850–1865*, 42; *New York Herald* (November 30, 1856), 4, (December 1, 1856), 8; *Phrenological Journal*, Vol. XXIII, No. 5 (May, 1856), 113, Vol. 65, No. 6 (December, 1877), 396; *Water-Cure Journal*, Vol. XVIII, No. 4 (October, 1854), 73, 82; Whitman, *New York Dissected, passim*.

30. *Life Illustrated*, Vol. I, No. 2 (November 10, 1855), 9.

31. *Ibid.*, Vol. I, No. 6 (December 8, 1855), 41.

32. *Ibid.*, Vol. I, No. 13 (January 26, 1856), 97.

33. *Ibid.*, Vol. I, No. 24 (April 12, 1856), 185f., 188.

34. *Ibid.*, Vol. II, No. 11 (July 12, 1856), 85, Vol. II, No. 12 (July 19, 1856), 93, Vol. II, No. 14 (August 2, 1856), 108f., Vol. II, No. 15 (August 9, 1856), 116, Vol. II, No. 16 (August 16, 1856), 125, Vol. II No. 17 (August 23, 1856), 133.

35. *Ibid.*, Vol. II, No. 18 (August 30, 1856), 140.

36. For the publication of the second edition of *Leaves of Grass*, see Allen, *op. cit.*, 178f.; Whitman Bennett, *A Practical Guide to American Book Collecting* (New York, [1941]), 118; Richard Maurice Bucke, *Walt Whitman* (Philadelphia, 1883), 140; Richard Curle, *Collecting American First Editions* (Indianapolis, [1930]), 196f.; Holloway, *op. cit.*, 145; Hungerford, "Walt Whitman," *loc. cit.*, 356f.; William Sloane Kennedy, *The Fight of a Book for the World* (West Yarmouth, Mass., 1926), 241f.; *A List of Manuscripts, Books ... in Commemoration of the One Hundred and Twentieth Anniversary of the Birth of Walt Whitman ... From the Whitman Collection of Mrs. Frank Julian Sprague* ([Washington], 1939), 9; Mott, *Golden Multitudes*, 111; Frank Shay, *The Bibliography of Walt Whitman* (New York, 1920), 9, 17; Carolyn Wells and Alfred E. Goldsmith, *A Concise Bibliography of the Works of Walt Whitman* (Boston and New York, 1922), 5f.; Whitman, *The Complete Writings*, VII, 143f.; [Walt Whitman], *Leaves of Grass* (Brooklyn, New York, 1856) [copy in New York Public Library], advertisement at end and *passim*; *Walt Whitman: A Catalog Based upon the Collections of the Library of Congress* (Washington, 1955), # 340; *Walt Whitman's Leaves of Grass: A Centenary Exhibition from the Lion Whitman Collection and the Berg Collection of the New York Public Library Compiled by Lewis M. Stark and John D. Gordan* (New York, 1955) 9f. Dawsons of Pall Mall recently (Catalogue 155, "Pot-Pourri," Item 323) listed the Louis H. Silver copy of the second edition, with a few inserted MS notes in Whitman's hand, at 240 pounds.

37. *Life Illustrated*, Vol. I, No. 7 (December 15, 1855), 53.

38. *Ibid.*, Vol. I, No. 11 (January 12, 1856), 87.

39. *Ibid.*, Vol. II, No. 3 (May 17, 1856), 20f. ("Fanny Fern's Opinion of Walt Whitman").

40. S. R. Wells to Friend Whitman, New York, June 7, 1856 (courtesy Mr. Charles E. Feinberg, Detroit, Michigan).

41. *Life Illustrated*, Vol. II, No. 16 (August 16, 1856), 124f.

42. *Ibid.*, Vol. II, No. 22 (September 27, 1856), 175.

43. *New-York Daily Tribune* (September 12–13, 15–20, 22–27, 29–October 4, 6–11, 1856), 1.

44. Conway, *op. cit.*, I, 216 f. See also Perry, *op. cit.*, 115.

45. Burroughs, *op. cit.*, 19.

46. Horace Traubel, *With Walt Whitman in Camden* (*November 1, 1888–January 20, 1889*) (New York, 1914), III, 115f.

47. Walt Whitman to Dear Friend, Brooklyn, July 20, 1857 (Henry E. Huntington Library). See also Allen, *op. cit.*, 217, and Rollo G. Silver, "Seven Letters of Walt Whitman," *American Literature*, Vol. VII, No. 1 (March, 1935), 78.

CHAPTER VIII

The Firm in the Fifties

1. For the Boston and Philadelphia branches, see *The Boston Almanac 1853–58*; D. P. Butler, *The Phrenological Delineator* (Boston, 1860), *passim*; Davies, *op. cit.*, 50f.; L. N. Fowler, *The Illustrated Phrenological Almanac 1855*, 42f.; Jones, *op. cit.*, 44f.; *The Massachusetts Register . . . Business Directory 1852–58*; Old Hickory Bookshop, Catalogue 165, Item 100 (Phrenology Broadside); Philadelphia directories 1854–60; *Phrenological Journal*, Vol. XIV, No. 4 (October, 1851), 93, Vol. XIV, No. 5 (November, 1851), 118, Vol. XVIII, No. 2 (August, 1853), 45, Vol. XIX, No. 1 (January, 1854), 19, Vol. XIX, No. 2 (February, 1854), 45, Vol. XXI, No. 1 (January, 1855), 15, Vol. XXI, No. 3 (March, 1855), 67, Vol. XXII, No. 4 (October, 1855), 91, Vol. XXIII, No. 2 (February, 1856), 32, Vol. XXXVIII, No. 6 (December, 1863), 165, Vol. 93, No. 5 (May, 1892), 218f., Vol. 96, No. 5 (May, 1893), 207ff.; Sizer, *Forty Years*, 300; Nelson Sizer to John Brown, Jr., New York, September 6, 1852 (Ohio Historical Society); *Water-Cure Journal*, Vol. XII, No. 4 (October, 1851), 91.

2. Ellwood Harvey, *Valedictory Address to the Graduating Class of the Female Medical College of Pennsylvania, for the Session 1854–5* (Philadelphia, 1854), [15].

3. O. S. Fowler, *Creative and Sexual Science*, 832, 949. For further details of Orson's withdrawal, which is variously dated 1854 and 1855, and his solo activity, see O. S. Fowler, *The Family* (New York, n.d.),

advertisement on title verso and *passim*; O. S. Fowler, Phrenological Character of Mr. L. N. Olden, Alton, March 1857 (courtesy Mr. Jack T. Ericson, Head, Manuscript Division, Syracuse University Library); O. S. Fowler, The Phrenological Character of Mr. J. Sullivan, Columbus, January 27, 1851 or 1857 (Ohio Historical Society); Growoll Collection, American Book Trade History, VI, 28; *Phrenological Journal*, Vol. 60, No. 6 (June, 1875), 353; Sizer, *Forty Years*, 300; Nelson Sizer to John Brown, Jr., New York, May 14–15, 1851 (Ohio Historical Society); S. R. Wells, *The Illustrated Annuals of Phrenology* [*1871*], 23.

4. For the Broadway Cabinet and its staff, see *Catalogue of Portraits, Busts, and Casts*, 36; L. N. Fowler, *The Illustrated Phrenological Almanac for 1851*, 33f.; O. S. Fowler to John Brown, Jr., New York, October 19, 1849 (Ohio Historical Society); Growoll Collection, American Book Trade History, VI, 28; Richard J. Hinton, *John Brown and His Men* (New York, 1894), *passim*; *Life Illustrated*, Vol. II, No. 6 (June 7, 1856), 44, Vol. IX, No. 14 (January 28, 1860), 108f. (courtesy Mr. Harold Celnick, New York); New York City directories 1854–60; *The New-York Illustrated News*, Vol. I, No. 14 (February 18, 1860), 211, 213, 220; *Phrenological Journal*, Vol. XII, No. 10 (October, 1850), 326, Vol. XII, No. 12 (December, 1850), 387, Vol. XIV, No. 1 (July, 1851), 23, Vol. XVIII, No. 3 (September, 1853), 69, Vol. XIX, No. 3 (March, 1854), 72, Vol. XIX, No. 4 (April, 1854), 88, 96, Vol. XIX, No. 5 (May, 1854), 109, Vol. XXI, No. 1 (January, 1855), 20, Vol. XXII, No. 2 (August, 1855), 40, Vol. XXVIII, No. 3 (September, 1858), 48, Vol. XXIX, No. 1 (January, 1859), 11, Vol. 78, No. 6 (June, 1884), 343f.; F. B. Sanborn (ed.), *John Brown . . . Life and Letters* (Cedar Rapids, 1910), *passim*; Nelson Sizer to John Brown Jr., New York, October 14, 1850, February 19, 1851, July 18, 1851, September 6, 1852 (Ohio Historical Society); Ver Nooy, "'Fowler's Folly,'" *loc. cit.*, 62; *Water-Cure Journal*, Vol. VIII, No. 1 (July, 1849), 24, Vol. XVII, No. 3 (March, 1854), 65, Vol. XVII, No. 4 (April, 1854), 87, Vol. XVII, No. 5 (May, 1854), 109, Vol. XVII, No. 6 (June, 1854), 121; S. R. Wells to John Brown, Jr., New York, October 3, October 18, October 31, 1849 (Ohio Historical Society).

5. *Phrenological Journal*, Vol. XXI, No. 5 (May, 1855), 106.

6. For the examinations performed, see Maturin M. Ballou, *Biog-*

raphy of *Rev. Hosea Ballou* (Boston, 1852), 222–27; L. N. Fowler, *The Illustrated Phrenological Almanac, 1854* (New York, [1853]), 29, *1855*, 43; L. N. Fowler, *The life, trial, confession, and execution of Albert W. Hicks . . . to which is added . . . his phrenological character* (New York, [1860]), *passim*; *The Illustrated Hydropathic Review* (New York, 1855), 715 (courtesy Mr. Harold Celnick, New York); *Phrenological Journal*, Vol. XIII, No. 2 (February, 1851), 30f., Vol. XVII, No. 2 (February, 1853), 46, Vol. XIX, No. 2 (February, 1854), 48, Vol. XXI, No. 3 (March, 1855), 55, Vol. XXI, No. 5 (May, 1855), 106, Vol. XXII, No. 3 (September, 1855), 49f., Vol. XXVII, No. 5 (May, 1858), 65, Vol. XXXVII, No. 1 (January, 1863), 1; Vol. XXXVIII, No. 6 (December, 1863), 165f., Vol. 79, No. 3 (September, 1884), 121–24, Vol. 96, No. 4 (October, 1893), 213; Sizer, *Forty Years*, 327; Nelson Sizer, Phrenological Character of Rev. M. D. Conway . . . New York . . . September 27th, 1856 (MS, Special Collections, Columbia University Library); John Townsend Trowbridge, *My Own Story* (Boston and New York, 1903), 121 ff. (courtesy Mr. Barrows Mussey, Düsseldorf, Germany); Wells, *New Physiognomy*, 700.

7. Nelson Sizer to John Brown, Jr., New York, July 18, 1851 (Ohio Historical Society).

8. Quoted in *Phrenological Journal*, Vol. XXVII, No. 5 (May, 1858), 75.

9. *Ibid.*, Vol. XXV, No. 6 (June, 1857), 122; Richard Emmons Thursfield, *Henry Barnard's American Journal of Education* (Baltimore, 1945), 185. See also Ruth M. Baylor, *Elizabeth Palmer Peabody: Kindergarten Pioneer* (Philadelphia, [1965]), 66.

10. For Melville and phrenology, see Harold Aspiz, "Phrenologizing the Whale," *Nineteenth-Century Fiction*, Vol. 23, No. 1 (June, 1968), 18–27; Merrell R. Davis and William H. Gilman (eds.), *The Letters of Herman Melville* (New Haven, 1960), 112; Tyrus Hillway, "Melville's Use of Two Pseudo-Sciences," *Modern Language Notes*, Vol. LXIV, No. 3 (March, 1949), 145–50; Herman Melville, *Moby-Dick or, The Whale* (New York, [1926]), 346f., (New York, 1952), 49. John C. Hoadley, who was to become Melville's brother-in-law, was examined by L. N. Fowler on June 24, 1845. The analysis, in O. S. Fowler, *Synopsis of Phrenology* (New York, n.d.), is in the Gansevoort-Lansing Collection, John Hoadley Papers, MS Division, New York Public Library.

11. For Holmes and phrenology, see Thomas Franklin Currier, *A Bibliography of Oliver Wendell Holmes* (New York, 1953), 618; L. N. Fowler, Phrenological Character of Oliver Wendell Holmes, Boston, July 1st, 1859 (courtesy Miss Barbara McDonnell, Librarian, Oliver Wendell Holmes Library, Phillips Academy, Andover, Mass.); O. S. and L. N. Fowler, *The Illustrated Self-Instructor in Phrenology and Physiology . . . with the Chart and Character of O. W. Holmes as marked by L. N. Fowler, June 22d, 1859* (New York, 1859), *passim* (copy in the Berkshire Athenaeum, Pittsfield, Mass.); O. W. Holmes, "The Professor at the Breakfast-Table," *The Atlantic Monthly*, Vol. IV, No. 22 (August, 1859), 232–43; *Life Illustrated*, Vol. VIII, No. 16 (August 13, 1859), 127; Hjalmar O. Lokensgard, "Oliver Wendell Holmes's 'Phrenological Character,' " *New England Quarterly*, Vol. 13, No. 4 (December, 1940), 711–18 (courtesy Miss Barbara McDonnell, Librarian, Phillips Academy, Andover, Mass.); Wallace Worth, "The Autocrat in Profile," *The Colophon*, N.S. Vol. I, No. 2 (June, 1939), 49–56.

12. *The Practical Phrenologist*, Vol. II, No. 8 (August, 1882), 3 (Landauer Collection, New York Historical Society); Sizer, *Forty Years*, 309. See also Oswald Garrison Villard, *John Brown: A Biography, 1800–1859* (Garden City, N.Y., 1929), 20.

13. *The Phrenological Magazine* (London), Vol. I (January, 1880), 7.

14. *Life Illustrated*, Vol. IX, No. 16 (February 11, 1860), 125; Sizer, *How to Study Strangers*, 46.

15. *Phrenological Journal*, Vol. XXI, No. 4 (April, 1855), 91 f. For further details of the Patent Office and the instruments and merchandise sold at the Depot, see L. N. Fowler, *Phrenological Almanac 1860*, 28; *Life Illustrated*, Vol. III, No. 6 (December 6, 1856), 47, Vol. III, No. 7 (December 13, 1856), 52, Vol. III, No. 8 (December 20, 1856), 61, Vol. VIII, No. 15 (August 6, 1859), 120, Vol. VIII, No. 18 (August 27, 1859), 139, Vol. IX, No. 19 (March 3, 1860), 151; *The New York Herald* (November 30, 1856), 4; *Phrenological Journal*, Vol. XXI, No. 2 (February, 1855), 40f., 43, Vol. XXI, No. 3 (March, 1855), 63, 66, Vol. XXI, No. 5 (May, 1855), 106, 115ff., Vol. XXI, No. 6 (June, 1855), 143f., Vol. XXII, No. 2 (August, 1855), 40, 45, Vol. XXII, No. 3 (September, 1855), 49, Vol. XXII, No. 4 (October, 1855), 92, 94, Vol. XXII, No. 6 (December, 1855), 134, Vol. XXIII,

No. 1 (January, 1856), 23, Vol. XXIII, No. 5 (May, 1856), 113, Vol. XXVII, No. 1 (January, 1858), 13, Vol. XXVII, No. 5 (May, 1858), advertisement; *Water-Cure Journal*, Vol. IX, No. 5 (May, 1850), 158, Vol. XVI, No. 1 (July, 1853), 23, Vol. XIX, No. 5 (May, 1855), 116, Vol. XXX, No. 6 (December, 1860), 95.

16. *Phrenological Journal*, Vol. XXII, No. 2 (August, 1855), 40, Vol. XXII, No. 5 (November, 1855), 108.

17. *Life Illustrated*, Vol. II, No. 13 (July 26, 1856), 104, Vol. IX, No. 6 (December 3, 1859), 43, 47; *Phrenological Journal*, Vol. XXII, No. 4 (October, 1855), 92; *Water-Cure Journal*, Vol. XXIX, No. 1 (January, 1860), 14.

18. *Life Illustrated*, Vol. I, No. 3 (November 17, 1855), 23. For the power presses, see *Phrenological Journal*, Vol. XVII, No. 4 (April, 1853), 95, Vol. XXIV, No. 6 (December, 1856), 137; *Water-Cure Journal*, Vol. XV, No. 4 (April, 1853), 93.

19. For the firm's periodicals, see Boardman, *op. cit.*, advertisements at end; *The Illustrated Hydropathic Review* (New York, 1855), *passim* (courtesy Mr. Harold Celnick); *Life Illustrated*, Vol. VIII, No. 10 (July 2, 1859), 76, Vol. VIII, No. 23 (October 1, 1859), 181, Vol. IX, No. 1 (October 29, 1859), 1, Vol. IX, No. 6 (December 3, 1859), 47 (courtesy Mr. Harold Celnick); *Phrenological Journal*, Vol. XII, No. 12 (December, 1850), 386, Vol. XIII, No. 1 (January, 1851), 1, Vol. XXI, No. 6 (June, 1855), 128, Vol. XXII, No. 1 (July, 1855), 20, Vol. XXII, No. 5 (November, 1855), 100f., Vol. XXIV, No. 6 (December, 1856), 121f., 136f., Vol. XXXVII, No. 1 (January, 1863), 17; N. Sizer to John Brown, Jr., New York, October 14, 1850 (Ohio Historical Society); R. T. Trall, *The New Hydropathic Cook-Book*, advertisements at end; *Water-Cure Journal*, Vol. X, No. 2 (August, 1850), 71, Vol. XII, No. 2 (August, 1851), 33, 39, Vol. XII, No. 4 (October, 1851), 89, Vol. XIV, No. 1 (July, 1852), 21, Vol. XV, No. 2 (February, 1853), 34f., 40, Vol. XVI, No. 2 (August, 1853), 45, Vol. XIX (1855), ii, Vol. XIX, No. 1 (January, 1855), 10, Vol. XXI, No. 1 (January, 1856), 23, Vol. XXII, No. 6 (December, 1856), 133.

20. N. Sizer to John Brown, Jr., New York, February 19, 1851 (Ohio Historical Society).

21. Sylvester Graham to S. R. Wells, Northampton, Mass., March

13, 1851 (Fowler Family Papers, Collection of Regional History, Cornell University Library).

22. For the firm's agents and imitators, see *Phrenological Journal*, Vol. XIX, No. 2 (February, 1854), 45, Vol. XXII, No. 6 (December, 1855), 129, Vol. XXVII, No. 6 (June, 1858), 95; Luximon Roy, *Grand Hindoo Poetical Phrenological Chart* (Cincinnati, 1854), *passim*; C. Townsend, *Improved Phreno-Chart* (Ogdensburgh, N.Y., 1859), *passim*; *Water-Cure Journal*, Vol. X, No. 6 (December, 1850), 241, Vol. XIII, No. 6 (June, 1852), 137, Vol. XXII, No. 4 (October, 1856), 73.

23. *American Publishers' Circular and Literary Gazette*, Vol. II, No. 38 (September 20, 1856), 583; [D. H. Jacques], *The Garden. Rural Hand-Books.—No. 1* (New York, 1858), advertisement at end; *Phrenological Journal*, Vol. XVII, No. 1 (January, 1853), 22, Vol. XXIII, No. 1 (January, 1856), 2.

24. William A. Clebsch (ed.), "Goodness Gold, and God: the California Mining Career of Peter Y. Cool, 1851–52," *The Pacific Historian*, Vol. X, No. 3 (Summer, 1966), 33 (courtesy Miss Gladys Tilden, Berkeley, California).

25. Besides the books themselves, see *American Publishers' Circular and Literary Gazette*, Vol. I, No. 1 (September 1, 1855)—Vol. II, No. 38 (September 20, 1856), *passim*; Thomas Gregg, *Fruit Culture for the Million* (New York, [1857]), advertisement at end; D. H. Jacques, *Hints Toward Physical Perfection* (New York, 1859), 102; M. Edgeworth Lazarus, *The Human Trinity* (New York, 1851), *passim*; O. O. Roorbach, *Bibliotheca Americana . . . 1820 to 1852, Supplement, 1852 to 1855, Addenda, 1855 to 1858, 1858 to 1861* (New York, 1939), *passim*; [Samuel Roberts Wells], *Domestic Animals. Rural Hand-Books.—No. 3* (New York, 1858), *passim*; [S. R. Wells], *Hand-Book for Home Improvement, How to Behave*, vii f., 17, 21, 23, 41; [S. R. Wells], *New Illustrated Rural Manuals: comprising The House. The Garden. The Farm. Domestic Animals* (New York, 1859), *passim*; [S. R. Wells], *The Right Word in the Right Place* (New York, 1860), 5.

26. [S. R. Wells], *Hand-Book for Home Improvement, How to Do Business*, 87.

27. R. T. Trall, *Tobacco: Its History, Nature, and Effects* (New York, n.d.), 22.

28. *American Publishers' Circular and Literary Gazette*, Vol. I, No. 7 (October 13, 1855), 105. For the firm's interest and publications in mesmerism, see also Boardman, *op. cit.*, advertisement at end; "Andrew Jackson Davis," *DAB; Phrenological Journal*, Vol. XIV, No. 2 (August, 1851), 33f., Vol. XXI, No. 2 (February, 1855), 32; Alfred Smee, *Principles of the Human Mind, Deduced from Physical Laws* (New York, n.d.), 5; *Spiritual Telegraph*, Vol. I, No. 23 (October 9, 1852), [4].

29. *Phrenological Journal*, Vol. XXI, No. 1 (January, 1855), 10.

CHAPTER IX

The Younger Fowlers

1. "Mesmerism," *Ciba Symposia*, Vol. IX, No. 11 (March–April, 1948), 836.

2. Seldes, *op. cit.*, 321. Davis' *The Philosophy of Spiritual Intercourse* was published in 1851 by Fowlers and Wells.

3. John W. Edmonds, *Letters and Tracts on Spiritualism* (London, [1875]), 13f.; W. G. Langworthy Taylor, *Katie Fox: Epochmaking Medium* (New York and London, 1933), 58f.

4. S. B. Brittan and B. W. Richmond, *A Discussion of The Facts and Philosophy of Ancient and Modern Spiritualism* (New York, 1853), 19; John W. Edmonds and George T. Dexter, *Spiritualism* (New York, 1853), I, 447; H. N. Fowler, *The Industrial Public*, 70; Charles Morris (ed.), *Makers of New York* (Philadelphia, 1895), 76.

5. Brittan and Richmond, *op. cit.*, 11–19; A. J. Davis, *op. cit.*, 147f; Edmonds and Dexter, *op. cit.*, I, 443–51; H. Mattison, *Spirit Rapping Unveiled!* (New York, 1853), 117f., 120; "Mystical Manuscripts," *The Shekinah*, I, 301–307 (courtesy Yale University Library); Frank Podmore, *Mediums of the 19th Century* (New York, [1963]), I, 232f., 236–39; N. Sizer to Mr. and Mrs. John Brown, Jr., New York, November 26, 1850, to John Brown, Jr., New York, February 19, 1851, July 18, 1851 (Ohio Historical Society); *Spiritual Telegraph*, Vol. I, No. 7 (June 19, 1852), [3], Vol. I, No. 9 (July 3, 1852), [3], Vol I, No. 13 (July 31, 1852), [2], Vol. I, No. 30 (November 27, 1852), [3]; M. B. Stern, "Poe: 'The Mental Temperament' for Phrenologists," *loc. cit.*, 160f.; *Water-Cure Journal*, Vol. XIII, No. 3 (March, 1852), 71; Charlotte Fowler Wells to John Brown, Jr., New

Haven, June 7, 1851 (Ohio Historical Society); R. S. [?] Wells to Mrs. John Brown, Jr., New York, August 4, 1850 (Ohio Historical Society); S. R. Wells to John Brown, Jr., New York, January 24, 1850 (Ohio Historical Society).

6. Emma Hardinge [Britten], *Modern American Spiritualism* (New York, 1870), 83f.

7. George Bush, *Heaven: A Sermon . . . with a Biographical Sketch of the Author* (London, 1850), i–vii; see also "George Bush," *DAB*. Lorenzo's analysis of Bush appears in *Phrenological Journal*, Vol. X (1848), 297–302; Poe describes Bush's phrenology in *The Literati*; Wells uses him as an example of the thinker in *New Physiognomy*.

8. "Mystical Manuscripts," *The Shekinah*, I, 305ff.

9. Lydia F. Fowler to Mrs. John Brown, Jr., New York, October 2, 1850 (Ohio Historical Society).

10. As reported in N. Sizer to John Brown, Jr., New York, February 19, 1851 (Ohio Historical Society).

11. Charlotte Fowler Wells, Report of Spiritualist Meetings, New York City, 1850–51, MS (Mrs. Charlotte Fowler Wells Miscellanea, Collection of Regional History, Cornell University Library).

12. Rodney Wells to John Brown, Jr., New York, November 26, 1850; S. R. Wells to John Brown, Jr., New York, July 1, 1851 (Ohio Historical Society).

13. R. S. [?] Wells to Mrs. John Brown, Jr., New York, August 4, 1850 (Ohio Historical Society).

14. N. Sizer to John Brown, Jr., New York, February 19, 1851 (Ohio Historical Society).

15. *New-York Daily Tribune* (January 30, 1914), 7; "New York Physicians. Edward Payson Fowler, M.D.," *The National Magazine*, Vol. XIX, Nos. 4–5 (February–March, 1894), 315ff.

16. H. N. Fowler, *The Industrial Public, passim.* Part 2 of this work consists of Samuel T. Fowler's *Genetics: A New System of Learning.*

17. *Ibid.*, 6.

18. *Ibid.*, 6f.

19. C. F. Wells, Report of Spiritualist Meetings, 3f.

20. *Ibid.*, 13–20.

21. *Phrenological Journal*, Vol. XVII, No. 1 (January, 1853), 1.

22. Besides the works mentioned, see Andrew Combe, *The Principles of Physiology applied to the Preservation of Health* (New

York, 1849), 4–page brochure tipped in at end concerning *The Spirit of the Age*; L. N. Fowler, *The Illustrated Phrenological Almanac for 1852* (New York, [1852]), 46, *1855*, advertisements; Clarence L. F. Gohdes, *The Periodicals of American Transcendentalism* (Durham, N.C., 1931), 132, 134ff.; [M. Edgeworth Lazarus], *Love vs. Marriage. Part I* (New York, 1852), advertisement at end; M. Edgeworth Lazarus, *Passional Hygiene and Natural Medicine* (New York, 1852), 13f., advertisement at end; *Life Illustrated*, Vol. VIII, No. 22 (September 24, 1859), 172; James J. Martin, *Men Against the State* (New York, 1957), 73f.; *Phrenological Journal*, Vol. XIII, No. 4 (April, 1851), 88; A. Toussenel, *Passional Zoology* (New York, 1852), advertisement at beginning.

23. John L. Capen, Phrenological Character of Miss Almira L. Fowler, August 2, 1855 (Fowler Family Papers, Collection of Regional History, Cornell University Library); James R. Chadwick, "The Study and Practice of Medicine by Women," *The International Review*, Vol. VII (October, 1879), 460, 463f.; information from Miss Ida J. Draeger, Librarian, and from Mrs. Dorothy L. Peuser, Registrar, Woman's Medical College of Pennsylvania, Philadelphia; Female Medical College of Pennsylvania, *Fourth Annual Announcement . . . for the Session 1853–54* (Philadelphia, 1853), 4, 14, 16, and *passim*; *Life Illustrated*, Vol. I, No. 3 (November 17, 1855), 23; *New-York Daily Tribune* (January 2, 1900), 7; *Phrenological Journal*, Vol. 109, No. 2 (February, 1900), 46; Frederick C. Waite, *History of the New England Female Medical College 1848–1874* (Boston, 1950), 124; *Water-Cure Journal*, Vol. XV, No. 3 (March, 1853), 70, Vol. XVI, No. 2 (August, 1853), 48.

24. For Lydia's medical work, professional activity, lectures, writings, and practice, see *The American Medical & Surgical Journal*, Vol. VII, No. 4 (April, 1855), 152; *The Eclectic Medical and Surgical Journal*, Vol. I, No. 5 (November, 1849), 160, Vol. I, No. 7 (January, 1850), 222f., Vol. I, No. 12 (June, 1850), 373f., 377, 379, 382, Vol. III, No. 2 (August, 1851), 61, Vol. III, No. 6 (December, 1851), 161 ff., Vol. IV, No. 2 (February, 1852), 65ff.; Phebe A. Hanaford, *Daughters of America; or, Women of the Century* (Augusta, Maine, 1883), 267f.; Hurd-Mead, *op. cit.*, 41 f.; *Life Illustrated*, Vol. I, No. 9 (December 29, 1855), 71, Vol. VIII, No. 10 (July 2, 1859), 79, Vol. IX, No. 18 (February 25, 1860), 141; New York City directory 1858–

59; *New-York Times* (February 10, 1879), 3; *Phrenological Journal*, Vol. XVIII, No. 2 (August, 1853), 46, Vol. XX, No. 6 (December, 1854), 137, Vol. XXI, No. 5 (May, 1855), 119, Vol. XXII, No. 4 (October, 1855), 95, Vol. 68, No. 3 (March, 1879), 159; Sizer, *How to Study Strangers*, 149f.; Nelson Sizer to John Brown, Jr., New York, May 14–15, 1851 (Ohio Historical Society); Frederick C. Waite, "Dr. Lydia Folger Fowler," *Annals of Medical History*, N.S. Vol. IV, No. 3 (May, 1932), 290–95; *Water-Cure Journal*, Vol. XI, No. 6 (June, 1851), 137f., Vol. XII, No. 1 (July, 1851), 21, Vol. XII, No. 5 (November, 1851), 120, Vol. XVI, No. 2 (August, 1853), 45, Vol. XIX, No. 2 (February, 1855), 43, Vol. XIX, No. 5 (May, 1855), 114, Vol. XXIX, No. 5 (May, 1860), 73; Weiss and Kemble, *op. cit.*, 153.

25. William Frederick Norwood, *Medical Education in the United States Before the Civil War* (Philadelphia, 1944), 412.

26. Lydia Folger Fowler, *The Heart and Its Influences* (London, [1863]), 12.

27. For the Central Medical College, see *The American Medical & Surgical Journal*, Vol. VII, No. 4 (April, 1855), 141–53; *The Eclectic Medical and Surgical Journal*, Vol. I, No. 7 (January, 1850), 223, Vol. III, No. 2 (August, 1851), 63; *Water-Cure Journal*, Vol. XI, No. 2 (February, 1851), 49, Vol. XII, No. 5 (November, 1851), 120; Alexander Wilder, *History of Medicine* (New Sharon, Maine, 1901), 580ff.

28. *The Eclectic Medical and Surgical Journal*, Vol. I, No. 12 (June, 1850), 373f.

29. *The Science of Health*, Vol. III, No. 13 (July, 1873), 35 (courtesy Mr. Harold Celnick).

30. Bettmann, *op. cit.*, 252.

31. *The Illustrated Water-Cure Almanac for 1857* (New York, n.d.), 3.

32. *The Journal of Medical Reform*, Vol. V, No. 3 (July, 1857), 68f.; *Phrenological Journal*, Vol. XIX, No. 2 (February, 1854), 47; Waite, "Dr. Lydia Folger Fowler," *loc. cit.*, 295; *Water-Cure Journal*, Vol. XVII, No. 2 (February, 1854), 46.

33. *The American Water-Cure Almanac for 1860* (New York, n.d.), advertisement at end; R. T. Trall, *The Alcoholic Controversy* (New York and London, 1856), prospectus at end; *Water-Cure Journal*, Vol. XVI, No. 4 (October, 1853), 94, Vol. XIX, No. 1

(January, 1855), 11, Vol. XX, No. 4 (October, 1855), 90, Vol. XXI, No. 1 (January, 1856), 20, Vol. XXI, No. 2 (February, 1856), 43; Weiss and Kemble, *op. cit.*, 35ff., 82.

34. Henry A. Archer, *Introductory Lecture to the Third Annual Course of the Metropolitan Medical College* (New York, 1855), 3f., 9.

35. *Water-Cure Journal*, Vol. XII, No. 6 (December, 1851), 136, Vol. XIX (1855), ii.

36. For the firm's homeopathic, hydropathic, and health interests and publications, as well as their attraction to women, see, besides the works mentioned, Carson, *op. cit.*, 19f.; Joel Shew, *The Hydropathic Family Physician* (New York, [1854]), iv; Alice Felt Tyler, *Freedom's Ferment* (Minneapolis, [1944]), 441; *Water-Cure Journal*, Vol. X, No. 6 (December, 1850), 241, Vol. XII, No. 4 (October, 1851), 91, Vol. XV, No. 3 (March, 1853), 70, Vol. XV, No. 5 (May, 1853), 115, Vol. XXX, No. 4 (October, 1860), 57, 63.

37. Fredrika Bremer, *America of the Fifties* (New York, 1924), 34f. See also, regarding Harriot K. Hunt, Fredrika Bremer, *The Homes of the New World* (New York, 1853), I, 93; Chadwick, "The Study and Practice of Medicine by Women," *loc. cit.*, 463f.; Female Medical College of Pennsylvania, *Fourth Annual Announcement*, 16; Harriot K. Hunt, *Glances and Glimpses* (Boston, 1856), 142ff., 217f., 235f., 265ff., 273; *Phrenological Journal*, Vol. X (1848), 95, 204.

38. *Phrenological Journal*, Vol. XXIII, No. 2 (February, 1856), 32. See also *Life Illustrated*, Vol. II, No. 3 (May 17, 1856), 19.

39. *Water-Cure Journal*, Vol. XVI, No. 5 (November, 1853), 120.

CHAPTER X

Radicals of Reform

1. L. N. Fowler, "Love, Courtship, and Marriage," *Lectures on Man*, 3.

2. O. S. Fowler, *Creative and Sexual Science*, 167.

3. L. N. Fowler, *The Illustrated Phrenological Almanac 1854* (New York, [1853]), 37; *Phrenological Journal*, Vol. XII, No. 10 (October, 1850), 318–22.

4. See, besides the books mentioned, M. Edgeworth Lazarus, *Comparative Psychology and Universal Analogy. Vol. I. Vegetable Portraits of Character* (New York, 1851), *passim*; Mrs. C. M. Steele, *A*

Mother's Thoughts on Parental Responsibility (New York, 1852), *passim.*

5. For the firm and Margaret Fuller, see *American Publishers' Circular*, Vol. II, No. 21 (May 24, 1856), 312, Vol. II, No. 26 (June 28, 1856), 387; *Life Illustrated*, Vol. I, No. 23 (April 5, 1856), 181; *The Literary World* (July 10, 1852), 31; *Phrenological Journal*, Vol. XV, No. 3 (March, 1852), 71, Vol. XV, No. 5 (May, 1852), 119, Vol. XV, No. 6 (June, 1852), 142, Vol. XXIII, No. 4 (April, 1856), 93; [S. R. Wells or D. H. Jacques], *How to Write* (New York, 1857), 86, 89, 141.

6. For Eliza Farnham and the firm, see Samuel Burhans, Jr., *Burhans Genealogy* (New York, 1894), 193; [E. W. Farnham], *Eliza Woodson* (New York, 1864), v and *passim*; Eliza Farnham to Fowler firm, Santa Cruz, California, November 15, 1850 (Collection of Regional History, Cornell University Library); Georgiana Bruce Kirby, *Years of Experience* (New York, 1887), *passim*; Georgiana Bruce [Kirby] to Charlotte Fowler Wells, [Santa Cruz, California, 1850] (Collection of Regional History, Cornell University Library); *Life Illustrated*, Vol. I, No. 24 (April 12, 1856), 189; *New-York Times* (December 18, 1864), 3; *New-York Tribune* (December 16, 1864), 4; *Phrenological Journal*, Vol. XXIII, No. 4 (April, 1856), 85, Vol. XXV, No. 6 (June, 1857), 133, Vol. 84, No. 4 (April, 1887), 224; Stern, "Two Letters from The Sophisticates of Santa Cruz," *loc. cit.*, 51–62.

7. Elizabeth Cady Stanton, Susan B. Anthony, and Matilda Joslyn Gage (eds.), *History of Woman Suffrage* (Rochester, N.Y., 1887), I, 178f.

8. *The Proceedings of the Woman's Rights Convention . . . at Syracuse . . . 1852* (Syracuse, 1852), 75.

9. For Channing and Charlotte Wells, see W. H. Channing to Charlotte Fowler Wells, Rondout, New York, September 21, November 20, December 15, 1851 (Collection of Regional History, Cornell University Library); Octavius Brooks Frothingham, *Memoir of William Henry Channing* (Boston and New York, 1886), 265–69 and *passim*; *The Proceedings of the Woman's Rights Convention . . . at Worcester . . . 1851* (New York, 1852), 58 and *passim*; Stanton, Anthony, and Gage (eds.), *op. cit.*, (Rochester, New York, 1889), I, 233f.; Madeleine B. Stern, "William Henry Channing's Letters on

'Woman in Her Social Relations,' " *The Cornell Library Journal*, No. 6 (Autumn, 1968), 54–62.

10. *Phrenological Journal*, Vol. XVIII, No. 1 (July, 1853), 11f.

11. Katharine Anthony, *Susan B. Anthony* (New York, 1954), 48f.; *Phrenological Journal*, Vol. III, No. 1 (January, 1901), 32.

12. Antoinette L. Brown to Charlotte F. Wells, Henrietta, N.Y., July 12, 1855 (Collection of Regional History, Cornell University Library).

13. K. Anthony, *op. cit.*, 102; *Phrenological Journal*, Vol. XV, No. 3 (March, 1852), 65; Stanton, Anthony, and Gage (eds.), *op. cit.*, I, 478,489f.

14. Lebbeus Armstrong, *The Temperance Reformation* (New York, 1853), *passim*; D. C. Bloomer, *Life and Writings of Amelia Bloomer* (Boston, 1895), 98ff., 102, 135; *New-York Daily Times* (February 8, 1853), 8; *New-York Daily Tribune* (February 7, 1853), 4, (February 8, 1853), 5; [*New York*] *Evening Post* (February 8, 1853), 2; *Phrenological Journal*, Vol. XVII, No. 3 (March, 1853), 69; Stanton, Anthony, and Gage (eds.), *op. cit.*, I, 490f.; *Water-Cure Journal*, Vol. XVI, No. 4 (October, 1853), 85, Vol. XVII, No. 4 (April, 1854), 89; *The Whole World's Temperance Convention Held at Metropolitan Hall . . . 1853* (New York, 1853), *passim*.

15. *Phrenological Journal*, Vol. XXI, No. 5 (May, 1855), 114. See also *Water-Cure Journal*, Vol. XIX, No. 5 (May, 1855), 112, 119.

16. *Phrenological Journal*, Vol. XXII, No. 4 (October, 1855), 88; *Water-Cure Journal*, Vol. XX, No. 4 (October, 1855), 80f.

17. *Life Illustrated*, Vol. I, No. 4 (November 24, 1855), 28, 30, Vol. I, No. 14 (February 2, 1856), 109, Vol. II, No. 4 (May 24, 1856), 28, Vol. II, No. 22 (September 27, 1856), 174.

18. For the Kansas Vegetarian and Octagon Settlements, as well as for Henry S. Clubb, see [Alfred Theodore Andreas], *History of the State of Kansas* (Chicago, 1883), 668; J. Christian Bay, *A Heroine of the Frontier: Miriam Davis Colt in Kansas, 1856* (Cedar Rapids, 1941), *passim*; Frank W. Blackmar (ed.), *Kansas: A Cyclopedia of State History* (Chicago, [1912]), II, 381, 842f.; Miriam Davis Colt, *Went to Kansas* (Watertown, 1862), *passim*; *Daily National Intelligencer* [Washington, D.C.] (February 9, 1856), [3]; Max Greene, *The Kanzas Region* (New York, 1856), *passim*; Russell Hickman, "The Vegetarian and Octagon Settlement Companies," *The Kansas*

Historical Quarterly, Vol. II, No. 4 (November, 1933), 377–84; *The Illustrated Vegetarian Almanac for 1855* (New York, 1855), 24, 38, and *passim*; *Life Illustrated*, Vol. I, No. 7 (December 15, 1855), 52f., Vol. I, No. 17 (February 23, 1856), 133, Vol. II, No. 4 (May 24, 1856), 29; *The Octagon Settlement Company, Kanzas* (New York, n.d.), *passim*; *Phrenological Journal*, Vol. XXII, No. 1 (July, 1855), 17, Vol. XXII, No. 2 (August, 1855), 41, Vol. XXIII, No. 3 (March, 1856), 49, Vol. 118, No. 12 (December, 1905), 379–82; *Water-Cure Journal*, Vol. XVIII, No. 5 (November, 1854), 105, Vol. XIX, No. 4 (April, 1855), 87, Vol. XIX, No. 5 (May, 1855), 120, Vol. XX, No. 1 (July, 1855), 10, Vol. XXI, No. 3 (March, 1856), 60, Vol. XXII, No. 2 (August, 1856), 37f., Vol. XXX, No. 4 (October, 1860), 63; Weiss and Kemble, *op. cit.*, 121.

19. *Life Illustrated*, Vol. I, No. 7 (December 15, 1855), 52.

20. N. Sizer to John Brown, Jr., New York, October 14, 1850 (Collection of Regional History, Cornell University Library).

21. *Phrenological Journal*, Vol. XXVI, No. 6 (December, 1857), 118.

22. *Orange [New Jersey] Journal* (May 28, 1859), 2.

23. *New York Times* (October 16, 1932), 38.

24. For details of the tour, see "Fifty Years of Phrenology," *loc. cit.*, 11, 14; *Prof. L. N. Fowler. A Sketch*, 5; *Life Illustrated*, Vol. VIII, No. 15 (August 6, 1859), 114f., 117, Vol. VIII, No. 18 (August 27, 1859), 140, Vol. VIII, No. 20 (September 10, 1859), 156; *Phrenological Journal*, Vol. XXVI, No. 6 (December, 1857), 123, Vol. XXVII, No. 1 (January, 1858), 12, Vol. XXVII, No. 5 (May, 1858), 75, Vol. XXXVIII, No. 6 (December, 1863), 165; Sizer, *How to Study Strangers*, 150.

25. Horace Greeley to Dear Sir, New York, July 9, 1860, copy (Collection of Regional History, Cornell University Library).

CHAPTER XI

Citizens of London, Boston, and the World

1. Dr. John Epps to Mr. Fowler, London, December 4, 1858, copy (Collection of Regional History, Cornell University Library).

2. J. Millott Severn, *The Life Story and Experiences of a Phrenologist* (Brighton, England, 1929), 104f. See also *The Phrenological Mag-*

azine (London), Vol. I (January, 1880), 6; Henry Robertson to S. R. Wells, Birmingham, September 13, 1861 (Collection of Regional History, Cornell University Library).

3. L. N. Fowler, "Love, Courtship, and Marriage," *Lectures on Man*, advertisement; *Human Nature* (London), Vol. I (April, 1867), 51 (courtesy Miss Joan I. Gotwals, Reference and Bibliographic Services, University of Pennsylvania Library); *Phrenological Journal*, Vol. 59, No. 5 (November, 1874), 327, Vol. 117, No. 5 (May, 1904), 158; George Francis Train, *My Life in Many States and in Foreign Lands* (New York, 1902), 123.

4. Sizer, *How to Study Strangers*, 150; Waite, "Dr. Lydia Folger Fowler," *loc. cit.*, 295.

5. L. N. Fowler, *The Illustrated Phrenological Almanac, 1854*, 27f.; L. N. Fowler, "Tact and Talent," [*Lectures*], 13; L. N. Fowler, "Thinkers, Authors, Speakers," [*Lectures*], 12.

6. L. N. Fowler, "Formation of Character," [*Lectures*], 7; *Phrenological Journal*, Vol. 109, No. 5 (May, 1900), 164, Vol. 117, No. 6 (June, 1904), 198.

7. Neider (ed.), *The Autobiography of Mark Twain*, 64ff.; Madeleine B. Stern, "Mark Twain Had His Head Examined," *American Literature*, Vol. 41, No. 2 (May, 1969), 207–18.

8. L. L. Fowler, [*Lectures*], *passim*; L. N. Fowler, *Lectures on Man*, *passim*; *Professor L. N. Fowler. A Sketch*, 7.

9. *Phrenological Journal*, Vol. XXXVII, No. 6 (June, 1863), 141, Vol. 40, No. 3 (September, 1864), 84.

10. L. N. Fowler, "Self-Made Men," [*Lectures*], 4; *Phrenological Journal*, Vol. 68, No. 1 (January, 1879), 7; Sizer, *How to Study Strangers*, 150.

11. Lydia F. Fowler, *The Heart, and Its Influences* (London, [1863]), 24 and *passim*; *The Illustrated Annual of Phrenology and Health Almanac, 1880* (New York, [1880]), 23; *New-York Daily Tribune* (September 4, 1896), 7; *New-York Times* (February 10, 1879), 3; *Phrenological Journal*, Vol. 68, No. 6 (June, 1879), 292; Sizer, *How to Study Strangers*, 150; Waite, "Dr. Lydia Folger Fowler," *loc. cit.*, 296; Winskill, *op. cit.*, III, 258.

12. L. N. Fowler, "Self-Knowledge," [*Lectures*], 16. For other details of Lorenzo's work in London, see Edmonds, *op. cit.*, title page;

"Fifty Years of Phrenology," *loc. cit.*, 11; Jessie A. Fowler, *Life of Dr. François Joseph Gall* (London and New York, 1896), 51f.; Jessie A. Fowler, *A Manual of Mental Science* (London and New York, [1897]), 145, 210; Jessie A. Fowler, *Practical Physiognomy* (New York and London, [1912]), 81; David George Goyder, *My Battle for Life* (London, 1857), 470; *Phrenological Journal*, Vol. 49, No. 8 (August, 1869), 321, Vol. 51, No. 2 (August, 1870), 150; *The Post Office London Directory for 1875*.

13. O. S. Fowler, *Creative and Sexual Science*, 934, 941.

14. O. S. Fowler, *Human Science*, 617.

15. For Orson's Manchester residence, see *The American Architect and Building News*, Vol. IV, No. 135 (July 27, 1878), 30; *Amherst College Biographical Record of the Graduates and Non-Graduates*, 30; Creese, "Fowler and the Domestic Octagon," *loc. cit.*, 89; Davies, *op. cit.*, 174; C. H. Webber and W. S. Nevins, *Old Naumkeag* (Salem, Mass., 1877), 290 ff.

16. *Amherst College Biographical Record of the Graduates and Non-Graduates*, 30; Jones, *op. cit.*, Chronological Table.

17. O. S. Fowler, *Life: Its Science, Laws, Faculties* (Boston, [1871]), advertisement at end (Harvard University Library).

18. O. S. and L. N. Fowler, *New Illustrated Self-Instructor in Phrenology and Physiology* (New York, 1868), tipped-in prospectus of O. S. Fowler's *Phrenological Journal* and Complete Revised Works on Man, *passim*; O. S. Fowler, *Religious Science* (Boston, [1871]), advertisement verso front cover.

19. O. S. Fowler, *Creative and Sexual Science* (New York, n.d.), 923.

20. O. S. Fowler, *Human Science*, 618.

21. For Orson's beliefs, teachings, and work in sexual guidance, see O. S. Fowler, *Creative and Sexual Science*, *passim*, from which the quotations originate; O. S. Fowler, *Human Science*, 217; O. S. Fowler, *The Practical Phrenologist* (Boston, [1876]), *passim*; O. S. Fowler, *Sexual Science* (Cincinnati, Memphis, Atlanta, [1870]), *passim*; O. S. Fowler, *Sexuality Restored, and Warning and Advice to Youth against Perverted Amativeness* (Boston, [1870]), *passim* (Harvard University Library); Adolf Growoll Collection, American Book Trade History, VI, 28.

22. O. S. Fowler, *Creative and Sexual Science*, 287.

23. *Ibid.*, 586, 590.

24. *Ibid.*, 90f.

25. *Ibid.*, 51.

26. O. S. Fowler, *Human Science*, 4, 8, and *passim*.

27. T. A. McNeal, *When Kansas Was Young* (New York, 1922), 124–28 (courtesy Mr. Ray Reynolds); *Phrenological Journal*, Vol. 120, No. 11 (November, 1907), 353.

28. *Phrenological Journal*, Vol. 67, No. 5 (November, 1878), 273; Ver Nooy, "More About Orson Fowler," *loc. cit.*, 101.

29. O. S. Fowler, *Human Science*, 1200. See also O. S. Fowler (ed.), *Fowler's Journal of Life, Health, Man, and Phrenology* (New York, [1876]), *passim* (Newberry Library); O. S. Fowler, *Life*, advertisement at end.

30. *New-York Daily Tribune* (January 2, 1900), 7.

31. *The Homœopathic Times*, Vol. III, No. 1 (April, 1875)–Vol. III, No. 7 (October, 1875), *passim*; *The Journal of the American Medical Association*, Vol. LXII, No. 8 (February 21, 1914), 630; *New-York Daily Tribune* (January 30, 1914), 7.

32. H. N. Fowler, *The Industrial Public*, 10; *Woodhull & Claflin's Weekly*, Vol. IV, No. 28 (May 25, 1872), 12, Vol. V, No. 22 (May 3, 1873), 6–7.

33. New York Medical College for Women, *By-Laws* (New York, 1865), *passim*; New York Medical College for Women, *Second, Fifth, Sixth, Seventh, Tenth Annual Announcement[s]* (New York, 1864, 1867–69, 1872–73), *passim*; *Phrenological Journal*, Vol. 51, No. 4 (October, 1870), 296, Vol. 58, No. 2 (February, 1874), 111.

34. John L. Capen to S. R. Wells, Philadelphia, December 1, 1874 (Collection of Regional History, Cornell University Library).

35. D. P. Butler, *The Lifting Cure* (Boston and New York, 1868), *passim*; *Phrenological Journal*, Vol. 48, No. 5 (November, 1868), 186, Vol. 93, No. 5 (May, 1892), 219.

36. "Fifty Years of Phrenology," *loc. cit.*, 14f.; Growoll Collection, American Book Trade History, XIII, 31; *New-York Daily Tribune* (April 14, 1875), 7; *Phrenological Journal*, Vol. 60, No. 6 (June, 1875), 353f.; *The Science of Health*, Vol. VII, No. 37 (July, 1875), 7.

CHAPTER XII
War and Panic, Fire and Flood

1. *Phrenological Journal*, Vol. XXXIII, No. 1 (January, 1861), 13, Vol. 49, No. 2 (February, 1869), 75.

2. For the changes in office personnel, see Isabel C. Barrows, *A Sunny Life: The Biography of Samuel June Barrows* (Boston, 1913), 53ff.; "Fifty Years of Phrenology," *loc. cit.*, 28f.; D. H. Jacques, *Florida as a Permanent Home* (Jacksonville, 1877), *passim*; *Phrenological Journal*, Vol. 44, No. 3 (September, 1866), advertisement at end, Vol. 46, No. 5 (November, 1867), 186, Vol. 48, No. 4 (October, 1868), 129ff., Vol. 52, No. 2 (February, 1871), 91; *The Rural Carolinian* [Charleston, S. C.], Vol. I, No. 1 (October, 1869), Vol. I, No. 3 (December, 1869), *passim*; Sizer, *The Royal Road to Wealth*, 74½.

3. *Phrenological Journal*, Vol. 39, No. 5 (May, 1864), 130. See also *Life Illustrated*, Vol. IX, No. 20 (March 10, 1860), 157; *New York Business Directory*, 1864–68; New York City directories 1864–74.

4. *Phrenological Journal*, Vol. 50, No. 1 (January, 1870), 39ff. The observer was Mrs. H. G. Pardee.

5. *Phrenological Journal*, Vol. 39, No. 3 (March, 1864), 79. See also *The Illustrated Physiological and Phrenological Almanac, 1863* [New York, 1863], advertisement verso of front cover; *Phrenological Journal*, Vol. 52, No. 2 (February, 1871), 132, 149, Vol. 57, No. 2 (August, 1873), 119; Wells, *The Illustrated Annuals of Phrenology*, [*1865*], 39.

6. *Phrenological Journal*, Vol. 48, No. 1 (July, 1868), 23.

7. *Ibid.*, Vol. 49, No. 1 (January, 1869), 30.

8. *Aesop's Fables. Illustrated. The People's Edition* (New York, 1867), advertisement at end.

9. C. Howard to Mr. & Mrs. R. S. Wells, Detroit, February 23, 1870 (Collection of Regional History, Cornell University Library); *Wells' New Descriptive Chart giving a Delineation of Character according to Phrenology and Physiognomy* (New York, [1869]), [3] (courtesy Mr. Ferenc Gyorgyey, Historical Library, Yale Medical Library).

10. Nelson Sizer, Phrenological Character of S. M. Blackstock . . . Dec. 30th 1869 . . . New York (MS, courtesy Mr. Jack T. Ericson, Head, Manuscript Division, Syracuse University Library).

11. M. F. Allen to S. R. Wells, East Jaffrey, N.H., April 10, 1868 (Collection of Regional History, Cornell University Library).

12. George Jarvis Geer to S. R. Wells, Norwich, Conn., August 20, n.y. (Collection of Regional History, Cornell University Library).

13. Foster Blodgett to S. R. Wells, Atlanta, Ga., September 25, 1871 (Collection of Regional History, Cornell University Library).

14. William Blaikie to S. R. Wells, Cambridge, Mass., December 28, [1866?] and Boston, January 24, 1867 (Collection of Regional History, Cornell University Library).

15. Clark Bell to S. R. Wells, New York, April 30, 1873 (Collection of Regional History, Cornell University Library).

16. [John Ward]. Five Phrenological Analyses at Fowler & Wells, 1868–71 (New York Historical Society).

17. G. Stanley Hall, *Life and Confessions of a Psychologist* (New York and London, 1923), 180. See also Curti, *The Social Ideas of American Educators*, Pt. X, 399; John K. Winkler and Walter Bromberg, *Mind Explorers* (New York, [1939]), 189.

18. James Parton, *The Life of Horace Greeley* (Boston, 1869), 573f.; *Phrenological Journal*, Vol. 55, No. 1 (July, 1872), 6; Lilian Whiting, *Kate Field: A Record* (Boston, 1899), 567f.

19. *Phrenological Journal*, Vol. XXXIII, No. 3 (March, 1861), 33.

20. L. N. Fowler, *The Illustrated Phrenological Almanac 1861* (New York, n.d.), 11.

21. Bronson C. Howard to Mrs. S. R. Wells, St. Paul, June 3, 1866 (Collection of Regional History, Cornell University Library).

22. *Phrenological Journal*, Vol. 38, No. 2 (August, 1863), 34, Vol. 38, No. 3 (September, 1863), 64, Vol. 39, No. 5 (May, 1864), 113, Vol. 40, No. 4 (October, 1864), 97, Vol. 40, No. 5 (November, 1864), 144, Vol. 41, No. 6 (June, 1865), 196. It is just barely possible that one of the Fowler brothers had phrenologized Grant when the latter was a boy. According to a letter from Jesse R. Grant to Robert Bonner, Covington, Ky., Jan. 20, 1868: "When Ulysses was about twelve years old [ca. 1834], the first phrenologist who ever made his appearance in that part of the country [southern Ohio or northern Kentucky] came to our neighborhood. He awakened a good deal of interest in the science, and was prevailed upon to remain there some time. . . . They blindfolded him, and then brought Ulysses forward to have his head examined. He felt it over for some time, saying scarcely anything more than to mutter to himself, 'It is no very common head. It is an extraordinary head.' At length Dr. Buckner broke in with

the inquiry whether the boy would be likely to distinguish himself in mathematics? 'Yes,' said the phrenologist, '*in mathematics or anything else; it would not be strange if we should see him President of the United States.*' " See *Newsletter* of the Ulysses S. Grant Association, Vol. VIII, No. 2 (January, 1971), 12 (courtesy Victor Jacobs, Dayton, Ohio, and John Y. Simon, Carbondale, Illinois).

23. Nelson Sizer to John Brown, Jr., New York, October 14, 1850 (Ohio Historical Society).

24. O. S. Fowler, *Human Science*, 322, 715.

25. *Phrenological Journal*, Vol. 38, No. 2 (August, 1863), 54.

26. *Ibid.*, Vol. 50, No. 3 (March, 1870), 192.

27. James L. Andem to Dear Friend, Opelousas, La., April 22, 1863; N. P. Banks to Fowler & Wells, New Orleans, March 7, 1863, copy (both in Collection of Regional History, Cornell University Library).

28. *Phrenological Journal*, Vol. 118, No. 12 (December, 1905), 382.

29. *Ibid.*, Vol. 42, No. 1 (July, 1865), 22.

30. *Ibid.*, Vol. 57, No. 1 (July, 1873), 1 f. at end, Vol. 57, No. 4 (October, 1873), 241, Vol. 57, No. 6 (December, 1873), 387; S. R. Wells, *The Illustrated Annual of Phrenology and Physiognomy 1869* (New York, [1869]), advertisement at beginning.

31. *The New Illustrated Health Almanac II (1874)* (New York, [1874]), advertisement; *Phrenological Journal*, Vol. 39, No. 3 (March, 1864), 83, Vol. 42, No. 1 (July, 1865), advertisement p. 31.

32. For Wells' publishing credo and output, see, besides the works mentioned, P. L. Buell, *The Poet Soldier* (New York, 1868), *passim*; H. S. Drayton (ed.), *Masterpieces: Pope, Aesop, Milton, Coleridge, and Goldsmith* (New York, 1889), General Introduction; *The New Illustrated Health Almanac I (1873)* (New York, [1873]), 1, *II (1874)*, 1; *Phrenological Journal*, Vol. 60, No. 6 (June, 1875), 353; *Publishers' Trade List Annual*, 1873–75 (Samuel R. Wells); *The Science of Health*, Vol. VII, No. 36 (June, 1875), 239f.

33. Jennie June Croly to S. R. Wells, [New York], January 9, [1871?] (Collection of Regional History, Cornell University Library).

34. For the periodicals under Wells' aegis, see Alex. Clark to S. R. Wells, New Brighton, Pa., April 1, 1863 (Collection of Regional History, Cornell University Library); F. W. Evans to S. R. Wells, Mount Lebanon, N.Y., February 10, 1867 (Collection of Regional History, Cornell University Library); Fowler & Wells to Dr. S. G. Howe,

New York, March 28, 1865 (S. G. Howe Papers, Harvard University Library); Phebe A. Hanaford to Fowler & Wells, Boston, March 28, 1867 (Collection of Regional History, Cornell University Library); *The Herald of Health and Water-Cure Journal*, Vol. I, No. 1 (January, 1863), 5; *Phrenological Journal*, Vols. 41–61 (1865–75), *passim*, especially Vol. 35, No. 4 (April, 1862), 17, Vol. 42, No. 3 (September, 1865), 85, Vol. 46, No. 1 (July, 1867), 15, Vol. 47, No. 4 (April, 1868), 128ff., Vol. 51, No. 1 (July, 1870), 43, Vol. 51, No. 4 (October, 1870), 232, Vol. 54, No. 5 (May, 1872), 340, Vol. 58, No. 3 (March, 1874), 191, Vol. 58, No. 4 (April, 1874), 236–42, Vol. 59, No. 6 (December, 1874), 377ff.; Anna Cora Mowatt Ritchie to S. R. Wells, London, July 12, 1867 (Collection of Regional History, Cornell University Library (she subsequently declined Wells' offer in a letter from London, January 18, 1868); *The Science of Health*, Vol. I (July–December, 1872), *passim*, Vol. IV, No. 23 (May, 1874), 178f., Vol. V, No. 26 (August, 1874), 55f., Vol. V, No. 27 (September, 1874), 108, 117f., Vol. VIII, No. 47 (May, 1876), 192 (courtesy Mr. Harold Celnick); Moses Coit Tyler to Samuel R. Wells, Poughkeepsie, N.Y., July 10, 1867 (Collection of Regional History, Cornell University Library).

35. Samuel R. Wells, *New Physiognomy*, *passim* and xxv, 169. The book was hailed by John Neal as a "great work" (John Neal to S. R. Wells, n.p., January 31, 1867 [Collection of Regional History, Cornell University Library]), and a European admirer asked for authorization to translate it into French (Ludovic Léchaud to Fowler & Wells, Havre, France, August 15, 1867 [Collection of Regional History, Cornell University Library]). See also [Samuel R. Wells], *Physiognomy, or Signs of Character* (New York, [1865]), *passim*.

36. *Phrenological Journal*, Vol. 41, No. 5 (May, 1865), 153. For details of the institute, see also Davies, *op. cit.*, 53; H. S. Drayton, *How to Study Phrenology* (New York, 1880), 6f., and advertisement at end; "Fifty Years of Phrenology," *loc. cit.*, 15; *Phrenological Journal*, Vol. 39, No. 3 (March, 1864), 79, Vol. 43, No. 3 (March, 1866), 87, Vol. 47, No. 3 (March, 1868), 106, Vol. 57, No. 4 (October, 1873), 237, Vol. 58, No. 2 (February, 1874), 118, 132–37; Sizer, *Forty Years*, 348ff.; Sizer and Drayton, *op. cit.*, advertisements at end; Nelson Sizer, *The Value of Phrenology* (New York, 1894), 44; S. R. Wells,

The Illustrated Annuals of Phrenology, [*1867*], 38; S. R. Wells, *The Illustrated Annual of Phrenology 1869,* 61 ff.

37. *Phrenological Journal,* Vol. 39, No. 1 (January, 1864), 23.

38. S. R. Wells, *The Illustrated Annuals of Phrenology,* [*1867*], 41.

39. S. R. Wells, *The Illustrated Annuals of Phrenology,* [*1868*], 6.

40. *Ibid.,* 61.

41. *Ibid.,* [*1867*], 15.

42. *Ibid.,* [*1872*], 61.

43. *Phrenological Journal,* Vol. 54, No. 1 (January, 1872), 56ff.; Madeleine B. Stern, "William N. Byers Had His Head Examined!" *Occasional Notes, Norlin Library, University of Colorado,* No. 10 (April, 1969), 1–3.

44. *Phrenological Journal,* Vol. 47, No. 5 (May, 1868), 195. See also George M. Ottinger to S. R. Wells, Salt Lake City, Utah, November 6, 1868 (Collection of Regional History, Cornell University Library); *Phrenological Journal,* Vol. 49, No. 3 (March, 1869), 109f., Vol. 51, No. 2 (August, 1870), 152, Vol. 52, No. 5 (May, 1871), 337–43, Vol. 53, No. 1 (July, 1871), 30–40; Charles R. Savage to S. R. Wells, Salt Lake City, Utah, June 27, 1871 (Collection of Regional History, Cornell University Library); Madeleine B. Stern, "A Rocky Mountain Book Store: Savage and Ottinger of Utah," *Brigham Young University Studies,* Vol. 9, No. 2 (Winter, 1969), 144–54.

45. George Francis Train to S. R. Wells, New York, February 11, 1867 (Collection of Regional History, Cornell University Library); Theresa Yelverton to S. R. Wells, San Francisco, September 8, n.y. (Collection of Regional History, Cornell University Library).

46. *The Science of Health,* Vol. III, No. 14 (August, 1873), 79. See also *Phrenological Journal,* Vol. 49, No. 2 (February, 1869), 83.

47. Rutherford B. Hayes, *Diary and Letters . . . ,* ed. by Charles Richard Williams (Columbus, 1922–24), III, 41. See also *Phrenological Journal,* Vol. 62 [i.e., 63], No. 5 (November, 1876), 405.

48. *Phrenological Journal,* Vol. 53, No. 5 (November, 1871), 328. See also *ibid.,* Vol. 51, No. 6 (December, 1870), 413–16, Vol. 52, No. 1 (January, 1871), 44.

49. For this transcontinental excursion, see *Phrenological Journal,* Vol. 59, No. 1 (July, 1874), 35–42, Vol. 96, No. 6 (December, 1893), 306f.; Henry T. Williams to S. R. Wells, New York, February 28,

1873, March 12, 1873 (Collection of Regional History, Cornell University Library).

50. *Phrenological Journal*, Vol. 56, No. 2 (February, 1873), 126.

51. *The Science of Health*, Vol. III, No. 17 (November, 1873), 198.

52. *Phrenological Journal*, Vol. 57, No. 6 (December, 1873), 383f.

53. *Ibid.*, Vol. 60, No. 5 (May, 1875), 336f. For details of the move, see also New York City directory 1875–76; *Phrenological Journal*, Vol. 60, No. 6 (June, 1875), 406; *The Science of Health*, Vol. VII, No. 34 (May, 1875), 194, Vol. VII, No. 36 (June, 1875), 239.

54. [S. R. Wells], *How to Read Character* (New York, 1875), Part II, A Delineation of the Character . . . of Saml J. Tilden as given by N. Sizer Dec. 30th/74 (New York Public Library).

55. *Phrenological Journal*, Vol. 60, No. 6 (June, 1875), 352ff., 406ff. For further details of Wells' death, see *New-York Daily Tribune* (April 14, 1875), 7; *The Science of Health*, Vol. VII, No. 36 (June, 1875), 238ff., Vol. VII, No. 37 (July, 1875), 7.

56. *Phrenological Journal*, Vol. 60, No. 6 (June, 1875), 406.

CHAPTER XIII

To the Fin de Siècle

1. For details of Charlotte's appearance, character, and life at this time, see Jessie Allen Fowler, *Brain Roofs and Porticos* (New York and London, [1908]), 131f.; information from Mr. Paul J. Howe, Ridgewood, New Jersey; *Phrenological Journal*, Vol. 120, No. 5 (May, 1907), 141f.

2. *Phrenological Journal*, Vol. 62 [i.e., 63], No. 3 (September, 1876), 188. See also Sizer, *The Royal Road to Wealth*, 514f.

3. Nelson Sizer and Henry S. Drayton, *Heads and Faces* (New York, 1887), advertisement. See also "Fifty Years of Phrenology," *loc. cit.*, 31; New York City directory 1880–81.

4. *Phrenological Journal*, Vol. 71, No. 4 (October, 1880), 220f.

5. For Charlotte's various attempts to modernize the firm, see *The American Kindergarten and Primary Teacher*, N.S. Vol. I, No. 1 (September, 1886), advertisement at end, Vol. I, No. 5 (January, 1886), p. 10 of advertisements at beginning, Vol. I, No. 5 (January, 1887), 150; Drayton, *How to Study Phrenology*, advertisement; Fow-

ler & Wells Advertising Card [1890] (Landauer Collection, New York Historical Society, courtesy Mr. Wilson Dupre); *Phrenological Journal*, Vol. 108, No. 9 (September, 1899), p. 7 at end, Vol. 112, No. 1 (July, 1901), 3; *The Practical Phrenologist*, Vol. IV, No. 2 (February, 1884), *passim*, Vol. IV, No. 3 (March, 1884), *passim*.

6. For details of these analyses, see Henry S. Drayton and James McNeill, *Brain and Mind* (New York, [1879]), 328 and advertisement; [Fowler & Wells Co.], *The Head and Face: A Mirror of the Mind* ([New York], 1891), *passim*; "Mirror of the Mind" (New York, [1880–87]), Landauer Collection, New York Historical Society; *Phrenological Journal*, Vol. 78, No. 6 (June, 1884), 340, Vol. 87, No. 3 (March, 1888), 180, Vol. 87, No. 6 (June, 1888), 318, Vol. 88, No. 4 (October, 1888), 223, Vol. 94, No. 6 (December, 1892), 287f., Vol. 98, No. 5 (November, 1894), 219f., Vol. 117, No. 5 (May, 1904), 158; *The Practical Phrenologist*, Vol. IV, No. 2 (February, 1884), 1 f., Vol. IV, No. 3 (March, 1884), *passim*; Sizer and Drayton, *op. cit.*, 145 and advertisement; Sizer, *How to Study Strangers*, 167, 171f., 283; Nelson Sizer, *Study of Character by Photographs* (New York, 1891), *passim*; [Samuel R. Wells], *How To Read Character* (New York, 1895), inserted leaf (recto and verso) after 142; *World* (New York) (July 8, 1881), 5. The most recent student of Guiteau appears unaware of Sizer's analysis, although he mentions other phrenological examinations of the assassin. See Charles E. Rosenberg, *The Trial of the Assassin Guiteau* (Chicago, 1968), 160 and frontispiece.

7. Frances E. Willard, *Glimpses of Fifty Years* (Chicago, [1889]), 529f.

8. Besides the works mentioned, see, for Charlotte's publishing activity, *The American Kindergarten and Primary Teacher*, N. S. Vol. I, No. 1 (September, 1886), 16 and advertisements at end, Vol. I, No. 4 (December, 1886), advertisement in Children's Supplement; Arthur M. Baker, *How to Succeed as A Stenographer* (New York, 1888), advertisements at end; [Anna Olcott Commelin], *Jerushy in Brooklyn* (New York, 1893), *passim*; Anna Olcott Commelin, *Of Such Is the Kingdom, and Other Poems* (New York, 1894), *passim*; M. L. Holbrook, *Eating for Strength* (New York and London, [1888]), advertisement at end; Dugald McKillop, *Shorthand and Typewriting* (New York, 1891), front cover; Hester M. Poole, *Fruits,*

and How to Use Them (New York, 1890), advertisements at end; *Publishers' Trade List Annual*, 1877–91, 1899; Sizer and Drayton, *op. cit.*, advertisements; Sizer, *How to Study Strangers*, 258n.

9. Emily Faithfull, *Three Visits to America* (New York, [1884]), iii–vi.

10. Susan B. Anthony to Charlotte F. Wells, Tenafly, New Jersey, August 10, 1876 (Collection of Regional History, Cornell University Library). For the firm's publishing of the *History of Woman Suffrage*, see K. Anthony, *Susan B. Anthony*, 341 f., 344, 370 ff.; *Phrenological Journal*, Vol. 75, No. 3 (September, 1882), 172, Vol. 109, No. 4 (April, 1900), 116.

11. *Phrenological Journal*, Vol. 75, No. 1 (July, 1882), 53. For details of the *Journal* during Charlotte's regime, see "Fifty Years of Phrenology," *loc. cit.*, 19; *Phrenological Journal*, Vol. 62 (1876)– Vol. 108 (1899), *passim* (several volumes courtesy Mr. Harold Celnick, New York); see especially, for quotations and specific references, Vol. 62 [i.e., 63], No. 4 (October, 1876), 313, Vol. 62 [i.e. 63], No. 5 (November, 1876), 404, Vol. 64, No. 5 (May, 1877), 400, Vol. 65, No. 5 (November, 1877), 323, Vol. 69, No. 2 (August, 1879), 67f., Vol. 73, No. 4 (October, 1881), 172ff., Vol. 75, No. 4 (October, 1882), 175–80, 207–10, Vol. 76, No. 5 (May, 1883), 234–39, Vol. 77, No. 1 (July, 1883), 47f., Vol. 84, No. 3 (March, 1887), 165, Vol. 89, No. 5 (May, 1889), 219, 224, Vol. 92, No. 1 (July, 1891), 20, Vol. 93, No. 2 (February, 1892), 74, Vol. 93, No. 5 (May, 1892), 242, Vol. 96, No. 5 (May, 1893), 234, Vol. 97, No. 1 (January, 1894), 52f., Vol. 103, No. 2 (February, 1897), 88f., Vol. 104, No. 5 (November, 1897), 239, Vol. 114, No. 3 (September, 1902), 298; *The Science of Health*, Vol. VIII, No. 47 (May, 1876), 192.

12. For the phrenographs and phrenotypes, see *Phrenological Journal*, Vol. 96, No. 5 (May, 1893), 199ff., Vol. 99, No. 2 (February, 1895), 89–96, 121ff., Vol. 100, No. 1 (July, 1895), 3–7, Vol. 101, No. 1 (January, 1896), 9, Vol. 101, No. 2 (February, 1896), 57–61, Vol. 103, No. 4 (April, 1897), 155–58, Vol. 104, No. 3 (September, 1897), 106ff., Vol. 108, No. 10 (October, 1899), 311ff., Vol. 108, No. 11 (November, 1899), 344ff.

13. "Fifty Years of Phrenology," *loc. cit.*, 31; Growoll Collection, American Book Trade History, VI, 27; *The Practical Phrenologist*, Vol. IV, No. 3 (March, 1884), 4.

14. Information from Mr. Hans Nussbaum, Business Manager, American Association for the Advancement of Science, Washington, D.C. See also American Association for the Advancement of Science, *Proceedings . . . Thirty-First Meeting, held at Montreal . . . August, 1882* (Salem, 1883), lxi.

15. Henry S. Drayton, *Light in Dark Places* (Philadelphia, 1879), *passim*; "Fifty Years of Phrenology," *loc. cit.*, 22f.; *Phrenological Journal*, Vol. 69, No. 3 (September, 1879), 141–44, Vol. 87, No. 6 (June, 1888), 318.

16. Sizer, *How to Study Strangers*, iii f.

17. Growoll Collection, American Book Trade History, VI, 27; *Phrenological Journal*, Vol. 84, No. 6 (June, 1887), 328; *The Practical Phrenologist*, Vol. VII, No. 5 (May, 1887), *passim*.

18. *The American Kindergarten and Primary Teacher*, N.S. Vol. I, No. 7 (March, 1887), advertisement.

19. *King's Photographic Views of New York* (Boston, [1895]), 536. See also *King's Handbook of New York City* (Boston, 1892), 291f.; New York City directory 1893–94; *Phrenological Journal*, Vol. 113, No. 5 (May, 1902), p. 4 at end.

20. For the institute, see *The Human-Nature Library*, No. 17 (January, 1891), 6f., 37, No. 29 (January, 1894), 19 and *passim*; *Phrenological Journal*, Vol. 69, No. 6 (December, 1879), 329, Vol. 76, No. 1 (January, 1883), 21–31, Vol. 76, No. 2 (February, 1883), 130, Vol. 84, No. 2 (February, 1887), "Institute Extra," No. 16, 1, Vol. 86, No. 2 (February, 1888), "Institute Extra," No. 17, 1f., 8f., 13, Vol. 89, No. 2 (February, 1890), 68, Vol. 96 [*sic*], No. 5 (May, 1893), 235, Vol. 96 [*sic*], No. 2 (August, 1893), 108, Vol. 105, No. 1 (January, 1898), 30; Charlotte Fowler Wells, *Some Account of the Life and Labors of Dr. François Joseph Gall . . . and . . . Dr. John Gaspar Spurzheim* (New York and London, [1896]), [5].

21. *Phrenological Journal*, Vol. 98, No. 3 (September, 1894), 113ff. For further details of Charlotte at this time, see *ibid.*, Vol. 87, No. 6 (June, 1888), 318, Vol. 112, No. 1 (July, 1901), 1ff.

22. Nelson Sizer to Henry W. Sage, New York, December 20, 1892 (Collection of Regional History, Cornell University Library). For details of the Cabinet and Building Fund, see also "Fifty Years of Phrenology," *loc. cit.*, 14; *Phrenological Journal*, Vol. 78, No. 6 (June, 1884), 340, Vol. 82, No. 1 (January, 1886), 60; Charlotte F. Wells,

To the personal friends of the late Samuel R. Wells and the friends of Phrenology (MS, Collection of Regional History, Cornell University Library).

23. *The Phrenological Annual and Record. 1888*, 11; *Phrenological Journal*, Vol. 61, No. 2 (August, 1875), 131 f., Vol. 68, No. 1 (January, 1879), 5–11, Vol. 84 [i.e., 85], No. 2 (August, 1887), 71 ff.

24. Lydia Folger Fowler, Death Certificate, General Register Office, Somerset House, London; *New-York Times* (February 10, 1879), 3; *The Times* (London) (January 29, 1879), 1; Waite, "Dr. Lydia Folger Fowler," *loc. cit.*, 296.

25. *New York Times* (October 16, 1932), 38.

26. For this and a subsequent visit, see *Professor L. N. Fowler. A Sketch*, 6; *The Illustrated Annual of Phrenology, 1880*, p. 1 of Publishers' Department at end; *Phrenological Journal*, Vol. 78, No. 3 (March, 1884), 181 f.

27. For Edward Fowler's accomplishments and characteristics, see Moriz Benedikt, *Anatomical Studies upon Brains of Criminals . . . Translated . . . by E. P. Fowler* (New York, 1881), *passim*; J. M. Charcot, *Lectures on Localization in Diseases of the Brain . . . Translated by Edward P. Fowler* (New York, 1878), iv f. and *passim*; Drayton and McNeill, *op. cit.*, 289, 291; Edward P. Fowler, *Annual Address before the New York Medico-Chirurgical Society . . . November 14, 1882* (New York, 1883), 7 and *passim*; E. P. Fowler, *Are Brains of Criminals Anatomical Perversions?* [New York, 1880], 31 and *passim* (courtesy Miss Gertrude L. Annan, formerly of the New York Academy of Medicine Library); Edward P. Fowler, *Medical Science against Exclusive Homœopathy* (New York, 1878), 8 and *passim*; *The Private Library belonging to Edward P. Fowler . . . to be sold by auction* (New York, 1876), *passim*; Charles Morris (ed.), *Makers of New York* (Philadelphia, 1895), 76; New York Medico-Chirurgical Society, *Transactions. 1878–9, 1880–1* (New York, 1882), *passim*; "New York Physicians. Edward Payson Fowler, M.D.," *The National Magazine*, Vol. XIX, No. 4–5 (February–March, 1894), 315 ff.; *Phrenological Journal*, Vol. 81, No. 4 (October, 1885), 210–17; Charles Richet, *Physiology and Histology of the Cerebral Convolutions . . . Translated by Edward P. Fowler* (New York, 1879), x ff. and *passim*. Charcot's *Lectures on the Diseases of the Nervous System*, translated by George Sigerson, had been published in London in

1877; Charcot's *Lectures on Bright's Disease* had been published in translation in New York in 1878.

28. H. N. Fowler, *The Industrial Public*, 10 f., Part 2, 76 and *passim*.

29. For Orson's later activities, tribulations, and death, see *Amenia* (N.Y.) *Times* (August 22, 1887), 3; *Amherst College Biographical Record*, 30; Max Bachert, *Is Prof. O. S. Fowler The Foulest Man on Earth?* (New York, 1881), *passim*; *Chicago Tribune* (June 10, 1881), 2, (June 16, 1881), 6, (June 27, 1881), 2; information from Mr. John D. Forbes, Office Manager, Woodlawn Cemetery, Bronx, N.Y.; O. S. Fowler, *Life: Its Factors and Improvement* (New York, [1880]), v, viii, and *passim*; O. S. Fowler, *The Practical Phrenologist* (Sharon Station, N.Y., [1885?] and [1887?], advertisements at end; O. S. Fowler, *Private Lectures on Perfect Men, Women, and Children, in Happy Families* (Boston, [1878]), *passim*; Jones, *op. cit.*, Chronological Table and 34ff., 91; *New-York Daily Tribune* (August 20, 1887), 5; *New-York Times* (August 19, 1887), 1, (August 20, 1887) 5; *Phrenological Journal*, Vol. 71, No. 4 (October, 1880), 199, Vol. 84 [i.e., 85], No. 4 (October, 1887), 196ff., Vol. 122, No. 11 (November, 1909), 365; *Poughkeepsie Daily Eagle* (August 19, 1887), 3; *Poughkeepsie Sunday Courier* (August 21, 1887), 3; Ver Nooy, " 'Fowler's Folly,' " *loc. cit.*, 80ff.; Ver Nooy, "More About Orson S. Fowler," *loc. cit.*, 101f.

30. Growoll Collection, American Book Trade History, VI, 27; *Phrenological Journal*, Vol. 101, No. 2 (February, 1896), 91.

31. For Charlotte's later activities, see Growoll Collection, American Book Trade History, XIII, 30; *Phrenological Journal*, Vol. 100, No. 6 (December, 1895), 293, Vol. 101, No. 2 (February, 1896), 94, Vol. 102, No. 6 (December, 1896), 200f., Vol. 106, No. 1 (July, 1898), 33, Vol. 106, No. 4 (October, 1898), 123–28, Vol. 108, No. 10 (October, 1899), 330f., Vol. 112, No. 1 (July, 1901), 1ff.

32. *New-York Daily Tribune* (October 19, 1897), 5; *New York Times* (October 19, 1897), 7; *Phrenological Journal*, Vol. 104, No. 6 (December, 1897), 251ff.

33. For the London office and Jessie's activities, see Jessie A. Fowler, *Life of Dr. François Joseph Gall* (London and New York, 1896), *passim*; Jessie A. Fowler, *A Manual of Mental Science for Teachers and Students* (London and New York, [1897]), 229; L. N. Fowler, *Mental Science, as explained by Phrenology* (London and New York, 1896), advertisement at end; L. N. Fowler, *Revelations of the Face*

(London and New York, n.d.), advertisement at beginning; *The Phrenological Annual and Record. 1888*, 4; *Phrenological Journal*, Vol. 84 [i.e., 85], No. 2 (August, 1887), 72, Vol. 87, No. 4 (April, 1888), 230, Vol. 88, No. 2 (August, 1888), 108f., Vol. 88, No. 3 (September, 1888), 169, Vol. 102, No. 10 (October, 1896), 149, Vol. 103, No. 4 (April, 1897), 151–55, 160 f., Vol. 105, No. 1 (January, 1898), 16f.; *The Phrenological Magazine* [London], Vol. I (1880), *passim*; Severn, *op. cit.*, 437; Winskill, *op. cit.*, III, 258. Almira Fowler and her second husband Edward Breakspear were vice-presidents of the Fowler Institute, London (see *Phrenological Journal*, Vol. 106, No. 5 [November, 1898], 164, Vol. 109, No. 2 [February, 1900], 45ff.).

34. Clara Barton to L. N. Fowler, February 20, 1886, Clara Barton Papers, Library of Congress, Vol. 7, Outgoing Correspondence after 1881, 206f.

35. J. A. Fowler, *Life of Dr. François Joseph Gall*, program at end; *New-York Daily Tribune* (September 4, 1896), 7.

36. For Lorenzo's visit to the United States and his death, see Lorenzo N. Fowler, Death Certificate, New Jersey State Department of Health; Growoll Collection, American Book Trade History, VI, 27f.; *New-York Daily Tribune* (September 4, 1896), 7; *New-York Times* (September 4, 1896), 10; *Phrenological Journal*, Vol. 102, No. 10 (October, 1896), 113ff.

37. For Jessie's incumbency in the New York firm and her activities, see Growoll Collection, American Book Trade History, VI, 27; *Phrenological Journal*, Vol. 102, No. 8 (August, 1896), 59, Vol. 105, No. 3 (March, 1898), 102, Vol. 108, No. 8 (August, 1899), 271.

38. *Fishkill Weekly Times* (August 11, 1897), courtesy Mr. C. R. Jones, New York State Historical Association, Cooperstown, N.Y.

39. *New-York Daily Tribune* (January 2, 1900), 7; *Phrenological Journal*, Vol. 109, No. 2 (February, 1900), 45ff.

40. *Newark Daily Advertiser* (January 29, 1900), 3; *Orange Chronicle* (February 3, 1900), 6; *Phrenological Journal*, Vol. 109, No. 3 (March, 1900), 96.

41. Growoll Collection, American Book Trade History, XIII, 30; *Phrenological Journal*, Vol. 112, No. 1 (July, 1901), 1ff.; information from Miss Kathryn L. Shafer, Rosedale Cemetery, Orange, New

Jersey; Charlotte Fowler Wells, Death Certificate, New Jersey State Department of Health.

42. C. F. Wells, Lecture on Phrenology, MS, Collection of Regional History, Cornell University Library.

43. Alexander Bain, *Autobiography* (New York and London, 1904), 237; *Phrenological Journal*, Vol. 79, No. 5 (November, 1884), 308.

44. Ralph Waldo Emerson, *Lectures and Biographical Sketches* (Boston, 1887), 318.

45. Quoted from *Elsie Venner* in *Phrenological Journal*, Vol. 74, No. 4 (April, 1882), 216.

46. William James, *The Principles of Psychology* (New York, [1890]), I, 28.

47. Dallenbach, "Phrenology versus Psychoanalysis," *loc. cit.*, 519.

48. Wilder, *op. cit.*, 289.

49. J. A. Fowler, *Life of Dr. François Joseph Gall*, 56f.; *Phrenological Journal*, Vol. 122, No. 12 (December, 1909), 401.

50. Quoted in *Phrenological Journal*, Vol. 89, No. 6 (June, 1889), 283.

51. Alfred Russel Wallace, *The Wonderful Century* (New York, 1899), 166, 193, and 159–93 *passim*. See also Frederic Whyte, *A Bachelor's London* (London, 1931), 148.

CHAPTER XIV
"The Wonderful Century"

1. [Jessie Allen Fowler], *Human Nature* (Philadelphia, n.d.), 12 (Landauer Collection, New York Historical Society). For Jessie's abilities, see also J. A. Fowler, *Brain Roofs and Porticos, passim*; *Phrenological Journal*, Vol. 120, No. 4 (April, 1907), 136, Vol. 122, No. 12 (December, 1909), 404f.; information from Mr. Henry Sellin, Lecturer, Woman's Law Class, New York University.

2. For Jessie's sales techniques, see *Phrenological Journal*, Vol. 110, No. 6 (June, 1900), 198, Vol. 111, No. 11 [*sic*] (July, 1900), advertisement at beginning, Vol. 111, No. 1 (January, 1901), 32, Vol. 114, No. 3 (September, 1902), p. 6 of advertisements at end, Vol. 117, No. 3 (March, 1904), p. 11 of advertisements at end, Vol. 118, No. 3 (September, 1905), p. 11 of advertisements at end, Vol. 118, No. 12 (De-

cember, 1905), advertisement on back cover, Vol. 121, No. 11 (November, 1908), advertisement at beginning, Vol. 122, No. 1 (January, 1909), p. 14 of advertisements at end, Vol. 122, No. 11 (November, 1909), 374, Vol. 123, No. 10 (October, 1910), 326; R. T. Trall, *The True Healing Art* (New York, n.d.), advertisement at end.

3. *Phrenological Journal*, Vol. 117, No. 1 (January, 1904), p. 7 of advertisements at end.

4. J. A. Fowler, *Phrenology. Its Use in Business Life* (New York and London, 1898), 25.

5. For Jessie's publications, see James Coates, *Seeing the Invisible* (London and New York, 1906), advertisements at end; Anna Olcott Commelin, *Twos and Threes and other stories* (New York and London, [1902]), advertisements at end; Richard J. Ebbard, *How to Acquire and Strengthen Will-Power* (London and New York, 1907), *passim* and advertisements at end; *Publishers' Trade List Annual*, 1905.

6. For the *Journal* during Jessie's incumbency, see *Phrenological Journal*, Vol. 115, No. 3 (March, 1903), 96f., Vol. 118, No. 11 (November, 1905), advertisements at end, Vol. 121, No. 9 (September, 1908), 273, 287, 293, Vol. 121, No. 11 (November, 1908), 352ff., 355, Vol. 122, No. 2 (February, 1909), 45–51, Vol. 122 [i.e., 124], No. 1 (January, 1911), 24f., p. 8 of advertisements at end.

7. For the institute at this time, see American Institute of Phrenology, *Announcement for the Season of 1916–1917* (Landauer Collection, New York Historical Society); American Institute of Phrenology, *The Charter* (New York, [1902]), *passim*; Davies, *op. cit.*, 173; *Phrenological Journal*, Vol. 111, No. 2 (August, 1900), 61, Vol. 116, No. 1 (July, 1903), 9, Vol. 117, No. 5 (May, 1904), p. 5 of advertisements at end, Vol. 118, No. 7 (July, 1905), 206ff., Vol. 118, No. 11 (November, 1905), 341–45, Vol. 122, No. 11 (November, 1909), 354f., Vol. 122, No. 12 (December, 1909), 398f.

8. Edgar C. Beall, *The Brain and the Bible* (Cincinnati, 1882), 243–63; Edgar C. Beall, *Practical Phrenophysics* (n.p., 1907), [40] and *passim*; [Jessie Allen Fowler], *Human Nature*, 14 (Landauer Collection, New York Historical Society); *Phrenological Journal*, Vol. 111, No. 6 (December, 1900), 180, Vol. 113, No. 4 (April, 1902), 103–106, Vol. 113, No. 5 (May, 1902), 137f., Vol. 113, No. 6 (June, 1902), 179, Vol. 114, No. 4 (October, 1902), 312f., Vol. 117, No. 1 (January, 1904), 1–4, Vol. 117, No. 12 (December, 1904), 375–84, Vol. 122,

No. 1 (January, 1909), 16–19, Vol. 122, No. 12 (December, 1909), 392f.; Madeleine B. Stern, "The Head of a Poet: A Phrenograph of Edwin Markham," *Coranto*, Vol. VI, No. 1 (1969), 6–12.

9. *Phrenological Journal*, Vol. 111, No. 4 (April, 1901), 103–106. See also Alan Gribben, "Mark Twain, Phrenology, and the 'Temperaments,'" typescript, citing, in Note 3, the entry from Mark Twain's Notebook in the Mark Twain Papers, Berkeley. Mr. Gribben also points out that Mark Twain read and copied passages from George S. Weaver's *Lectures on Mental Science*, and states, with supportive quotations, that "he made use of its [phrenology's] terminology and tenets in a minor but surprisingly persistent manner in his literature" (p. 2). See also Madeleine B. Stern, "Mark Twain Had His Head Examined," *loc. cit.*, 207–18.

10. *Daily Graphic* (London) (January 12, 1907). See also Neider (ed.), *The Autobiography of Mark Twain*, 63, 66 n. 2; Stern, "Mark Twain Had His Head Examined," *loc. cit.*, 217 n. 13; Whyte, *op. cit.*, 152, 155.

11. *Phrenological Journal*, Vol. 123, No. 6 (June, 1910), 190.

12. For Jessie's activities, see J. A. Fowler, *Brain Roofs and Porticos*, 46f., 87, 89; J. A. Fowler, *Character Types* [chart], Landauer Collection, New York Historical Society; [J. A. Fowler], *Chart of Brain Centers* (New York, 1916), Landauer Collection, New York Historical Society; Jessie Allen Fowler, *Practical Physiognomy* (New York and London, [1912]), *passim*; *Phrenological Journal*, Vol. 120, No. 8 (August, 1907), 259, Vol. 120, No. 11 (November, 1907), 353, Vol. 122, No. 2 (February, 1909), 45–51.

13. J. A. Fowler, *Brain Roofs and Porticos*, 97.

14. *Phrenological Journal*, Vol. 113, No. 5 (May, 1902), p. 4 at end. See also New York City directory 1902–1903.

15. *Publishers' Weekly*, Vol. LXV, No. 1 (January 2, 1904), 22.

16. Information from L. N. Fowler & Co., Ltd., 1 Tudor Street, London, E.C. 4; Stackpool E. O'Dell, *Phrenology: Its Truthfulness and Usefulness* (London, n.d.), 3.

17. *Orange Advertiser* (May 16, 1913), 5.

18. Edward Payson Fowler, Death Certificate, New York State Department of Health; *The Journal of the American Medical Association*, Vol. LXII, No. 8 (February 21, 1914), 630; *New-York Daily Tribune* (January 30, 1914), 7.

19. For the firm's split, changes of address, and later work of the American Institute of Phrenology, see American Institute of Phrenology, *Announcement for the Season of 1916–1917* (Landauer Collection, New York Historical Society); [J. A. Fowler], *Human Nature*, 16 and *passim* (Landauer Collection, New York Historical Society); New York City directories 1916–25, 1928–30.

20. Jessie Allen Fowler, Death Certificate, City of New York Department of Health, Bureau of Records and Statistics; *New York Herald Tribune* (October 17, 1932), 13; *New York Times* (October 16, 1932), 38.

CHAPTER XV

Appraisals

1. See in this connection Iago Galdston, "Hypnosis and Modern Psychiatry," *Ciba Symposia*, Vol. IX, No. 11 (March–April, 1948), 846.

2. *Should Woman Obey? A protest against improper matrimonial and prenatal conditions. . . . Together with a special chapter by Prof. L. N. Fowler, entitled, Love, Courtship and Marriage* (Chicago, [1900]), *passim*.

3. William H. Murray, *Christian Mothers* (Boston, [1950]), verso of half-title and *passim*. In 1970, Chelsea House Publishers issued a Fowler phrenological reprint.

4. Introduction to William Windsor, *Phrenology: The Science of Character* (Big Rapids, Mich., 1921), ix.

5. *Ibid.*, 24.

6. Horace N. Fowler, *The Industrial Public, passim*.

7. Karl M. Dallenbach, "Phrenology versus Psychoanalysis," *The American Journal of Psychology*, Vol. LXVIII, No. 4 (December, 1955), 519; Jones, *op. cit.*, 94.

8. Carl W. Ritter, "Character in Handwriting," *San Diego Union* (October, 1967), clipping, courtesy Mr. Ray Reynolds, Grossmont College, El Cajon, California.

9. Coptic Fellowship of America, *The Science of Physiognomy* [Hollywood, 1945], 16.

10. Bernard Hollander, *The Revival of Phrenology. The Mental*

Functions of the Brain (New York and London, 1901), iiiff. and *passim*.

11. Edwin G. Boring, *A History of Experimental Psychology* (New York and London, [1929]), 565.

12. Whyte, *op. cit.*, 155.

13. *Engineering Outlook at the University of Illinois in Urbana*, Vol. 10, No. 8 (April, 1969), [2]. See also *ibid.*, Vol. 9, No. 1 (January, 1968), [2].

14. Dr. Robert S. Morison's review of *The Biological Time Bomb*, by Gordon Rattray Taylor, appeared in the *New York Times Book Review* (September 15, 1968), 3.

15. See, for example, John Finley Scott, "Who Marries Whom and Why," *New York Times Magazine* (October 30, 1966), 27.

16. David Perlman, "The Search for the Memory Molecule," *New York Times Magazine* (July 7, 1968), 8f., 33–37.

17. Seldes, *op. cit.*, 314.

18. Dallenbach, *op. cit.*, 521.

19. *Ibid.*, 512.

20. Erwin H. Ackerknecht, " 'Mesmerism' in Primitive Societies," *Ciba Symposia*, Vol. IX, No. 11 (March–April, 1948), 831. As J. C. Furnas put it, "Bumps yesterday—complexes today—perhaps glands tomorrow. *Plus ça change, plus c'est la même chose*" (in "Sermon in Skulls," *The Virginia Quarterly Review*, Vol. 8, No. 1 [January, 1932], 58). See also Richard H. Shryock, "The History and Sociology of Science," *Social Science Research Council Items*, Vol. 10, No. 2 (June, 1956), 16.

21. See, for an interesting commentary, *New York Times Magazine* (January 28, 1968), 28–40.

22. Karl Menninger, *The Crime of Punishment* (New York, 1968), *passim*.

23. Hammacher Schlemmer, *Mid-Winter Specialties* (1969), 14.

24. Graham Greene, *The Comedians* (New York, [1966]), 25.

25. Creese, "Fowler and the Domestic Octagon," *loc. cit.*, 100.

26. Information from the Pentone Co., Inc., New York City.

27. Information from Miss Marion Sauerbier, Cohocton, New York.

28. Galdston, "Mesmer and Animal Magnetism," *Ciba Symposia*,

Vol. IX, No. 11 (March–April, 1948), 833.

29. See Boring, *op. cit.*, 55f.; G. Elliot Smith, *The Old and the New Phrenology* [Edinburgh, 1923], 1–4.

30. Oscar Handlin, review of paperback edition of Gilbert Seldes' *The Stammering Century* in *Washington Post Book Week* (May 1, 1966), 20f.

31. Phrenology has long played some part in scholarly interpretations of the past. See, for example, William B. Walker, "The Health Reform Movement in the United States, 1830–1870" (Ph.D. Dissertation, Johns Hopkins University, 1955), and Francis W. Weeks, "Some Aspects of Pseudo-Sciences in Nineteenth Century American Literature" (Master's Thesis, Columbia University, 1939). Now the popularizers of straight, as distinguished from offbeat, history are beginning to include brief discussions of phrenology in their documentations of the nineteenth century. See, for example, American Heritage Press, *American Manners & Morals* (New York, 1969), "Making Headlines," and J. C. Furnas, *The Americans: A Social History of the United States 1587–1914* (New York, [1969]), 445–49.

INDEX

· ·

The paper on which this book is printed bears the watermark of the University of Oklahoma Press and has an effective life of at least three hundred years.

348